LIVES IN PROGRESS

LIVES IN PROGRESS
A Study of the Natural Growth of Personality

Third Edition

ROBERT W. WHITE
Harvard University

HOLT, RINEHART AND WINSTON
New York • Chicago • San Francisco • Atlanta • Dallas
Montreal • Toronto • London • Sydney

Library of Congress Cataloging in Publication Data

White, Robert Winthrop.
    Lives in progress.

    Includes bibliographies.
    1. Personality—Cases, clinical reports, statistics. 2. Genetic psychology—Cases, clinical reports, statistics. I. Title.
BF698.W46   1975   155.2   74-20758

ISBN: 0-03-089403-4

234 008 987

PREFACE

It is appropriate that a book on lives in progress should itself show evidence of progress. The original plan called for intensive study of three lives chosen to exemplify the natural growth of personality. These histories furnished a factual foundation, but they were used to introduce and illustrate the general ideas, drawn from a variety of sources, that go to make up a theoretical account of personal development. In this third edition I have continued the narratives of the three subjects, who have now reached middle age. I have also undertaken to bring up to date, as well as brief compass permits, the theoretical ideas illustrated by their lives. Like the subjects, who have grown without losing identity, like the ideas, which have enlarged without losing historical connection, this book exhibits natural growth without losing its original ground plan.

How can a person best be introduced to the general subject

of personality? My preferences can be indicated by mentioning four features of the book.

First, I have concentrated on three case histories rather than trying to summarize a larger body of material. This reflects my view that the initial facts of personality are the lives of people, and lives cannot be adequately understood unless they are described at considerable length. The case histories are designed to provide a solid foundation of fact on which to anchor the discussion of concepts and theories. I have tried to maintain a close connection between general ideas and their particular embodiments in these three lives.

Second, the lives reported here were studied on my initiative rather than that of the subjects, and they were studied at more than one point in time. These circumstances are important in making the case histories broadly representative of the facts of personality. Our knowledge is overweighted with clinical case records taken at a time when the patient, overwhelmed by difficulties, is preoccupied with the problem of getting well. Clinical histories are necessarily concentrated on understanding the origin and nature of the disorder; rarely can justice be done to the fact of change, except as this occurs under the artificial circumstances of psychotherapy. Yet temporal development is one of the central facts and central problems of personality.

Third, I have favored a broadly inclusive approach to the understanding of lives. Personality is open to a multitude of influences, shaped by a multitude of forces. Repeatedly we say that it is complex, and this means that it cannot be properly envisioned from a single provincial point of view. I have represented this diversity by speaking of social, biological, and developmental views of man. Formerly I called the third view psychodynamic and drew its substance from psychoanalysis, but it now seems clear to me that the psychoanalytic theory of growth belongs with developmental psychology, where research has been moving impressively forward.

Finally, I have laid stress on natural growth and constructive activity. Personality does not stand still; under certain circumstances it evolves in directions of greater maturity and effectiveness. Nor is the person always a passive victim of the forces that influence him. He is himself a center of energy and an active agent in changing his material and human surroundings. The study of relatively normal people at more than one point in time provides favorable conditions for examining natural growth.

The life histories in this book are not fiction. They represent a painstaking attempt to describe faithfully the three principal characters. Of course, I have taken steps to conceal the identities of these three people, and the purpose of the disguise would be defeated by explaining how it was done. On this point I must ask to be trusted for having fulfilled my obligation to the subjects without making changes that would significantly alter one's understanding of the cases. The subjects have seen the chapters about themselves and have consented to the publication of their histories. "Nothing requires a rarer intellectual heroism," said George Santayana, "than willingness to see one's equation written out." This book is dedicated to the three subjects, with my respect and affection.

The gathering of case histories is an enormous task, and I have had the assistance of well over a hundred people in working on it. I am greatly indebted to the staff members, research assistants, volunteer workers, and graduate students who at various times formed part of the diagnostic team. When working on the case materials for the first edition, I was frequently reminded of my helpers by seeing their names on the reports of test sessions and interviews, and I realized how often I was using their thoughts in piecing together my own. Of outstanding importance were the contributions of Professor Donald W. Fiske, Dr. Annette R. Silbert, Dr. Pauline B. Hahn, Dr. Ruth-Jean Eisenbud, Dr. Margaret M. Riggs, and Dr. Robert M. Ravven. I should like to acknowledge also the helpfulness of Professor Robert W. Leeper, who sent me a thoughtful and detailed commentary on the first edition. My wife, Margaret L. White, had a part in gathering and interpreting the case material and in improving the clarity of the text.

R.W.W.

Marlborough, New Hampshire
November 1974

CONTENTS

1

THE
UNDERSTANDING
OF LIVES

> To know the truth partially is to distort the Universe.
> . . . An unflinching determination to take the whole
> evidence into account is the only method of preserva-
> tion against the fluctuating extremes of fashionable
> opinion.
>
> A. N. WHITEHEAD

Human nature and the human condition must always be matters of serious concern, never more so than in our own time. To learn about them
calls for studies of many kinds, approaches from many directions. One
possible route to understanding is the intensive study of individual lives.
This book is an attempt to take a forward step through life studies of a
somewhat unusual kind. The three people whose histories take up more
than half this book were studied on several occasions: first when they
were college students, a second time five to ten years later, and (in two
cases) on subsequent occasions extending past their fiftieth birthdays.
None of the subjects was met as a clinical patient seeking help; the initiative came entirely from those who were making the studies. The extent
to which these three people should be considered normal, healthy,
mature, successful, admirable is a judgment that each reader will want
to make for himself. Clearly the subjects are too few to qualify as a rep-

.resentative sample of anything, even of the university they attended. They are simply three individuals, not much alike, whose good will and curiosity disposed them to share the story of their natural growth.

The study of lives has one advantage over more specialized approaches to personality. The goal of understanding a person as a whole over time effectively opposes narrow observation and oversimplified thinking. It is natural to start from biological concepts such as constitution, motivation, and learning. Each person, in this view, starts life with a certain inherited biological individuality; each is activated by needs shaped by the evolutionary past; each makes use of an enormous capacity for learning to adapt to the environment. These concepts are indeed important, but their promise of simplicity vanishes the moment we think about what is implied by environment. The surroundings most fateful for development are the human ones, and they can be bafflingly complex. Early in life the child must begin to grasp and cope with the individual peculiarities of the people around him, who are certainly not cut to standard patterns. As soon as possible he must learn about the complicated relations that exist among people, whether in family relations, in the neighborhood, or in institutions like school. He must learn to respond in some way to a large weight of expectations, spoken and unspoken, on the subject of how to behave, expectations characteristic of the society and culture in which he is embedded. To understand a person's life requires understanding the society in which that life is led. Students of personality cannot hope to comprehend their subject without covering the whole biosocial range from organic foundations such as drive and constitution to social shaping forces such as class status and cultural pattern.

Central to the purpose of this book is the often neglected task of bringing these diverse contributions to bear all at once on the study of the individual. Equally central is the goal of keeping in view the true nature of the person's response. As strongly as behavior is influenced by past and present forces, it cannot be correctly described as the simple consequence of these forces. As a living organism, a person is himself to some degree a center of force capable of having effects on his environment. Much as we are molded by circumstances, it is not entirely beyond us to do some molding of our own. Especially when viewed over time, human behavior exhibits qualities of selecting, construing, testing, organizing, and persisting, all of which tend to produce movement toward bettering one's personal situation. Individual lives progressing normally amid natural circumstances are especially well suited to disclose this constructive aspect of behavior. Because they are not acutely problematical, as are handicaps, neurotic hang-ups, or mental illness, they have not been extensively studied. Likewise there are few systematic case records of great fortitude, rare heroism, unusual contribution to the arts or to science, or special success in grasping and solving important social problems. Thus it happens that the natural growth of personality and the higher flights of human achievement are still poorly represented in current science-based thinking about human nature.

In this book we shall examine three lives in progress. Our first goal will be to understand them as fully as possible in the light of existing ideas derived from biological research, psychology, psychoanalysis, and the social sciences; our second goal, to name some of the ideas that need to be added in order to account for natural growth. Before we begin the study of our first example it will be well to assemble in a brief survey the ideas that make up our current stock in trade. In later chapters these ideas will receive fuller evaluation in the light of the case studies. Here we can do little more than call the roll and quickly sketch the origins.

The Biological View of Man

One of the major revolutions in scientific thinking occurred in 1859, when Charles Darwin published *The Origin of Species* with its impressive evidence for a theory of evolution. The effect of this work was to plant man firmly in the animal kingdom. His cherished notion of himself as a separate kind of creature, endowed with altogether superior faculties, had to be abandoned in the face of evidence that he had evolved from an earlier primate form. Instead he was forced to regard himself as one of the animals, distinguished from the rest of the kingdom only by certain quantitative advantages, such as his more mobile hands and more spaciously developed brain. However great these advantages, the roots of his being and the reasons for his existence were identical with those of all living creatures. He could be studied just as animals or plants were studied without invoking special principles such as soul or spirit. This general idea, now implemented by a century of research, constitutes what we shall here call the biological view of man. It underlies the momentous accomplishments of the biological sciences, including experimental psychology and medical research.

Motivation If man is an organism, he is engaged on the task that is common to all organisms: growth, maintenance, reproduction. Taken over a short span of time the activities of an organism seem adequately covered by the concept of homeostasis, the maintenance of an internal equilibrium in the face of changing tissue needs and changing external conditions. Body temperature, for example, has to be maintained within narrow limits, and the tissues must be kept nourished by periodic taking in of water and food. Viewed over a longer period, the life of an organism can be seen to exhibit further trends: growth to maximum size and efficiency, and reproduction of its kind. In all such transactions the organism takes an active part, responding sometimes with great vigor to conditions both internal and external, especially those that seriously threaten its well-being. Its energies are not called forth in random and indiscriminate fashion; rather, there are certain conditions to which it is highly sensitive, which release large amounts of energy, and which make for persistent behavior until the situation is changed. The concept of *drive* refers to this selective mobilization of energies.

Considering the matter abstractly, one might suppose that the biological view would necessarily be founded on a clear understanding of innate drives. If these could be listed, we would know the raw material out of which experience fashions the complex motives of adult life. The earliest attempts at such a listing emphasized the continuity of man and animals by using the concept of *instinct*, but it soon became apparent that man possessed none of those clear-cut unlearned sequences of behavior that appear, for example, among insects. The concept of *drive* thus came to be preferred in describing human urges, which are initially more blind than instincts but capable of great elaboration through learning. The goal of preparing an exhaustive catalogue of drives, however, has shown itself to be something of an illusion. The concept of innate drive seems most appropriate when it is possible to specify bodily structures and tissue conditions that set off persistent lines of behavior. These tissue conditions can be approximately specified for certain important visceral drives, such as the needs for air, food, water, sex, and lactation. But there are other kinds of persistent behavior that have no apparent relation to bodily deficits or unpleasant tensions. Tendencies to explore and manipulate the environment, so conspicuous in young animals and children, are examples of persistent, absorbing activity that does not lead to definable bodily changes or relief from distress. Little as they resemble other drives, these investigat-

ing tendencies must be included in any systematic account of motivation. Their effects upon development are of no small significance.

In spite of the difficulties of establishing a definitive list of
human urges, the concept of drive has been of large service in understanding behavior. Its value becomes fully apparent when it is placed in
conjunction with learning. Man with his highly developed brain is the
animal above all others capable of learning elaborate channels of
expression for drives. He can learn the most complex routes to their
gratification; he can delay and deflect them, combine them in patterns
of joint satisfaction, build them into motives many steps removed from
their original sources. Yet even when all this complex organization has
been achieved, it remains important to understand the elements of primitive drive that may still be contributing to behavior. However susceptible to change through learning, the human motivational system has
roots in the simple necessities of growth, maintenance, and reproduction. The value of this idea is particularly apparent with respect to the
sex drive. Some parts of nineteenth-century society treated this need as
if it could be wholly subordinated to motives of other kinds. The difficulty in working such a policy became clear first through the study of
neurotic illness and then through biological research on the nature of
drives. During the last half century these two influences have revolu-
tionized the attitude of our culture toward sex.

Learning The scientific investigation of learning is one of
the chief concerns and accomplishments of experimental psychology.
An early landmark was Ivan Pavlov's well-known work on the condi-
tioned reflex. This was the starting point for an array of researches on
animal and human versatility in picking up cues that are of service in
the pursuit of satisfaction or safety. The dogs used in Pavlov's experiments learned to respond to bells or buzzers as signals when these
sounds regularly preceded a natural reward such as food, or a punishment such as electric shock. These responses could then be unlearned or
extinguished when the signals were no longer followed by food or
shock. Even such simple instances are not without relevance to the
young child's learning the signals in parental behavior that betoken the
satisfaction or frustration of his needs. The conditioning experiments
have also been of service in understanding the nature of neurotic
anxieties, and sometimes in extinguishing them.

Edward Thorndike established another landmark by his studies
of the efforts of hungry cats to get out of cages in order to reach food.

The cats' slow but successful mastery of the intricate mechanical problem—their gradual learning of the effective sequence of acts and their abandonment of the ineffective ones—seemed to imply that the reward of reaching the food strengthened the last few acts before the cage opened. In more general language, the selective reinforcement of certain responses resulted from their having just preceded a reduction in the tension inherent in a drive. This version of Thorndike's original "law of effect" has wide applicability in understanding how children acquire sequences of behavior that are instrumental in securing what they want or avoiding what they fear. It places the burden of explanation on reinforcement, and it has encouraged a sharp lookout for rewards and frustrations as determinants of individual development.

Useful as they have proved to be, these simple models of the learning process cannot easily represent behavior in its more organized forms. Even in their early years children begin to put things together. They learn to coordinate eye and hand, to master complex motor performances like jumping and climbing, to test relations among objects by persistent manipulation. With increasing age, operations of this kind can be accomplished largely in thought with a minimum of overt acts. The results can best be described as the formation of a cognitive map representing the environment and the possibilities for action within it. Typically, behavior comes to be governed by plans to produce changes in the environment or in one's relation to it, and the execution of the plans is guided by feedback as to what is being accomplished. Even a simple intention like hammering a nail fits this description; much more so the characteristically human purposes of making a good record in school, getting along with one's fellows, and preparing for an occupation.

The vast amount of learning required to develop cognitive maps and sustain effective intentions brings us back again to the question of motivation. The human infant is born conspicuously incompetent. He has everything to learn about his surroundings and how he can affect them. Behavior activated by drives like hunger, sex, and avoidance of pain will teach him a number of things about the environment, but it is through play, manipulation, and exploration that he rounds out his cognitive map and perfects his capacities. Human beings are often active even when their drives are at rest; they reach out toward the environment and expose themselves to it. It is therefore useful to think of exploratory and manipulative behavior as representing a form of persistent motivation, the biological function of which is to develop competence in dealing with the environment. To the extent that competence is actually achieved, it contributes to feelings of efficacy which are an important ingredient of self-esteem.

Constitutional Endowments The study of personality is in part the study of individual differences. Inasmuch as each person has his own particular history of learnings we would expect him to be different from anybody else. Biological research, however, shows plainly that no two individuals of the same species are precisely alike in their structural properties. Present knowledge about the laws of inheritance shows that the genes are combined in constantly novel patterns rather than being arranged to produce a standard article. Just as we would like to work out an exhaustive list of innate human drives, so we would like to have a complete account of those differences in natural endowment that might affect the development of personality. But the goal of completeness is here even less practicable, partly because our knowledge of basic properties is not sufficiently refined, partly because inherited qualities soon merge their effects with those of learning in a way that makes analysis difficult.

Constitutional origins have been attributed to a number of *traits* in which people conspicuously differ, traits such as sensitivity, impulsiveness, liability to mood swings, and extraversion-introversion. One of the most carefully studied variables is activity level. Marked differences can be observed in newborn babies, and these differences show at least some tendency to persist in later years. Activity level has decided effects on the character of experience. A highly active child gets around more, tests his competence more often, interacts with more people, gets into more trouble, and is more likely to try his parents' patience. A passive child is less of a care, may seem to develop more slowly, but may be superior in observational learning and stability of behavior. The significance of activity level thus lies partly in its effects on learning, but the innate element may still be important in adult life. Breakdowns in health and happiness can occur when there is a discrepancy between available energy and external requirements. The demands of an exacting job may produce unbearable strain in a quiet person, whereas a person with buoyant energies may become frantically restless with monotonous desk work.

Differences in *ability* seem also related to natural endowment. We recognize this easily in outstanding athletes, whose striking success cannot plausibly be laid just to greater practice or motivation. We recognize it also in certain types of genius, as represented by infant prodigies in music or in mathematics. No ability has been more persistently tested than intelligence, and for a long time the IQ was interpreted as a fairly close measure of intellectual endowment. Recently this view has been widely challenged by research showing the significant part played in intellectual performance by environmental influences, but these findings do not wholly eliminate an hereditary component. It will be a great boon to guidance programs when the innate element in this and other aptitudes can be better disentangled.

The Contribution of Psychoanalysis

Psychoanalysis has had a strong influence on present thinking about human nature. It was largely created by Sigmund Freud during the early years of this century. A physician interested in the cure of neurotic patients, Freud began his labors at a time when doubt was first beginning to be cast on the organic or diseaselike character of neurosis. Instead of being, like other diseases, the surface manifestation of a disordered bodily state, neurosis appeared to have its roots in the patient's thoughts and feelings, and there were a few bits of evidence that exploration of the thoughts and airing of the feelings might produce a cure.

Method of Discovery Freud's career of discovery really began when, after several false starts, he invented a way to surmount the obstacles offered by patients to having their intimate thoughts and feelings explored. His invention, the technique of free association, seems an amazingly simple device to have produced momentous consequences. It consisted of nothing more than asking the patient to put aside his usual goal of reporting about himself with logic, order, coherence, and propriety; instead, he was to give his thoughts the utmost freedom, telling the listener about the images, feelings, and daydreams that streamed through his mind, no matter how haphazard and insignificant they seemed to be. The material produced in this way soon proved to be anything but meaningless. By eliminating the effects of logical habits and of fixed pictures of the self, Freud successfully brought into the open the feelings, impulses, anxieties, and defenses that operated all the time behind this customary façade and that under just the right combination of circumstances produced a neurosis.

Free association is not as easy as it sounds. Patients mobilized all kinds of resistances against yielding to the flow of their thoughts. As they became less anxious, however, they began to recall one emotionally charged topic after another, often going far back into childhood, laying bare whole chains of frustrating and frightening situations that had caused development to take a neurotic course. Moreover, the patients experienced again the tangled patterns of love, hate, and fear that had generally characterized these incidents, acting out in their relation to the physician the crucial struggles with parents and other important figures of their earlier years. This renewal of contact with the emotions and urges they had earlier shut out of their development sometimes appeared to promote new growth toward health. As a method of treatment, psychoanalysis is too long, uncertain, and expensive to have a wide impact, but its character as a thorough exploration of a person's emotional life made it a highly significant contribution to the study of human nature.

Leading Ideas The ideas developed by Freud to explain the findings of psychoanalysis did not remain the property of specialists but entered widely into contemporary thought. Foremost among these ideas is the notion of the constant play of impulse beneath and through the rational, conscious, goal-directed activities of everyday life. The central place is given to motivation rather than rationality, to drive rather than intellect. Beneath the surface of awareness lies a zone of teeming emotion, urge, fantasy, from which spring the effective driving forces as well as various disrupting agents in our behavior. At first it seemed that this zone was chiefly inhabited by sexual impulses, but soon the finding was generalized to include aggressive urges, dependent tendencies, and any other strivings which, for reasons either external or internal, could not be permitted free egress into behavior. The new image of man was beautifully dramatized by Eugene O'Neill in *Strange Interlude*, in which the characters speak to each other in ways dictated by reality and propriety but also give long asides to the audience in which they display their hates, fears, vanities, and sexual involvements. The centrality of striving, the understanding of behavior by finding out how it is motivated even though the operation of the motives be devious and unconscious, remains one of the main ideas of psychoanalysis.

Another leading idea is that of defense mechanisms. Freud was aware of two stages in the development of his thinking: one in which the chief interest lay in unmasking the patient's unconscious strivings, another in which the focus of inquiry shifted to the defenses set up to check and control these strivings. This advance was necessary in order to understand the neuroses, many of the symptoms of which represent the effects of overworked defenses rather than the disguised expression of impulse. The defense mechanisms that Freud first recognized in his work with patients—such things as repression, projection, and reaction-formation—were gradually expanded to accommodate some of the more complex aspects of personality organization. Alfred Adler, for example, pointed out that various common traits such as vanity, deference, or a preoccupying concern with one's ailments served often to maintain fictions of superiority and to avoid tests that might reveal inferiority. Adler and later Karen Horney studied the whole personal style of life as in part a defensive operation. A consuming struggle for professional success, for instance, sometimes carried the latent meaning of a vital personal vindication, a denial of inferiorities that had produced rage and panic in childhood; thus the person became highly vulnerable to even the smallest hint that his success was incomplete, and he drove himself relentlessly to make his triumph perfect. In such ways the whole pattern of personality came to be perceived as accomplishing not only the satisfaction of urges but also the maintenance of defenses.

A third major tenet is that the earliest learnings are extremely important in the shaping of personality. The free associations of neurotic patients led back constantly to the earliest years and to memories in which the members of the family circle played a paramount part. The first five years of life, formerly brushed aside as a time when the child was too young for serious learning, suddenly sprang into focus as the period in which the great problems of impulse and defense received their vital first solutions. Parents and siblings served as chief characters in the infant's emotional dramas, giving him his first experiences in human relationship. Repeatedly it was found that neurotic difficulties in adult years arose from the continuing effects of infantile learning. A male patient's troubled relation to his women friends, for example, would prove to come from an almost literal repetition of the attitudes and expectations he had learned in his childhood experiences with his mother. Such behavior could be understood not only by perceiving the impulses and defenses that were involved but also by discovering the historical origin of the pattern in the learning situations of the nursery. Particular significance came to be attached to the manner in which major frustrating episodes were traversed: weaning, toilet training, punishments and discipline, birth of siblings and adjustment to their presence, jealousies and rivalries including the "eternal triangle" of child and parents that Freud picturesquely called the Oedipus complex. Much research eventually came to be directed toward understanding parent-child relations during the earliest years.

Ego Psychology One of Freud's ventures in conceptualization was a threefold division of personality into id, ego, and superego. The id signified the realm of impulse or drive, including fantasies to which these gave rise. The superego represented childhood conscience, the imperious "do's" and "don't's" that make up a child's understanding of parental expectations. These two sets of forces, largely unconscious and often conflicting, could be guided only by the ego, the part of ourselves that appraised reality and tended to steer behavior into sensible and rational channels. Psychoanalysis was most startling when it unveiled the subterranean conflicts of id and superego, but a theory of behavior could not be complete without accounting for adaptation to reality. The outstanding contribution to ego psychology came in 1950 in Erik Erikson's *Childhood and Society*, wherein a scheme was worked out for describing ego development through eight stages during the course of life. This book did a great deal to connect psychoanalysis with other branches of thought. Understanding the growth of the child's behavioral capacities means turning to the experimental psychology of development, while the emphasis Erikson put on mutual regulation— between mother and child in infancy, between individual and society in later years—requires consulting the resources of the social sciences.

In historical perspective Freud and psychoanalysis will doubtless be reckoned a powerful influence upon contemporary culture. Literature was profoundly affected. Values have changed in directions similar to those of psychoanalytic treatment, which stressed honesty about one's feelings, openness in human relations, and greater freedom for the expression of impulse. While its influence was at its height, psychoanalysis was treated as a special body of knowledge not closely connected with other kinds of investigation. Its findings were designated *dynamic psychology*, a title that reflected the emphasis put on motivational forces and their conflicts. Strife between urgent id and repressive superego, as disclosed in protracted free associations, could indeed be aptly described as a battle of forces. Ego, however, is quite another matter. The ego in psychoanalytical theory is clearly a process of learning, the seat of maps and plans. There is thus no theoretical justification for distinguishing a dynamic psychology from one that is not dynamic. All psychological research is firmly grounded in common principles of motivation and learning.

The Social View of Man

An individual's career of learning takes place in an environment well populated by other human beings. From the start there is large dependence on human ministrations. Learning is first closely guided by those who provide for immediate wants, later increasingly by larger segments of the society. For the most part the voyage of life does not cross unexplored oceans; it goes along dredged and buoyed channels, guided by a carefully prepared social chart.

The Culture Concept Our rapid sketch of the social forces that shape personality will begin with the concept of *culture*. This concept has been put forward primarily by anthropologists as a means of understanding some of the features of primitive societies. It has had an enormous influence on the understanding of personality. It opened another of those areas to which we had previously paid little heed. Not that the effects of culture are remote and obscure; quite the contrary, they are everywhere in our daily lives and were overlooked simply by being taken for granted. The comparative study of primitive societies necessitated the emergence of culture into our consciousness.

The culture concept in anthropology refers to the training that an individual receives because of his membership in a human society. This includes routine matters such as eating with the fingers or with chopsticks or with knife and fork. It includes beliefs about the nature of the world and the means of propitiating hostile forces: ceremonial dances, or employment of medicine men, or support of scientific research. It includes ideal patterns of conduct, such as gentle cooperativeness or warlike assertiveness or individual enterprise and self-reliance. In this sense no societies, however simple, are without a culture, and no individuals are uncultured. The concept of culture refers to the total way of life of a society, the heritage of accumulated social learnings that is shared and transmitted by the members of that society. To put it another way, a culture is a set of shared plans for living, developed out of the necessities of previous generations, existing in the minds of the present generation, taught directly or indirectly to new generations. Without such plans the life of a society would become impossibly chaotic. The culture provides pretested solutions to many problems and allows us to learn without endless trial and error what to expect of others and of ourselves.

The most dramatic examples of the quiet but forceful impact of culture on our lives come from comparisons with other societies where customs are radically different. Rattlesnake meat is in some places a delicacy; by fancying our own reaction to this tempting dish we can appreciate the horror and disgust felt by members of other cultures on seeing us eat the unclean pig or the flesh of the sacred cow. The religious practices of other societies, or their customs as regards the burial of the dead, serve further to remind us of the wide differences that exist in what is felt to be right and natural.

More important for the understanding of personality are those parts of the plan for living that have to do with the socialization of children and the setting of ideal standards of behavior. Some societies train children through sharp punishments and the evoking of fears; others are more lenient, using gentle persuasion and bribery. Some cultures make courtship and marriage a matter for individual enterprise; others assign matrimony to parental decision, regarding mutual attraction and romantic love as irrelevant to this grave social institution. As Ruth Benedict, Margaret Mead, and others have shown, some societies train children to shun individual success and prominence. The goal of life is to be pleasing, generous, cooperative; to put people at their ease, be thought a good fellow, and avoid all signs of arrogance or strong emotion. As adults, children trained in this tradition try to avoid marks of distinction and consider it a miserable sacrifice if they are elected to public office. Other cultures look upon such behavior as repulsively weak and abnormal; they train their children instead to climb to the top through sharp practice, theft, and the use of magic. Elsewhere the prescribed route to self-esteem may be individual excellence in hunting edible game, in human head-hunting, or in accumulating wealth, which is then wastefully destroyed in a public display. Thus the culture bears down on its individual members, indoctrinating them with the plan of life they will be expected to follow.

The study of culture, mostly in simpler societies, and psychoanalysis, working mostly with neurotic patients, seem to have little in common; but in certain respects they have had a similar impact on the understanding of personality. Both challenged man's claim to conscious, rational self-direction. Psychoanalysis disclosed the irrational grip of urges, anxieties, and overworked protective devices. The study of cultures brought out a similar tyranny, this time of custom, belief, and moral precept learned half unconsciously from the older members of the group. Large sections of our behavior were unmasked and found to be anything but expressions of free choice or adjustment to the clear dictates of reality. The culture concept shows us how closely we live according to the habitual life plans prevailing in our society, even when changed conditions make these plans inappropriate.

In another respect psychoanalysis and the culture concept have made an overlapping contribution. Both have turned a searchlight upon the earliest years of life and upon learnings that take place within the family circle. For the child the first transmitters of the culture are his parents, just as they are the first participants in his emotional development. The initial impact of the culture comes through the behavior and attitudes of the parents. It comes charged with all the importance and authority that the young child necessarily attributes to his parents. For this reason cultural dictates often acquire the force of moral imperatives and become resistant to critical appraisal. They become part of an irrational superego.

What first impinges on the child is always a parental version of the culture, possibly somewhat different from the overall pattern that is characteristic of the society as a whole. In a small and uniform society it is not likely that parental versions will stray far from the general pattern. When it comes to understanding a person in our own vast and differentiated society, however, we have to specify with great care the portion of the culture, the particular subculture, that the parents represent. Cultural pressures vary widely among different regions, social classes, ethnic and religious groups. But the search for these subculture patterns quickly takes us into the whole question of the social structure and its effects upon personality.

Social Structure If a society is to operate successfully there must be a division of functions among its individual members. Even the simplest society does not make the same demands upon all, for instance, upon men and women, or upon infants, children, young adults, and older people. Age and sex put the individual in a definite position with respect to the other members of his society. Different behavior is expected from the occupants of different social positions, and the individual personality cannot be fully understood without taking these expectations into account. With a more complex division of labor, future social and occupational positions can often be anticipated in advance, so that from the very beginning the child is trained for a specific part. Our own society favors the abstract ideal that each individual shall be free to choose his life work. Nevertheless it is obvious that the child of wealthy professional parents and the child of an itinerant farm laborer are not reared in the same framework of expectations for the future. In a society with highly developed division of labor, the specialized position occupied by the individual member becomes a major influence in the shaping of his personality.

Much light has been thrown on this problem by studies of *social class*. Our democratic ideals incline us not to speak openly of classes and barriers, but there is no doubt that social stratification exists and that it exerts a powerful influence on individual behavior. Students of social structure, beginning with W. Lloyd Warner and his associates, have been active in working out the precise nature of social classes in various American communities. Marked social stratification was found in every community, and its effects were pervasive. Other workers, in particular A. Davis and J. Dollard, have pointed out that each social level has its own set of values and ideals, which differ sometimes sharply from those of adjacent levels. A child grows up not merely in the American culture but in the subculture of his social class; we cannot hope to understand him without taking account of these direct pressures and traditions.

Similarly, we cannot expect to understand an adult without taking account of *occupational status*. The more organized occupations, especially the professions, tend to impose definite roles upon their members. Living within the role means for the most part restricting one's goals and one's notions of success to those favored in the occupation. An occupational role confers numerous privileges but it also imposes a series of obligations, which are maintained not only by standards within the occupation but by the expectations of everyone on the outside. Each occupational group is privileged to work with its clients in one particular way and is not expected to go outside definite limits. Thus we would be startled, if not outraged, if our lawyer asked us about habits of eating and excretion, if a loan officer inquired into our sexual life, or if our doctor wanted to know the terms of our will. The whole pattern of privileges and obligations provides a framework which affects the individual course of life.

In such fashion personality is shaped by social forces. Much of the shaping takes place unconsciously. Through the constant process of social interaction a person comes gradually to know what others expect of him, what he may expect of others, what roles he can play satisfac-

torily, and how these roles fit into the roles of other people. In this subtle process of learning, memberships in groups play a significant part.
Second only to the impress of the family is the molding influence of
groups in childhood and especially in adolescence. In attempting to
understand an individual life it is important, though often difficult, to
work out the history of group participations and to establish their effect
in forming personality. Equally important is the appraisal of current
memberships, which often have a great deal to do with stability, contentment, and the person's conception of himself.

An Illustrative Problem: Adolescence

The need for a multiple approach to the study of human nature is well
illustrated by the problem of development during adolescence. There
is a tradition in our culture that adolescence is a period of emotional
storm and stress, marked by difficult behavior, a rebellious outlook, and
a great deal of internal conflict and suffering. In the nature of things,
according to this tradition, adolescence is a trying period that must be
endured as best one can. Let us now briefly consider what the biological, psychoanalytical, and social views have contributed to understanding this phase of growth.

   Viewed biologically, adolescence signifies the attainment of
adult stature, strength, and mental capacity, together with the final mat-
uration of sexuality and reproductive functions. The child finishes the
period of growth and becomes ready to assume an adult role. Studies of
intelligence show that mental capacity reaches its maximum during the
teen years; the youngster becomes as bright as he will ever be, though
naturally not as wise nor as experienced. The attainment of this mature
level of mental capacity produces rapid cognitive development with
expanding mental horizons: there is so much to be taken in and assimilated by a mind freshly able to perceive things in their full dimensions.
The strengthening of the sex drive upsets not only the accustomed pattern of interests but also the established balance of the endocrine system. Adolescence can be perceived as a kind of biological turning
point, and its problems are in part the results of this crisis in organic
growth.

   When we take the psychoanalytical point of view the problems
of adolescence appear in a somewhat different light. The adolescent
must learn to manage a newly strengthened and somewhat tumultuous
drive, but difficulties in doing so spring chiefly from the fact that this

drive has a previous history that has channeled it in ways no longer
wholly suitable. The sexual interests of early childhood, to some degree
forgotten during the so-called latency period from the sixth year to
puberty, are reanimated by the waxing sex urge. But now they are a
source of even more severe conflict, especially if they continue to involve
family members or friends of the same sex. Anxiety and guilt are frequently by-products of infantile sexual interests, and these painful feelings return to plague the adolescent while he is attempting to get used
to his new erotic status.

A second important problem is that of outgrowing dependency
needs. The surly and exaggerated rebellion that is sometimes displayed
may well represent an angry attempt to cut the ties that still inwardly
bind the adolescent to the benefits and exemptions of childhood. Self-
respect requires that they be cut, but the young person may wonder and
worry about the resulting freedom; growing up creates pressure to discover and develop one's own sense of identity. Parental reactions need
to be added in order to complete the picture of adolescent development.
It is not easy for parents to withdraw protective supervision at an appropriate rate, to respect the new-found powers of their young, or to avoid
disquieting contrasts between the fresh energy of youth and their own
advancing middle age.

These problems could easily be misconceived, however, if we
failed to transcend the limited perspective of our own culture. To what
extent are such stresses biologically and psychologically inevitable? It
is here that anthropology makes a significant contribution. Field studies
among primitive peoples show that adolescence is by no means always a
period of storm and stress. In some societies it is traversed with a calm-
ness quite at odds with our own expectations. The problems of adolescence are highly relative to the values of the culture. Many societies
have elaborate puberty rites that serve to mark sharply the entrance of
the erstwhile child into full adult status. Very likely the young person
ceases to live at home and becomes the object of a wholly different set
of attitudes on the part of other people. This institutional recognition
makes it easier for the adolescent to break with childhood and move
toward adult identity, just as it makes it easier for parents to change
their expectations and relinquish parental roles. Puberty rites create a
very different situation from that which prevails in our society, where
there is no clearly defined transition from childhood to adult status.
Cross-cultural studies reveal also great differences in the cultural attitude toward sex. When this attitude is highly permissive there seem to

be no signs of the latency period assumed in our own culture to be more or less biologically determined. Sexual interests flourish throughout childhood without becoming a deep preoccupation. The latency period turns out to be a cultural rather than a biological phenomenon, and the difficulty of redirecting the sexual urges of childhood seems to be smaller when guilt and anxiety are less involved.

How fixed are the attitudes of our own culture toward adolescence? Historically they are of fairly recent origin. The Victorian attitude toward sex was considerably more repressive than those prevailing before the second half of the nineteenth century. Furthermore, adolescence is in a certain sense a cultural invention brought about by developments in industry and education. Under simpler conditions of life, children were absorbed gradually into adult work, which they were often well able to manage during their teen years. After the industrial revolution this once natural practice became cruelly exploitative and was progressively delayed by law. Simultaneously the need for more extended education became urgent, and opportunities were provided by expansion of public schools and colleges. It was no accident that adolescence emerged as a problem, heavy with storm and stress, only when these developments were well under way, for it was only then that long years came to intervene between puberty and entrance into adult roles of work and marriage. This turned adolescence into a true age-status, occupied by people in many respects mature but treated by the rest of society as not yet adult. Such a status can easily engender stress, particularly with respect to dependence and independence.

These considerations emphasize the importance of social structure in understanding adolescent development. In the course of establishing independence from adult constraints, the adolescent in our society tends to identify very strongly with other adolescents. Both boys and girls tend to become loyal and highly conforming members of the local youth culture. This conformity, often so at odds with a negative attitude at home, suggests that an emotionally difficult process is going on, and we can grasp this difficulty when we notice three features of the American social structure: the small isolated family with its strong emotional ties, the urban impersonality of the world beyond, and the still highly competitive economic system with its requirement of independent enterprise. The adolescent may experience this transition as leaping from a family nest into a vast wasteland, where it will be necessary somehow to find occupation and set up an independent home. No wonder that for a time many young people feel disoriented and become excessively dependent on the circle of peers. The transition is particularly sharp in large cities and changing suburbs which offer so little emotional anchorage or sense of security.

The problems of development during adolescence make sense only when seen in these multiple ways. It is essential to include the biological, the psychoanalytical, and the social evidence, remembering that man, the animal, is a very complex being living in a society that has a history and tradition as well as a contemporary structure. Human nature cannot be understood from a limited viewpoint. Perhaps it cannot be understood without widening our vision still more. We may not yet have taken enough into account.

The Place of Activity and Initiative

What seems to be most poorly represented in the ideas thus far reviewed is the conception of the person as an active agent. The three subjects to be described in this book, like the rest of us, experience themselves as capable of initiative and efficacy in leading their lives. They tell of times when they reflected on their experience, perceived things in a new light, and decided to try some new line of behavior. They describe the effects their behavior had on other people. They relate critical occasions when they had to oppose the expectations of others and decide what was right for themselves. This way of reporting one's experience, sometimes dismissed as an unscientific claim to free will, is congruent with the biological view that a living organism is a system which grows, expands its boundaries, resists deformation, and exerts effects on its surroundings. We may be deceived about the extent of our influence, but it would be dogmatic, indeed, to declare that we have none.

The neglect of individual activity and initiative is in fact an unintended by-product of scientific zeal. By training, if not also by deep temperamental preference, those who approach things scientifically want to deal with objective facts and connections that can be tested. Like anyone else, the scientist prefers victory to defeat. He wants to work with facts that can be controlled, with determinants that can be determined, with outcomes that can be predicted and measured. He wants to arrive at general concepts and general relationships, searching out the lawfulness beneath the multitude of surface events. In consequence of this bias, the scientist is inevitably disposed to deal selectively with human nature. He can do little with the fact that each person is acted upon by a tremendous multiplicity of influences, becoming as a result a unique individual. He can do hardly more with the circumstance that both person and environment undergo continuous change—that personality is a constantly evolving system. He is extremely reluctant to go beyond the task of explaining the forces that affect the person in order to consider how the person in turn affects his environment. The scientific approach to personality, therefore, has thus far greatly favored the simpler and less flexible aspects of behavior, giving scant attention to multiplicity, individuality, continuous change, or to the person as a source of action.

The extent of this bias can be appreciated by contrasting the scientist's approach with that of the novelist, dramatist, or writer of biography. The literary man is usually interested in the changes that occur in his characters as they live through a series of complex important events. He tells us about the way such events affect the characters and the way the characters affect the events. Growth is a prominent theme in novels of strongly autobiographical flavor, and it becomes particularly insistent for the writer of biography, who usually sets himself the task of understanding a life marked by noteworthy accomplishment. If his work is to be complete, the biographer must try to account for transformations such as that of Abraham Lincoln from a moody, reluctant, indecisive young man into a President distinguished for powerful conviction and vigorous leadership. Change, whether it be growth or disintegration, is a central concern in literature. Of a writer who does not depict change in personality we are apt to say a little scornfully that he deals only in caricature. The minor characters of Dickens, like Mr. Micawber, who at each appearance reiterates his bland assurance that something will turn up to rescue him from poverty, illustrate this inferior though often amusing treatment of personality. An artist would certainly be overlooking the richest qualities of his material if he made his central characters behave with such monotonous rigidity. The scientist, however, is under tremendous temptation to practice the art of caricature. It would be vastly easier to explain and predict behavior if everyone acted like Mr. Micawber and if no one had any particular effect on the conditions surrounding him. It is not surprising, therefore, that scientific study has achieved its triumphs chiefly with the fixed, the repetitive, the unrealistic, and the unspontaneous in human relations.

Most of the ideas discussed earlier in this chapter put emphasis on the kind of learned behavior that is unwitting and irrational. The subtle impress of the culture is most readily perceived when it produces automatic behavior that is not adapted to existing conditions. Behavior indicative of social class is unconsciously absorbed from the environment and sometimes occurs in contradiction to the person's professed ideals. Role expectations are not laid down in black and white to be learned by conscious act; they seep into a person's life from sources he does not always recognize and with a force he may sometimes regret. It is much the same story with emotional attitudes early learned in the family circle and with the unconscious conflicts, anxieties, and defenses that figure in neurotic maladjustment. Similarly the biological foundations of behavior have been examined in their more primitive manifestations where their command of conduct is most autocratic. In short, the scientific student of personality has been most interested in what enters the learning process through channels not consciously discerned nor rationally appraised. These processes most easily fit a cause-effect model in which the person's behavior can be cast as effect.

In the pages that follow it is important to be aware of this bias. The three lives to be examined were indeed strongly affected by cultural and social expectations, by family members and friends, and by urges and wishes over which they had little or no control. We cannot understand them without doing full justice to these powerful shaping influences. But we must recognize this without slipping into the dogma that a person is always a result and never a cause of what happens around him. Special importance should perhaps be attached to the idea of an inherent tendency or motive toward activity, taking the form of exploration, manipulation, and playful testing of surroundings, and having the biological significance of attaining competence in dealing with the environment. This is by no means all that lies on the side of personal activity, but it helps to restore to the person what we all experience as initiative and efficacy in leading our lives. As will soon become clear, we cannot do justice to lives in progress without including the changing, growing, designing, farsighted, creative aspects of behavior.

SUGGESTIONS FOR FURTHER READING

The social view of man will be considered at greater length in Chapter 4, the biological view in Chapter 6, and some aspects of the psychoanalytical contribution in Chapter 8 on the course of growth. Suggested further readings are given at the end of each of these chapters.

The most pertinent book to suggest for further reading at this point is Erik H. Erikson's *Childhood and Society* (New York: W. W. Norton &

Co., 2d ed., 1963) which undertakes to build bridges between the study of society and the study of the individual. A similar integrative purpose animates Ralph Linton's small but illuminating classic, *The Cultural Background of Personality* (New York: Appleton-Century-Crofts, 1945).

Two recent books on adolescence will be of service in making vivid the problems of this period of development: G. W. Goethals and D. S. Klos, *Experiencing Youth: First Person Accounts* (Boston: Little, Brown and Company, 1970), and N. C. Ralston and G. P. Thomas, *The Adolescent: Case Studies for Analysis* (San Francisco: Chandler Publishing Co., 1974). A standard textbook on the subject is K. C. Garrison's *Psychology of Adolescence*, 6th ed. (Englewood Cliffs, N. J.: Prentice-Hall, 1965). Two books develop the historical theme that adolescence is not so much a biological event as a modern cultural invention produced by industrial conditions and prolonged education: J. H. van den Berg, *The Changing Nature of Man* (New York: Delta Books, 1964), and F. Musgrove, *Youth and the Social Order* (Bloomington: Indiana University Press, 1965).

The place in personality of agency, initiative, and the power to choose is taken up in Ernest Keen's *Psychology and the New Consciousness* (Belmont, Calif.: Brooks-Cole Publishers, 1972).

2

HARTLEY HALE,
PHYSICIAN AND SCIENTIST

> I like the world as it is. For as it is it offers competition and insecurity, and it's the battle to overcome each of these that makes life worthwhile.
>
> HARTLEY HALE

In the fall of 1939, twenty Harvard undergraduates were engaged through the student employment office to serve as paid subjects in extensive studies of personality. One of these young men was Hartley Hale, a twenty-one-year-old junior who was concentrating in biology and planning a career in medicine. The studies proceeded at a leisurely pace up to the time of his graduation. Ten years later, just after his thirty-third birthday, he came to Boston to read a paper at a medical meeting. He was prevailed upon to extend his visit so that he might be made the subject of a second study, compensation being offered at a rate appropriate to his current earning capacity. This time the interviews and tests were packed closely together, but all the sessions were recorded, and this together with Hale's good-humored and generous participation permitted the study to be searching and comprehensive. What we know about this man thus rests upon two separate series of observations, one made when he was a premedical undergraduate, the other when he had become a physician and scientific investigator well established in his profession.

To understand as well as possible the natural growth of even a single personality is a task of no small magnitude. In order to concentrate fully upon it we shall not stop to make explicit in this chapter either our methods of examination or our guiding concepts. These problems will occupy us later. Our present purpose will be more strictly biographical. We want to understand one man, Hartley Hale, as well as it is possible to understand him with the materials at our disposal. We want to know the story of his life and to search behind that story for whatever we can find by way of explanation. Before we can move in a responsible manner in the realm of general ideas, it is necessary to become exhaustively acquainted with at least one fact; and if personality is our theme this fact can be nothing smaller than a person's whole life in all its uniqueness and all its complexity.

PART ONE: THROUGH COLLEGE

The Hale Family Circle

One of the first tasks assigned to Hale in the undergraduate study was that of preparing an autobiography. He started with the family circle. He told of his paternal ancestors, who herded cattle in the Scottish lowlands, and of his grandfather, remembered as a "stern straight-laced old Scotsman," who settled in a fair-sized midwestern American city and established his own wholesale business. He described his father's career at a large university, a career which included both scholastic attainments in the classics and success in the hockey rink. After a short period of teaching, the father was persuaded to enter the wholesale business, where he "started at the bottom" and "struggled upward" until he became, on the grandfather's death, general manager of the company. Hale's father was forty when he met and courted his future wife, an artist of twenty-seven for whom "critics were predicting a bright future." Born in Iowa, this talented young woman had received most of her education and all of her artistic training in Chicago, and had but lately moved to the smaller city with her mother following the latter's second marriage. So energetic was the father's courtship that she was persuaded to drop her career in favor of marriage. Three years later a daughter was born and after another five years, when the father was forty-eight and the mother thirty-five, Hartley arrived on the scene. "As my mother remarked many years after," he wrote, "I was late on this occasion just as I have always been late for everything else."

Hale's father conducted his business with energy and devotion. Most of the profits were plowed back into the company to expand and strengthen its position. But he was much more than a businessman. His son wrote:

> Dad is a scholar in the old meaning of the word. The house is filled with bookcases, which in turn are filled with books, all of which he has read. He even sometimes picks up Latin books and reads them. He is young-minded, forward-looking, interested. His mind is sharp and fast; his temper, when roused, likewise. He is seldom unreasonable. Operated on for appendicitis two years ago (when 69) he was sitting up in bed smoking a cigar on the second day, home and around on the sixth. He is half a head shorter than I; thin, active, a burner of midnight oil.

Hale admitted later that his father's quick temper was sometimes disturbing. The father's scholarly tendencies, perhaps also the fact that he was by no means a young man while his children were growing up, caused him to want peace and quiet in the home and to be unduly irritated by noise. "He'd get quite angry at us," Hale declared; "it always used to sort of shock me when he'd get that angry." What shocked him most in these incidents, however, seems to have been his father's lapse from a standard of reasonableness which at other times conferred a considerable feeling of security. On the whole he considered his father an unusually just man as well as a model of energy and competence.

The mother appeared in the autobiography in a somewhat less favorable light. The son's pen sketched as follows the contrasting personalities of his parents:

> Mother is undecided, opposed to unknown change. She is afraid of airplanes, having never been in one. Dad went up in an open two-seater when I was four years of age, just to see what it was like. Mother's mind usually makes a quick stab at the answer, and then retreats while she thinks it over and answers again. Dad's mind pauses momentarily and then comes out with the right answer. This point is readily apparent when one plays bridge with the two of them. I can never remember seeing Dad play the wrong card. Mother often plays and then gasps as she sees that she has played the wrong card.

If the father's standards of quiet were a little high for a growing boy, the mother's standards of cleanliness were even more formidable. In the second study Hale told us that she kept the house "absolutely spotless," cleaning it twice a day, polishing the furniture, insisting "that no piece of dirt be allowed to lie in a place for more than thirty minutes." She was also "a great dictator: she told you when the weather was cold, what you should put on, whether it was myself or my father, and that's a very irritating quality." In other ways, however, she figured as an interesting and satisfactory member of the household, where on the whole the children felt themselves to be liked and cherished. This was summarized as follows in the autobiography: "Mother is interested in art, music, books; Dad in nearly everything; both in Connie (my sister) and me."

Different as were the two parents, they managed for the most part to present a united front in matters of discipline. "They pretty much got together on punishments," Hale told us; they always carried out whatever disciplinary measures they had threatened to use, and this gave to the punishment program a reliable character that allowed the boy as he grew older to weigh in advance the pleasure of misbehavior, the pain of punishment, and the chances of being caught. He felt that his punishments were deserved and that there was no particular favoritism between himself and Connie. Methods of punishment included spanking, scolding, being sent to his room, denial of some pleasure, being made to feel that he had fallen short of expectations; but no methods were used, as far as he could recall, which emphasized sibling rivalry or possible loss of the parents' love. Hale looked upon his father as the final authority and as the more reasonable disciplinarian. If his father lapsed from rationality, the boy protested angrily and might even refuse to obey. He recalled an incident in his adolescence when his father had forbidden a radio in the car. This unjustified ruling he evaded by hooking up his own portable radio temporarily when he had the car for the evening, and his father, though well aware of the ruse, never caught him in the act and never punished him.

Both parents seem to have played a part in creating what Hale rather oddly described as an "atmosphere of cultural unrest." This expression signified an emphasis on intellectual and artistic accomplishment; for instance, "I had read, or had read to me, most of Shakespeare, had learned to draw and play the piano, and could quote quite a few poems by the time I finished with primary school." He claimed to have memorized almost the whole of *Horatius at the Bridge* before he could read. Artistic and musical instruction was undertaken by the mother, but she was an impatient teacher whenever the learning progressed slowly. Hale's early literary heroes were Horatius, Ben Hur, and several of the characters of Kipling. He wrote that he "liked and admired justice, hated injustice and cruelty."

The high cultural standards of the home did not preclude interests of a more childlike and spontaneous kind. Hale wrote:

> I loved animals. Any kind of animals. I used to read stories about them by the hour, draw pictures of them, own as many of them as I could convince the family we had to have. This included several birds (one of which we had for 13 years, and which would come out of the cage and sit on our fingers), two dogs, white rats, turtles, goldfish, a cat. They vetoed a skunk. An English setter was, and is, my idea of a perfect pet.

That his parents limited the domestic zoo only by prohibiting the skunk suggests that his father's love of peace and his mother's devotion to neat cleanliness were counterbalanced by considerable appreciation of the natural interests of childhood.

In one important respect the family circle failed to provide a feeling of security. Every so often its harmony was disrupted by a parental quarrel, and these disputes frequently started over Hartley's misbehavior and disobedience.

> But there was a general tension in my home life. I was a rather stubborn, know-my-own-minded little child. I used to distress Mother no end, which distressed Dad no end, which led usually to an argument. Dad, an introvert, would say things and then sit there reading; Mother, an extrovert, would go upstairs (where I then went) and tell me what she felt, upon which I would act as a sort of peacemaker. I, strangely enough, felt malice toward neither of them; partly because harmony between the two of them was uppermost in my mind, and partly because I felt that Mother was wrong in saying what she did in the first place, and then that Dad was wrong in saying what he did. So that about evened the score. These "outbreaks" didn't happen often, but I had a certain fear that they might at any time. It was a tension.

Nothing further was said in the autobiography, but in the second study a decade later Hale told us a great deal more about these quarrels. "I never felt that things were too safe and too happy," he said; the whole thing seemed to "make my own future so uncertain, as a result I spent a lot of time thinking about it." From the later vantage point he was able to see the relation between these quarrels and the recurrent nightmares which he had reported in his autobiography:

> Our house was a big wooden frame structure. I was born in the very room I occupy when I'm home. I always loved the house, and the only nightmare I can remember having fairly often was the one that would cause me to run crying to my parents' room to be reassured that we weren't going to move out of the house.

When in the second study we reminded him of this excerpt, he said that his parents sometimes talked of moving, especially his mother, who wanted a smaller house. He said:

> Whenever they did talk about that, it used to scare me, used to scare the hell out of me, I didn't want to move, I was very much attached to the old house. For no special reason; it had no particular gratifying features about it; big frame ugly house with high ceilings and poor heating, no heating as a matter of fact until I was about 14, and there wasn't much to recommend it except that my sister liked it . . . I never felt too secure about life in general, and the talk about moving was taking away the most secure part of my life, which was that house.

The effect of these quarrels on Hale's development was evidently a profound one, especially from his tenth to twelfth years when they came to their peak. We shall return to them when we reach that point in his career.

It was important that his sister liked the house. From this remark we might infer that his sister occupied a position of prestige and respect. Connie resembled her father, having his "quick mind and temper"; she got high grades in school but also excelled in the art and music first taught by her mother. "She was very good looking," wrote Hartley, "and I liked her, though we were never especially close due to age differences." One of her endearing traits was her tendency to stick up for him when he was out of parental favor. But her most drastic influence occurred in what we shall refer to as the "backbone incident."

> Probably the greatest influence she exerted on my young life was the installation of a backbone in me. I shall never forget the incident:
>
> I was thin and small when young. One day when I was about 8, I guess, I was playing with my cousin, a girl half a year older than I. One of the bullies of the neighborhood came over and began

making unpleasant remarks about what he was going to do to me. Betty (my cousin) stuck up for me and held him off until I could make my escape. I ran home as fast as I could. Mother wasn't home, but Connie was. I told her the story, expecting sympathy. To my utter amazement she accused me of cowardice and shamed me for "hiding behind a woman's skirts." She told me if I had any courage I'd go back there and assert my rights. This I did, I must admit with fear and trembling inside of me, and when I called his bluff with no changes in my anatomy occurring I found that my terror of him vanished; and from that time on I never again feared him and never again ran from fright in a fight.

Hale attached to this incident an importance almost equal to that of the parental quarrels. Before we attempt to evaluate its part in his development, however, we must consider in more detail the events and chronology of his childhood.

Early Childhood

Hale remembered two episodes that occurred when he was two years old. One of them involved the enjoyment he felt in playing around a country summer cottage with a little girl of his own age. In the other we find him in the role of investigator: he stood on his kiddy car to peer through a garage window in order to see what was going on inside, but the car went out from under him so that he fell and cut his head. For the next year his memories were more numerous. His sister and and another girl wanted him to ride in a baby buggy and pretend to be a baby; though greatly offended, he consented in return for a suitable bribe. He recalled swinging and riding a tricycle, eating grapes from the vine, and picking dandelion greens with the family. These scattered early memories presently give place to more definite and more connected episodes. An important landmark was the Christmas when he was four years old:

> I got a fire engine, a wagon I could sit in and ride, with a ladder sticking way out behind. For four years I went all over the neighborhood. Everyone in the neighborhood used the fire engine. Next summer I got an Indian suit. I couldn't decide whether to be an Indian or a fireman.

Noteworthy in this memory is the easy making of the masculine identifications implied by the nature of the gifts he received. Also to be inferred from this recollection, as from his earliest memory of the little girl, is an easy and comfortable feeling about other children: he expressed no fear or resentment over the borrowing of the cherished fire engine, basking instead in the popularity and distinction it conferred upon him.

By the end of his fourth year his memories begin to testify to a tremendous interest in things mechanical. The mastery of machines is the theme of a whole series of pleasurable recollections. When he entered kindergarten, the blocks with wheels, holes, and axles arrested his attention: "I built carts every day and rode on them." He used to slam the cupboard doors after putting the blocks away, but one day he happened to close them quietly and the teacher praised him and held him up as a good example, after which he took the lead in quiet closing. His memories of machines continued with the receipt of an electric train for Christmas. This gift had hitherto been considered too dangerous by his parents, so although he was dubious about the existence of Santa Claus he decided to go over his parents' heads by writing a direct letter.

> The train was there, with a letter from Santa Claus saying how we had foxed my parents. I was jubilant; I wouldn't leave the train for a minute, and it was hard to shake my faith in Santa Claus after that. I was just about nuts.

Before he could read, a friend of the family gave him a book on electricity, which his parents read to him while he looked at the diagrams. Thus instructed, he tried to build a motor that would run without an outside source of power, but he experienced all the difficulties that beset earlier inventors of a perpetual motion machine. At seven his appendix was removed, an event he remembered chiefly because it prevented him from celebrating the Fourth of July. During convalescence he continued to design the machine, even though his nurse said that it looked like a mouse trap.

> I was all pepped up again about my machine. So I sold stock, 5 shares at a nickel, which gave me a quarter. I worked all summer and it wouldn't work. The stockholders began to clamor for their quarter. So I talked to Mother about it. She usually tried to shut me up on things she didn't think I could do. So she said if I could make a boat that would go twice around the bathtub she'd give me a dollar. I got a clock motor and did it, and the stockholders got twenty cents on their nickels.

Later in the year he began building model airplanes, a craze in which he was joined by two other boys. At nine he received a book on radios and built first a crystal set that did not work, then a one-tube set that was a great success. Quite early he seemed to possess the spirit of a true mechanic. He did not require quick success; it was the planning and building and tinkering and experimenting, together with the vision of some ultimate success, that kept him on fire with enthusiasm.

Meanwhile he was going to school, where his studies were successful but his deportment record horrible. He used to "act up in class" and "raise as much hell as possible," as a result of which he spent a great deal of time standing in the corner or sitting in the principal's office. "I got interested in girls about this time," he said; "I used to grab them when they came into the coat closet and kiss them." At six he worshipped from afar a platinum blond three years older than himself. At seven, however, his affections came to rest on a young lady a year younger who was "cute," whom he "led around by the hand." From this point on he was never without a girl friend. He was equally unabashed about investigating the possibilities of tobacco. At eight he and his cousin Betty were irked because his parents would not let them join in a game of bridge. To get even they smoked a couple of cigarettes. When Hartley's mother detected the smell of smoke, he expected a severe punishment, but instead she merely explained why it was an undesirable thing and told him not to do it again. Soon afterward, however, he resumed cigarette smoking, sometimes with Betty, but more often alone behind the barn. It is interesting to note that by the time he reached college he had become a moderate smoker who chiefly enjoyed an occasional pipe.

Hale's proficiency as a fighter, first demonstrated in the "back-bone incident," received considerable development in the years immediately following. He wrote:

> The neighborhood, though fine to the west of the house, became a very tough district only a block to the east. Gangs came out of the east to cloud our youthful horizon, and many a heated fight occurred. I still felt afraid while we were bandying words, but as soon as the actual fight started the fear vanished, and I bored in with a verve that earned me a better-than-average percentage of wins. I grew stronger.

His parents differed in their attitudes toward this phase of his social development. "Mother didn't like me to fight," he told us. "Dad didn't care too much; he actually paid to have me take some boxing lessons at one time, which helped quite a lot."

Later Childhood

Although Hale's interest in mechanisms continued unabated through the later years of childhood, the events that stood out in his mind between the ages of nine and thirteen had to do mainly with athletic and social ventures. His school career continued to be tempestuous. According to his own account his behavior record became worse and worse. Without much effort he was able to keep up such a good scholastic record that he skipped half a grade in the fourth grade and stayed consistently on the honor roll. He said little about this and seemed inclined to attribute it more to his skill in human management than to either scholastic aptitude or effort: "When I wasn't cutting up I played the teachers for all I was worth."

At the age of nine Hartley joined the YMCA and went to "Y" camp the summer he became ten. Here he met a boy named Dan, who was for many years his best friend: "a hellion, a daring sort of a chap; we got into more trouble than anyone who ever lived." Following Dan's bold example, he would perform feats such as diving from the top of a windmill tower into the water tank many yards below. It was also in Dan's company that Hartley overcame a long-standing fear, that of moths alighting on his face. One night at camp they got the cabin full of moths so that Hartley even swallowed one while talking. Dan lived only four blocks from the Hales, but in an easterly direction so that Hartley's parents did not know his parents. At the end of the camp period, he joined with Hartley and the two friends of the model airplane days to make an adventurous foursome.

It was at the "Y" that still another fear dropped by the wayside. Attempts had been made since the age of four to teach Hartley to swim, but he was deathly afraid of the water.

> At the "Y" I began playing at the shallow end of the pool. One night there was a swimming meet of 10-year-olds, and one side was a man short. So the instructor asked me to join but I said I couldn't swim. So he coaxed me to dive across the pool, which I did, struggling across to the other side. Then they put me in the 60-foot race and I beat the fellow I was against. I almost dropped dead from surprise.

There was one branch of learning that Hartley pursued with vigor during his later childhood, choosing for the most part his own sources of instruction.

I was from the earliest time curious about sex. Due to my insistent demands my mother started to teach me something about it, but the gutter was so much more rapid that I finally abandoned instruction in favor of it. When I went east a block, I found that knowledge and near-knowledge were quite easily attainable, and with my natural curiosity the two of us soon got together. When I learned a new word one day I went and looked it up in the Century Dictionary which was on our library shelf, and the paragraph about that mentioned some other word, and so on, so that in two hours' time I had learned all the scientific names, though I wasn't just exactly sure how the whole thing worked yet. By the time I was twelve I had read a book on prenatal care, one on childbirth, and one on "what every married man should know," and that, added to all the jokes I had heard, gave me a pretty comprehensive knowledge for one of my age. I was thinking about it one day when I realized that of course my parents must have done it, but though it seemed sort of strange to think about it, it didn't shock me at all.

His knowledge served to immunize him against terror on the subject of masturbation, about which he merely felt that "it was something I shouldn't tell anyone"; but at puberty he gave up, at least for the time being, both masturbation and smoking when he read that they interfered with athletic ability. Of his first nocturnal emission, which occurred at about thirteen, he said: "It didn't worry me because I had been expecting it ever since I read about it the year before."

He felt that he was on the whole quite popular with other children. "Among my close friends in youth," he wrote, "I was more often than not the goat, but this really never bothered me—I sort of liked it." The role of goat is not usually a child's spontaneous first choice, and the willingness to play it can usually be interpreted as a sign of urgent need for acceptance by the others. With the passage of time, however, Hartley was no longer obliged to swallow his pride; he became increasingly "competitive and outspoken." "I was cocky," he said in the autobiography. "As I grew older, approaching twelve, I was very very cocky. This almost always antagonized older people with whom I came in contact. But the few older people who took the trouble to break under the shell of cockiness became among my staunchest friends."

One highly important problem of Hale's childhood was completely omitted from his autobiography. In fact he did not disclose it at all during the undergraduate study; it came to light only in the last interview of the second study when, to the utter amazement of the interviewer, he suddenly said:

When I was very young I stuttered extremely badly. I stuttered badly all through grade school, and I stuttered pretty badly all through high school. Although I was able to overcome it on a few occasions and get myself up on the stage, it was always with a great deal of effort, and I usually forced myself to do those things with the hope that I would ultimately overcome those feelings, but it didn't work out as rapidly as I thought it was going to, and I was stuttering when I came to college. I didn't have as much difficulty when I was among friends as I did when I got myself out on a limb, when I was in class or something of that sort. But I've done a reasonably good job of overcoming it now.

Asked if it was not quite a handicap when he was in grade school, he replied:

Oh boy! I'll say it was tough. It was very tough. And I'm sure it arose from the general insecurity of my home surroundings. That's why it started, I'm sure. But even that knowledge, even the fact that I had that knowledge, even when I was a little kid, didn't help me as far as the stuttering was concerned. Nothing I could do about it myself, no one I could go to to help me. And as a result it's been tough.

Hale did not, of course, stutter in any of the undergraduate interviews. Nothing in his speech suggested a history of stuttering, even to interviewers accustomed to take notice of such things. It is interesting to inquire why he suppressed this particular piece of information when he seemed otherwise so free in relating the facts of his life. Evidently he found the speech difficulty peculiarly humiliating. We can assume that as a child he had been mercilessly ridiculed. His difficulty in wielding the weapon of speech doubtless contributed to his anxiety when a fight was in the stage of "bandying words" and his joyful relief when he could bore in with his unstuttering fists. At the time of the first study he was still not quite sure that his victory over stuttering was securely won. He preferred to tell us about his historic victories: his conquest of the fear of moths, his mastery of swimming, his triumph over cowardice in fights. There was no evasion of his failures and setbacks provided he had finally mastered them, but he was not disposed to bring into the discussion a personal battle in which the issue was still in doubt. Stuttering bears a peculiar relation to the building of a favorable self-picture. It lets one down and exposes one to ridicule precisely at those moments when one is attempting self-display, assertion, and competitiveness. It is also involuntary and uncontrollable, likely to be made worse by effort and tension, and thus resistant to those techniques of vigorous direct action and mastery that Hale used so successfully upon his other problems. Here, then, was a source of grave feelings of inferiority and helplessness, a severe blight on the career of an energetic growing boy. We can better understand his hunger for respect, his earlier willingness to play the goat, his pride in mastering adversities, and his omission of the still dangerous weakness when painting for us the picture of the man he hoped he was becoming at the age of twenty-one.

Hale himself related his stuttering to the insecurity of his life at home. The parental quarrels constituted another threat which he usually could not control. In the second study, further removed from their impact, he was able to tell us a great deal more about these squabbles, which reached their height when he was ten to twelve years old. Apparently his mother and father came fairly close to an actual breakup during this period. He attributed the difficulty to their differences in temperament. As mentioned before, he himself was one of the main causes of strife, which made the situation all the more trying. He said:

> I was a bone of contention because my mother was a very cautious person, and her general reaction to anything new is a negative one. And her general attitude toward me was one of protection and of not wanting me to do anything that was bad for me or anything, and I was by nature slightly venturesome, so this attitude used to annoy me considerably. And as a result, instead of calming me down any, it made me considerably more venturesome than I would have been. And I went out of my way to do things that I knew would—that she didn't want me to do, simply because she didn't want me to do them. I'd go ahead and do these things anyhow and then I'd usually go them one better, and that would get her very upset. She'd get very upset, and then that would upset my father because he didn't like upsetting things. . . . He never liked to have arguments at the dinner table, it was very annoying to him, so then he'd get mad at my mother, and then she'd get mad at him for getting mad with her, and then they'd forget about me.

One of the worst features of the quarrels, especially after Connie had gone away to school, was that the entire burden of restoring peace fell on Hartley's shoulders. "It was difficult being caught in the strife," he said, "and having to take care of it and not having anybody to help me." As with the stuttering, he did not see what he himself could do and he could not turn to anyone for help. He felt responsible for the continuing existence of the family.

> The thing that used to bother me the most was the uncertainty of when the thing was going to explode. I could never be quite sure. I didn't like to go to bed, and I used to read until I could hear my parents coming upstairs, and I'd put out the light and lie there, and I could hear them as they were getting undressed, and I'd never be sure when they'd start talking about it, they could almost never talk without there being some kind of an argument. And I could always recall lying there in bed wondering whether it was going to develop into an argument or whether it wasn't, a point about which I am so conscious that we make it a very definite point now with my own children never to argue in front of them.

Hartley's anxiety was clearly intense, but it is significant that he did not discontinue the venturesome and defiant behavior which was so often the immediate cause of the arguments. Whatever his initial bewilderments, he eventually placed the whole problem on a reflective plane and consciously decided against toning down his own behavior.

> I realized that if I were the model child perhaps that would quiet down the arguments, because it was always—it was often made fairly clear to me that I was the cause of the arguments. But I quickly discarded that thesis and decided that after all I couldn't go that far. I decided that I had my own life to live after all, and by God I was going to live it, and by God I did. An awful lot of the things that I did were things that I wouldn't have done if it hadn't been for this opposition; I just went that much further as an extra effort of defiance.

He was inclined to agree to a suggestion that in some respects his early trials might have had a stimulating effect on his development. "I think that probably by birth I was endowed with some of my mother's qualities, caution," he said, "which without that opposition might have held me back to some extent." He was clearly resentful of what he described as "being held down," resolving not to give in at any cost. Describing his own eldest child, he said:

> She is very much like I was when I was young, very anxious to be grown up, and very anxious to assume responsibilities for things, and likes very much to be around grown people and so on. I was myself always held down in those things, anything I wanted to do

I was held back in, used to irritate the hell out of me, with the result that I usually went ahead and did it anyway, and I always made up my mind that if I had any children that wasn't going to be the case with them.

In some of our tests in the earlier study that called upon him to make up or to complete stories, he utilized the theme of being held down and made his heroes stubbornly pursue their own way to worthy ends. We also noticed at that time that all the marriages which came into his plots were either explicitly or implicitly unhappy.

To accomplish his extensive program of resistance and rebellion Hartley fortified himself with a large circle of friends. We have already noted the strengthening effect of his daring friend Dan, who was, however, merely the most prominent representative of his many contacts to the eastward. Hartley's choice of friends often upset his mother and thus led to quarrels at home, but he rejected the friends she preferred for him and found a welcome life of his own among the gangs and on the baseball teams of the less pretentious end of town. He said:

> I got a chance to get a circle of friends around me that sort of buffeted me from my family, that my family had no connection with. . . . It gave me a circle of friends of my own which I could use between my family and myself. . . .
>
> Once I got into high school I was able to build up my own circle of friends against my family. Then I wasn't so much embroiled in the family as I had been. And then I was happier.

In this case also it seemed to him that his departure from family ideals had a beneficial effect on his development. He learned about the rougher side of life, proved his capacity to deal with it, and at the same time gained sympathy and respect for people living in economic circumstances less favorable than his own.

High School: The Happiest Years

Hale remembered his high school years as the happiest time of his life. "I was struck with the idea," he wrote, "that one should try to indulge in as many outside activities as possible, raise hell, have a good time. This I did." In later retrospect he attributed his happiness to "the complete and utter irresponsibility of those years": "nobody did much work, there were a lot of outside interests which made it happy. I enjoyed working on theatrical productions, working on the newspapers, going to parties, driving an automobile rapidly around corners, things of that sort." He looked back on high school as a place where he had learned nothing but had had a wonderful time.

He was still able to make good grades in his studies without serious effort. Disliking chemistry, he did no work and got a "D"; but the courses he enjoyed, such as physics and English, yielded him a harvest of good grades that offset his failures. He carried extra courses and could have graduated half a year early except that his parents thought him too young and he himself wanted to graduate with his class. When he graduated, it was with considerable distinction: he had achieved an average of 90 and was also voted the most popular boy in the class.

His heart was in extracurricular activities. He took particular pleasure in dramatics, in which he rose to the position of stage manager. Quite a little space in the autobiography was given to describing the up-to-date high school auditorium, which had stage facilities to delight the heart of a mechanically inclined manager. "Working out startling lighting effects and staging plays," he wrote, "was one of the major joys of my life, and I worked hours on it." He did not participate as an actor, which is not surprising in view of his tendency to stutter, and in the second study he told us of an incident that must have given him a decidedly poor reputation as a public performer. The wording of a stimulus phrase in one of our association tests struck him as funny; he responded humorously and then became seized with a fit of uncontrollable laughter. When he finally brought his mirth under control he explained the seizure as follows:

I've always had trouble with laughing. When I was a kid in school I used to get started laughing and couldn't stop. The more the teacher would get mad at me and try to make me stop, the harder I'd laugh, and it was just fantastic, and I was afraid I was going to get started again, I haven't done that for years. I was afraid I might laugh half way through a record for you. The first time I was ever on the stage, one of our school plays, my lines were after several other people had spoken, and I thought to liven up the ceremony a little bit I'd shoot a spit ball at one of the other characters on the stage. So I rather surreptitiously shot the spitball, and it hit him right behind the ear, and he let out a howl—this was before about 1500 people—and just about the next instant was my line, and I got so convulsed with laugher that they had to bring the damn curtain down and call the whole thing off; I couldn't go on.

Even if this yarn contains a bit of picturesque exaggeration it testifies to a number of interesting traits in our subject and certainly suggests that he was better placed behind the scenes than in front of them.

Equal in attraction to Hale's work as a stage manager were his activities as a high school journalist. He became humor editor of the monthly magazine, editing the humorous contributions and drawing cartoons. He also wrote an anonymous column filled with spicy bits of gossip and scandal. It amused him to hear the persons who appeared in this column expressing their annoyance and saying what they would like to do to the author, but the editor-in-chief, who alone knew the authorship, faithfully kept the secret. Hale was irked that some of the most fascinating gossip was deemed unsuitable for publication in the school magazine. To remedy this situation he got out a single sheet of his own, prepared by hand and circulated among the students. He was asked about it in detail during the second study, and said:

> That was a sort of little scandal sheet. I'd collect embarrassing things about people and then make some drawings and write it up and circulate it. It would circulate to most everybody in the school except the person about whom it was written, who would get it only at the last minute and be quite angry but generally keep the paper. I got a big kick out of it and I think most of the other people did too.
>
> I would try to find out something about someone that nobody else knew, sort of scout around and see what was going on, see what they were up to, and trail them around for a while. Sometimes I'd go and follow them in the car at night and see what they did and where they went. It was especially nice when I could get something they thought nobody else knew, and which they were trying definitely to keep secret. The sort of thing that I particularly liked was somebody who would be going steady with some gal and two-time her, go see some other gal, something of that sort. That was especially choice.

The authorship of this sheet was no secret, yet Hale was not disqualified from being chosen the most popular boy in the class. It is justifiable to assume that his relations to his fellow students contained friendlier elements which did not, however, lend themselves so well to lively narrative when viewed in retrospect.

That Hale was not wholly occupied with hell-raising comes out in his description of his girl friends. He started having dates at thirteen but went always with the same girl for the next three years and was therefore "considered slow." This girl was a year older and did not take much interest in her young suitor; their relationship was somewhat shy and distant. It was in fact with another girl, a casual acquaintance met while crashing parties at the age of fifteen, that Hartley overcame his shyness about kissing.

> She said it was New Year's Eve and it was the custom to kiss girls on New Year's Eve, and, well, I'd been brought up to be a gentleman. I must have been pretty poor because she asked me if she was the first girl I had ever kissed, and I just barely recovered in time to say "Don't flatter yourself" and really kiss her.

This incident is curiously parallel to the "backbone incident" at eight years. Again the woman defines the masculine role, in which Hartley is failing, and again he meets the challenge by swift direct counteraction. At sixteen he met a girl a year younger with whom he fell in love, "if one may be said to do that at sixteen." He described this girl as very good looking.

> She was likewise very emotional, though reserved and cautious. She held her head high, talked easily, said the right things, danced well. I walked home with her every night, a mile out of my way, and I saw her "by accident" between every class.
>
> One night after I had known her about a month (but had only had three dates with her because she was very popular) I called her on the phone. During the conversation she mentioned that she was having trouble with her mathematics. I really wasn't supposed to go out on school nights, but then . . . it didn't take long to solve the problem; I had had the course the year before. It took longer to solve the problem of leaving. I wanted to kiss her, but had talked that very day with someone who was usually successful along those lines and who had failed when he tried it with her. But she seemed co-operative, and I finally got up enough nerve to try. I was successful, and from that time on it was just a question of gaining momentum.

He went with this girl steadily until his second year in college when, although they had considered themselves engaged, they both agreed to call it off in view of his prolonged absences and formidable course of professional training. The relationship was a source of great happiness to him:

> We seldom quarreled. We laughed too much to quarrel. We both liked the same things and we were both crazy about each other.

Neither of us could stay mad about anything for long. Sexually I think I shall never meet anyone who appeals to me more. The only emotion I can ever remember having had after a sex experience with her was one of intense pleasure. Neither of us ever felt shame, remorse, or revulsion.

The decision to part was a hard one, made several times and then reversed before it finally stuck. Discussions about it sometimes made him feel so weak that he could hardly talk or stand. The discovery of an enjoyable and lovable girl companion, who put him ahead of her other male friends and with whom quarrels could be avoided, seemed to do a lot to soothe and stabilize the rambunctious young man whose path through high school so closely resembled one of his responses on the Rorschach inkblot test: "A bullet going through mud, splattering, traveling at high speed."

College: The Emergence of Serious Purposes

Graduating from high school at seventeen, Hale went for a year to a nearby junior college before making application to Harvard. His experience with the high school magazine, and a course in journalism, which he found "sensational," had caused him to select advertising as his life work. He enjoyed the idea of selling things, of "presenting things in attractive form," of writing copy and making drawings, and in addition he liked the prospect of what he called "the hectic life, the upside-down hours, the peculiar existence." At junior college, however, he elected a course in biology, more to round out a program than because of any previous interest in the subject, and this brought him into contact with a teacher who had a marked effect on his career. When questioned in the second study about people who had influenced him he spoke as follows:

> Some people that I admired most were my teacher of physics in high school and my teacher of biology in junior college, both of whom were men and both of whom were very inspiring teachers. Both were intensely interested in the subjects that they taught and both were intensely interested in individuals, which is a rare quality in a teacher, and I did well in those subjects because I liked both teachers so much.

Evidently these two men broke through the shell of his cockiness; certainly they became his very good friends with whom he visited whenever he returned to his home city. To the biology teacher he assigned credit for getting him into Harvard: as a result of his tutelage Hale wrote an entrance examination in biology that earned highest honors.

> This guy got me so darned interested in the course that I used to sit up nights looking through the microscope, and I went out into the field to collect things and all that kind of thing. By the time I got done I'd really learned a little biology, and gotten intensely interested in it.

The thought of changing to medicine crossed his mind, but he was still, headed for the advertising business when he entered Harvard.

The news of his admission to Harvard was one of the major positive events in his life. But when he learned that his best friend Dan had also been admitted, he was completely overwhelmed. "I have never regretted," he wrote, "the tears of joy I shed" upon hearing the second piece of glad tidings. The two boys continued to be friends at college, but they made the decision not to room together, their plan being that each should build up his own circle of friends and then share it with the other. Apparently the plan worked well, and the friendship was still in force at the time of the second study. Hale was enchanted to find that there were no required courses. "That's wonderful," he said, "it gives you a wonderful sense of freedom and it makes you very enthusiastic. You can wade out into the middle of things and get as wet as you want to in as many things as you want to." He used his freedom chiefly to take extra courses in biology.

During his freshman year he plunged more heavily than before into athletics. This had some curious consequences. He worked hard all season to make the freshman football team, but on the morning of the final game he was so late for the bus that the team had to leave without him so that he never got his numerals. He then worked furiously for the track team and was in every meet except the one with Yale, for which he failed to qualify by the narrowest last-moment margin. "That was a bitter pill to swallow," he wrote, "but fortunately my spirits don't stay down for long." That he should twice have failed on the very threshold of success suggested that athletic achievement was not entirely free from conflict and anxiety. He told us that he never lost sleep over sports but that he was always very nervous, in fact "practically a wreck," just before an important game. He also said that he often deliberately made himself late so that he could drown the

anxiety by rushing around and arriving ready at the last possible moment. But his anxieties did not generally interfere with top performance;
quite the opposite, they added energy to the battle and zest to the ultimate victory. He was not sure that sports would be worthwhile if they
did not contain the element of anxiety and its conquest. The two incidents of the freshman year were certainly not typical of Hale, not typical even for the rest of his athletic performance that same year. Yet
they happened, and they gave him a severe feeling of frustration; furthermore, they found an echo in several of the plots he devised two
years later in our tests of creative imagination.

Given the picture of a man climbing a rope, for example, and
asked to make up a story for which the picture might be an illustration,
he told of a powerful young black athlete who sneaked into the gym-
nasium reserved for white people because his own gym was not equipped
with a rope. The story continued:

> He is nearly at the top when the door of the gym opens and the
> keeper comes in. He sees him from his lofty position and his brain
> gropes madly for a method of escape. He fears that if he does not
> find any the rope will be around his neck rather than in his hand.
> But he is only severely reprimanded and sent back to his own gym
> where he contents himself with doing push-ups.

The very next picture in the test showed a man bent over a table, his
face buried in his arm, surrounded by strange hovering birds and bats.
Hale perceived the man as an author who is also an opium fiend; the
author is "approaching the climax of his most brilliant story" when his
drug-poisoned body collapses "and his mind is filled with horrible
visions," as a result of which "the story remains unfinished." Hale's
reported anxiety connected with competitive struggle, the two instances
of last-minute failure, and these two unusual imaginative plots, together
suggest the presence of an inner obstacle which is occasionally large
enough to trip him up at the threshold of success, although for the
most part he functions with great effectiveness in competitive situations. We shall return at a later point to this curious problem.

It was also during his freshman year that Hale came to his
decision to be a doctor. His conversion, we learned in the second study,
occurred in a quite unusual way. Across the hall in the dormitory lived
a student who enjoyed argument. Hale also enjoyed argument, and he
particularly liked debating with this neighbor, who was always rea-

sonable and therefore did not irritate him and throw him into stubborn negativism. As a result they sometimes spent most of the night in arguments. Hale reconstructed for us as follows the crucial incident:

> One night for some reason or other, this was out of the clear blue sky, I don't know why or what brought it up, he decided, he got it in his mind, that I should be a doctor instead of going into advertising. And so he started to argue with me about it, and when morning came I agreed that he was right. He did a very logical, very thorough job on me, and so I went down the next day and I changed my field of concentration to biology. Then I called up my family and told them what I'd decided, which they didn't like.

Asked if he could recall the course of the argument, he said that his friend began by declaring him to be chiefly interested in medicine. Hale countered by pointing out that he was concentrating in English, going into advertising, and not taking a premedical program. His friend then called attention to his honors entrance-grade in biology and observed that he must like his biology course the best of any he was taking because he spent the most time on it and talked about it at the greatest length.

> And after thinking it over pretty seriously I had to admit that I was pretty interested in that course. And he said, "Now look what you've outlined for next year, all these biology courses, why are you doing that?" And I had to argue, had to admit that he was right, that perhaps I was slightly interested in the subject. And then I went on to the fact that it was going to take too damn long, that I didn't want to go through all the business of going through medical school, and that in addition the field was overcrowded, and so on, and he went on to argue that that didn't make for much difference, that if I did well at it I wouldn't have any trouble getting ahead, and that doctors don't usually starve. And he said that in addition it was his personal conviction that I was suited psychologically to be a doctor, so I went on to argue that I wasn't in the slightest suited to be a doctor, and . . . I've forgotten just what points he brought up about it but he made a pretty good case.

It is not without interest that Hale forgot the content of the arguments just at the point where they involved his own personal characteristics. He may have halted here because the friend's arguments were filled with embarrassing praise. We learned with surprise that the friend was not himself going into medicine but into law, for which he considered himself psychologically better suited. His only connection with medicine was his great admiration for the doctor in his home town, a man who had done a great deal for the community and stood as a "very heroic figure in his mind." It was this picture of the medical man with which the friend enticed Hale, who had always previously thought of doctors as "a little too stolid and fixed," "tied up in their work," "not very interesting people," "dull people." Hale thought that his tremendous interest in biology might eventually have led him to choose medicine anyway, but the argument with his friend greatly hastened his seeing of the light.

Hale was not in the habit of responding submissively to the advice of others. In the early study he did not mention the part his friend played in the shift from advertising to medicine, allowing the decision to sound like one that he reached of his own accord. Why was he so decisively influenced on this particular occasion? Partly because he respected reasonableness and could see that his friend had no ax to grind. Partly because an appeal was made to inclinations already at work though not formulated in his own mind. But perhaps the strongest impact came from the element of flattering challenge that was implicit in what his friend had to say. The friend was arguing, in effect, as follows: "Medicine is a great career, an heroic one, not a dull one; I have been observing you, and you have the qualities that fit you for this great and heroic career." Through the combined appeal of logic, fact, and the display of personal interest, Hale was converted from a lower to a higher calling. Advertising represented to him an easy, exciting, profitable way of continuing the brash irresponsible life of his high school years. Medicine appealed to something different in his personality, the thing that had been touched by the physics teacher and the biology teacher who had broken through his shell of cocky rebelliousness. It mobilized his capacity for deep, absorbed interest, patient continuous work, dedication to goals of discovery that transcended the immediate satisfaction of personal needs. It eliminated certain doubts he had entertained about the ethics of advertising, and it gave to his college career a feeling of purpose and direction.

Having overcome, in what was for him routine fashion, his parents' objections to the new and bolder plan, Hale plunged enthusiastically into his biology courses. Sometimes his other work was neglected, especially if he did not see its relevance to his career, but he continued to do first-rate work in biology. He presently began work with a teacher who resembled his two previous models: highly competent and enthusiastic in his field, but also interested in his students and what they could accomplish.

During his junior year Hale became interested in a research project involving bone growth in animals, and his teacher allowed him to pursue it the following year as a senior honors thesis in spite of the fact that he had failed in sociology and therefore did not have quite the grades required to qualify as a candidate for honors.

> As it turned out it was all right. I got two A's and two B's. That was really a lucky break in which he sort of took a gamble on me. There've been a few people along the line who've taken a gamble on me, it's been necessary two or three times, and I always feel a great sense of responsibility toward those people, and I think that every time that's happened I've come through.

Interestingly enough, although he "came through" with more than the required grades, the honors thesis itself was not completed on time. We inquired closely into the reasons and were forced to discard our first guess that once again he had been compelled to fail on the threshold of success. His research problem was sound, but the technical difficulties were very great and he did not have time for all the false starts, changes of method, and checking and rechecking of results, that go with honest scientific inquiry. If again he did not "get his numerals," so to speak, it was this time because he was too good a scientist, and he did not lose the esteem of his teachers for holding back an incomplete piece of research.

Hale's busy life as a premedical student cut into his athletic career, but he did not allow it to interfere too seriously with his social life. He took an active part in the affairs of his House, knew and regularly spoke to at least 250 of the 300 students who lived there, and was always seen in the dining hall in lively conversation with the students around him. He also made time for two or three dates a week. His dates would generally be with some favorite girl of the moment; "usually," he said, "it would take a minor upheaval to get going on a new track." These friendships did not supplant the relationship with the girl in his home city until the beginning of his junior year. When that relationship was finally terminated, he gave his full attention to a new girl who was still his regular date up to the time of graduation. He was quite fond of this girl but not at all inclined to consider marriage in view of the long professional training that lay ahead. During our senior year interview in which his girl friends were under discussion he rather unexpectedly volunteered the following piece of information:

> One other girl I liked better than any I've ever met. She's the only one I'd consider asking to marry me. She was the sister of a kid I grew up with and used to play with ever since I was five. She was about eight years older but she was at ease with us as with anyone else. She is more unselfish, more gracious, more talented than any I've ever met. There is so much more to her. She paints and plays the piano. She has the rare quality of making anyone from one to ninety feel that there is nothing more interesting in the world than talking with them. She has the disposition of an angel and a marvelous sense of humor.

Now nearing thirty, married, and with her own children, this "girl" was obviously not a potential partner. Some of her qualities were those of an ideal mother, yet Hale described his interest as being anything but ethereal.

Hale's conception of himself at the time of the undergraduate study can best be conveyed by quoting the closing words of his autobiography.

> I like the world as it is. For as it is it offers competition and insecurity; and it's the battle to overcome each of these that makes life worthwhile. When one gives up the fight he's through with this "mortal coil," and with security comes senility.

> The world thinks of me as happy, as seldom worrying; they laugh at and with me and I like it. They usually respect my judgments. They like me, I think.

> I swear too much, I procrastinate, I tend to exaggerate, I dramatize, I'm stubborn, I daydream, I'm optimistic, I'm honest (except when exaggerating), I'm fair. Life is sweet.

Analysis of responses on self-rating questionnaires did not substantially change this picture. He gave himself fairly high ratings with respect to most abilities, though quite low ones on a few. He pictured himself as intense and impulsive yet also capable of endurance, but he made only modest claims to organization and continuity. In the sphere of motives he thought of himself as highly active, assertive, dominant, yet friendly and nurturing; his low self-ratings piled up in the area of dependence, avoidances, and fears. He felt that he had won most of his developmental fights up to the present and could face those of the future with confidence and zest.

Available Capacities and Existing
Limitations as a College Senior

Before we undertake to deepen our understanding of Hale's development and to carry his career forward another decade, we must stop to
take a brief cross-sectional view of his capacities and limitations. In
making this appraisal we do not assume that we are dealing with fixed
innate endowments. We are concerned rather with the capacities and
skills, whatever their origin, that were available to him and capable of
mobilization at the time he was a college senior.

Physical Traits Hale was of average height and weight, with
a body build well suited to athletic achievement. He carried no
excess weight, was broad in the shoulders, narrow in the hips, muscu-
larly strong in arms and legs. When younger he had been of less than
average stature, but a marked growth spurt at fourteen brought him
well up to average. He had participated in a great many different sports,
usually with considerable success though rarely with outstanding distinction. No unusual or serious illnesses had marred his excellent health
record. He seemed full of restless energy, describing himself as "a very
impatient sort of fellow" who hated to sit and wait and always wanted
to take action of some kind. His preference for vigorous action showed
itself in many ways, serving among other things as his chief method
of dealing with obstacles and frustrations.

Affective Qualities Hale's days were full of events, from most
of which he received satisfaction and pleasure. His prevailing mood
could best be described as zestful. From rare experiences of dejection his spirits tended to bounce back quickly. It was interesting to
notice that in his imaginative productions there were frequent themes
in which dejection and despair visited the characters as a consequence
of failure, isolation, and the lack of an appreciative audience. Sometimes his characters were so overwhelmed by these misfortunes that
they elected to kill themselves. It was evident that Hale was not a
stranger to dark moods, but it was equally clear that his energetic and
sociable way of life effectively counteracted most of the conditions
which proved so disastrous to his fictional characters. Hale said that
sad stories and sad scenes in the movies never made him feel like crying; they simply depressed him. He was more apt to cry when flooded
by sudden happiness, as when he learned that his best friend was

admitted to college, or when transported out of himself by beautiful music. He specified as follows the most specific stimulus to tears: "when somebody goes out of their way to do something nice for me," or when a character on stage or screen "goes out of his way to be awfully good to someone who doesn't expect it." He was also able to specify the condition most conducive to furious anger: "when I think some injustice has been done." His temper could be easily aroused, though if necessary he could control it by being "very quiet and very firm." For the most part he believed in expressing his anger and then forgetting about the episode, lasting resentments being unusual in his experience. Mention has already been made of his anxieties in competitive situations and his control through procrastination and distracting activity at the last moment.

Intellectual Characteristics Hale's intellectual competence has already been attested by his effortless climb up the educational ladder and by his occasional outstanding performances such as the entrance grade in biology. Standard intelligence tests placed him in the *very superior* category with an IQ of 130; performance on the different parts of the tests showed a fairly even distribution of skills with no areas of marked weakness. Characteristically he used his mind in rapid, direct, concrete fashion, sometimes even to the extent of a careless disregard for details and a willingness to leave hasty replies uncriticized. He showed little disposition toward either cautious planning or complex theorizing; his test performances were those of a doer rather than a thinker. He seemed to have difficulty, relative to the rest of his capacity, in organizing separate items and in arriving at general patterns. In tests of imagination he was free and creative. His stories characteristically took full account of whatever facts were offered him in the first place. If he was shown a picture, for example, he told a story that included everything that was in the picture; he unleashed his imagination only after having paid full respect to the objective stimulus. Impressive also was his preference for objects as against human figures in the Rorschach inkblot test. He managed to find quite a few mechanical objects in the roughly formed, unmechanical inkblots. His test performances showed the same mechanical and objective preferences that had appeared in his autobiography. We were reminded of his extensive description of the stage in the high school auditorium and his objective way of contrasting the characteristics of his parents through their behavior in a bridge game.

Special Abilities   Hale's history gave abundant evidence of his early and lasting interest in the understanding of mechanisms. When he said that he put a reverse switch on his electric train at the age of seven, we thought of his remark that he was always honest except when exaggerating; but even if he did it only at nine or ten, we must still count it as testimony to considerable aptitude. The record is full of his fascination with mechanical objects, his rapid but patient mastery of their intricacies, his creativeness in thinking of new devices and working out new triumphs of technique. His absorption in biology seemed to be a continuation and development of the same kind of interest, shifted from the inanimate machine to the even more intriguing machinery of the living organism. In interviews he was more apt to talk about his dramatic adventures in the social sphere, but his hours in the laboratory were clearly a deep and lasting source of satisfaction.

In the arts Hale preserved a more completely amateur standing, but his interests and energies overflowed even in this direction. Though not really a good singer, he got considerable pleasure out of his efforts and found time to write a number of songs during his college years. He greatly enjoyed good painting and good music, to which his parents had introduced him early in life. Occasionally he turned his hand to poetry and to drawing, the latter talent eventually being diverted into the making of biological drawings in his courses. Considering the high artistic standards of his home, he seemed to have accepted relative mediocrity in the arts with fairly good grace. He could usually take pleasure in artistic activity regardless of the competitive merit of the product.

Social Skills and Attitudes   It was plain from his school and college histories and from our own observation of his behavior that Hale was unusually gregarious. Companions and friends were involved in almost everything that he did; in fact, he expressed a definite distaste for being alone, and it was the lonely characters in his stories who fell prey to dejection and despair. Even his most absorbing mechanical and scientific interests were apt to be shared with others, especially in subsequent conversation. He reported several incidents in which he displayed social initiative, though he confessed that his first enthusiasm sometimes waned before the project reached its fulfilment. He said, and we observed, that he could often keep the whole table laughing in the dining hall, and he enjoyed presiding or serving as master of ceremonies at meetings. Those of our questions that were designed to bring out his capacity for intuitive, empathic understanding of other people he reinterpreted in more congenially objective terms. "I can't know anyone without analyzing him," he said; "I tear people to pieces all the time in my own mind."

Then he spoke of his quickness to detect unpleasant traits such as "social climbing," "selfishness," "narrow-mindedness," and "excessive ambition, not the kind that inspires you to work hard, but an overreaching one." With regard to such traits he was a determinist: "It's pretty hard to change them, almost impossible. I've tried." These excerpts, taken together with the fact that he never felt moved to tears by sorrowful scenes, suggest a low capacity for sympathetic understanding and a tendency to look upon people objectively, with emphasis on the annoying features of their behavior. Nevertheless, we noted that his companionship was valued and that his friendships with both men and women tended to be of long duration.

First Interpretive Summary

Before making Hartley Hale's life story any longer let us attempt to strengthen our grasp on what we already know. Closer inspection and a search for the significant connections among events may help us to understand better how he came to be the kind of person he was at twenty-two. In making this closer inspection, we shall inevitably find ourselves attempting to reconstruct his past history. This always contains a substantial amount of guesswork; we cannot be certain of what really happened. Nevertheless we are justified, taking all the evidence at our disposal, in trying to weave into an intelligible fabric the loose strands of event, attitude, and feeling that make up the narrative of Hale's career.

In clinical work the central task is to understand the patient's complaints. In a study of natural growth the purpose is different: we want to understand our subject as a person in all his individuality, strengths as much as weaknesses. This means, in Hale's case, accounting for a pattern that includes unusual independence and self-reliance, serious interests, popularity, brash and sometimes aggressive social behavior, together with anxieties and ways of dealing with them. As a starting point we shall follow Hale's lead and examine what he himself thought to be critical in his childhood: the quarrels between his parents and the insecurity they engendered.

Hale's parents often made it clear to him that his own venturesome and mischievous behavior was the subject of their quarrels. The sequence of events usually started with some act of rebellion on his part; then followed upset feelings in his mother, which upset his father, which precipitated a quarrel in which Hartley was forgotten. The mother then retired to her room, whither the son followed with a view to restoring peace, but there was little he could do beyond listening to her self-justifications. Hale told us that his sympathies were evoked on both sides, that he judged both parents to be wrong in losing their tempers, but that he did not feel resentment against either of them. This is surprising, especially when we recall that he himself had often been sent to his room for the very same crime of losing his temper. But the situation aroused anxiety: there was danger that the mother would leave and the home break up, and there was fear that he would not be able to make peace in these quarrels, which obviously involved more than his own misbehavior. If he did not feel anger, it must have been because he did not dare to feel it lest he heighten the quarrel and ruin his own efforts at conciliation. Experienced marriage counselors do not consider it easy to deal with marital strife, even in the subsequent detachment of the consulting room. Hartley was called upon to cope with the problem in its moments of white heat, himself fully involved, his own security hanging in the balance, and with only a child's resources for understanding what it was all about. The foundations of self-respect as well as the cornerstone of security must have been severely shaken as he struggled with these unmanageable situations.

If this sequence of events and emotions occurred in a quite young child, it would probably bring about an inhibition of the stubborn rebellious behavior that precipitated so many of the quarrels. When assertive behavior brings on the threat of parental desertion, feelings of anxiety become insupportable and the child strives to become everything that his parents desire.[1] In Hale's case we have to explain why this did *not* occur. He refused to relinquish his right to independence and rebellion; quite consciously he decided not to become a model child. This means that he was in some way able to control the anxiety set off by the quarrels. We can reject on his own showing any hypothesis that Hale was naturally fearless: he feared water, moths, fights, and a reasonable number of other threats. His power to control anxiety must be explained in some other way.

[1] This outcome is well illustrated in the case of Albert Rock, who also was forced to deal with parental quarrels. This case is described by M. B. Smith, J. S. Bruner and R. W. White, in *Opinions and Personality*, New York: John Wiley & Sons, 1956.

One method by which he supported his independence and controlled his fear was to form an active alliance with friends of his own age. He was quite explicit in pointing out this function of his circle of acquaintances. His friends became an alternative source of human support, taking the place of that which was threatened by the parental quarrels. To emphasize the opposition he chose friends of whose social class his parents disapproved. Many of his adventures, much of his growing self-assertion, took place in the company of these friends and enjoyed their express approval. Bold companions like Dan helped him greatly to overcome his shortcomings and master his fears. Even though he carried the grave social handicap of stuttering, he poured great energy into his activities with others and derived great satisfaction from them. He did not have to sustain single-handed his refusal to become a model child. Probably he could not have done so—like his fictional characters he would have fallen into deep dejection—if he had found himself without friends, without audience, without some measure of success.

Once again, however, we encounter something of a paradox. When a child's feeling of security is heavily dependent on his social relationships, we can expect a marked hunger for group approval and a strong fear of group rejection. Conformity becomes peculiarly urgent when group membership is being used to ward off anxiety and guilt. Hale's relation to his age-peers does not seem to have shown this compulsive quality. It is true that he sought group approval by active means —humor, hell-raising, defying the teachers—but apart from evidence that earlier he played the goat, he does not appear to have been inhibited from expressing self-assertion, cockiness, and aggression in relation to the group. He declared himself to have been outspoken and competitive with his friends even at the time when the parental quarrels were at their worst, and he certainly ran chances of group disapproval by his eagerness to win and poor acceptance of defeats. We must conclude that he could control anxiety in relation to the group as he could control it in relation to his parents.

These considerations force us to look back to the earlier part of his childhood. Can we find evidence that before stuttering began, before the gangs from the east clouded his youthful horizon, Hale developed a feeling of confidence and self-reliance which could not be wholly shaken by later events? On what, in his case, could such secure confidence be based? There is evidence, in the first place, that his parents were interested in their children, fond of them, and able to discipline them without creating a fear that love would be withdrawn. In the second place, there is evidence that Hartley was happy and comfortable in his early relationships with other children. Here were two conditions highly favorable to the development of a feeling of security and confidence. Furthermore, inspection of his record suggests that several conditions existed which encouraged him to rely on his own power of mastery. Consider the punishment program, for example. He remembered his punishments as realistic and reasonable, clearly related to the offenses, a sort of transaction with his parents who defined standards to which he must live up but who did not threaten catastrophic consequences if he failed. Sometimes his father allowed him to choose a form of punishment appropriate to the offense, and always he felt that he could object and perhaps convince if the punishments appeared unreasonable. Conducive also to his feeling of strength was the knowledge that his sister would sometimes lend aid. Both the father, as in the case of the boxing lessons, and the sister, as in the backbone incident, appear to have held standards of assertive accomplishment before him but left him to fight his own battles. In particular we must not overlook certain incidents which show clearly that Hartley's parents respected him, understood his interests, and were not disinclined to let his initiative prevail. They let him persuade them to keep pets; they allowed him to feel that he had outwitted them in the matter of Santa Claus and the electric train; and they encouraged him to substitute a still-challenging mechanical achievement, the boat that would go twice around the bathtub, when his perpetual-motion project was stalled.

From such evidence it seems permissible to hazard the guess that quite early he was able to build a firm core of self-respect. Though it took effort, he was successful in memorizing the poems and making the drawings that his parents expected of him; he was also successful in mastering the intricacies of the mechanical world. He took pleasure in using his skills and increasing his mastery over things; the story runs consistently from the block carts in kindergarten, through model airplanes and radio, to his stage managership in high school, and his work in the college biology laboratories. Any sequence of events that ran from bafflement to mastery gave him great satisfaction. When the emotional climate grew more difficult, his reliance on his own competence was put to severer tests. He was peculiarly gratified when he found it possible to master human situations by action and manipulation: his physical fear by counterattack, his shyness by kissing, his poor deportment record by playing the teachers. The advertising business he saw as a lively continuation of his pleasure in manipulating and mastering the human environment. In contrast, he was peculiarly frustrated when either his human environment or he himself proved refractory to such treatment. The parental quarrels he could not seem to master, nor could he bring under control his own tendency to stutter.

Our search into early childhood has thus yielded one possible reason for Hale's ability to maintain his independence: he was actually encouraged along lines of mastery and self-respect. His independence was seriously challenged, however, by his mother's cautious, apprehensive, but dictatorial attitude of protection and restraint. As the scope of his boyish venturesomeness increased, he felt more and more held down by his mother's tidy rules and fears of danger. He seems to have felt that his father did not disapprove of his independence but that it was difficult to win open support against his mother because of his father's distaste for argument and domestic upset. Thus the mother seemed likely to prevail in her attack on Hartley's cherished delight in mastery. In short, the early alliance between his parents and his assertiveness broke down into serious opposition. We need to scrutinize this situation with some care. It was here that he launched forth on the career of rebellion and defiance which we found him so sturdily maintaining in the stormy years of later childhood.

We should first notice that the behavior of which he most complained in his mother was not such as to imply that she did not or would not love him. On the contrary it was marked by great solicitude and fear lest he come to harm. The danger, as he first sensed it, was probably not that she would desert him but that she would fatally interfere with his urges to activity and his enjoyment of masculine roles such as fireman, Indian, and adventurer. His rebellion was first directed against a smothering of his initiative and assertiveness, privileges worth defending even at some risk. We can hardly assume, however, that a young child could oppose a generally loving mother without emotional cost. He took the bold rebellious way, but there is every evidence that in doing so he experienced severe conflict and had to carry on a running campaign against his own feelings of guilt. The situation must have created a powerful temptation to give in and preserve affectionate harmony as well as an urge to break out and continue the life of adventure. That his mother's restraints could make him so uncomfortable probably added to his hostility toward them. To compromise, to give-

and-take in a situation of this kind, would certainly be difficult for a young child. We can make the guess that Hartley was forced into a radical solution, that of affirming and asserting his independence while attempting to repress his guilt and his longings for a dependent relation with his mother.

The probability that this guess is correct would become greater if we could show (1) that the assertive and independent behavior became forced and exaggerated, (2) that there were signs of general tension, (3) that dependence, guilt, and anxiety were strongly denied in word and deed, but (4) that these tendencies reappeared in some indirect form such as dream and fantasy. All of these manifestations were characteristic of Hale, although it is not now possible to pin them all down to the time in his childhood, say the third to the eighth years, when the hypothetical development took place. That his assertive independence was exaggerated came out in his own testimony that the desire to outrage his mother kept forcing him into ever wilder enterprises, and that his deportment in school was practically the worst on record. That he felt great tension is suggested by the fact that stuttering began during these years, and is certainly demonstrated in the school mischief and laughing jags whereby he infuriated his teachers. Dependence, guilt, and timid avoidances were systematically denied in his self-ratings as a college junior and were admitted to his autobiography only when they led up to a masterful triumph. The reappearance of anxiety was shown in the nightmare that the family would move, and the continuing existence of dependent longings came to light in certain features of his fantasy life. His cherished image of the much older girl whom alone he would want to marry, who made him feel that he was the most interesting person in the world, probably harks back to the mother as she was remembered to be before he began the battle for independence.

An interesting sidelight on rebellion and guilt in relation to the mother is furnished by a story that Hale derived from a test picture that is often perceived as a son breaking bad news to his mother. The mother, he said, had long hoped that her only son would become a doctor or lawyer.

> One fateful night he comes home to tell her that he has become a boxer. She can't believe her ears and is stunned by this statement. He feels badly that he should have to thus wreck her hopes but he knows that boxing is the only thing for him. Though he later rises to the top of the boxing pile, she never quite forgives him this breach of faith.

The same picture was used in the retest ten years later, and once again Hale represented the young man as disappointing his mother but going firmly away to do what he had planned. The second version differed only in that the emotional tension was not so fully concealed.

> She has undoubtedly said, "If that's what you want to do, all right, go ahead, don't worry about me," in a voice that implies he ought to be worrying about her, and he is therefore upset at the dilemma in which he finds himself.

But he has already decided what he is going to do, and he does it anyway.

We have now worked out two possible reasons for Hale's independence. He was early encouraged, in a secure environment, to develop initiative and self-respect, and he was then able to defy his mother's apprehensive interferences because the gravest threat, loss of the mother's love, did not present itself as an imminent danger. By the time parental quarrels became severe it seems likely that a new complication had entered the picture, one that may have made it easier for him to hold his own course and that counterbalanced the increased danger created by the sister's absence and the real possibility that the family would break up.

Hale's account of the later quarrels made it clear that he sensed issues between his parents that were much more far-reaching than his own fractious behavior. In the course of their arguments they forgot him and went on to deeper grievances. His picture of himself listening nervously for an argument to start when his parents came upstairs to undress and go to bed suggests that sex was one of their bones of contention, and that Hartley was extremely curious, baffled, perhaps frightened and perhaps angry about this mysterious element in their lives from which he was completely excluded. We know that Hartley became inordinately curious about sex, that during childhood he combed the available literature, that in high school he trailed couples at night in order to obtain copy for his scandal-sheet. Very likely he perceived still other issues between his parents, but this one was peculiarly apt to create jealousy and a feeling of exclusion. It seems important that the parental quarrels reached their peak at a point where Hartley was old enough to discern that matters beyond his own misbehavior were involved. He must have felt a burning sense of injustice when his parents blamed him for their quarrels, and he must have felt an added urge to defy, even at the cost of great anxiety, the people who blamed him and did not tell him what was really at stake.

We have already considered the fact that Hale counterbalanced his disappointments at home by means of an active, gregarious life. We need to explain, however, his uneasiness in the competitive aspects of this life, as shown in the anxieties he reported in connection with athletic contests and presumably also in the two curious incidents of last-minute failure during his freshman year. The available evidence on the origins of his fear of competition is not very clear, but two things at least must have contributed to a sharp feeling of inferiority: the early incursions of tough and menacing boys from the east, and his own stuttering. We can infer that during the middle years of childhood, in contrast to the earlier ones, he had a hard fight to establish respect, and with it self-respect, among boys of his own age. He triumphed in this campaign, but it is not inconsistent with victory that there should be residues of anxiety in the presence of any new challenge.

One of the most significant sequences in Hale's life was his progress from a brash, irresponsible high school student to a young man of rather serious purposes in college. In general such a sequence is not unusual, though sometimes with a serious-minded high school student it works in exactly the opposite way. Development does not have to be exceptional, however, in order to deserve explanation, and in Hale's case there is the added interest that the progress involved a change of vocational goal to one of the hardest and most exacting professions, a thing that must have astonished most of his high school teachers and friends, though perhaps not his physics and biology teachers.

The understanding at which we have arrived shows Hale as relying heavily upon himself. He had learned to depend a great deal upon his power of action and mastery, his ability to attack and solve problems, his capacity to check and counteract emotions that might otherwise betray him. He was certainly successful, but any adjustment must be regarded as a not wholly stable balance, liable to tip in one or another direction whenever the weights are changed. Looking at Hale's career we can observe a rather frequent, though by no means fatal, tendency of his adjustment to shift in the direction of greater assertiveness, self-display, and aggression, with the resulting danger that he would become separated and isolated from his human supports. We know from his statements and from his imaginative productions that he dreaded such isolation, associating it with depressed feelings and despair. But it was hard for him, given an audience, not to overplay his bid for applause, hard also not to mingle in his assertive self-display a large measure of hostility. It was difficult for him, for instance, to keep his humor from hurting as well as entertaining, and to prevent his outspokenness from angering others as well as winning a certain respect. His development had left a legacy of hostile feelings that had a tendency to creep into his relations with other people. When his adjustment tipped in this direction, he became uneasy, drove things all the harder, and was unable to relax sufficiently to pursue constructive interests.

From this situation he could be rescued only by a real display of kindly personal interest. The interest might be directed toward him as a person, as was the case with his girl friends, or it might be directed toward his skill and capacity for learning, as was the case with the three teachers who affected him so profoundly. That he really hungered for this kind of thing was indicated by his statement on what most readily made him cry: someone's going out of his way to be unexpectedly kind. At all events the effect of another person's deep interest was to calm him down, remove his uneasiness, and free him for absorption in some kind of continuous work. One of Hale's assets was his capacity to become deeply absorbed and fascinated by scientific pursuits. This capacity, however, could actually operate only in a situation that contained a definite income of reassuring esteem. Whenever he was forced into cockiness, his power of productive work was impaired. Whenever he felt assured of some respected person's esteem, whenever he felt that someone was willing to take a gamble on him, his productiveness sprang into high gear. One of his stories, set off by a picture showing an older man talking to a younger man, bears striking testimony to this connection:

> The younger man in the picture is an intern who has been working since graduation from medical school in a large and very modern hospital. Like all young interns he is ambitious and has already formulated many ideas about how to better the medical profession. His favorite scheme has met with rather cold disdain from the higher-ups in the hospital. He feels bitter about this rebuff and is contemplating changing hospitals when an older doctor, who when he was the age of the young intern felt the same way and who realized how the young man must feel, knocks on his door. The young man opens the door and the doctor comes in. The older doctor talks to him and shows him why his scheme was not accepted, and explains to him that every young man in his position must expect

to meet with many rebuffs before one of his suggestions is finally met with approval. The young man loses his bitter feeling to some extent and determines to go back and work even harder on his experiment.

Perhaps it was not coincidence that between the ages of sixteen and twenty-one, during which time he enjoyed the affectionate interest of his first important girl friend and had successive gambles taken on him by the high-school physics teacher, junior-college biology teacher, friend who urged him into medicine, and college tutor in biology, his stuttering steadily declined so that we did not observe it in our interviews.

PART TWO: FROM TWENTY-THREE
TO THIRTY-THREE

Medical School

Hartley Hale's career as a medical student began with a series of frustrations. He had wanted above all things to get his medical training at a leading school in New York, but his overall college record was not quite good enough and his application was rejected. This was, he said, "a pretty bitter pill to swallow; in fact, one of the major failures of my life." He found himself living in a city where he was a complete stranger, attending a medical school that, though excellent, was not his first choice. The living conditions were uncongenial. "I was in a room by myself," he said, "which I never like; I don't like being alone." His freedom was restricted by grave financial embarrassment. His father, having reached the age of seventy, was in process of liquidating his business and for the time being could give him no help. Hale obtained a tuition scholarship, but he had to take on outside jobs, such as washing dishes in a restaurant, that totaled forty hours a week. He was also obliged to enroll for an extra course that most of the medical students had already taken. "I hated to have to go over there when nobody else did," he told us, and as a result he skipped the final exam, failed the course, and lost his scholarship. The first term at medical school was "pretty unhappy," indeed one of the darkest periods of his life.

Hale's response to these discouraging circumstances was as usual an active one. He made friends with several of his fellow medical students and had beer parties with them on his weekly night off. When the school authorities expressed distaste for beer cans strewn outside the windows on Sunday mornings, he and two friends seized the opportunity to take an apartment off campus. Required to repeat the course he had failed, he this time gave it full attention and secured a very high mark. The most important step that he took, however, was made possible by the research he had done during his junior and senior years at Harvard. He approached one of the medical professors whose own research lay in the same field, explained the work he had done on the growth of bone cells, and asked whether he might have the opportunity to continue it. He was soon provided with space and equipment, and shortly thereafter with a small paid job as assistant in the laboratory, which helped to ease his financial difficulties. In spite of his extremely crowded schedule he was able, mostly during the night, to keep up a certain amount of work on his research.

By the time he reached the third year things began to go really well. He enjoyed clinical experience much more than book work, and he felt that this part of the training was particularly well handled inasmuch as "the teaching was personalized," "we got a lot of attention," and "we were let do quite a lot of things." His record had been good but not outstanding during the first two years, but his success with practical work in the clinics eventually placed him among the top five men in his class. The wartime shortage of medical personnel was already beginning to be felt, and this opened unusual opportunities for responsible work. On one occasion near the end of his third year, for example, replacement of an intern was delayed for several weeks; Hale volunteered to assume the duties during the interim, and carried them off in a way that delighted the astonished chief of the service. "I've felt many times since," he remarked, "that it was very lucky for me that I went to that school. It was one of those things which started out badly and turned out well."

For a while he was neutral toward surgery. "The student's-eye view of surgery," he said, "is that of holding the retractors and standing long hours in the operating room, looking over somebody's shoulder and not seeing much." He preferred to work on the general medical service, where the diagnostic problems seemed to be more difficult and challenging. During the fourth year, however, his preference swung definitely to surgery. "I've always liked to do things with my hands," he reminded us, and then he enlarged on the differences in personality between men who go into general medicine and men who go into surgery. The former, in his view, "like to sit around and talk about things and think about things," whereas the surgical people "like to go and do something about them." As his medical course drew to a close, Hale became increasingly certain of where he belonged, and he applied without hesitation for a straight surgical internship.

We shall later describe in detail the subject of Hale's marriage, but in order to keep the chronology straight we must insert here the information that his wedding occurred in the middle of his fourth year at medical school. At this time he was serving as a paid assistant in a laboratory course for first-year students, and he was hoping to be relieved for a fortnight's honeymoon. Shortly before he planned to put in his request, however, the professor in charge of the course announced that he was going on a two-weeks' vacation and asked Hale to take over his sections of the laboratory course. "So there I was," said Hale, "and we had only seventy-two hours for a honeymoon."

Professional Apprenticeship: Intern and Resident

Feeling that his medical school record had been strong, Hale restricted his applications for internships to three hospitals in New York City. "I suppose because of my failure to get in there in the first place," he said, "I set my heart on going to New York." In spite of wartime restrictions on travel he took the initiative in securing interviews and pressed his cause so successfully that he received one of the most coveted appointments. Upon arrival at the hospital, he was immediately thrust into a terrific round of duties which kept him going all day and most of the night, so that although in theory he was entitled to every second night off it was actually several days before he saw his wife again. The pace did not continue quite so vigorously, but everyone in the hospital was overworked, and each new assignment seemed to plunge him into a thousand obligations. Earlier than usual he was assigned to the outpatient department.

> At first I was pretty lost down there, but I got to liking outpatient a lot because I was left to my own devices and I could do what I wanted to, and I could see the patients and make diagnoses on them, which was fun, and we did a lot of minor surgery down there. And I had time to read, I stacked a lot of books down there and read about things I didn't know about, in fact I used to sleep down there a lot of the time on one of the cots because then I could be there when the patients came in and I could read until they came in.

Because of this reading he was able to recognize that one patient, treated unsuccessfully for many previous weeks, had been wrongly diagnosed and actually had a rare disease seldom seen at the hospital. This disease was treatable, though by a different method, and Hale soon had the satisfaction of seeing the chronic patient become a well person. "I had a good time there," he said; "things went very well."

In the operating room things went if anything even better. "When we finally got to operate," he reported, "I found that it was very easy for me, I did quite well in the operating room." The wartime shortage of personnel was a real boon to this part of his training, because there was no choice but to press promising young surgeons as rapidly as possible toward more difficult assignments. "I love to operate," he told us, "so I used to stick around at odd hours and do things when other people would go to bed, so I got to do more than the others." This helpfulness was much appreciated by the harassed staff. "They welcomed enthusiasm, and I was nothing if not enthusiastic at that point."

When the period of internship ended, Hale found himself retained for another year as assistant resident, a rare honor for someone not trained in the leading metropolitan medical schools. His work was praised by some of the visiting physicians. The residency was a stimulating experience. Sometimes he was in the operating room most of the day and part of the night. Little time was left over to be at home and to make the acquaintance of his small daughter.

> As you can imagine, I didn't see much of either my wife or my child. As a matter of fact I never saw the child when it was awake until it was a year old, I think, because I always got up at around four-thirty or five in the morning, and even on my nights off I didn't get home until nine or ten, so I never saw the kid except when it was asleep, but it seemed to be a fairly quiet, nice baby.

The young lady here referred to as "it" was thus badly handicapped in working her way into her father's affection, the more so, no doubt, because he had really wanted a boy and felt quite outraged at first that fortune had decreed otherwise.

At the end of his residency Hale was called into the service and assigned to a military hospital in the South. His first placement was not in a surgical service, but the chief encouraged him to examine patients who might be in need of surgery, and all of the older staff members were impressed by the thoroughness of his work. His training at the hospital in New York had been extremely rigorous. The most careful checking and rechecking, the greatest exactitude, was expected in every case, no matter how routine, and the interns and residents received merciless criticism if their work showed haste or carelessness. "I thrived pretty well in that system," he commented, "I don't mind working that way; in fact I actually like it; it's a challenge to get everything as perfect as you can." His detailed and up-to-date knowledge also proved to be a great asset. One day a patient was brought to the military hospital in coma. The commanding officer, an earnest man but not very well trained, could not determine the cause, and in great agitation lest the patient die he summoned all staff members on duty to his aid. Hale had seen a few such cases in New York and quickly administered the proper treatment; within an hour the patient was markedly improved and well out of danger. This incident led to Hale's being put in charge of a ward of his own and gave him a second opportunity to astonish his chief. He was transferred to his ward at three o'clock in the afternoon. Next morning the commanding officer made rounds and discovered that Hale knew each of the hundred patients by name, had talked with each one, knew the contents of each record, and had examined all the relevant X-ray plates. One might suspect that in telling this story Hale was exaggerating again, but the sequel shows that at all events the commanding officer was greatly impressed. He wrote to Washington about Hale, and as a result the next assignment was to an overseas rear hospital specializing in some of the most difficult branches of surgery.

In his new post Hale continued to work and to learn. Typical of his devotion to his work was his handling of a patient who had been in an extremely severe jeep accident and had "everything in the books wrong with him." Since the patient obviously could not be pulled through without constant care, Hale put a cot in his room and attended him almost without interruption for four days and nights until he was out of danger. In the course of three months, five operations were necessary, but the patient finally made a complete and lasting recovery.

At the end of his overseas service Hale returned to New York, where he picked up the threads of the research he had done in medical school on bone growth and development. The research went well, and this strengthened his desire to become an orthopedic surgeon.

Marriage and Family Life

The foregoing narrative of a crowded medical life naturally begins to make one wonder what was happening to young Mrs. Hartley Hale. Before we inquire how she managed the difficult assignment of being Dr. Hale's wife we must go back to find out how she came on the scene and how her predecessor in his affections left the scene. It will be remembered that he went fairly steadily with one girl during his last two years of college. She was to accompany him to his much anticipated senior spread. The day before the spread she telephoned to say that she had a good business offer in New York and was leaving at once. Hale commented:

> Of course there was no possibility of getting anyone else at that time. I was without a date to my own senior spread. That was quite a blow. And I was a little disappointed that she thought more of her career than she did of coming to senior spread with me, although I realized that that was a selfish point of view.

Correspondence continued during the summer, but Hale became sidetracked from a projected visit because of his growing interest in a new girl, several years younger than himself, who had previously been a casual acquaintance. The girl in New York began to repent her haste and offered, when Hale went to medical school, to have herself transferred to another office so located that they could live together. In the loneliness of his first year Hale "thought about that for a long time," but he finally decided that it was "not really very fair to her" inasmuch as he had pretty well decided not to marry her.

In the next two years letters and occasional visits strengthened his interest in the new girl. One summer they had a month together and became engaged. In speaking about their courtship Hale mentioned the attraction of her family circle, so different from his own.

> One of the things that attracted me, oddly enough, was her family situation. I mean her family always had such a good time, and they always seemed so happy, and they always had so much fun together, that it made it very pleasant to be with them, and I would still much rather be with her family than with mine.

His future wife, however, possessed numerous pleasing qualities in her own right. In retrospect he enumerated them as follows:

And I was very strongly physically attracted to her; she's good-looking, and she's very very attractive. And then another thing was the fact that things didn't bother her too much, they didn't seem to bother her too much when I was courting her, at least. If we decided at ten o'clock at night to go for a sail we went, and that was fine and nobody got excited about it; and if we decided to jump off the end of the dock and take a swim, why, nobody was upset, and that all seemed great. And then she has some insight into the trials and tribulations of doctors because of her father being one. I think that those are the main things that attracted me. She likes parties, likes to go out, likes to see people. She's very gregarious.

Reviewing these grounds for attraction one cannot escape the feeling that Hale already sensed something of the terrific demands he would make upon a wife, both because of the nature of his profession and because of his own absorbed devotion to it and determination to do well. It is almost certain that he did not reason it out in this way, but he seems to have tried to select a girl who would make him a blithe, happy, sympathetic companion while not being bothered by erratic hours nor demanding of his time and attention.

Whatever his wife may have known about the trials and tribulations of doctors, she had little conception of what being a doctor meant to Hartley Hale. Frequent moves to new places, cramped wartime housing, and a husband who practically never came home from the hospital, soon began to bother her a good deal. "Our marital life," Hale admitted, "was fairly strained for the first few years." His wife, he now began to realize, had been accustomed to much loving care and protection at home. "To be out in the cold, cold world all alone was quite a shock to her, and she hadn't been very well suited for that sort of life." Throughout his internship and first residency it was impossible to get off for more than a single afternoon at a time. When he was called into the service he managed to get a fortnight's vacation and for the first time got acquainted with his fourteen-months-old daughter. It was not until he became established in research, however, that the marital situation really began to improve. They took a house in a pleasant suburb where they were more or less surrounded by professional people and where for the first time Hale could be at home long enough to take an interest in his family and community. His wife at last found a congenial circle of friends and a chance to do things occasionally in her husband's company. But if she hoped that his interests would stay in the

laboratory and not encroach upon their domestic life she was soon disappointed. He set up a photographic workshop in the attic and began
to process pictures for his experiments.

> I often come home at 10 o'clock and go up to the attic and work
> until 2. My wife likes to go to bed at 8:30 or 9, so that it usually
> irritates her when I come home at 9, say, and go up to the attic. I
> put an easy chair up there for her and I got a radio, and I try to
> induce her to come up and sit in the chair and listen to the radio
> while I work. She does sometimes, but occasionally I've got to take
> her out or come downstairs and talk to her, occasionally I have to
> do that. So that's the only cloud on the horizon; she hates to see me
> get buried in the attic. I spend a lot of time up there; I enjoy it
> very much.

In spite of the cool self-centeredness of the last declaration, Hale
was not entirely at peace with his own proclivities. In one of our free-
association tests his thoughts arrived at the topic of buying an expensive new piece of equipment for his shop. This called up misgivings: he
considered it "pretty purely selfish" to want such elaborate equipment,
and he told us how "miserable" it usually made him feel to buy articles
for the shop when the money could have been used for things around
the house that would benefit the whole family. In another part of the
tests, when associating to the phrase *others expect*, he said, "Well, my
wife expects me to spend more time with the family." What he admitted
his wife might rightfully expect of him, however, still looked small when
compared to what he expected of her, as shown in his associations to
the phrase *a wife should*. Her primary duty was bearing, bringing up,
and providing for the children. "Her secondary job is taking care of the
husband" by getting his meals, running the house, and so forth.

> And, thirdly, I think that wherever possible she should be com-
> panionable, should go along with the things her husband likes to do
> as much as she can, and be enthusiastic about the things that he
> does. And I think, fourthly, that she should as much as she can
> remain attractive, and make herself desirable as far as her husband
> is concerned, and do everything that she can to make him proud of
> her so that he's anxious to show her off to other people.

In several of our conversations Hale contrasted his own and
his wife's temperaments. His wife differed pleasantly from his mother
in that she took care of the house in a casual spirit, getting the
work done reasonably well without fussing over details. Hale's own

thorough and meticulous tendencies, derived from his mother, have often bothered him considerably. "I realize why I do it and I still can't stop it," he said, "and it's been a hell of a thing for me." Another difference between them was their attitude toward adversity: his wife was somewhat timid and unaggressive, inclined to retreat from difficulties and "fold up when things get bad," whereas he, "stubborn and obstinate," was more apt to "go charging ahead in the face of adversity." "She has no spirit of competition," he complained, a trait which seemed to irk him considerably. At another point he remarked: "She's very feminine and has most of the feminine shortcomings which, oddly enough, rather attract me."

Real difficulty had arisen over their differences in daily cycles of energy. His wife arose cheerful in the morning, while he himself was then tired and irritable. Early in the evening, however, his wife became tired and wanted to go to bed, whereas he was all ready for several hours in the attic. A good many times Hale mentioned this problem with respect to the hour of retiring. Usually it was solved by his wife's going to bed early while he stayed up until twelve or one o'clock; fortunately, he added, she was not averse to being waked up when he came to bed. "I think she's reasonably happy these days," he judged. "We like long walks and riding, we both like the kids, we like to go to parties, and we like the same people, so that's quite a lot in common." The main problems appeared to him to have been solved. "It looked bleak for a while," he concluded, "but it all worked out very well."

At the time of the second study Hale had three children, two girls and a boy. He had been quite disturbed by the birth of his second daughter. Having a girl rather than a boy the first time had been something of a disappointment, causing him to feel, as he put it, "slightly cheated," but the news that he had had a second daughter left him "completely crushed." "I wasn't prepared for anything like that at all," he told us, "and it took quite a while for me to get over it." He was naturally overjoyed when the third child proved to be a boy. "I wanted to have a boy sometime," he said, "at least one boy." He considers his children a source of great enjoyment.

The two things I enjoy most about my children are the fact that they seem happy in their surroundings and the fact that they're always glad to see me, the fact that they're nice to me. This is very pleasant. And I enjoy teaching them. They very often come to me and ask me questions, and I like to sit down and talk to them; they

> seem to enjoy it, I enjoy it. I like to tell them stories. I like to take them with me walking and riding.

He undertakes to provide for them a better home atmosphere than that which he remembers to have prevailed in his own childhood. In particular he avoids open argument with his wife, tries not to hold down the children's venturesomeness, and does what he can to be more companionable with his children than his own much older parents were with him. He believes that on the whole his children are developing excellently. "I'm very proud of them," he remarked; "I like to see them develop along the lines I think they ought to."

Dealing with his children has made Hale aware that he sometimes involuntarily behaves as his own parents used to behave.

> The thing that usually tips me off is that the children act exactly the way I did under the same circumstances. And I stop and think, "Well, now, why is that child acting like that?" and then I suddenly realize that I've done exactly what my parents would have done in the same situation. Then I usually make a conscious effort not to act like that.

He perceives that his elder daughter works hard to be considered mature and independent, just as he himself did as a child. Sometimes this independence makes him angry:

> I get angry when my children don't do what I've told them. The oldest child in particular is inclined to do exactly what I did as a child, and that is to go out of her way to appear unimpressed by what I tell her to do, and to make every effort to show me that she's doing it not because she thinks that I'm right but only because she has to. She can sometimes be very very annoying in that respect. The case in point especially is when you tell her to hurry, when she's doing something, and she then proceeds at the slowest possible pace, just barely moving one foot in front of the other. This makes me quite angry.

The vigorously assertive older girl and the charming and popular baby boy do not show signs of insecurity, but the second little girl is not without her troubles. Caught between the greater privileges of the older sister and the greater indulgent attention received by the baby, she alternates between belligerence and thumb-sucking and has become the object of no little parental solicitude. "She definitely has a feeling of insecurity," Hale told us, "and we all work on it all the time. I often go out of my way to take her by herself some place so that she'll feel that she's the center of attention for once." He assumes that "every family has that sort of problem" and is optimistic about the outcome of his own and his wife's efforts to do something about it.

Hale is much pleased with the suburban community where his home is now located. He described with pleasure the backyard picnics at the outdoor fireplace and the friendly way in which neighbors, young and old, drop in for casual conversation. He has participated in public meetings summoned to discuss the affairs of the borough, such as the zoning of school districts. Much as he likes his dwelling place, he goes ahead in fantasy to what he calls his "ultimate house," which without being isolated from other homes or inconveniently remote from his work and from shopping centers would enjoy some of the advantages of the country. He imagines a hill and a view, a good-sized garden, perhaps a barn and some animals, certainly a stream or pond that could be stocked with trout. He also cherishes the fantasy of going off somewhere to write a book, not necessarily a medical book although he hopes later to contribute to the professional library. To some extent he keeps up his singing, and he owns a good many records. He gets great pleasure out of drawing, but this art has been wholly subordinated to his professional activity. The exacting demands of his profession have restricted considerably the range of his outside activities, but his restless energy still pushes out in fantasies of new territory he would like to explore sometime.

Growing Responsibility and Power

Although Hale was happy in a life centered on research, he felt that his professional future depended upon holding at some time the position of orthopedic resident in a hospital. This post was recently offered to him, and he gladly accepted it. He was at once precipitated into a schedule of work more demanding than anything he had yet encountered. "You don't really get to the top in surgical matters," Hale informed us, "until you run the whole show yourself, and you don't really run the whole show until you're the resident." He described as follows his life in this new and gravely responsible position:

> You run the ward, you see all the patients, you decide what's going to be done to them, and you decide who's going to operate on them, who's going to help who, who you want to do yourself, and you make rounds every day on every patient, decide what portion of their treatment you don't like, what you want changed, and that

sort of thing. And you're always on call, you're never off, and although I go home almost every night I don't usually get home until nine or ten o'clock, because when you finish the day's work you have consultations on the medical service, and sometimes they're problem cases and it takes you a while to work things out and get X-rays. And then some nights you've got patients that are pretty sick and you stick around to see what's going to happen, and we do quite a lot of emergencies, night work, and although I don't operate on most of those patients, the interns do that, I always want to see every patient, just so I can say "O.K., go ahead with it," so that they're protected in case anything happens, and I usually stick around until after the operation is done just in case something turns up that's unexpected so that they need me.

It's a busy time but it's a good time. You do what you want to, and it's a chance to really get out and do surgery that you might not ever do elsewhere.

Among the duties of the orthopedic resident is the training and supervision of residents and interns. Hale tries to deal with his subordinates as he himself liked to be dealt with when he occupied a similar position. When a new man comes into his charge he tries to put him on his mettle. He tells him in explicit detail how he would like to have things run, emphasizing that he would like to have the younger man take just as much responsibility as possible. He indicates that he will be appraising efficiency especially when rounds are being made. If everything seems well organized and if questions about the patients and their treatment can be promptly and adequately answered, so that the rounds proceed with dispatch, he will judge his subordinate favorably and give him opportunities to do more surgery. He explains that there are always twenty things to do in a ward and that time must be carefully organized to get the important things done first and all the things done in the end. Hale laughingly admitted that this matter of organizing time had been one of his own most difficult problems. He tries to help his subordinates with it, but some do not seem to be able to achieve good organization. He pictured for us his impatience when rounds went slowly and the needed information had to be pried out of the intern or sought from the nurse.

It just makes rounds pretty tedious and I don't like it, and it's hard on them, the intern feels he isn't doing a good job, in fact he isn't, whereas with other boys they'll learn so that you can make rounds on the ward in fifteen minutes, and they'll have all the facts for you; they'll just reel it out as you stop at each bedside, and you can just nod to the patient and move on. The boys who don't ever get that I'm sure feel somewhat browbeaten, because I usually am a little hard on them. But the ones who do a good job feel very happy; I usually give them a lot of responsibility in the operating room, and they get a good deal out of it.

Hale enjoys the respect of his subordinates not only for his skill but also for his defense of their interests in conflict with the hospital management. No novice at battling with authorities, he takes a strong attitude when things are needed to improve the efficiency and comfort of the service, and this makes the house staff feel that he is on their side.

Hale's strictness and his tendency to be angered by inefficiency come to their fullest expression in dealing with the nurses. When given the phrase *I hate* as a stimulus to free association, he said, "I hate stupidity," and when pressed to continue his associations he mentioned the nurses at the hospital. "I sometimes get very angry at them," he said, "when they do stupid things, which they do about twenty times a day." Elsewhere he described himself as sometimes screaming at them and frequently criticizing them, with the result that he was far from popular with most of the nursing staff. Good nurses he respects, taking active steps for their advancement, but the poor ones become the chief targets of his irritation. Hale is not perfectly at peace with the idea that the poorer nurses dislike him. He says that he quickly forgets his own outbursts and harbors no grudges, and he reassures himself that "most of them know it so that there aren't too many who really dislike me intensely." The same misgivings cross his mind about those interns and residents who receive his disapproval. He expresses his belief that their resentment is "fairly quickly forgotten," since they show no sign of it at social gatherings. On such occasions he himself steps widely out of his professional role in favor of fun and conviviality.

Among his patients Hale has the reputation of being the kind of doctor who cares about their lives as well as about their diseases. A number of people whom he first treated on the ward have come to him later as private patients. More than once he has lent a hand in finding a job or helping to solve some other personal problem. At the time of the first study, we believed that Hale had little capacity for empathic response. The desire to help people, however, always formed part of his motive for entering medicine, and in the relationship of doctor to patient he seems to have found a welcome opening for his nurturing needs.

Values and Ideals

To the value which he esteemed most highly in his professional life Hale gave the name "integrity." When asked to specify this value in more detail by giving an example of behavior that lacked it, he first mentioned doing a careless job in working up a patient's diagnosis. He remarked:

> I sometimes stop and ask myself whether I'm being honest with all my patients and I sometimes find that I am starting to slide over things a little bit, and I force myself to go back and double-check on everything to be sure that I'm not missing anything.

As discussion continued, he amplified his conception of integrity so as to make it include the willingness to attempt a difficult operation when you judged that it stood a fair chance of prolonging the patient's life but knew that a bad outcome would injure your reputation. He blamed a feeling of insecurity about one's reputation for any lapse of this kind from the standard of integrity. In general it appeared that he identified integrity with an absolute subordination of oneself to the welfare of the patient, a devotion into which the physician's ease, comfort, timidity, and concern for reputation must never intrude. This is, of course, the spirit of the Hippocratic Oath, and if Hale gave it a personal slant it was only in the intensity of his affirmation and in his choice of examples. He had been somewhat upset in the earlier days of his medical work to see the extent to which petty rivalries, jealousy, and factionalism discolored the atmosphere of hospitals. "It's like anything else," he commented, "but that isn't the way it's made to appear." The image of the completely dedicated physician had evidently served him as a strong guiding ideal, and it was his purpose to keep his own behavior close to this formidable standard.

We asked Hale whether he would still have made integrity his central value if he had gone into advertising. He laughed uproariously at such an idea, but then revealed that he had done quite a lot of thinking about the ethics of advertising during the time when he expected to make it his life work. He greatly disliked, even in those days, the idea of selling people things they did not need, of entangling them in installment buying, and of creating anxiety as a means of inducing people to buy. He had solved the problem in this way: he would select first-rate and necessary products, then go out and actively solicit the advertising for them, knowing that the sales he might bring about would be at the expense only of rival manufacturers whose products were not as good. His service would be that of promoting better products in situations where people were likely to buy something anyway.

Hale began an interview devoted to his opinions on public affairs by disclaiming any proper knowledge. He represented that a man who spent most of his time in a hospital, in an attic studio, or reading medical journals could hardly have well-crystallized views on the world at large. The exposition of his ill-crystallized views, however, occupied nearly an hour and was characterized by definiteness of statement and vigor of partisanship. Ten years earlier the most marked feature of his opinions had been his uniform opposition to government interference of any kind. He seemed to treat government interference with the same angry contempt that he had shown toward maternal interference. In the course of a decade his opinions had become better differentiated, but he still viewed with disfavor anything that suggested interference with freedom of enterprise, especially when it touched his own activities. The two objects of his bitterest wrath were socialized medicine and Communism. His views on the latter, though vehement, were not out of line with widespread American opinion in the early 1950s, and he rejected extremes such as the proposal that the United States should engage in a preventive war to thwart Russian imperialistic designs.

Although firmly a Republican, Hale was severe in his criticism of Republican policies, which he characterized as a stupid mixture of waving the flag for the good old days and trying to outdo the Democrats in conferring federal benefits. "We've got to stop screaming to get the labor unions throttled," he said; "it's more a matter of getting them managed well, actually helping them rather than hindering them." Labor leaders he considered too powerful, but he was not at all sure that the real interests of labor were sufficiently represented in the American economy. He interrupted us when, thinking that he had finished with this topic, we suggested another one:

I'd like to say one final word. I have a very definite feeling that labor was not getting the break it deserved in the past, one of the reasons being that I worked on a lot of jobs with a lot of people, and I've gotten a pretty good idea of what it was like, and I worked many hours for 35 cents an hour while other people were doing work which was a great deal easier and no more skilled and getting 3 dollars an hour. It's a very annoying thing, and a very unfair thing, I think. It's a good thing that wages have come up the way

they have, so from that point of view I'm more in favor of getting
the labor unions organized and supporting that part of the system.

The ideal in Hale's mind was clearly the establishment of a fair balance between the interests of management and those of labor. He did
not believe that large-scale government interference was the proper
method of achieving such a result.

Second Interpretive Summary

Toward the end of the final interview we asked Hale, mildly deprecat-
ing the journalistic sound of our question, to what he attributed his
success. His answer to this question may well form the starting point
for our second interpretive summary. Certainly his still young career in
medicine has been by all ordinary standards a tremendous success, and
it is just as much our task to understand success as to understand failure. Hale was of the opinion that the decisive thing in his career had
been his research. He said:

> I didn't do brilliantly in medical school. I think that the only reason
> that I've gotten most of the things that I wanted was because of the
> research I did. If I hadn't done that I wouldn't have stood out
> above anybody else. When I came to get an internship, certainly.
> It gave me a chance to get myself a little above my classmates.

He traced the crucial role of his research interests, showing how in
medical school they drew the attention of certain professors, brought
him a chance to assist in teaching, and led to strong recommendations
for the internship. His present prospects and growing eminence in the
profession depended, he believed, more on his work as a research scientist than on his ability as an orthopedic surgeon. He considered it a
"lucky break" that part of his experiments had come out well and that
they had "dovetailed so neatly" into other research, a circumstance
which enabled him to obtain financial support for continuing his investigations. His research was the central reason for his success, but he did
not deny the importance of his surgical skill and devoted hard work,
especially at the critical point where, following his initial internship, he
was retained at the hospital in the capacity of assistant resident.

> That choice came out in my favor mainly because I was enthusiastic
> and worked hard and enjoyed the work, and because I was also
> lucky again, I was able, without much difficulty, to do pretty well
> in the operating room.

When asked whether he had put an unusual amount of energy and time into his work he denied being a hard worker, characterizing himself as in most respects "a lazy guy at heart." He attributed his zeal at the hospital to an intense interest in everything that was going on.

Hale's own account of his success does full justice to the elements of good fortune in his career: his luck with the research, and the advantage of being trained in wartime when opportunities opened more rapidly than would have been possible under normal conditions. What he did not perceive so clearly, or at least emphasize so strongly in the interviews, was the contribution of his own personality to the success of his career. He called it "luck" that he was able to do well in the operating room, but this is certainly an insufficient explanation. Perhaps he had unusual dexterity, but we know that ever since early childhood his hands had been practicing the delicate manipulation of mechanisms and the art of drawing, and his research in college involved refined surgery on experimental animals. Skill in surgery, furthermore, is not simply a manual skill; it involves qualities of boldness, confidence, self-reliance, freedom from squeamishness, and willingness to assume responsibility in a situation where life is at stake. Hale did not sense that he possessed such qualities in rather unusual measure, just as he did not sense that, relative to others, he seemed practically a stranger to fatigue and welcomed the challenge of those critical situations that constantly arise in the daily and nightly life of a large hospital. He also did not think it unusual that he was capable of the absorbed interest, patience, and eternal struggle with baffling problems that characterized his behavior as a research worker. Like most people, indeed like most students of personality, he took for granted a great many of the qualities that are responsible for success.

Hale's behavior as a physician and scientist was not created suddenly as a response to the demands of the profession. His traits go far back in his history; we have already discussed all of them when summing up his personality at the end of his college years. The profession of medicine influenced him in a favorable direction, bringing forward his steadier and more constructive qualities and permitting his disorganized rebelliousness to recede. It exerted a selective effect, but the selection was made from a pool of qualities already well developed. Before he became a doctor he lived a life marked by high energy and zestful interest, by wide gregarious contacts, by deep absorption in scientific problems, by lasting curiosity and a joy in mastering mechanisms, by direct action and counteraction in the face of difficulties, by self-reliant independence, and by subordination of feelings of guilt, anxiety, and inferiority. When he was in college we noticed his relative obtuseness toward the inner feelings of other people, and we were not surprised to learn a decade later that he had never liked nor respected psychiatry. His desire for challenging action first inclined him to general medicine but later, when he graduated from passively holding the retractors, swung him decisively toward surgery. Thus even the pattern of his interests within medicine reflected traits that were clearly discernible during the undergraduate study.

To what extent, it may be asked, was Hale's success the result of calculated ambition? Did he, in medical school and later, behave in a way that corresponded to "playing the teachers" in his earlier school career? This question can be more sharply specified by asking whether he deliberately chose to play up research and whether the alleged interest that caused him to be at all times an "eager beaver" was in fact a design to impress his superiors and secure his advancement. In Hale's case the answers to these questions seem fairly clear. The ability to do creative scientific research is not a thing that can be conjured into existence by even the most flaming ambition. Hale possessed this special pattern of interests and skills before he entered medicine, and a great deal of his satisfaction in doing this kind of work must be rated as strictly intrinsic. Much the same can be said for his skill as a physician. Thus it appears that Hale was well able to deliver the goods as a physician and scientist because of qualities that were clearly apparent before he decided to enter medicine. Granting this, however, it is also true that he cared a great deal about success. It was extremely important to him to stand out above the others. Finding in himself the power to deliver the goods in so many respects, he did not hesitate to use it as a means of impressing his superiors. Still another of his preexisting traits, however, made this a natural and spontaneous, rather than a cynical and calculated, way for him to behave. As we have already noticed, he took great satisfaction in the interest and respect of older men, reaching his best level of constructiveness when some mentor became willing to give him unqualified encouragement. Hale's whole personality was so well adapted to making a success that we do not need to accuse him of devious design in forwarding his career.

The roots of his ambition can best be understood by considering some of his faults. We asked him the reasons for his success but we did not spare him questions about the things in himself that had hindered success. The fact that a person accomplishes a job and fulfills a role does not mean that there is nothing further to say. We must be on the lookout for signs of wear and strain in even the most smoothly working life pattern.

Hale was able to give us, both in interviews and free associations, quite an extensive account of his faults. He complained, for instance, about a trait which he described as "my constant procrastination which keeps overcoming me." He related his struggles against it, especially when he was an intern and found himself overwhelmed by the number of things to be done. Often he would get behind schedule; then he would make out a list, forcing himself to cross out each item before going to bed even if that meant, as it several times did, that he stayed up all night. "So that was a hard thing to fight against," he concluded. Then he mentioned a quality of obsessive neatness that had bothered him a great deal. It struck him as strange that in some respects he could be very untidy, for instance with clothes and with things around the house, but that when it came to making anything, whether bookshelves, drawings, or pieces of apparatus, every detail had to be absolutely perfect. Even in school he used to tear up drawings and start afresh because he had made some tiny mistake. He believed that his "meticulous attention to details" was derived from his mother, whose extreme neatness we have already described. Today he still sometimes finds himself completely unable to check this trait, even when he realizes that speed is the main requirement, and he characterized it as "a terrific handicap" and "a hell of a thing for me."

Hale complained also about a certain inefficiency in the workings of his mind. His memory does not always serve him with the facts and details it would be convenient to have available, especially in scientific arguments. He furthermore deplored what he called his "vagueness," a quality possessed by his mother but admirably absent from his father and sister. He reflected as follows on this trait:

> I'd like to be somewhat less vague than I am, somewhat more like my father than I am. He very rarely made a statement that wasn't right, or that he didn't have pretty good proof for. . . . The thing that I principally don't value is the general tendency to speak first and think afterwards, and the tendency to be somewhat vague, as against knowing what you want to say at once and knowing what you want to do at once, and not having any indecision. I would rather be as decisive as my father than the way I am, although I'm nowhere near as indecisive as my mother, fortunately.

We were not surprised, in view of his history of stuttering, that he included among his ideals that of being "an easy and gifted speaker who is never at a loss on his feet, able to say whatever he wants to at any moment." It was clear, however, that Hale's feelings of inferiority had roots deeper than his stuttering, however much this handicap may have enhanced such feelings. In the family circle he had perceived the contrast between his alert, self-possessed, ever-competent father and his vague, fussy, indecisive mother. He had apparently felt the same contrast between his clear-minded sister and himself. The desire to be unlike the mother and equal to the father and sister seems to have been a spur to action, yet left him with a frequent sense of shortcoming, residues of which persist today. Even now, when he enjoys the respect of colleagues and the outspoken admiration of patients, he is not always satisfied concerning his adequacy. The bothersome thought now and then crosses his mind that people think he is better than he really is, and when he sits down to analyze himself he is forced to conclude: "I never am quite as good as they think I am." The ambition that has carried him so far, that has made him fight so hard to subdue his stuttering, vagueness, procrastination, and obsessive meticulousness, seems to spring from a deep-rooted necessity to prove himself a masterful human being.

It was interesting to discover that Hale feels disquieted when everything is going well. He spoke as follows:

Everything is just a little bit too smooth now. I don't like it like that, I feel a little nervous about it. I don't have any real problems right now, and that's not good. . . .

It's always been much harder for me to be on top of the pile than to be down in the pile. Once I get on top of the pile I don't know what to do with myself, and I very soon don't do anything, and it very soon catches up with me again. And I feel more at home when I'm submerged and when things are closing in on me, when I feel myself cornered. Then I sort of gird my loins and look for ways out and there always seems to be one. It's a miserable way to live; I don't know why I do that, but I've always done it that way. . . .

There's almost nothing that I've ever done that held any sustained interest for me that I was not also afraid of. It's true even in my present position. It's true of horseback riding; I love to ride, but still being on horseback often sort of scares me. But the general sort of situation that I find myself propelling myself into, whether it's by obsession or desire I don't know, is one in which I'm in the middle of a situation which terrifies me—not necessarily terrifies me, but frightens me to a certain extent—but which I can ultimately set to rights and get out of. I don't know what force propels me into them, but I've always gotten in them and I seem to always get out of them.

Hale described vividly his terror at stages in operations when everything seemed to be getting out of hand. He is able to fight down panic by working all the harder, by reminding himself that the responsibility belongs to him alone, by urging himself to keep going as best he can. He always prepares himself with the utmost care for a difficult operation: reviewing the relevant anatomy, searching the relevant scientific papers, making exhaustive tests on the patient. He told us also that a certain anxiety was involved in his research activities. When offered in one of our tests the phrase *my greatest fear* as a stimulus to free association, he thought immediately of his current research. He fears that his findings will not be confirmed by the work of others. He reported being very upset when another laboratory published results at variance with his work, then much relieved when still another laboratory brought out findings in agreement with his own. "Quite a lot of one's career depends on research," he remarked, "and I would hate to see the whole thing come tumbling down like a house of cards."

These disclosures demand the most careful analysis. Let us begin by noting that Hale does not seem to be quite accurate when he relates all sustained interest to anxiety. His original interest in biology and his undergraduate research grew under circumstances virtually free from threat. His fears about research seem to arise from the possibility of finding himself alone and rejected by other scientists and from the possibility that failure might wreck his career. We should further note that Hale's remarks about being at the top of the pile do not seem to imply anxiety specifically at being ahead of other *people*. He uses the analogy of a pile to suggest circumstances, demands, crises, details that require attention, in short the whole impact of events as one feels it in a busy institution such as a hospital. Having made these two reservations, however, we must still be impressed by what Hale has here told us. He has said, in the first place, that he feels impelled to get into a turmoil of events, not knowing what to do with himself and even experiencing nervousness when this external pressure is lacking. Secondly, he has declared that anxiety and the chance to conquer anxiety are very important elements in his satisfaction with life. It almost seems as if the sequence of inviting anxiety and then conquering it had become an end in itself. He attested its presence in riding, a pure recreation unrelated to the serious concerns of his life.

The need for outside turmoil and pressure suggests a certain lack of internal organization. We can infer that when Hale's life is not forcibly structured for him by the pressure of events he falls into the grip of his various "faults"—procrastination, meticulousness, vague indecisiveness—and is unable to pull himself together for effective action. Mild weakness in the organization of his mental processes appeared in the results of his intelligence tests, and his choice of surgery rather than general medicine revealed his strong preference for dramatic action together with his distaste for elusive diagnoses and slow methods of treatment. Hale seems to need pressure and excitement to energize and direct his action. It is not easy to be certain of the cause of such a trait. Perhaps he is innately impulsive; perhaps his restless impatience is a part of constitutional endowment. On the other hand the nature of his "faults" suggests that certain emotional intrusions might be at work to hinder organization and disturb peace of mind. The obsessive character which he himself recognizes in these "faults" counts as evidence in favor of this interpretation. He needs external pressure in order to neutralize and dispel these intrusions.

Hale's need to invite and conquer anxiety represents a slightly different though probably not unrelated problem. It will be recalled that his undergraduate autobiography contained several incidents in which he felt anxiety but was able to emerge victorious. His interest in college athletics was, he believed, to some extent dependent on the fear he experienced before a contest and the joyful triumph over fear that could be achieved by vigorous competition. This long-standing pattern of behavior might be interpreted as a habit broken loose from its original importance, repeated merely as a matter of pleasure. Its force, however, suggests that it has a more strictly contemporary function in Hale's adjustment to life. He seems to require constant proof that he can repeat his old triumphs over fear, as if some traitor within his personality kept whispering that he could not win. One way to beat these hidden traitors is to look for external threats and keep proving that one is their master. Perhaps what he is really proving is that he can still rule the household of his personality.

Concerning the origin of the obsessive traits and anxieties that bother Hale we can offer the following hypothesis. In his earliest years he was encouraged to become self-reliant and to take pride in his power of accomplishment. In the course of time, however, maternal solicitude and autocracy began to insult this pride. He reacted by rebelliously increasing his independence, but the inner conflict and hostility generated by this bold course led to the appearance of obsessive traits and indecisiveness which constituted a still further insult to his pride. The inner stress gave rise also to inexplicable fears of the dark and of water, later on of having to move to a new house. Pride was again insulted when stuttering appeared, a grave and uncontrollable social handicap. The final insult came when he could not control his fear of the boys from the neighborhood to the east, and his ultimate conquest of this fear, in the "backbone incident," stood out as the major triumph of his childhood. It is slow work to overcome traits that have been implicated in the emotional crises of childhood. Hale still needs to strengthen his mastery of anxiety by inviting and overcoming it, to counterbalance his earlier speech handicap by volubility, and to beat out his obsessive traits by immersing himself in a turmoil of dramatic and demanding events.

One of the traits that Hale criticized in himself was his general irritability. He said:

> I'd like to have a somewhat more even temper. I get fairly annoyed at some situations, and I think it's very advantageous not to be bothered by little details that keep cropping up; lots of little things annoy me, and that's very wearing, to be annoyed by lots of little things. I'd rather not be.

It seems reasonable to assume that Hale's associates share his negative attitude toward this trait and that everyone would be happier if he could change it.

We have already discussed, in the first interpretive summary, his association of solitude with dejection, his need of friendly social support, and his tendency to injure social relationships by too free a display of assertiveness and aggression. His attitude toward solitude and toward being set apart from the group came out with striking clarity during the unhappy first year at medical school, but it appears that from now on solitude is likely to be the least of his worries. The only danger that is today actively present is that of alienating the group and creating a sense of isolation by being too critical and too aggressive. In the past this tendency has been balanced by the presence of older men who were willing to take a chance on him: professors at medical school, commanding officers in the service, senior physicians in the hospital. His term of duty as orthopedic resident, when he runs the show more or less alone, is a crucial test of his ability to function without the active support of an older man and still to check himself from assertive and aggressive displays toward his staff. Like most things in life the test is not pure, because he enjoys the implicit support of the surgeon-in-chief who granted him the flattering appointment, but he has never before faced so clearly the relative isolation that is the lot of a top administrative officer. We have seen that he experiences distinct strain. He is irritable, he criticizes his less competent lieutenants sharply, he is at times violently aggressive with the nurses, and he is anxious about the effects of all this, hoping that his victims harbor no grudges and doing his best in the relaxed atmosphere of social occasions to cancel any injuries he may have inflicted.

When we turn our attention to Hale's children, we discover a realm in which he is making progress. Although at first it seemed that he had scarcely time to become aware of his children, later he began to take considerable pleasure in their company, giving them trips and instruction in return for their gratifying quality of being nice to him. From his eldest daughter's annoying displays of independence he is slowly learning not to repeat his mother's errors in child rearing, and his sympathy for the insecurity of the second child has somewhat opened his mind to the sort of problem that is dealt with in psychiatry. Hale's own life has been built on action and the mastery of the external world. It is through bringing up his children that he is beginning to learn more about the inner world of feelings.

The point of least progress in Hale's life seems to be his relationship with his wife. Attention has already been called to the unusual features of his courtship: the appeal of his girl friend's harmonious family life, and the subtle influence of his estimate, doubtless unconscious, that his girl would be able to endure the slim emotional pickings of being a doctor's wife. She was charming, erotically attractive, and congenial to the gay social life he hoped to lead when off duty. The trouble was that once he got launched in his medical career he literally had no time off duty. Even on the occasion of the honeymoon he placed considerations of being a good medical subordinate ahead of spending time with his new wife. When this kind of thing seemed likely to continue indefinitely, his wife showed signs of rebellion, but Hale seemed to have great difficulty in contemplating that her complaints might be justified. Only slowly has he conceded that it is necessary for him to give more thought to her happiness.

In many ways his lack of consideration can be traced directly to his relationship with his own mother. Because of her oversolicitude and threat to his boyish spirit of adventure, he was obliged to develop a precocious capacity for independence, suppressing both his dependent longings and his feelings of guilt over his own defiance. He became an expert in leading his own life regardless of a woman's demands. Hale thus acquired a kind of insensitivity which carried over into his own married life when that life began to replicate the original pattern of stress: domestic demands versus the man's right to do what he wanted.

At first glance one might suppose that the conflict was simply between incompatible duties, the claims of a wife and the claims of a hospital with its sick people for whom the husband is professionally responsible. Every doctor's family knows this kind of conflict. Closer inspection shows, however, that the freedom Hale expected went far beyond the legitimate demands of his job. He was not required to do the photographic work connected with his experiments and scientific papers. He did these things because he wanted to, and it was hard for him to realize that a wife's objections sometimes had to be taken seriously. Occasionally he was aware of guilt feelings over his preoccupation with the attic workshop. But he was an old hand at disposing of that kind of guilt feelings.

In considering the life adjustment of a single individual, we are inevitably drawn into weighing the correlated adjustment of those people who constitute his social orbit. Hale's way of leading his life involves certain strains in himself, although these are for the most part well mastered and do not interfere with successful accomplishment. It also involves strains in others, particularly his wife, the hospital nurses, and the less competent members of the hospital's house staff. For them, adjustment to Hale must often be a difficult and vexing problem. But if we are to include the social orbit, it is hardly fair to consider the strains Hale imposes upon it without remembering also the services that he renders. He does much to advance the fortunes of the better nurses and more gifted house-officers, he runs his section of the hospital efficiently, he contributes possibly lasting benefits to mankind in his research, and he takes care of his patients. Our portrait of him includes his night-long study in preparation for a difficult piece of surgery, his four-day vigil at the bedside of the injured jeep driver, and his casual remark that "some nights you've got patients that are pretty sick and you stick around to see what's going to happen."

PART THREE: FROM THIRTY-THREE
TO FIFTY-SIX

When the chapter up to this point was completed, it was sent to Hale with a request for permission to publish. Lack of response for a while seemed consistent with his tendency to procrastinate, but when silence continued an appointment was sought with him at his office in New York. He said that he had read the typescript and that its publication seemed to him utterly impossible. Although he had earlier given permission to report results of the research, he had never supposed that this meant putting his whole life story into print. He felt that his privacy was invaded and that recognition of his identity, should the disguise prove fallible, would be acutely embarrassing. When told of the purposes of the book, however, he agreed to read the chapter again; and after making certain corrections of fact and amendments of disguise he consented to publication, but on condition that the study should never be carried further.

Hale's reluctance and his prohibition of further study is easy to understand, however much we may lament the absence of detailed information about the next twenty-three years of his life. Many readers may well agree that in like circumstances they would have felt the same reservations, if indeed they had ever allowed themselves to be studied in the first place. There are no follow-up interviews; but we can slightly reduce the inevitable sense of incompleteness by mentioning the known external shape of his career.

Hale continued to work in New York for several years, during which time he became well known in his profession. As a surgeon he was conspicuously successful. In his research field he became an authority, one of those regularly called upon to contribute papers at professional meetings. Teaching in a medical school was included among his duties, and his administrative talents were not allowed to languish. His mechanical inventiveness enabled him to devise individual orthopedic appliances that made all the difference to patients with unusual patterns of handicap. Presumably he stood a chance of reaching the top in New York, but a position came his way that promised greater immediate scope, responsibility, and freedom. Not yet forty, he moved to the Northwest as full professor at a medical school and surgical chief at the associated teaching hospital. At once he began to build up the research laboratories and enlarge the training program for surgical interns. As he worked for these objectives he also found time for a good deal of technical writing, through which he became still better known in his field.

The Hale family, husband, wife, two daughters, and son, has remained intact. The new location made it possible to live in the country where his fantasy of the "ultimate house" seems to have been substantially realized. Somewhat later a visitor described the lively atmosphere produced by numerous animal pets and the boisterous activity of the now teen-age children and their friends. Mentioned also was the host's pleasure in the heavy work of clearing additional land for cultivation and pasture. Hale had taken up skiing, perhaps repeating once more his search for anxieties to overcome. There was evidently plenty in his life to engage the energies of a man who thrived on action.

Because our information is purely external, it tells us little about the inner course of natural growth. We might suppose that Hale's unusually successful career would entail, as before, strains both in himself and in others. We might imagine moments of crisis at home, though these fell short of disrupting the family circle. On the other hand, we might wonder whether or not Hale's development had moved out in new directions: widening appreciations, increasing empathy, a mellowing and deepening of his personal relations. Of all this we know nothing, but what we do know reveals frequent continuities with Hale's previous life. From small matters, like the houseful of pets, to large issues, like his choosing a position where he could be more on his own, he continues to exhibit themes that started in his early years. Studying natural growth means being on the lookout for change, but change in personality occurs against the background of much that stays constant.

3

RESOURCES
FOR
UNDERSTANDING

> To know that we know what we know, and that we
> do not know what we do not know, that is true
> knowledge.

CONFUCIUS

In order to concentrate fully on describing and understanding Hartley
Hale we excluded from the last chapter any discussion of the sources
of our knowledge. No doubt this created an air of omniscience with
which no one should remain satisfied. In this chapter we shall try to
clear the air by stating how the information was collected. It will at
once become apparent that our study falls far short of being a definitive
investigation. By subjecting Hale twice to extensive studies, and by
reflecting carefully upon the results, we have been able to understand
certain things about him that would not otherwise be apparent. But we
had to use such tools as were practicable for us. As in any scientific
investigation, what we know is the kind of thing our methods made it
possible to know. An explicit statement of resources for understanding
must always accompany the claim that something has been understood.

When the object of study is another person, and when the purpose is to understand his life in detail, the first thing to consider is the other person's motivation for taking part. Unless interest is enlisted to a rather unusual extent, the subject is not likely to be disposed toward wholehearted participation and candid self-disclosure. Even when cooperation is perfect, a further difficulty arises from the nature of the material. No interviews or tests, no methods of observation, can possibly be considered complete or definitive. Many angles of approach must be used and their results combined. Information of this sort leaves much to be judged and interpreted by the examiners. In this way the frailties of the examiners enter the study and constitute a liability in reaching valid conclusions. It clearly behooves us to reflect a little on what is involved in trying to understand another person.

Methods of Gathering Information

The methods used in this study were adapted from those described by Murray in *Explorations in Personality*.[1] Subjects were invited to take part in studies of personality that would occupy fifteen to twenty hours. This meant that they dropped in frequently at the research center and became friendly with the people there. The sessions were conducted by several different workers, exposing the subject to examiners of both sexes and different ages, to whom he was likely to show different aspects of himself. The resulting diffuseness of the contacts was somewhat mitigated by having the chief investigator responsible for engaging the subject in the first place, conducting several interviews, seeing him when the schedule had been completed, and doing all subsequent correspondence. The scheme of multiple examiners makes it possible to pool the findings and ideas of several workers and to make the understanding of the subject's personality a matter of consensus.

Interviews Any attempt to study other people must rely heavily on interviews. There can be no adequate substitute for the obvious procedure of asking the subject to tell all that he can about himself and his environment. The present project began with a written autobiography, but the subject's story was then amplified by means of extensive interviews covering the family circle, the personalities of the parents, discipline and ideals, early memories, school and college his-

[1] H. A. Murray, *Explorations in Personality* (New York: Oxford University Press, 1938), especially Chapter 6.

tory, social relationships, health and sex, emotions and their control, current interests and problems, opinions and general outlook on life. A similar series of interviews, this time recorded, formed the backbone of the second study. We began with the history of the intervening years, then sought more detailed information concerning relationships with parents and siblings, marriage and family, ideas and practices as regards bringing up children, occupational satisfactions and frustrations, social life, amusements, participation in community affairs, opinions about world events, personal values and ideals. Abundant time was allotted to the interviews so that both subject and examiner could feel free to explore whatever topics entered the conversation.

It is sometimes felt that the interview method puts the examiner at the mercy of whatever fictions the subject chooses to set forth. When we ask someone to tell us what he considers to be the characteristic and essential features of his life, we certainly give him an opening to regale us with falsified pictures, selected events, and highly colored interpretations. Even when he intends to tell nothing but the truth, we cannot expect him to cancel his unwitting defenses or set aside his cherished illusions. Under favorable circumstances, however, this very real defect in the interview method can be greatly diminished. Much depends on the subject's motives and the relationship he establishes with the examining staff. Some people do not really like to have their personalities studied. They feel defensive and would prefer to study the examiners while keeping secret their own true qualities. Others participate willingly so long as they can fathom the purpose of the procedures but become resentful if they suspect the examiners of trying to learn something which they themselves do not know. The subjects described in this book were relatively free from these forms of resistance. The process of being studied was congenial to them, satisfying important needs and thus evoking their fullest cooperation. The pattern of favorable motives was quite different in each case, as we shall see in later chapters, but it was always such as to dispose the subjects toward judicious candor in discussing themselves.

For Hartley Hale an important attraction was the opportunity to talk about his successes. He felt encouraged to describe exploits which it would have been boastful to relate under ordinary circumstances. Finding himself appreciated, he progressively relaxed his defenses and became able to discuss his faults and even his failures. He gained needed reassurance from the discovery that his faults were accepted calmly, without censure or criticism. Hale thus obtained both pleasure and increased confidence from putting his personality under the microscope. It was also important to him that his chief listener in both studies was a man older than himself. The situation resembled those earlier ones in which an older man took a chance on him, respected his ultimate worth despite current defects, and thus brought out the best features of his personality. The money he earned was convenient rather than necessary; and Hale, whose standards of research method were very high, rejected the idea that his life story so blithely told could make a contribution to scientific knowledge. What prompted him to stay with the first study and return for the second was mainly a favorable pattern of inner needs.

Motivation of this kind goes a long way to minimize the faults of the interview method. It would be a mistake, moreover, to think of interviews merely as fact-gathering procedures in which the examiner has no way of sifting out the truth. The subject's behavior includes much more than the imparting of information; he displays feelings and gives the examiner abundant opportunities to read between the lines. Especially when the session is recorded so that the transcript can be studied at leisure, the examiner will observe peculiarities of phrase, odd sequences of topics, abrupt changes of theme, errors and self-corrections, hints of anxiety, and many other signs that indicate how the subject feels about the things he is discussing. Close inspection will reveal unspoken assumptions and unwitting ways of looking at things that may be of great importance in the subject's personality. Hartley Hale never told us, for instance, that he regularly placed the demands of his profession ahead of the demands of his wife, but this generalization was obvious from specific events he described and from the character of his transitions between the two topics. Only toward the end of the study did he speak of his strong conscience with regard to patients and his sharp anxiety over difficult pieces of surgery, but these feelings could easily be inferred from his earlier narrative of events.

Tests and Systematic Observations In spite of the central position of interviews and the richness of understanding to be derived from them when subjects are favorably motivated, the study of personality would be incomplete without a considerable use of other methods. There are plenty of things that people cannot tell about themselves and that cannot very well be inferred from interviews. Standardized tests for which norms have been established for the population as a whole, or for relevant parts of it such as college students, provide an easy way of placing the individual case in relation to the performance of others.

In attempting to assess the abilities of our subjects we relied upon a combination of standard tests and performance in everyday life. With respect to physical abilities we obtained standard somatotype photographs according to the technique devised by Sheldon, and we took careful note of the health and athletic histories.[2] For an estimate of intellectual status we used the Wechsler-Bellevue Adult Intelligence Test, generally supplementing it with several other measures.[3] One of these supplemental examinations was the Vygotsky test, a difficult problem in concept formation which generally creates considerable frustration and tension before the correct solution is reached.[4] A test of this kind has the special value of showing the extent to which intellectual processes become disrupted by stress. It is of interest that Hartley Hale dealt rather successfully with this problem. Baffled for a while, he showed distinct signs of mounting annoyance and confusion, but he firmly pulled himself together and worked with resolute concentration until he had mastered the problem. In estimating intellectual competence we included the school history, the imaginative productions, and such evidence as we could obtain by discussing intellectual interests with the subjects. We sought in these ways to draw a qualitative picture of the subject's actual use of his mind.

To facilitate comparisons between our subjects and larger populations we used a certain number of standardized self-rating scales, particularly the Bernreuter Personality Inventory and the Allport-Vernon Study of Values.[5] The fullness of our interview material, however, freed us from having to depend heavily on self-ratings in understanding the individual cases. Self-rating questionnaires have to be used as a matter of economy when a research project calls for large numbers of subjects, but the information they typically yield is of the sort that can be gathered much better, with less risk of distortion, in favorably moti-

---

[2] For a description of Sheldon's ideas see C. S. Hall and G. Lindzey, *Theories of Personality*, 2d ed. (New York: John Wiley & Sons, Inc., 1970), Chapter 9.

[3] A. Anastasi, *Psychological Testing*, 3d ed. (New York: The Macmillan Company, 1968), Chapter 11.

[4] S. L. Garfield, *Introductory Clinical Psychology* (New York: The Macmillan Company, 1957), Chapter 4. For fuller information consult E. Hanfmann and J. Kasanin, "Conceptual Thinking in Schizophrenia," *Nervous and Mental Disease Monographs*, 1942, No. 67.

[5] Garfield, 1957, Chapter 5; G. W. Allport, *Pattern and Growth in Personality* (New York: Holt, Rinehart and Winston, Inc., 1961), pp. 296–299.

vated interviews. During the undergraduate study the subjects participated in whatever experiments were going on in the laboratory, for example, hypnotic susceptibility, level of aspiration, and tests involving competition and frustration. Such participation provided further opportunities to observe their behavior under various pressures.

One of the most interesting ways of approaching the individual case is to make a study of imaginative productions. The general idea behind tests of imagination—*projective tests*—is to confront the subject with ambiguous material of some kind and ask him to do something with it. In the Rorschach test, for instance, he is asked to tell what he perceives in a series of actually meaningless inkblots, while in the Thematic Apperception Test he is shown pictures susceptible to many different interpretations and is invited to make up stories about them. The ambiguous character of the material precludes merely conventional answers and forces the subject to fall back on his own preferred ways of doing things. He is thus apt to reveal certain covert features of his personality, for example, his unsatisfied desires, suppressed anxieties, preferred patterns for perceiving the world and the people around him.

Hartley Hale made a strenuous effort in the Rorschach test to perceive mechanical objects in the unmechanical inkblots. He also had difficulty in achieving good organization among his percepts. Both of these clues pointed to traits that were important in understanding his personality. In his stories for the Thematic Apperception Test he regularly attributed dejection, despair, and suicidal thoughts to lonely characters, thus significantly amplifying his direct statement that he hated to be alone. Significant also were those plots in which sons ran counter to their mothers' wishes, showing determined independence but also traces of uneasy regret.

The Rorschach and Thematic Apperception Tests were regularly used in the studies described in this book.[6] They were supplemented, especially in the earlier studies, by several other procedures involving imaginative production: sentence completions, story completions, story alterations, cloud pictures, and so forth. By these techniques we hoped to extend and deepen the abundant information gathered in the interviews. We also used with each subject one or both of two procedures based on Freud's original idea of free association. The first of these procedures called for continuous free association for an hour with a mini-

[6] Garfield, 1957, Chapter 6; Anastasi, 1968, Chapter 19.

mum of prompting. The second technique varied from the classic pattern by offering brief but significant phrases as a stimulus to association.[7] Examples of the phrases used in the latter session, and of the associations they stimulated in Hartley Hale, have already appeared in the preceding chapter.

Comparison with Other Methods

These were the methods used, the sources of our knowledge. It hardly needs saying that we did not learn everything about our subjects and cannot certify that our understanding is either complete or accurate. A brief look at other methods will show what can be done under different circumstances and with different resources.

For reconstructing personal history nothing compares in thoroughness with the technique of psychoanalysis. This means two or three years of daily meetings between patient and analyst; it means the persistent use of free association as a way of disclosing the patient's emotional life. Although the method is not proof against unwitting suggestion by the analyst, in careful hands it can produce a wealth of information about the childhood origins and affective undertones of present personality. In the last chapter we inferred from certain evidence that Hale's rebellion against maternal interference was accompanied by guilt which still occasionally disturbs current behavior. This is the kind of problem on which psychoanalysis could be expected to supply more abundant and more reliable evidence. But no person would willingly submit to a process so painful and protracted unless driven by the most powerful motives: to recover from a grave emotional disorder or to learn to help others recover. The probing of emotional depths cannot be part of a study such as ours.

The best information about actual behavior, especially behavior under stress, comes from direct observation. During World War II, in a program to select men for difficult assignments from among volunteers, Murray and the Assessment Staff of the Office of Strategic Services developed a series of lifelike tasks requiring action, alone or in groups, under genuinely trying conditions.[8] Such methods yield information about coping behavior that is hard to obtain reliably through inter-

[7] R. M. Ravven, *The Phrase Association Interview*, 1951, unpublished thesis, Harvard College Library, Cambridge, Mass.

[8] O. S. S. Assessment Staff, *Assessment of Men* (New York: Holt, Rinehart and Winston, Inc., 1948), Chapters 3 and 4.

views. Since that time there have been many studies based on contrived situations intended to simulate real life. Conditions have been
arranged to create frustration, produce anger, awaken anxiety, start an
argument, provoke ingratiation and other social strategies, test honesty,
and encourage affiliative and supporting behavior. Valuable information can result from seeing a subject in action, but care must be taken
in interpreting the results. Is the situation construed as a real happening
and a genuine test of worth, or is it, at the other extreme, taken as a
game which the subject will obligingly play or perhaps try to spoil? It is
not always easy to invest a contrived situation with real seriousness.

The study of social behavior and the social orbit is best carried
on when the examiners can function as participant observers and can
secure expressions of opinion about the subjects from the people
amongst whom they live. An early high standard in this respect was set
by Jones in the Adolescent Growth Study at Berkeley.[9] Ratings made by
teachers, reputation among classmates, position in the pattern of friendships, and spontaneous behavior observed at the school clubhouse all
contributed in this study to a detailed knowledge of each subject as a
member of the school society. Such excellence can be achieved, however, only when the research project has invaded the community and
secured a rather unusual degree of cooperation from everyone concerned.

Still another important branch of personality study, parent-child
relationships, calls ideally for a similar kind of participant observation.
The studies of child development carried out over many years by the
Fels Foundation at Yellow Springs, Ohio, have brought to a fine point
the observation of parents and children at home and the systematic
recording of their interaction.[10] Periodic visits are made to the home
by social workers who record their observations immediately afterwards
with the aid of long-tested check lists. This technique again calls for
unusual community cooperation and is probably most successful when
the children are young. It has been widely used in studies designed to
trace the growth of personality from the earliest years.

It is instructive to call to mind at this point the methods used
by professional writers of biography. The biographer considers his
work badly done if he has not made an exhaustive search for personal
documents, such as diaries or letters written by, to, and about the sub-

[9] H. E. Jones, *Development in Adolescence: Approaches to the Study of the Individual* (New York: Appleton-Century-Crofts, 1943), Chapters 3 and 4.

[10] A. L. Baldwin, J. Kalhorn, and F. H. Breese, "Patterns of Parent Behavior," *Psychological Monographs*, 58 (1945), No. 3.

ject. Personal impressions of contemporaries, actual interviews if some of these are still living, must be scrupulously sought, and every attempt must be made to construct a complete chronology of the events of the subject's life. If he left writings, these will be scrutinized with great care. In addition, the author must try to grasp the subject's view of the world and of himself at different points in his career; he must try also to get in tune with the subject's feelings and emotions. Information about these inner states is partly a matter of inference, but without it the biography will not seem to "come alive." The research and reflection demanded of themselves by good biographers set a standard that merits our respect.

The preceding paragraphs have called attention to a number of ideal methods for studying personality. If in so doing they have constituted a criticism of the case studies reported in this book, which rivaled none of these ideals, we are the more justified in mentioning a special virtue of our own enterprise. By using an abundance of interviews, by evoking strong personal interest in the proceedings, and by giving respectful attention to the subject's self-estimates, his hopes and fears, his plans and daydreams and deepest aspirations, we have been able to learn a great deal about the inner integrations that are so important in giving overall form and direction to a life. Furthermore, by starting with relatively healthy and able young people and by carrying the study on into their more settled young adulthood and approaching middle age, we have been in a special position to observe the process of natural growth. Whatever potentialities there may be in human nature for self-direction, spontaneous insight, and constructive change, our methods have helped us not to overlook them. And these are the most neglected aspects of personality.

Precautions in Interpreting Information

The final point to consider with regard to method is the judging and interpreting activity performed by the examiners. It is impossible to study another person without making evaluations, and it is hard to keep these evaluations from being seriously distorted by one's personal reactions to the subject. Hartley Hale, for example, is a man who evokes strong feelings in the people who become acquainted with him. These feelings in turn call forth definite preferences as to the interpretation of the case material. Some of Hale's qualities are likely to evoke approval and admiration: his successes, his rapid advance up the ladder

of professional status, his vigorus self-confidence and capacity for masterful action, his service and self-dedication in the field of medicine. But
such qualities can also generate feelings of envy and resentment, so that
we look for flaws in the flattering picture. It may be felt, for instance,
that Hale had a pretty easy time of it in comparison with young men
who face acute financial difficulty or ethnic prejudice. We all tend to
have preconceived attitudes toward people who get by in school without
working hard or even behaving well, and toward people who take great
pains to win the approval of their superiors. Even Hale's treatment of
clumsy subordinates and of his long-suffering wife, while not generally
popular, may receive widely different evaluations in the pattern of his
life. At one extreme these qualities may be considered minor fail-
ings inevitable in so busy and useful a life—after all, we cannot be perfect—while at the other extreme they may be read as profound failures
in human feeling, suggesting affective shallowness in all the rest of his
activities.

The study of personality is one of the most difficult branches of
knowledge in which to achieve a judicious outlook, free from invasion
by personal preferences and personal feelings about the subject matter. Even when the more obvious kinds of prejudiced thinking are overcome, there is still the danger of projecting unwitting attitudes and problems of one's own into the judgment.

The procedure devised by Murray, whereby several different
workers collaborate as a diagnostic council in making the interpretations, is intended to reduce these difficulties to relatively harmless proportions. Especially if the workers are of somewhat different backgrounds and training, they can cancel each other's personal rigidities of
judgment to a considerable extent. Working together in this way progressively teaches the examiners to perceive their own tendencies toward
bias and to achieve greater judiciousness. The studies described in this
book are the handiwork of a large number of examiners. Several different people participated in giving the tests and conducting the interviews. The interpretation and integration of the findings were done in
staff conferences attended by ten or a dozen workers. While this plural-
istic procedure does not guarantee complete impartiality, it serves at
least to diminish those errors of judgment that must be laid at the door
of the examiners.

SUGGESTIONS FOR FURTHER READING

Further study of methods for the understanding of personality can well begin with the brief systematic survey given by G. W. Allport in *Pattern and Growth in Personality* (New York: Holt, Rinehart and Winston, 1961), Chapters 17 and 18. A concise introduction to the difficult question of measurement is provided by E. L. Kelly, *Assessment of Human Characteristics* (Belmont, Calif.: Brooks-Cole Publishers, 1967). A searching analysis of the problem, valuable for anyone who foresees doing research in this area, is given by D. W. Fiske, *Measuring the Concepts of Personality* (Homewood, Ill.: The Dorsey Press, 1970).

H. A. Murray in *Explorations in Personality* (New York: Oxford University Press, 1938) describes a wide variety of methods designed to approach personality from all angles; see especially Chapter 6. Methods developed by Murray and associates for the purpose of assessing personnel for strategic wartime services are given in Chapters 3 and 4 of *Assessment of Men* by the O. S. S. Assessment Staff (New York: Holt, Rinehart and Winston, 1948). Stress is laid on the performance of lifelike tasks in a social setting that permits frequent informal contacts between observers and candidates. C. A. Dailey in *Assessment of Lives: Personality Evaluation in a Bureaucratic Society* (San Francisco: Jossey-Bass, Inc., 1971) argues in favor of the life history as a whole, rather than tests and credentials, as a basis for employment and the prediction of future performance.

Those who are interested in particular procedures will be well guided by Anne Anastasi, *Psychological Testing*, 3d ed. (New York: The Macmillan Company, 1968) and by L. D. Goodstein and R. I. Lanyon, *Personality Assessment* (New York: John Wiley & Sons, Inc., 1971).

4

THE SHAPING
OF LIVES
BY SOCIAL FORCES

Society and individuals are inseparable phases of a common whole, so that wherever we find an individual fact we may look for a social fact to go with it.

C. H. COOLEY

The plan of this book is to alternate between intensive case studies and the discussion of general ideas. This chapter will be devoted to *the social view of man*: the ways in which an individual is shaped by the culture and society of which he is a member. We shall examine some representative ideas about social shaping forces, using Hartley Hale as a case in point. During the last fifty years the social sciences have built up impressive evidence for the importance of these ideas. Man is a highly social animal, and we need to understand the large part played in individual development by the ever-present social and cultural environment.

The General Influence of the Culture

The broad influence of the culture as a whole provides an appropriate starting point. How do the values and ideals of American culture affect the course of individual development? To what extent, more specifically, can we see in Hartley Hale's personality the imprint of the culture in which he grew to manhood? This culture, we must bear in mind, has changed substantially in the course of thirty-five years. Hale grew up between the two world wars; we must try to picture the cultural influences of that time, while taking the occasion to examine some important historical changes.

Competitive Enterprise "The pattern of the culture," wrote Lynd in 1939, the year when Hale was first studied, "stresses individual competitive aggressiveness against one's fellows as the basis for personal and collective security. Each man must stand on his own feet and fight for what he gets—so runs the philosophy of the culture—and in this way the common welfare throughout the entire culture is best achieved."[1] For the most part, success in the struggle is measured by money, but money easily serves as a symbol for other values such as prestige and power. The sharp cultural accent on individual enterprise had its origin in the conditions that prevailed on the frontier and in a rapidly expanding economy, but it tended to outlast these conditions. In the atmosphere engendered by this ideal the individual is encouraged to be much concerned about his competitive prowess and to seek constant proofs of his adequacy. He also tends to feel alone and isolated from others, who are his rivals rather than his associates in a common enterprise. To be able to compete successfully he must hold in reasonable check his dependent tendencies, his sympathies, and his desire to be loved by others. The ideal calls for high self-sufficiency and freedom from hampering restraints.

Hale exemplifies to perfection the ideal of competitive enterprise. His early independence and self-reliance, his embattled course toward childhood self-respect, his drive, his desire to rise above his fellow medical students, his suppression of the softer side of his nature, his conception of a proper economic order, all testify to the impact of this cultural ideal. His father was in competitive business and had taken part in com-

---

[1] R. S. Lynd, *Knowledge for What? The Place of Social Science in American Culture* (Princeton, N.J.: Princeton University Press, 1939), p. 71.

petitive sports. Presumably a personality such as Hale's might be found in places other than the United States, but it is easy to think of cultures, for example, the Chinese, Hindu, and Russian, in which a like pattern would be so heavily discouraged as to become all but impossible.

Faith in Material Progress A long-standing feature of the American culture pattern is an optimistic faith in material progress. As Commager put it in 1950, the American's culture is "predominantly material, his thinking quantitative, his genius inventive, experimental, and practical."[2] In this cultural climate there is scant encouragement for contemplation, theorizing, or artistic endeavor, which tend to be identified with the idle and the useless. Virtue resides rather in action directed primarily to changing the material environment for the better. Thus the industrial pioneer and the enterprising businessman served for several generations as culture heroes because they conspicuously augmented the supply of material goods; the inventor was honored because of his extensions of technical mastery. Unbroken material progress long stood as an article of American cultural faith.

Again the description of a cultural characteristic sounds at the same time like a description of Hartley Hale. A few points will sufficiently recall the whole striking resemblance: his description of the ample high school stage and of his joy in inventing new lighting effects, his research activities which included the building of apparatus, and his ultimate preference for surgery because of its active attack on the material sources of illness. The channels of Hale's interest and the directions taken by his energies were again harmonious with the American cultural terrain and were undoubtedly encouraged by it.

Action and Rationality Optimistic faith in material progress is usually accompanied by a like faith in the energy and rationality of human beings. Making an effort and behaving with realistic common sense are values that are deeply enshrined in the American tradition. In Kluckhohn's words, "our glorification of science and our faith in what can be accomplished through education are two striking aspects of our generalized conviction that secular, humanistic effort will

[2] H. S. Commager, *The American Mind: An Interpretation of American Thought and Character since the 1880's* (New Haven: Yale University Press, 1950), p. 410.

improve the world in a series of changes, all or mainly for the better. We further tend to believe that morality and reason must coincide."[3]

With respect to this feature of the cultural outlook Hale was again in perfect accord. He feels almost completely detached from religion, declaring that he can get more inspiration from being out of doors than from being in church. Whenever we attempted to draw him into a discussion of moral and spiritual values, he plainly showed that he considered such topics both fuzzy and unimportant. In common with most of his sophisticated contemporaries he had dislodged sex from its pre-Freudian status as the cardinal sin and accepted it as a pleasurable part of man's biological endowment. If it is true, as Commager maintains, that Americans on the whole lack "either a sense of sin or that awareness of evil almost instinctive with most Old World peoples,"[4] then Hale must again be rated as a typical American. But this does not mean that his conduct is without moral control. He has a sharp sense of fairness. Injustice is the thing above all others that makes him angry, and it was on grounds of unfairness that he refused to live with the girl he had decided not to marry. In his dedication to this value, he exhibits yet another culturally accented trait. According to Erikson, a common type of young American "does not know any kind of indignation in the positive sense of the violation of a principle, with the exception of unfairness."[5] Hale's morality does in fact reach a little further. His indignation can easily be fired by any lapse from that high code of professional ethics which he applies relentlessly to his own conduct. The codes of both medicine and science are severe, but they are secular codes in which morality is pretty much identified with effort and reason.

Hale's competitive enterprise, faith in material progress, and reliance on action and rationality are not wholly of his own making. He may have had qualities that fitted this pattern especially well, but the pattern itself was there long before him, a cultural guide developed over many years of American experience.

Conformity General cultural values are influential but not all powerful in shaping individual behavior. The next value to be con-

---

[3] C. Kluckhohn, *Mirror for Man: The Relation of Anthropology to Modern Life* (New York: McGraw-Hill, Inc., 1949), p. 232.

[4] Commager, 1950, p. 410.

[5] E. H. Erikson, *Childhood and Society*, 2d ed. (New York: W. W. Norton & Co., 1963), p. 315.

sidered proves to be hardly at all characteristic of Hartley Hale. For more than a century foreign visitors accused Americans of excessive conformity in matters of speech, dress, manners, behavior, and ideas. The ideal of equality, however imperfectly realized in practice, produced what was sometimes called "the cult of the average man." Most Americans, in spite of their interest in getting ahead, seemed in most respects loath to stick out from the crowd and preferred to think that they were doing things in ways of which everyone approved. Conformity, of course, is not consistent with competitive enterprise; this conflict has often been pointed out as a clear source of strain in our culture. The inherent conflict shows most plainly in those individuals who simply split their lives, competing ruthlessly in business but conforming rigidly in the domestic and community spheres. Hale was not a conspicuous nonconformist; he "liked the world as it is." But no one would choose him as an example of the American tendency toward a leveling of individuality. At thirty-three as at twenty-one he was guided by ideals of professional achievement, and he made rather small concessions to smooth social participation.

Men and Women Anthropological studies have disclosed great cross-cultural differences in the definition of male and female roles. In the America of Hale's youth, these roles were generally considered to be quite different. Breadwinning and homemaking called for different virtues, and the interests of men and women only partly overlapped. Some progress had been made toward equal rights for women, but the culture reserved many important privileges for men. In spite of this basic inequality, observers in the 1930s talked of a tendency of American men to spoil their wives, idealize them, assign them superior cultural and spiritual attributes, and at the same time permit them to exert no little tyranny in the home. The idealizing tendency found its most extreme expression in sentimental rhapsodies on Mother's Day. The acceptance of petticoat rule could be discerned in the cartoonist's stock figures of dominating wife and henpecked husband, a family pattern that contrasted sharply with most European cultures.

Hale may have experienced the impact of this latter attitude. His adolescent description of certain girl friends puts them a little on a pedestal. In the main, however, he exhibited no tendency to spoil women, idealize them, or submit to their domination. At best, he treated them as companions with whom pleasures could be shared; at worst, as inferiors who could be ignored or made targets of angry criticism. In the family circle of his childhood, he had perceived his forthright father as an unsentimental authority and he had himself forcefully rebelled against fussy maternal dominance. His personal image of the culture was consistent with the idea of female inferiority but not with the idealizing of women.

Changes in American Culture Description of these cultural values prevailing between the two world wars provides us with a base for examining several directions of change. During the 1940s observers began to notice a decline of emphasis on competitive enterprise and a corresponding rise in the value attached to conformity. The increasing prominence of large-scale organizations in American economic life took the emphasis away from individual success and favored the ideal of cooperative membership in groups and on teams. A transitional phase was noticed by Fromm in his account of a "marketing orientation."[6] Success in an organization had come to depend less on what a person could do, more on how well he could sell himself as a cooperative, genial, agreeable person who worked smoothly with others for company goals. The shift from values of individual achievement to social adjustment was perceived more broadly by Riesman.[7] "Increasingly," he wrote, "other people are the problem, not the material environment," and this had the effect of training each person to guide his conduct by paying close attention to the signals of approval and disapproval that emanate from others. The high value placed upon conformity and the anxiety experienced when one felt conspicuous were particularly obvious in adolescent groups, but Riesman maintained, and others confirmed, that a similar outlook was invading many spheres of adult concern.[8] Riesman described the trend as a movement from "inner-direction" to "other direction." Applying these concepts to Hale, "inner-direction" is indicated in the steering of his conduct by his own interests, ambitions, and decisions; he does not display such "other-directed" characteristics as sensitivity to signals from others, and he has certainly never objected to being conspicuous. We may well wonder how he would have fared

---

[6] E. Fromm, *Man for Himself* (New York: Holt, Rinehart and Winston, Inc., 1947).

[7] D. Riesman, *The Lonely Crowd: A Study of the Changing American Character* (New Haven: Yale University Press, 1950).

[8] W. H. Whyte, Jr., *The Organization Man* (New York: Simon & Schuster, 1956).

in the blandly tolerant yet leveling atmosphere described by Frieden-berg as characteristic of many American high schools of the 1960s.[9] Would his continual hell-raising and his scandal sheet have been consistent with popularity, or would his schoolmates with kindly condescension have suggested that he talk to the school psychologist? But even in his own time Hale leaned far more toward competitive enterprise than toward conformity.

During the early 1960s another traditional value came under challenge. The basic faith in material progress, while it still holds its place in the minds of many members of the culture, has lately been the target of searching criticism. The rapid forward march of technology has revealed serious dangers and injuries to the quality of life. It has entailed reckless depletion of natural resources and careless polluting of the environment. It has led to vast concentrations of wealth, power, and corruption. Trust has been undermined by cynical manipulation of public opinion and by advertising designed to create more and more material wants. Some observers describe the economic system as a destructive juggernaut moving toward chaos rather than salvation. To the extent that action and rationality are seen as linked to this dehumanizing process, they share in the fading esteem of material progress.

Meanwhile a new set of values began to emerge as an alternative. Emphasis began to be placed on openness in human relations, sincerity of feeling, freedom to enjoy the pleasures and beauties of living.[10] For some, these goals seem to imply a sharp break with traditional occupations and social institutions, but the influence of the new values has been widely felt among those who do not move so far. One consequence has been a change in the definition of masculine and feminine roles. The movement for women's equal rights is again active, and the differences between sex roles tend to diminish, as outwardly symbolized by the growing similarity in dress and hair styles.

Hartley Hale's children went through college during the 1960s and must have been well exposed to these changes in the culture. Their father lived in a different time and was affected by a different cultural climate. But he was not a literal product of prevailing values. We learn from his case that the general influence of the culture is indeed general,

[9] E. Z. Friedenberg, *Coming of Age in America: Growth and Acquiescence* (New York: Random House, Inc., 1965).

[10] C. A. Reich, *The Greening of America* (New York: Random House, Inc., 1970).

leaving wide scope for other shaping forces and for a certain amount of choice. The culture encourages certain patterns of behavior and expectation without prohibiting a considerable range of variations from the norm. If we consider Hale's personality as a whole we are justified in calling him very American, yet he certainly is not typical in the matter of conformity.

Better understanding of social shaping forces requires going beyond values that characterize the culture as a whole. The inquiry must be pushed to include those subcultures represented by social class, which will be found to differ significantly with respect to value patterns. It must be pushed further to take account of more specific roles such as those associated with occupation. We would fall far short of taking the social view of man in the case of Hale if we failed to consider him not only as an American but as an upper-middle-class American who has become a physician and scientist.

The Effects of Social Status

It is a well-established fact that American society is highly stratified. The cultural ideal of democratic equality and "the cult of the common man" have not prevented the existence of marked social stratification based largely, though not entirely, on differences in wealth. In recent years social scientists have invaded a number of representative communities and remained there long enough to become thoroughly familiar with the status hierarchy. Information is derived chiefly from the residents of the community, who seem to experience little difficulty in ranking their fellow citizens with regard to social status. Questions about the relative importance of people in the community draw from most informants a ready assignment of all the people they know to definite social positions, and there is surprising agreement among the assignments made by different informants.

Agreement is smaller when it comes to grouping the people of the community into social classes. Only in the South, where skin color was made the basis for a rigid caste system, has stratification been clearly institutionalized. Otherwise American society, though riddled with status differences, has not developed sharp criteria for separating social classes. The democratic ideal is preserved in the notion that status can be improved by individual effort, and the motive of upward mobility proves to be strong and pervasive in American life. It is actually no easy matter, however, for a person to improve the status to which he was born. Social obstacles, sometimes expressed with open cruelty but more often taking the form of ill-recognized prejudices, serve in fact to restrict mobility and perpetuate the existing stratification.

The seriousness of these restrictions was well shown in a study by Hollingshead, which concentrated particularly on class structure as it affects young people of high school age.[11] The social status of parents was found to exert a powerful influence on the formation of those groups that are so important in the lives of American adolescents. The "crowds" or "bunches" to which one might belong were almost wholly restricted according to class status. Sometimes this rigidity of groupings even defeated the efforts of teachers to organize classless recreations at the school. The teachers themselves, however, were not exonerated of class prejudice. Mostly of middle-class origin, they were found to favor the upper parts of the social scale and to discriminate against lower-class pupils, whom they considered crude and unpromising. Feeling this rejection both by teachers and fellow students, lower-class young people withdrew as early as possible from school, took unskilled jobs, and thus perpetuated the stratification. Studies of intelligence and school achievement can hardly be adequate without taking into account the pervasive effect of social class on motivation to succeed in school.

The study of individual lives stands to benefit in several ways from this knowledge of social stratification. Upward social mobility is a motive often disguised and denied, but we are now in a much better position to look for it between the lines. We are also in a better position to estimate the strength of the social barriers with which an individual is confronted, a necessary step in building up his picture of the world and explaining the channels taken by his own strivings. The most important benefit, however, comes from realizing that the conditions under which personality develops are not at all the same at different levels of society. The simple circumstance of the mother going out to work, for example, greatly changes the character of the home as an agent in shaping the child's personality. Values, ideals, and goals, moreover, vary widely with social class. As Davis and Havighurst have expressed it, "the social class of the child's family determines not only the neighborhood in which he lives and the play-group he will have, but also the basic cultural acts and goals toward which he will be trained. . . . Thus the pivotal meaning of social class for students of human devel-

[11] A. B. Hollingshead, *Elmtown's Youth: The Impact of Social Classes on Adolescents* (New York: John Wiley & Sons, Inc., 1949).

opment is that it defines and systematizes different learning environments for children of different classes."[12]

Characteristics of Social Classes   In the following descriptions
we shall follow the five-class scheme that has been widely used in
sociological studies. In this scheme, the *lower class* is defined occupationally as the level of unskilled manual labor. Limited education,
irregular employment, poor living conditions and constant economic
insecurity are characteristic at this level. The proportion of broken
homes is large, and the disciplinary regime is apt to consist of
alternations between harsh punishment and neglect. Free competition
with other children on the streets leads often to defeat and frustration,
though it may become the basis for premature independence and self-
esteem. Claude Brown in the story of his Harlem boyhood points out
that the culture of the streets calls for building up, rather than suppressing, one's aggressive tendencies. Especially for boys, but even for girls,
fighting is expected, encouraged, and made the basis for respect.[13]
Most important for lower class members is the feeling of not belonging
in the larger society as represented by its schools, its agents of law and
order, and its employment opportunities. It is not surprising that group
delinquency sometimes becomes a satisfying way of life when neither
family nor society holds the promise of security and self-respect.[14]
Oscar Lewis, in *The Children of Sanchez*, a study of four lower-class
young people in Mexico City, advanced the idea that there is a "culture
of poverty" which is more or less the same the world over, regardless of
national characteristics. This culture tends to be local and provincial,
"only partially integrated into national institutions"; its members occupy
a small world of relatives and acquaintances, and suspicion and hostility
prevent much extension of friendship. Lewis described "a sense of resig-
nation and fatalism based upon the realities of their difficult life situation," and attributed to this the "strong present-time orientation with
relatively little ability to defer gratification and plan for the future."[15]

[12] A. Davis and R. J. Havighurst, "Social Class and Color Differences in
Child-Rearing," in C. Kluckhohn and H. A. Murray, *Personality in Nature, Society, and Culture*, 2d ed. (New York: Alfred A. Knopf, Inc., 1953), p. 309.

[13] Claude Brown, *Manchild in the Promised Land* (New York: The Macmillan Company, 1965), Chapter 10.

[14] A. K. Cohen, *Delinquent Boys: The Culture of the Gang* (New York:
The Free Press, Inc., 1955).

[15] O. Lewis, *The Children of Sanchez: Autobiography of a Mexican Family*
(New York: Random House, Inc., 1961).

Children reared in such an environment learn little that prepares them for more hopeful and planful living.

In an advanced industrial economy like that of the United States, the lower class may not be numerically large. It is overshadowed in size by the *working class*, which may include as much as half the population in a given area. This large segment of the population, engaged occupationally in skilled and semiskilled manual labor, differs greatly from the historical idea of a disorganized proletariat. Its members are frequently traditional and unadventurous in outlook, asking not much more for themselves and their children than security, respectability, and a decent standard of living. Their sources of information and entertainment are limited to radio, television, and the daily paper. They do not take an active part in community life, even in the labor unions that represent their interests. To college-trained observers their outlook seems restricted. Professional workers, who owe everything to higher education, can hardly believe that working class clients do not care about their children going to college. Upward mobility is typically not a strong motive; parents are content if their children are neat, obedient, reliable, and pleasing to adults who may be their future employers. This is the pattern of behavior that best fits people for life in the working class.[16] Its faithful acquisition by children increases the probability that they will remain in working class status.[17]

It is when we turn to the *middle class* that upward mobility shows as a frequent and at times stress-producing motive. Middle status is customarily subdivided: *lower middle class* is represented occupationally by white collar workers in jobs such as secretary, draftsman, and accountant, or in modest professional status, such as public school teacher. Education typically includes several years beyond high school, for instance two years in a business course or four years at a teachers' college. In general, lower-middle-class occupations do not lead on to higher status. This may or may not be a cause of disappointment, but typically there are higher aspirations for the children, who are expected to go to college and as far beyond as is necessary to achieve the better life denied their parents. Lower-middle-class values, however, are colored by the circumstance that job security depends largely on satisfying one's employers. The outstanding virtues are to perform efficiently, to be sta-

[16] M. L. Kohn. "Social Class and Parent-Child Relationships: An Interpretation," *American Journal of Sociology*, 68 (1963), 471–480.

[17] A. C. Kerckhoff, *Socialization and Social Class* (Englewood Cliffs, N.J.: Prentice-Hall, Inc., 1972).

ble and reliable, to get along well with others, and to be well thought of in the community; it is less important, perhaps even risky, to be assertive and competitive. Everyone knows the sad fate of school teachers whose unconventional behavior or whose classroom innovations shocked the superintendent and outraged the community. The ambition that lower-middle-class parents feel for their children is tempered by values appropriate to being an acceptable employee.

The designation of *upper middle class* goes to salaried executives in large firms, to owners and operators of moderate-sized enterprises, and to doctors, lawyers, and other relatively independent professionals. These generally occupy large apartments or good-sized houses most commonly located today in affluent suburbs. Typically, upper-middle-class adults participate extensively in civic affairs and are concerned about the community in a way that is foreign to both lower and working classes. Upward mobility tends to be at its strongest at this level. Success in career is of great importance; as Kahl expresses it, "the husband's career becomes the central social fact for all the family."[18] At no social level is competitive enterprise more highly valued. Strong pressure is placed on the children to excel in school—to get the highest grades, to be socially prominent, to be a successful athlete—thus starting the climb to outstanding success. Earlier observers reported that this ambitious pressure included stress on respectability, control of impulses, and postponement of present satisfactions for future goals. Upper-middle-class parents are readers, however, and have become psychologically well informed. Recent research finds them often respectful of their children's feelings, concerned about their happiness as well as their future status. Parents may even use permissive methods, hopeful that initiative, competence, and self-control will be the result.[19]

The scheme of social stratification is completed by an *upper class* or elite. In most communities the members of this class do not number more than 3 or 4 percent of the population. In the United States, where there is no formalized aristocracy, the upper class is generally defined by the possession of wealth through two or more generations. The upper class is often imagined to possess all the expensive objects displayed in the advertising pages of slick magazines, even as being made happy by these material advantages. At the same time its members are seen as exerting unfair control over the channels of power in

[18] J. A. Kahl, *The American Class Structure* (New York: Holt, Rinehart and Winston, Inc., 1957), p. 194.

[19] M. L. Kohn, 1963.

the community and as being committed to conservatism and social exclusion. There is some measure of truth in these images, but research
has shown also a prevailingly high sense of civic responsibility in the
upper class and a stronger development of esthetic values.[20] Because
getting ahead is less urgent for those who in the economic sense are
already there, conditions are more propitious for appreciating arts, recreations, and other ways of enjoying life.

Application to the Case of Hale In applying these findings
about social status to the study of individual cases, it is first necessary
to establish the status of the subject's family. Although we do not
have a community study of the midwestern city in which Hartley
Hale was raised, it was fairly similar to a much-studied community
called Jonesville by Warner and Elmtown by Hollingshead.[21] The evidence contained in the interviews places the Hale family rather definitely
in the upper middle class. The father did not inherit wealth, although
he did have the opportunity to work his way to the top in the moderate-
sized business started by the grandfather. He was college-educated and
had started out as a teacher before entering the business. He sent both
of his children through college, helped pay his son's expenses at medical school, and lived on the income of invested capital after liquidating
his business. The Hales lived in a good residential neighborhood. Like
many upper-middle-class members, they occupied a large house of older
type, which contrasted with the smaller, more standardized homes usually favored by the lower middle class.

Hartley was distinctly aware of a class above his own as well as
of lower classes in the neighborhood that began a block to the east.
Asked in an oral questionnaire during the undergraduate study whether
he would marry a girl from "the top ranks of society," he said that he
would do so only if she were able to "break through her artificial life"
and accept his own social position. When put the same question with
regard to a girl "of lower social position" he replied that he would marry
such a girl if her status were lower only for financial reasons but not if

[20] A. B. Hollingshead and F. C. Redlich, *Social Class and Mental Illness:
A Community Study* (New York: John Wiley & Sons, 1958) ; C. C. McArthur,
"Personality Differences between Middle and Upper Classes," *Journal of Abnormal
and Social Psychology*, 50 (1955), 247–254.

[21] W. S. Warner and associates, *Democracy in Jonesville: A Study in Quality and Inequality* (New York: Harper & Row, Publishers, 1949) ; Hollingshead,
1949.

there were any "hereditary reasons." In this last reservation he partly accepted what Hollingshead has shown to be a common belief of all classes except the lowest, namely, that the people below them have remained in lower status because of innate inferiority.

In many respects the Hale family can be understood as a typical product of its class status in a somewhat industrialized midwestern community. But there was one important divergence. The Hales showed little of the drive toward civic leadership that was found characteristic of the upper middle class in Jonesville. Hartley's father seems to have felt small interest in the Chamber of Commerce, Rotary Club, and other power-wielding organizations that generally attract the energies of upper middle businessmen. With considerable justification, in view of the father's literary tastes and the mother's artistic attainments, the Hales felt themselves to represent more than an economic status. They stood for cultural values—for scholarship, literature, art, and music—and their identification was with professional and artistic people rather than with the world of business. They did not, to be sure, feel separated from business, and they supported Hartley's first choice of advertising as a life work, but they thought of business as a means of making a good enough living so that one could enjoy the higher things of life. This weakened the interest in upward mobility that might otherwise have been expected. People who identify themselves with intellectual and cultural values do not feel that there is any class above them. They are not likely to be wholly immune to the charms of wealth, power, and prestige in the business and political spheres, but they are less vulnerable than people who are working only for such goals without fully attaining them. The Hales could afford to look on business success as merely instrumental.

The force of Hartley Hale's rebellion against his mother caused him to make havoc of his youthful social status. He rejected the playmates she chose for him and exhibited downward social mobility in finding companions more to his taste. His ability to play a manful part was seriously challenged by the gangs from the east; he was not satisfied until he could match these lower-class boys in fights and athletics, thus winning their recognition and acceptance. He thus used a lower social status as a place to develop and assert those masculine qualities that seemed threatened by his mother's philosophy of cleanliness and caution. In retrospect he valued these experiences, as he valued his summer jobs, for the insight they gave him into the outlook and problems of ordinary people. Traces of these democratic contacts could still be found in his otherwise somewhat rightist political views. With the passing of the need for rebellion against his mother, however, and with his moving away to college, he swung back again to the social status of his origin. His wife came from approximately the same social position, his home was established in the best residential section he could afford, and in his daydreams the "ultimate" dwelling began to assume the proportions of an ample country estate.

It may seem paradoxical, especially in view of the fancied country estate, to suggest that at thirty-three upward social mobility was not an important motive in Hale's life. He certainly was competitive, he certainly wanted to rise to the top; he sought power, prestige, and an income that would permit a little conspicuous spending. But it would represent a serious failure to analyze the facts if we set this all down to upward social mobility in the ordinary sense of the term. Hale is a doctor and a scientific investigator. To describe his upward mobility as social would imply that he cares a great deal about the social hierarchy, wanting to frequent the best circles, join the best clubs, be invited to the best houses. Hale does not care about these things. The motive that was really strong in him can best be characterized as upward mobility in his profession. He wanted to be outstanding as a surgeon and scientist; insofar as his country estate was to be a symbol, it was to signify that he had reached the professional top. Hale is an example of a man whose energies have been poured almost entirely into the channels of a profession. At the age of thirty-three he was influenced more by his occupational role than by his position in the general hierarchy of social status.

Social Roles

The concept of role has proved to be an important one in linking the social and psychological sciences. "One of its most alluring qualities," writes Levinson, is that it concerns "the thoughts and actions of individuals, and at the same time it points up the influence upon the individual of socially patterned demands and standardizing forces."[22] As usually defined, role involves the related idea of social position. The meaning of these two terms can be most easily grasped through the example of a highly organized social subsystem such as a hospital. Here

---

[22] D. J. Levinson, "Role, Personality and Social Structure in the Organizational Setting," *Journal of Abnormal and Social Psychology*, 58 (1959), 170–180.

the several positions of superintendent, business manager, doctor, resident, intern, nurse, nurse's aide, orderly, bookkeeper, and volunteer, representing both a hierarchy of power and a division of functions according to trained skills, are sharply defined; the duties and privileges that go with each position are specified in considerable detail. These duties and privileges exist in everyone's mind regardless of the particular occupants of the positions. They are there even if a position is temporarily vacant; and when someone is appointed to the vacancy, he is expected to behave in such a way as to fulfill the functions of the position. It is through these expectations about behavior that the concept of the role can be defined: in Newcomb's words, role refers to "the ways of behaving that are expected of any individual who occupies a certain position."[23]

The example of the hospital throws the ideas of position and role into sharp relief, but it hardly suggests the wide range of social roles in the shaping of behavior. Age and sex are also social positions: different expectations are associated with being male or female, with being young or old, with the statuses of husband, father, wife, and mother, with the positions of friend, neighbor, and associate in work or play. These broadly conceived social positions carry with them definite expectations concerning behavior. Mothers are assigned primary responsibility for keeping the children washed and clothed and fed, and for caring for them when they are sick. Fathers are expected to earn the money to pay for food and shelter. Even when sex differences are minimized and the sharing of parental roles is highly valued, the mother will probably be less blamed for a leaking roof, while the father will be given greater leeway in keeping the children washed. Social roles, and the expectations that give them shape, exert their formative influence on a great many aspects of individual behavior.

It is obvious that social roles are learned in the course of life. In the study of individual lives it is a matter of great importance to work out in as much detail as possible the role expectations and role models that were influential in childhood. Children learn about roles by absorbing the expectations communicated to them by parents and other people who become important to them. They learn about roles also by copying available role models. A girl can acquire her feminine role by copying her mother and by gathering from her father, whom she does not copy,

[23] T. M. Newcomb, *Social Psychology* (New York: Holt, Rinehart and Winston, Inc., 1950), p. 280.

what he values as feminine behavior. The learning of roles involves an active element of trying them out, seeking to enact them in play or in earnest. The social responses, favorable or unfavorable, that are elicited by these attempts eventually shape the behavior in the direction of social expectations.

Although the influence of role expectations is widespread and important, we must not make the mistake of assigning them dictatorial power. They exist in the structure of society only in a somewhat metaphorical sense. Their true locus is in the minds of the people who make up society, and it is by no means likely that they will exist in every mind in identical form. A research study of one particular social position, that of superintendent of schools, brought to light a poor consensus of expectations: school boards and teaching staffs saw the duties of the office in quite different ways, and in both groups there were individual differences as to what should be expected of a superintendent.[24] Role expectations are typically not tight-fitting rules that define behavior down to the last detail. It is more correct to say that they describe ranges of behavior that are considered suitable for occupants of a position. As Kelvin puts it, "When we talk about the behavior associated with a role, we refer to the more or less adequate performance and *completion of a task*. The role specifies *what* is to be done; it rarely specifies precisely *how* it is to be done. . . . It would be better to consider roles as sets of task expectancies associated with a position, rather than as sets of behavioral expectancies."[25] There are many different ways of being a satisfactory mother or father, or a competent teacher or physician. Furthermore, role expectations can be changed when an occupant of a position, through initiative and invention, makes something out of it that has never been made before. The shaping influence of role expectations does not preclude creative individual enactments. Each person, as Levinson points out, brings to any given position a *personal role definition* that is influenced by his characteristics and early history, and this gives individuality to his role performance.[26]

Hartley Hale seems to have found no difficulty in discovering

[24] N. Gross, W. S. Nason, and A. W. McEachern, *Explorations in Role Analysis* (New York; John Wiley & Sons, Inc., 1958).

[25] P. Kelvin, *The Bases of Social Behaviour* (New York: Holt, Rinehart and Winston, Inc., 1971), p. 149.

[26] Levinson, 1959.

male role models. His father served well in this capacity, as did later his bold friend, Dan, and still later there were the teachers who set him examples of fidelity to science. It is noteworthy that in the significant "backbone incident" he was strongly influenced by his sister's forthright statement of the masculine role: he must go back and fight the bully and not hide behind a woman's skirts. It was an order backed by the full force of society's expectations. As she made no offer to assist him, it also served to differentiate more sharply the feminine role, which his helpful girl cousin had ignored. The incident dramatizes the manner in which children learn through experience what is expected of them.

Learning through Social Interaction

Cultural values, social class outlooks, and role expectations are obviously not learned like lessons out of a book. They exist largely in people's minds and find their way into the behavior of the next generation through processes of human interaction. They are learned from experience; the most relevant experiences are those that occur in the course of interacting with the individuals and groups who make up the immediate human environment.

Social scientists have found it useful to distinguish between primary and secondary groups. According to Cooley, who was the first to emphasize the importance of this distinction, a group qualifies as primary when it is "characterized by intimate face-to-face association and cooperation."[27] For a young child the family constitutes the most important primary group, but neighborhood playmates and school groups soon start to make their impact upon his social development. Secondary groups, in contrast, are organized according to special interests of one kind or another, and they do not depend either upon propinquity or upon more than occasional face-to-face association. Political parties, religious bodies, school systems, labor unions, medical associations can all be used as examples of secondary groups. Memberships in such groups are an important feature of adult life, but it is the primary groups that play the crucial part in the early shaping of personality. Within the circle of his family and within the orbit of his playmates and school com-

[27] C. H. Cooley, *Social Organization* (New York: Charles Scribners' Sons, 1909), p. 23.

panions the child receives his direct training as a member of society. It is here that he learns, often without realizing it, his social habits and attitudes and his conception of himself as a social being.

The Family Circle Learning through social interaction is no different in principle from learning about the physical world. A child has to learn what to expect from everything around him, what it will do in response to his own action, how he can influence it in favor of his desires. Dependent as he is, however, upon the ministrations of others, he soon learns to take a special interest in the people who provide for his wants and produce beneficent changes in his environment. He becomes especially concerned with what he can expect from his mother. Thus his earliest experience of social interaction is surcharged with the pressure of his basic needs; a great deal of his feeling of security becomes attached to predicting and controlling what will happen in his immediate human environment. Social learning begins in the relationship of the infant to his providers.

This circumstance contributes importantly to the acquisition of cultural norms, class values, and role expectancies. Children become sensitized early to signs of pleasure and displeasure in their caretakers. Long before real understanding is possible, these signs tell them what is good and what is bad, and the motive of eliciting parental pleasure is strong enough, except in moments of rage, to cement an alliance with what is good. Adults often recall with embarrassed astonishment how automatically they accepted certain values which on mature reflection seem senseless. The communication of values from one generation to the next takes place under circumstances that favor strong, lasting, but uncomprehending acceptance. Thus values become enshrined, and it is far from easy to secure their rational examination in later life.

The role learning that is possible in the family circle is not that of strict equals. Except in the case of multiple births, everyone in the family circle is either older or younger; and the parents, however hard they work for a democratic and respecting atmosphere, cannot really abdicate the power that is theirs because of age, experience, and capacity to provide. The presence of brothers and sisters, however, creates conditions that often lead to role differentiation. It sometimes happens, for example, that two children become firmly cast as the "good" child and the "bad" child. The "good" child conspicuously adopts and espouses parental values, while the "bad" child gets as much satisfaction as possible out of relative freedom to misbehave.[28] The role differentiations that develop among siblings, and especially the rivalries and jealousies, are not easily outgrown. Like cultural values, they are over-learned because of the high emotional stakes in what happens in the family circle.

Effects of Group Membership It is among playmates outside the family that a child carries on the social learning that best trains him for interaction with peers. Here he encounters a somewhat different set of social shaping forces. There is less emphasis on good behavior and conformity to adult standards, more on individual prowess, adventuresomeness, and willingness to share in whatever is going on. At first, interactions are apt to be tentative and discontinuous; each meeting with any other child has somewhat the character of a new experiment. In the course of time these fragmentary contacts build up into more lasting relationships. The child behaves with greater con-sistency toward each friend, and he gradually learns to react to more than one friend at a time. Children's groups at first lack permanence and structure, but as time goes on they become increasingly organized and increasingly important in the shaping of the individual personality.

Group membership affects the individual in a variety of ways. It is a little too simple to pass this off by saying that it teaches him to give and take. There is a positive side to membership that is scarcely implied in this stock disciplinary phrase. Under favorable circumstances partic-ipation in a group may produce a notable increase in the sense of per-sonal worth and personal strength. Pooling of initiative and sharing of responsibility enable the group to accomplish many purposes far beyond the resources of any individual member. They enable the group to re-sist pressures before which individual members would feel helpless. If a member successfully performs his part, he receives an income of approval and esteem that greatly surpasses anything he would be likely to secure by playing a lone hand. The strength that comes from group membership is strikingly illustrated in small groups such as air combat units, which develop strong cohesiveness through exposure to major stress. It was the conclusion of psychological studies made during World War II that morale was a group phenomenon, not an individual trait,

[28] R. W. White, *The Enterprise of Living: Growth and Organization in Personality* (New York: Holt, Rinehart and Winston, Inc., 1972), Chapter 5, especially pp. 103–111.

and that loyalty to one's unit rather than hatred for the enemy produced the truly courageous feats of arms.[29]

The formative influence of groups is all the stronger because of benefits that go with membership. The nature of this influence can best be indicated by saying that the group teaches the individual to operate within shared norms. It visits approval on what is considered loyal and good, disapproval on what is rated disloyal and bad. Furthermore, the group helps the individual to sort out the particular roles that it is practical for him to play. It rewards with approval those roles that the person can play well and that at the same time forward the harmony and purposes of the group, but it pours contempt and ridicule on attempts to play disruptive, incompetent, or presumptuous roles. A variety of informal roles is required for the successful functioning of any group. Positions are available as leader, right-hand man, follower, idea man, clown, and water boy; the group needs them all. The participating individual has a chance to discover what roles he is able to enact and what ones it is necessary to discard. Homans has described social life as being analogous to exchange: it has values but it also has costs.[30] Each individual must discover his own balance between values received and costs incurred by attempting to enact different roles. To be a group's humorist, even to be its useful water boy, may be a better deal than struggling tensely with rivals to become the right-hand man.

The shaping of individual behavior by group memberships is particularly well illustrated in street-corner gangs.[31] These spontaneous groups are little influenced by tradition, parental standards, or the dictates of the larger society, with which they are often enough at odds. Nevertheless, they are extremely effective in upholding group norms and shaping the behavior of individual members in the direction of appropriate roles. Participant observers can usually work out the status of each member with respect to all the others, and it is clear that individual behavior is sharply affected by the expectations of the rest of the group.

One of the corner gangs studied by Whyte went in heavily for bowling. It was apparent that a man's bowling performance, especially in stressful moments of the game, was considerably influenced by how

[29] R. R. Grinker and J. P. Spiegel, *Men under Stress*, (New York: McGraw-Hill, Inc., 1945), especially Chaps. 2, 3, 6, 8, 15.

[30] G. C. Homans, "Social Behavior as Exchange," *American Journal of Sociology*, 63 (1958), 597–606.

[31] W. F. Whyte, *Street Corner Society*, (Chicago: University of Chicago Press, 1943).

well his teammates expected him to do. One man, who occupied a status close to the leaders of the group, had a reputation for dependable good bowling; another, located low in the status hierarchy, could occasionally make the highest score of anyone, but was considered certain to go to pieces under stress. These judgments were doubtless based on real initial differences, but in the course of time they acted with increasing social compulsion. The erratic man could often beat the steady man when they played alone, but at the Saturday night matches, with the whole group present, the dependable bowler always turned in the higher score. Bowling scores were significantly affected by a man's social position in his group.

The differences between group pressures at home and those encountered on the playground and at school are important in the child's social education. At home he finds one set of norms and plays one set of roles; outside he meets a different set of norms and finds opportunity to play a different set of roles. Parents can often scarcely believe that their child, a very devil in the home, rates as a helpful and responsible citizen in school, or, conversely, that their well-trained model child has been caught by the police stealing fruit and breaking windows. As a child's memberships multiply, he begins to discover that different groups take different attitudes toward him; he begins to realize that he himself behaves and feels differently as he moves from one company to another. This type of experience is crucial for more complex social learning. Through it the child arrives at a relativity of perspectives, realizing how widely people differ in outlook and interest. Such insight is an essential ingredient of mature social behavior and a mature moral code.

The case of Hartley Hale exemplifies many of these general ideas. While it is impossible to reconstruct an adequate history of his social participations, there can be little doubt about the importance of group memberships in his development. This was particularly true in later childhood, when parental quarrels increasingly made the home atmosphere intolerable and when the evolution of self-esteem required recognition as a "he-man" capable of boldness, confidence, and athletic success. Because of his stuttering Hale was constantly exposed to ridicule; we can assume that group pressure had a good deal to do with assigning him the roles of stage manager and behind-the-scenes editor during his high school years. Hale himself testified, particularly in his discussion of labor unions, to the importance of memberships in different groups as a means of deepening perspective and increasing understanding of other people.

Occupations and Occupational Roles

It is a matter of common belief that people are influenced by their occupations. We are all familiar with such stereotypes as the crabby hair-splitting lawyer, the dry precise bookkeeper, the vague absentminded professor, the blunt outspoken army officer, the bossy rule-bound schoolmistress, the erratic but colorful actress. The force of these linkages between occupation and personality can be demonstrated by trying to rearrange them. An erratic but colorful bookkeeper, a vague absentminded army officer, a crabby hairsplitting actress certainly strike us as unlikely if not impossible types. For the most part the familiar linkages are not arrived at by direct observation of the people who hold different jobs. Such observation would surely reveal a considerable variety of personalities within each occupation. There would undoubtedly be erratic but colorful lawyers, blunt outspoken lawyers, perhaps even absentminded lawyers, as well as lawyers who are crabby and hairsplitting. The linkages are based rather on a kind of analysis of the job as generally conceived and on the further belief that the requirements of a job forcibly shape the personality of its holder. Bookkeeping calls for dry and precise figuring; therefore the person who daily performs the job of bookkeeper must necessarily become dry and precise.

These stereotypes ascribe to occupations a greater shaping force than they actually possess. Occupation certainly does a great deal to shape a person's life, determining where and how he will spend his time, what sorts of skills he will employ, what kinds of contacts he will have with other people. Often a man's occupation exerts a decisive influence on his political philosophy. But the fact that a person's *life* is strongly molded by occupation does not necessarily imply that his *personality* is deeply affected. Occupation does not, like the general cultural atmosphere or like social status, influence the individual during the most formative part of his development. We must therefore conceive somewhat differently the shaping effect of occupations and occupational roles. There is, in the first place, a certain amount of selection whereby occupations attract to their ranks people who already have an appropriate personality structure. The requirements of the job and its associated role then act to reinforce certain characteristics while more or less suppressing others. To a considerable extent people fall out of the occupation if their personal qualities prove inappropriate, or if they find it difficult to endure the expected roles. In most occupations, however, there is room for individual variation; the job can be done in several different ways. All these points must be taken into account when we study the action of occupational roles and search for the processes whereby their influence is exerted.

Among occupational roles none are more highly organized than those represented by the professions. A profession is entered only through a long course of training that is designed to equip the candidate with the knowledge and skill requisite for subsequent practice. As Hughes points out, however, "the training carries with it as a by-product assimilation of the candidate to a set of professional attitudes and controls, a professional conscience and solidarity. The profession claims and aims to become a moral unit."[32] The law student, for example, not only learns the theory and technique of law but also acquires, through contact with teachers and fellow law students, a sense of membership in a professional group having its own ideals and ethical constraints. In this respect the professions contrast somewhat with trades, crafts, and business enterprises, still more with the large realm of more or less unskilled jobs. Except in rare circumstances the professional man is in his occupation for life. He must submit to obligations but at the same time he can usually expect to find within it the opportunity to use his full capacities in building up a satisfying career. He can often find a large part of his happiness in his work. In sharp contrast is the wage earner who grinds away at a tiresome task, or flits from one job to another, looking for happiness only when the day's work is done. Occupational role exerts a far stronger shaping force on the professional man than it does on the unskilled wage earner.

The Role of Physician The socially expected role of the physician is on the whole very clearly defined. It is based on his specific competence, acquired through long and difficult training, to understand and to alleviate sickness. He is not supposed to be a general wise man or sage, or an expert on political and economic affairs. His competence is specifically that of healing the sick, and his technique for discharging this duty is that of applying scientific knowledge. He is expected therefore to perform his work in a relatively impersonal fashion, not involving himself in deep emotional relationships with his patients. Even when he practices psychotherapy, in which the doctor-patient relationship becomes the central part of the cure, he performs as a trained

---

[32] E. C. Hughes, *Men and Their Work*, (New York: The Free Press, Inc., 1958), Chapter 2.

expert who points out the patient's emotional reactions, not as an ordinary person who becomes blindly involved in them. A striking feature of the role is its emphasis on service. The patient's health is supposed to be given regular precedence over the interests and comfort of the physician. The specifications of the role are thus clear, requiring the doctor to apply in faithful but strictly rational fashion the scientific knowledge that is at his disposal.

Inherent in the situation of curing disease, however, are many irrational elements. As Parsons has pointed out, it is hard for the doctor in actual fact to function simply as an impersonal applied scientist.[33] Often his knowledge is insufficient and uncertain; at other times he recognizes with certainty that there is nothing he can do for the patient. When thus helpless in a situation where life itself is often at stake, he is placed under the strain of not being able to meet the high hopes and tense expectations placed on him by patients and their relatives. He is also subject to irrational pressures because of the intimate nature of his work. He has the right to discuss very personal matters and to see and examine the patient's naked body. Doctors are pretty well accustomed to exert these privileges with impersonal detachment; but the patients are not similarly trained and may react with a variety of fears, resistances, sexual fantasies, and other personal feelings that interfere with the businesslike pursuit of diagnosis and treatment. The doctor's job might become incredibly involved and entangled if his occupational role were not sharply and strongly formulated. He can do his work properly only because of the protection he receives from his well-understood professional role. Both his own behavior and that of his patients are defined and controlled by this role.

It is important to notice that the role of physician does not derive its whole force from law or from the professional code of ethics. There are legal safeguards to the practice of medicine, and there is a strong professional code, but these institutionalized controls are invoked only on rare occasions. Informal controls, based on strongly felt social expectations both inside and outside the profession, actually maintain for medical practice its current high repute. The surgeon's decision to operate may be taken as a case in point. Few decisions are more crucial, yet this one is typically reached by the surgeon and ratified by patient

---

[33] T. Parsons, *The Social System* (New York: The Free Press, Inc., 1951), Chapter 10.

and relatives without appeal to state authorities or professional com-
mittees. Medical men argue among themselves about "unnecessary operations." One school of thought believes that surgical intervention tends
to be made too promptly, without sufficient regard for spontaneous
recuperation. We know that Hartley Hale took the opposite stand, and
that he did so on the highest moral grounds, believing that the decision
to operate was often postponed through the physician's timidity and
selfishness. Whatever the merits of this controversy, it is remarkable
that the public is content to leave it in the hands of the profession.
Nothing could testify more eloquently to the silent force and effectiveness of the physician's occupational role.

The role of physician contrasts in many respects with that of
the businessman. Perhaps the most central difference lies in the attitude
toward personal profit. The businessman is expected to make a profit
for his company and for himself. He is expected to consider the likeli-
hood of profit when he undertakes a new enterprise, and he is not supposed to get mixed up with poor credit risks. The physician is allowed to
make generous charges to rich patients, but he is not permitted to refuse
a patient on the ground of poor credit risk, nor may he bargain before-
hand over fees. Advertising is closed to him except for a sign at his door
and a modest card in the paper. "The general picture is sharp segregation from the market and price practices of the business world, in ways
which for the most part cut off the physician from many immediate
opportunities for financial gain which are treated as legitimately open
to the businessman."[34] Some return for this restriction comes from the
fact that the role of patient is conceived quite differently from the role
of businessman's client. A patient is not expected to shop around among
different doctors, secretly comparing what they have to say about his
treatment and trying to decide which doctor will give him the most for
his money. He is expected to have confidence in his own doctor, and
unless he decides to shift outright to another practitioner he may seek
additional advice only by asking his own doctor to invite a colleague for
consultation.

Occupational Role in the Case of Hale This contrast between
the occupational roles of physician and businessman has particular
interest in the case of Hartley Hale, who at one point in his career

[34] Parsons, 1951, p. 464.

deliberately chose between them. He was at first strongly drawn to the advertising business, but he shifted to medicine when shown by a persuasive friend how well he fitted the requirements of the profession. Both occupations genuinely attracted him, though they appealed to somewhat different aspects of his personality. Both appealed to his love of activity, excitement, and competition; both offered an opportunity to rise to the top. The special attraction in advertising was the chance it would give him to utilize his writing and drawing skills and to gratify his somewhat cynical delight in influencing people. But medicine seemed to him a more important service, and it drew fully on his absorbing passion for the biological sciences. More clearly than most undergraduates he foresaw what was involved in occupations and made his choice on the basis of genuine preference. Hale thus exemplifies the process whereby occupations draw to their ranks individuals whose pattern of personality is already appropriate for the fulfillment of the occupational role. The selective process continued even after he had entered medicine. His urge for decisive action drew him to surgery; his liking and capacity for independence contributed to his success in research. His preference for a mechanistic outlook and his lack of empathic responsiveness to others doubtless aided these decisions and certainly steered him far away from psychiatry.

The influence of the medical role in Hale's case can best be appreciated by trying to contrast what might have happened to him in advertising with what did happen in medicine. We saw that he approached advertising in an ethical spirit, hoping to accept business only when convinced of the genuine superiority of the products. It is hard to believe that this self-imposed limitation would not have brought serious conflict with his strong desire for competitive success. In an occupational role in which profits and a flourishing business are the marks of success, he would soon have been forced to clip either his conscience or his ambitious wings. In medicine he was not pushed into any such position. Here the conditions for success were skill, eagerness, hard work, and devotion; little could be gained by anything that smacked of sharp practice or cynical deception. Another contrast can be drawn with respect to his relative neglect of wife and home. No doubt Hale would have gotten himself overworked and absorbed in any occupation, but when the job is at a hospital and forms part of the physician's role of dedication to sick people it can be used to justify a much greater neglect of other obligations. It seems likely that Hale's personality has been definitely influenced by his profession and that certain of his traits would have developed toward a different ultimate pattern if he had gone into advertising.[35]

The Self

The concept of self is extremely important in the theory of personality. It is an integrative concept, needed to account for the fact that unity is preserved even under the most diversifying social influences. The unity of the organism is inescapable. The self-image has its point of reference in one body, one consciousness, one continuous series of personal memories; it cannot be separated from our enduring sense of personal identity. Differently as someone may behave on different occasions, flexibly as he may respond to social atmospheres, he remains always to some extent the same person, the same self. Although the concept of self is rooted in biological fact, it is from social scientists such as Cooley and Mead that we have learned how the concept must be elaborated.[36]

These writers, devoted to the social view of man, considered that the self achieved its development through social interaction. They were dealing, of course, not with the self as active ego but with the person's idea of himself; as Mead put it, not with the agent called "I" but with the object called "me." A person builds up his conception of himself out of the ideas he perceives other people to have about him. This perception is grounded in how they act toward him. Through social experience he has to learn whether he is brave or cowardly, handsome or homely, quick-witted or deliberate, likable or surly, leader or follower, prophet or clown. In childhood the process often works in a fairly open

[35] In an autobiographical study of experiences in a psychiatric residency, D. S. Viscott in *The Making of a Psychiatrist* (Greenwich, Conn.: Fawcett-Crest, 1972) describes a more or less enforced neglect of wife and children that is highly reminiscent of Hale. A contrast between Hale and a young business executive, Olin Larson, can be drawn from W. R. Dill, T. L. Hilton, and W. R. Reitman, *The New Managers* (Englewood Cliffs, N.J.: Prentice-Hall, Inc., 1962), Chapter 2. Larson is as successful in his environment as Hale is in his, but there are important differences in the demands of the two environments. The relation between personality and occupation can be brought to sharp focus by the mental experiment of putting these two men in each other's occupation.

[36] C. H. Cooley, *Human Nature and the Social Order* (New York: Charles Scribners' Sons, 1902); G. H. Mead, *Mind, Self, and Society* (Chicago: University of Chicago Press, 1934).

fashion: children are not backward in calling each other names and classifying each other's behavior. Later the judgments of others are more apt to be inferred, but they still operate to retouch in various ways the picture one has of himself. Thus even the concept of self, central and integrative in personality, cannot be formulated without reference to social interaction.

We should not misunderstand the proposition advanced by Cooley and Mead—that the self arises in social interaction—to mean that a person takes no active part in the forming of his self-picture. He cannot learn much from the way others respond to him unless he puts forth some behavior of his own. He need not, moreover, take all responses as of equal weight, and he need not rest content with unflattering self-images. Hartley Hale did not accept all the judgments made about him by others. He did not accept as final, for example, the judgment that he was cocky and rude, knowing that he could be very different in what seemed to him the important relationships with adults. Moreover, he refused to accept what seemed like the clear fact that he was a stutterer. Unlike the erratic bowler of the street corner gang, whose score was adversely affected by group expectations, he clung to the ideal image of himself as one who would not stutter, and eventually, by hard struggle, he turned this image into a true fact. What people thought of him, how they reacted to him at any one time, contributed to his perception of himself but did not prevent him from working for an improved self-picture in the future.

Further light on the concept of the self can be gained by recalling that Hale sometimes rejected as too favorable the opinions held of him by others. Referring to the admiration expressed by some of his patients and colleagues, he said: "I never am quite as good as they think I am." Again, he deplored the vagueness of his mind and fuzziness of his memory, qualities which certainly did not figure in the judgments made of him by other people. It was clear in this case that he was comparing himself to his clear-minded and decisive father, that he was using an ideal standard created by identification with an important admired figure, and that he was thus to a considerable extent impervious to the picture of him held by others in his environment.

These illustrations serve to show that the development of the self-picture does not take place through a simple averaging of the evaluations that are sensed to proceed from other people. It is necessary to consider the relative importance of these other people. Nor must we forget that a person has inner information for evaluating himself. He may

know full well that he was nervous even when he kept up an outer
appearance of self-possession. He may know that a piece of work was
done in careless haste even though his friends call it as good as his best.
Similarly, he may know that an act took great inner courage and sacrifice even though others suppose it was done quite easily. The development of the self-concept is highly dependent on social interaction, but it
is also a product of internal selection and organization, and it includes
ideas not only of what the person has become today but of what he
may become tomorrow.

Shaping Forces and Individual Freedom

The study of social shaping forces produces insights that are not always
welcome. As we saw early in this chapter, American values have
changed, and one of the most important changes calls for honesty in
human relations, openness of feeling, and freedom from conventions
that are without personal meaning. To such aspirations the social
sciences seem inhospitable. Telling us how much we are products of
American culture, social class outlook, role expectations, early family
indoctrination, and group membership training, social scientists seem
constantly to downgrade the possibility of developing into an authentic
person whose behavior and feelings are his own. It may be illuminating to understand the full range and effectiveness of social shaping
forces, but this does not necessarily make it welcome.

The social view of man needs to be balanced by the biological
view, in which living organisms are perceived as themselves centers of
force. But the social view, as we have seen throughout this chapter,
leaves a good deal of room for the activity of the person. To an adolescent engaged in building a self-concept that includes autonomy and
authenticity, it is easy to picture social shaping forces as enemies with
hostile designs on one's freedom. Douvan, in a paper on commitment,
describes adolescent distrust of conventional forms and manners, indeed
of any expected or role-inspired behavior which is not expressive of a
real human relation.[37] The high level of personal authenticity to which
many people now aspire makes it difficult to see role expectations, for
instance, as anything more than unwelcome constraints. But role specifications exist to insure that necessary tasks will be done, tasks like bring-

[37] E. Douvan, "Commitment and Social Contract in Adolescence," *Psychiatry*, 37 (1974), 22–36.

ing up children and healing the sick which we all want done. We could hardly get along at all without the order and reliability which they introduce into behavior. Furthermore, role expectations do not preclude individuality and creativity in any given person's role enactment. Respect for social shaping forces need not diminish one's respect for individual choice and freedom.

Once again we refer to the life history of Hartley Hale, this time on the subject of personal choice. Many situations could be cited in which his behavior was not a simple consequence of social pressures. Not every boy subjected to maternal overprotection responds with rebellion and downward social mobility, thereby developing empathy for people in lower status. Not every young fugitive from battle, taunted by someone older, forces himself back to the fray. Hale's choice of medicine can hardly be interpreted as bowing to social pressure; his selection of surgery was in no sense a consequence of role expectations. Other young men in his time might have accepted the chance to live with an agreeable girl whom they did not intend to marry. Plenty of doctors gladly accept their patients' good estimates and do not, like Hale, look beyond to an ideal of greater clear-mindedness. In each of these and straints; there was room for optional response. Hale chose the behavior many other incidents, social-shaping forces did not act as total conthat felt right to him, that suited his preferences, and that seemed to promise a personally congenial future. From such choices comes the individuality that makes each of us a unique person.

SUGGESTIONS FOR FURTHER READING

The pattern of American culture at the time our personality studies were begun was allotted a chapter in each of two books by anthropologists: R. S. Lynd's *Knowledge for What? The Place of Social Science in American Culture* (Princeton, N. J.: Princeton University Press, 1939), Chapter 3; and Clyde Kluckhohn's *Mirror for Man: The Relation of Anthropology to Modern Life* (New York: McGraw-Hill, Inc., 1949), Chapter 9. Suggestive observations are made in Erik H. Erikson's *Childhood and Society* (New York: W. W. Norton & Co., 2d ed., 1963), Chapters 8–10, where the German and Russian cultures are compared with the American. Somewhat different approaches are made by the historian H. S. Commager in *The American Mind: An Interpretation of American Thought and Character Since the 1880's,* and by David Riesman in *The Lonely Crowd: A Study of the Changing American Character*. Both books were published at New Haven, Conn., by the Yale University Press in 1950. Too numerous to mention are accounts of changes currently going on, but interesting ideas on this subject and on the individual's role in social change will be found in Charles A. Reich's *The Greening of America* (New York: Random House, Inc., 1970).

The effects of social class are well described by W. Lloyd Warner and associates in *Democracy in Jonesville: A Study in Quality and Inequality* (New York: Harper & Row, Publishers, 1949) and by A. B. Hollingshead in *Elmtown's Youth: The Impact of Social Classes on Adolescents* (New York: John Wiley & Sons, 1949). These are studies of a whole community; for the effects of social class position in individual cases one should turn to *Children of Bondage* by A. Davis and J. Dollard (Washington, D.C.: American Council on Education, 1940). More recent works on the subject are Alan Grey, *Class and Personality in Society* (New York: Atherton Press, 1968) and A. C. Kerckhoff, *Socialization and Social Class* (Englewood Cliffs, N. J.: Prentice-Hall, Inc., 1972).

A good source of information on social roles is *Social Psychology: The Study of Human Interaction* by T. M. Newcomb, R. H. Turner, and D. E. Converse (New York: Holt, Rinehart and Winston, Inc., 1965). A stimulating reformulation of the concept is offered by P. Kelvin in *The Bases of Social Behavior* (New York: Holt, Rinehart and Winston, Inc., 1971).

On social interaction and group memberships an illuminating work is *The Human Group* by George C. Homans (New York: Harcourt Brace Jovanovich, Inc., 1950). A book by Abraham Zaleznik and David Moment, *The Dynamics of Interpersonal Behavior* (New York: John Wiley & Sons, Inc., 1964) makes extensive use of studies of small work groups. A collection of unusually valuable essays edited by W. G. Bennis, E. H. Schein, D. E. Berlew, and F. I. Steele, is to be found in *Interpersonal Dynamics* 3d ed. (Homewood, Ill.: The Dorsey Press, 1973).

The sociology of occupations is engagingly discussed by Everett C. Hughes in *Men and Their Work* (New York: The Free Press, Inc., 1958). For a sociological analysis of the medical profession consult Talcott Parsons, *The Social System* (New York: The Free Press, Inc., 1951), Chapter 10. Case studies of young business executives are given in *The New Managers* by W. R. Dill, T. L. Hilton, and W. R. Reitman (Englewood Cliffs, N.J.: Prentice-Hall, Inc., 1962) Psychological aspects are stressed in Anne Roe's *The Psychology of Occupations* (New York: John Wiley & Sons, Inc., 1956).

Classic works on the self are C. H. Cooley's *Human Nature and the Social Order* (New York: Charles Scribner's Sons, 1902) and G. H. Mead's *Mind, Self, and Society* (Chicago: University of Chicago Press, 1934). An excellent summary is given by Kenneth J. Gergen in *The Concept of Self* (New York: Holt, Rinehart and Winston, Inc., 1971).

5

JOSEPH KIDD, BUSINESSMAN

> It dawned on me after a while that I was knowing
> what I wanted. I was able to make up my mind.
>
> JOSEPH KIDD

Joseph Kidd was eighteen years old when he became a paid subject in the studies of personality. In contrast to the well-poised Hartley Hale, he was passing through a crisis in the development of self-determination and self-respect. At his lowest point he suffered from acute and lasting distress in social contacts. He was troubled by severe self-consciousness, painful uncertainty as to his standing in the opinion of others, and an irresistible submissiveness designed to win everybody's favor. He felt that he had no personality of his own, and he therefore lacked any stable object of self-respect. The turmoil of his emotions made it impossible for him to concentrate upon his studies. He fell further and further behind, so that the college required him to withdraw temporarily, his return being made conditional upon a good job record for twelve months and successful course grades in the ensuing summer session.

Kidd met these conditions and returned not only to college but to the interrupted studies of personality. It was possible to repeat several tests after an interval of three years, so that the study became, even in this first period, an examination of development over the course of time. He went from college into four years of military service, then returned to the family home to become for the time being his father's business assistant. He was still thus employed when we asked him, eleven years after his first visit, to return for another extensive study.[1] Subsequently he granted us two lengthy follow-up interviews in which he continued his life story first to the age of forty-three and then to fifty-three.

PART ONE: THROUGH COLLEGE

The initial autobiography was submitted very soon after the first meeting, an encouraging sign that Kidd was interested in his duties as a psychological subject. It was written with considerable feeling, unusual frankness, and marked self-depreciation; plainly, its author was baffled by his own nature and welcomed the chance to share with a trained observer the results of his intense self-scrutiny. The opening paragraph, to be sure, had something of the propriety and exaggeration of an obituary notice, but it was not long before he related his social misfortunes, his trials over masturbation, his growing feelings of worthlessness, and his wish that he could live the last six wasted years over again. If there was self-deception in this document, it took the form of too harsh an indictment against himself.

The Kidd Family

Following an outline given him for guidance, Kidd began his autobiography with a description of his parents:

> My parents for as long as I have known them have been the most ideal couple I've ever seen. They have never to my knowledge had an argument, bitter or small; their differences are none; their respect for each other has always been the greatest. Their educations, likes, dislikes, habits, desires, and emotions always coincided.

[1] A full report on the first set of studies was published in 1943: R. W. White, "The Personality of Joseph Kidd," *Character & Personality*, 11, 183–208, 318–360. Part One of this chapter is largely reprinted from that report, by permission of the Duke University Press.

We need not assume that these lines were written for decency's sake alone. Later material shows plenty of conflict between parents and son and plenty of ambivalence in the latter's attitude, but everything indicates that the parents had reached a good working relation and that the home life offered many satisfactions.

The mother was born in Ireland, went to school through six grades, and came to America at the age of sixteen. Until her marriage a few years later she was a domestic servant; her son, as if to give her vicarious social status, named two prominent Worcester families by whom she had been employed. The father, also of Irish descent, was born in Worcester, and went through the second year of high school. Trained for no particular line of work, he held a meagerly paid office job with a large wholesale florist at the time of his marriage. He established his modest home in a fairly crowded but respectable Irish Catholic neighborhood in the city of Worcester.

When he was thirty-five his financial fortunes turned sharply upward with the arrival of a modest inheritance. This wholly unexpected windfall came from an uncle who had emigrated from Ireland to Australia, prospered there, and was a widower with no children at the time of his death. With this money Mr. Kidd bought out the business of an elderly German florist who had built up a considerable reputation as a floral decorator, and whom Mr. Kidd had known through his work at the wholesale house. This man was often engaged on a contract basis to take full charge of the flower arrangements at big weddings, dances, and banquets. He thus considered himself something more than a retailer and referred to his shop as a flower studio. Kidd told us that his mother was largely responsible for the purchase of this business, encouraging the father to make the bold plunge. The business presently yielded such a substantial income that a college education and professional training could be planned for all five children. These plans were also the mother's work, although the father gave willing assent to her ambitious designs. It was decided that the four boys should be, respectively, a lawyer, a doctor, a banker, and a priest.

In describing his parents, Kidd placed special emphasis on the ideals for which they stood. After mentioning his mother's education and employment, he continued as follows:

As long as I can remember she has held religion primary with education secondary. She is extraordinarily religious and has kept her family so, and never tolerates any deviations of any sort from our faith, which is Roman Catholic, in any detail. She isn't fanatic about it but just staunch. My father is just as if not more staunch than she, and both try to attend mass every day. As for education it is almost secondary religion to her in that she'd sacrifice her all that her children might all become pinnacles of knowledge for her to look up to.

So far there is no hint of resentment against this staunch regime, but the adjectives chosen to describe the father suggested that it may more than once have proved irksome.

He is as obstinate as my mother concerning religion and education, but he reaches extremes sometimes and holds these as the only two factors in early life with life itself beginning at twenty-five. He is positively fanatic on the subject of liquor; never having taken a drop himself, he has stated on various occasions, "I'd rather see you dead than touch it sociably or otherwise." This is mainly because of the city environment which displays only too often the results of indulgence.

The topic of family discipline seemed to throw Kidd into a sharply ambivalent state, if the testimony of the following disjunctive sentences can be accepted:

Their discipline is strict and spankings and such aren't uncommon; by strict discipline I mean that their rules, though few, are just ordinary but forceful. I haven't stressed the fact that freedom is extensive to a certain degree as long as we're doing what's right.

In a later interview he discussed the question more coherently. Parental discipline was based on the precept that "father runs the family," his punishments being more dreaded, more effective, more harsh, and less reasonable than those of the mother. The father used spanking, denial of pleasures, and withholding of affection as his principal weapons, while the mother, always "exceptionally just," maintained her standards by reasoning, scolding, denying affection, and making the culprit feel that he had fallen short of what was expected of him. It was the denial of affection that exerted the strongest pressure, for when asked how he reacted to disciplinary measures, Kidd declared, "I tried to punish them back by denying them affection, not eating my supper, and so forth, but it didn't much work; I couldn't keep it up." Parental discipline evidently carried considerable weight in the Kidd family, the psychological weapons being particularly effective.

Since his venture into floral decorating, Joseph Kidd's father had been an unusually good provider with rising aspirations for his children. These aspirations emerged in Joseph's description of the family:

> Our family consists of five children besides the two parents, four boys and one girl. The family income is rather good, but because my father tries to give us the best besides education our surplus is usually low. I am the second oldest of the family; the oldest is a student at Wesleyan, Michael. Younger than I is Tom (17), and Mary (15), who are in high school, then Peter (12), who is in grammar school. And my father hopes to send each to college, Tom to business school and Peter to the priesthood. There is no direct discord in this family, just normal, each independent of the other pursuing his or her own likes and dislikes.

> Our family life was always rather close, and cooperative till about five years ago when suddenly independence spread to each member rather suddenly much to my regret, leaving the home just an overnight stop almost.

The closeness of family ties was heightened by the parents' attitude outside their home. They were "cold" to other people; the mother especially did not build up a circle of friends, while the father was at ease in groups only when playing the piano and singing. The family group provided a sufficient outlet for their feelings and interests.

The mother was described as an easygoing, overloving, generous person with nothing nervous or erratic in her nature. When the children were small, she used to give them candy to take to school, and Joseph thought that he could still get "a thousand dollars out of her" if he asked for it. Mingled with this devotion and kindness there was a marked streak of dominance in Mrs. Kidd, and this was sometimes a source of annoyance to her children. "She would rather not have us independent," said Joseph; "sometimes I could slight her for not leaving me alone and stop butting into my affairs and opening my mail." When he was a freshman in college a girl called up to ask him to a dance; Mrs. Kidd, answering the telephone, "flew off the handle and said he don't go out with girls, he don't dance." Even when Joseph began to live at college his mother wanted to go on providing things, had to know all about his roommate, and was very much afraid "some waitress" might snatch him. Since the mother was herself a waitress before marriage, her anxiety on this score is an impressive sign of her interest in upward social mobility. Michael and Joseph learned to introduce all their girl friends as college girls; when this was not true, the ruse was nevertheless temporarily successful because their mother, shy with strangers and not sure but what they might really be college girls, tried at once to make the best possible impression. Mrs. Kidd adapted herself unwillingly to the growing independence of her children. She painfully learned to reseal their letters after reading them, to refrain from voicing her suspicions about the use of alcohol, and to joke about their friends without inquiring too closely.

The father's personality was somewhat less smoothly organized. "One minute," said his son, "he'd give you the shirt off his back and the next he'll start ranting up and down." There were times when he did not like to be interrupted and would urge Joseph to look out for himself, but these outbursts gave him feelings of guilt so that the next day he would take his son to a show. On the whole, like the mother, he expected devoted submission and resisted the growing up of his children. "He puts no stock," Joseph complained, "in my judgment or ideas." No less than the mother, he was preoccupied with the children, especially the three older boys, and above all Joseph, who resembled his side of the family. So deep was his interest that signs of independence genuinely hurt him and aroused his resentment in a way that was highly important, as we shall see, in his second son's psychological development. Joseph used the word "senile" to describe his father's condition at forty-five; this seemed to refer to a contractive tendency in his father, who had "a limited mind as far as holding many things is concerned" and who, as if disgruntled at the growing up of his boys, became "more and more retiring." Mrs. Kidd "treated him rather like a baby" and recognized that he would rather "live and take his pleasures and leave everything else to her." At times she even advised her sons as to the best way to get money out of him. In spite of his theoretical position as the one who ran the family, the father seemed to have been all along pretty much guided and dominated by his wife, and the tendency was steadily increasing.

For a time Joseph Kidd was perfectly happy in the affectionate devotion of his parents. He was clearly the favorite of both parents, a more beautiful and more responsive child than either of his nearer brothers. Yet there was enough competition for parental favor and enough transient loss of it through his own misbehavior so that he never accepted it as a matter of course. "I'd feel rottenly guilty," he said, "when I did certain things"; and again, "I have a great fear of hurting my parents; my life is guided by what they want, not what I want." The steadier devotion of his mother made him like her better than his father, his love for the latter being mingled with fear and tempered by a willingness to deceive: "I don't dare cross him directly, I'd rather out-trick him; I'd say I needed six dollars for books instead of four dollars."

Although both parents were brought up in poverty, both came into considerable contact with the upper class. Education became their second religion because it was associated with upward social mobility. Neither parent was familiar with college studies, but the people for whom they worked were college graduates, and it was easy to believe that education and money were responsible for the splendid lives that these employers appeared to live. Later on, Joseph complained that his parents cared nothing for what was going on inside him; they thought only of degrees and other outward symbols. This complaint was probably just, for the goals of upward social striving are defined by external marks such as the people with whom one associates and the signs of wealth one is able to display. The Kidd parents were devoted to their children, sacrificed much for them, and earnestly wanted them to have a good life. But their vision of a good life was contaminated by their idea of how it could be attained, with the result that the social acceptability of the children obtruded itself in their minds at the expense of subjective values. Their eyes were fixed on passports to the upper class.

Memories of the First Five Years: A Center of Attention

In his autobiography Kidd accounts for the first five years in a single paragraph, but he amplified this considerably in an interview devoted to early memories.

I was born eighteen years ago in the West Avenue Hospital in Worcester. As far as I know, everything about my early life was normal such as birth, weaning, teething, growth, etc. I had no physical or mental defects. I know I was always exceptionally intelligent (not conceit but fact) though I was handicapped to make the most of it. Being second son, I was pampered and petted a little and always was on my father's side since I resembled him a lot. He favored me more than the others always till about five years ago. My brother and I were close and were given everything. I had long golden curls and was prized. A recollection of that "adorable" age of about one and a half is clear to me and is supplemented by my mother and father. It was that I was able to pedal a bike and I can still picture myself pedaling it along, still with curls, and many people watching me and patting me on the head. My early life was a very happy one. I was always treated well by my parents and continually pushed along.

In the interview on early memories the bicycle scene was again the first thing that came to Kidd's mind. He now dated it somewhere in the third year and added the following details:

> Father was standing beside me outside our yard. My feet couldn't reach the pedals. He got a kick out of my trying to ride. Some remarks were made that I was very good to be able to ride so young.

Later in the interview he mentioned that he "was always called very smart and very intelligent." The first son, Mike, was considered a homely boy, and the parents were frankly and audibly elated at the attractiveness of their second child, an attitude he did not fail to register.

During the winter when Kidd was two-and-a-half, his mother took him to the school principal and tried to get him admitted to kindergarten. "He'll be three pretty soon," the mother argued, but the principal refused to waive the usual rule, and Kidd's school life did not begin until after his third birthday. In retrospect, and probably at the time, he reacted to his mother's educational zeal with mixed feelings. "At the rate she had children," he remarked, "she had to get rid of one as fast as she could to make room for another one." With entrance into kindergarten the stream of memories began to widen.

> One time I sat in the middle of a ring of children while the teacher was out. I was showing off: I took off my shoe and threw it around the room. I remember lots of faces at kindergarten, how the girls were dressed and how the boys were dressed. On the day of promotion to the first grade we were lined up and taken to the floor above. It was that day my mother dressed me in a velvet suit with lace collar. The teacher stood me up on a desk in front of the class so everybody could see it.

The memory of a Halloween party where he ducked for apples that contained "nickels and cents" probably belongs to his fifth year.

> I got very tired and fell asleep at the end. I was dressed in a Buster Brown collar and a blue serge suit. The collar propped my head up when I fell asleep.

He recalled also the blue overalls with red cuffs that he and Mike wore when playing in the yard.

The most noteworthy feature of these memories is the repeated mention of clothes and, what is probably more important, the recurrence of the situation of being seen and admired, whether for prowess in riding or for beauty as the possessor of golden curls and fine garments. We are entitled to be surprised that a young man's early childhood memories should be so loaded with items of adornment and scenes of exhibition. Kidd's interest in clothing appeared not only in his memories but also in his imaginative trends. Twelve responses in the Rorschach test had to do with costume, and one of the Thematic Apperception stories turned on the almost magical importance of good clothes. In this story Kidd described a haggard young transient, willing to work but so unpresentable that nobody cares to employ him; one day he accidentally finds a good suit of clothes, and his immediate success teaches him that "it is clothes that make the man."

Kidd was a beautiful and clever child who delighted his parents. They praised him, dressed him up, showed him off, and tried to advance him in school. He was given what may be described as a high esteem-income, the payments coming at moments when he was the center of attention. He was clearly favored in this respect over his less attractive brothers Mike and Tom. It is important to notice that he seems to have been praised more for gratuities than for accomplishments—for beauty and cleverness that he unaccountably possessed more of than his brothers. In the story just mentioned, the hero's willingness to work counts for nothing until he is granted the gratuity of fine clothes. Perhaps Kidd was thus predisposed to feel both *helpless* and *self-conscious* when during adolescence his esteem-income suffered a sharp decline.

Further memories amplified the statement that "my brother and I were close." Joseph remembered asking Mike "if mouses grew into cats, cats into dogs, dogs into horses, and horses into elephants," and being amazed at the wisdom of the reply. Evidently the two boys were much together, so that at five Joseph felt very badly when Mike alone was asked to a party; Joseph walked down the street with his brother and sadly watched him disappear into the house. This incident was one of two memories which involved deprivation; the small number confirms the statement that Kidd had a happy and well-provided childhood. The other occasion was a party given by the teachers for the parents. The parents were given crackers and cream cheese, and Kidd remembered "sitting there and not being given any." He seems to have enjoyed parties and felt injured when for some reason they did not include him.

The memories of kindergarten did not include acts of aggression. One of the older boys once kicked the teacher in the shins, but

Kidd looked upon this act as "very, very bad." He recalled various scenes of boys being given the rod, scenes which appear to have impressed him strongly. By the time he reached the first grade, however, he had begun to show the belligerent tendencies that flowered in his childhood; he had a fight at the back of the classroom and was kept after school for it.

Childhood: A Period of Forced Advancement

Introducing his childhood with statements suggested by the outline, Kidd enumerated his illnesses and accidents, then passed directly to an event he considered of major importance in his life: a double promotion in school.

> I've had all the illnesses of a child such as whooping cough, measles, mumps, and scarlet fever. I was struck by an auto when I was about six and received a fractured leg; that is the only accident I've ever had. I received a double promotion from the fourth to the sixth grades in grammar school and though it seemed marvelous then I now consider it the biggest mistake my parents made. They too thought it grand, still do, that I'm so young in my third year of college. Right now I'd rather be back in my last year in high school, with fellows my own age. At any rate this double promotion put me in the same class as my brother and such didn't appeal any too well with him.

Kidd blamed many of his later troubles on the double promotion, which made him younger than his classmates. The circumstances surrounding this event give us a new insight into the forces at work in his family. The fourth and fifth grades occupied the same room; and Kidd, finishing up his fourth grade lessons quickly, would sit watching the fifth graders until the teacher allowed him to move over and take part in their lessons. This proved embarrassing because one of his classmates coveted his seat and he had to keep moving back to claim it. The teacher, however, was a friend of his mother's, so that the news of his mental promise reached home and generated a parental striving. Neither Kidd nor the teacher wanted a double promotion, but the mother began to exert such a persistent pressure upon both that the child became "more and more thrilled with the idea" and the teacher consented to the step. Since education was the mother's "secondary religion," it is not hard to understand her zeal, which was quickened by rivalry with her husband's sister, whose only child, a boy of Mike's age, had recently skipped a grade in the same school. At all events, during the following year Joseph was in the sixth grade with Mike, a situation that, he said, "inflated my ego so that I acted like a baby, very spoiled." Whereas Mike was quiet and reserved, Joseph "always acted wild" and often won the condemnation of the teacher.

> Once the teacher said if anyone dropped a pencil he would get three slaps. I dropped mine three times, by accident, and got nine slaps.

The evil effects of the promotion, however, did not fully show themselves for several years to come. Joseph and Mike were still close friends, who played and roamed with a congenial group of boys.

> Our "click" still held together and we played all sports together. We fellows never had a thing to do with girls in any way; all were bashful except me and I used to chase after them in my spare time and as a result had a flock of them following me (not conceit but fact).

Was it perhaps easier to win the admiration of a female audience? Kidd's interest in female company was certainly stronger than that of his boy companions, but it was a minor theme in the affairs of childhood.

> My marks were very good, and the difference in age between my classmates and I never bothered me, I always had my brother beside to help me. I was sensitive, very sensitive, ignorant of sex, mischievous, exceptionally so and was always getting in trouble while my brothers were very quiet. I was very fond of movies and sports and was very healthy. I had very many friends and close ones; as boys we stuck together. I never had any future desires as for occupation, nor hero-worship to speak of. I wasn't timid but very straight-forward and aggressive. Sports then were our only interest and amusement. And I never liked to see any of our fellows with others or others to try and get in our "click."

On the whole, it seems clear that during the childhood period Kidd was energetic, happy, sociable, and aggressive. It is worthwhile to stress these traits because they were all soon to disappear. At the time when the study began he seemed passive and even sluggish, distinctly unhappy, socially withdrawn, and anything but aggressive. By contrast, his early childhood history includes a record of some ten fights, seven or eight of which he won. According to his own account he was "always rarin' for a fight" and could completely lose his head in one, although there were instances when he backed out because he was afraid of his opponent. Curiously enough, the only fight he recalled in detail during the interview on early memories was a defeat rather than a victory. His brother Tom came over to the third-grade yard to report that a fellow had said he could lick Joseph. Kidd accepted the challenge, the fellow being no older than himself; he did well while they fought with fists, but when it turned into wrestling he was finally downed. However, even after the double promotion, when he began to associate with boys a little older, he does not seem to have been at any serious physical disadvantage. From then until adolescence he was an active member of a congenial, closely knit gang which spent most of its time at sports. The breaking up of this gang was a severe disappointment to him.

Adolescence: A Period of Growing Frustration

Early adolescence was a crucial and painful period for Joseph Kidd. The gang started to break up: "We spread to different parts of the town as our hangouts." This process began when the two eldest Kidd boys were sent to a somewhat distant high school, and it continued rapidly when Mike, now fourteen, "started to leave the 'click' we grew up with for dances, parties, girls, and a wilder bunch."

> My brother (14) and I (12) were sent to Central High School. The first year we were together; I studied hard and got better marks and then he became independent and indifferent towards me because he wanted different associations and I suppose jealousy was beginning to get him. By this time I had begun to note and be affected by the marked differences between the ages of my classmates and I yielded, becoming childish in my actions and bragging about my age. I had acquired masturbation by this time and practiced it excessively since I studied hard, but I didn't have the slightest idea of what I was doing. I kept this up throughout high school excessively and have only stopped over a year ago. Because of this my high school marks were very low and I managed to get out of there by the skin of my teeth. Because of this I began to give up my friends, sports, and everything and used to stay in the house all day listening to the radio and studying. I became soft—soft as a banana.

This was a rather striking change of behavior, and Kidd was not entirely wrong when he traced it back to the double promotion. Being in the same grade with his brother, he had come to depend upon him for companionship, initiative, and even defense. When sexual maturity carried the brother into a new circle of activities, Kidd felt deserted and helpless; he was faced by the new task of making his own way, a task for which his being more than a year younger than the group was at this age a serious handicap. His accustomed social attitudes were now revealed as wholly unsuitable. He described as follows his junior year, when he was fourteen:

> I fooled away my time in school, and acted like a young kid of about eight, laughing, being childish and all, till all the fellows looked down on me and all the teachers especially. . . . I gave up everything, friends, sports and all the outside world. I stuck to my home and my studies. Meanwhile my brothers were out and around and I was becoming sissylike.

In a later interview, discussing fears, he mentioned a fear of losing friends and a "terrific fear of teachers; that came from Central High School":

> I was ultra-dependent, and felt more inferior toward teachers than any fellow in the classroom. Anyone whom I'm under, any authority like a teacher, I'm very submissive.

The Latin teacher earned his respect along with fear; he required that things be written out hundreds of times and "pounded it into" the pupils, a pressure to which Kidd responded by winning a prize in Latin. The English teacher, on the other hand, "a very refined fellow," stormed and threatened capriciously.

> He hated my guts because I raised Cain and was silly. He called me the kid and threatened me with high heaven. He told me I was foolish to go on to Harvard. My dislike of English was fostered by that teacher.

During his senior year, now fifteen years old, Kidd was "more childish and silly than ever."

> I had all my teachers reporting me till they were blue in the face. They all banded together once and censured me for throwing milk bottles down the ventilator; but much to their regret they couldn't throw me out. I was pretty much of a stooge for them and they got a big kick out of me at my expense. During my senior year even my brothers looked down on me but didn't make it evident.

Bored by his studies, Kidd worked erratically at them and barely passed his college entrance examinations. He was not quite sixteen when he graduated from high school, and he had to lie about his age in order to get a job in the post office for the summer. He was the only boy from his school to enter Harvard College in the fall. He chose medicine for his life work "because it's always appealed to me and I'd prefer it to any other profession"; we know, however, that it was his father's choice for him and favorite among the professions. His adviser suggested that he concentrate in biology, and thus his field of concentration was chosen, though without much enthusiasm since his poorest grades were in that subject. Outside of his field he took a lot of sociology courses because "they were easy and seemed interesting." He frankly admitted that he did almost no studying in college, which was enough to destroy his liking for any course. Before examinations he "crammed," frequented tutoring schools, used borrowed notes, and even handed in copied term papers. A course in anthropology momentarily aroused his interest because it presented the theory of evolution and distinguished the provinces of science and religion on this theme, thus touching a question disputed in the Kidd family. He became more deeply interested in embryology, which held an unexplained fascination for him. On the whole, however, the intellectual side of the college experience meant almost nothing to him, and the chief lesson he learned was how to get along without working.

Although he blamed the double promotion for part of his troubles during high school, Kidd felt that his history centered around his developing sex life. He masturbated "excessively" from twelve to sixteen and believed that on this account his school work suffered and his social life practically ended. Evidently there was a great deal of shame, much more than we can attribute to a strict church or family attitude, since his brothers were not similarly affected. Because he discovered the pleasures of masturbation while lying on his back and continued to practice it in that position, he did not at first fully identify it with sex and thought that he had stumbled upon a vice peculiar to himself. It is clear, however, that he believed it injured his masculinity, for he used expressions such as "soft" and "sissylike" to describe its effects. He was surprisingly upset when the true facts about sex came to his attention. At the end of his sophomore year at high school he worked at a camp for the summer.

Here I *was* shocked because up until that time I still thought that the stork brought the babies to the hospital and mothers went there and got them and stayed a while. I really couldn't believe all I learned down there at once, because everything came to me like a bolt and I was dazed. Even though I was *fourteen* I just learned down there all at once all about sex even to menstruation.

I associated with a fellow who was about three years older than me; he told me all about the many aspects of intercourse, till it seemed to me something extremely pleasurable and only that. What the church said against it only went in one ear and out the other. He twisted and warped my mind tremendously. Girls seemed to me nothing but a lust and none of them any good because what these fellows would say as conversation would affect me, and I'd absorb it and think about it.

Why did Kidd feel so strongly about masturbation? It seems likely that there were three contributing causes that strengthened the ordinary guilt feelings: (1) his self-consciousness, (2) feelings of inferiority connected with enuresis, and (3) his submissiveness. (1) In early childhood he was trained to feel the importance of appearing well before the eyes of others; the idea of being looked at was connected with the highest gratifications. This heightened consciousness of an audience made it difficult for him to conceive of a secret vice; he felt almost as much disgraced by masturbating as if he had done it in public. A little later he was an easy victim of the notion that masturbation leaves visible signs on the genital organ. For a while he shunned the locker room and swimming pool and did his best to avoid being seen undressed. When asked in one of our tests to complete a story about a boy suffering from an inferiority complex, Kidd gave an explicit elaboration of this theme. The complex, he declared, came from "a physical defect caused by masturbation"; the hero endured much joking, avoided the swimming pool, "ran if anybody said anything to him," and felt that "everyone was talking about him" wherever he went. Self-respect was regained only when the hero stopped the habit and learned to "kid the other fellows back." (2) Feelings of inferiority had been slowly mounting for some years on account of his failure to control bedwetting. His parents tried to take this problem calmly, and his father offered the supposedly comforting thought that he himself had wet the bed at a like age and beyond. Mike and Tom, however, were often merciless and occasionally reduced their brother to tears. Enuresis probably predisposed Kidd to perceive in masturbation another sign of genital inferiority and childishness. (3) Further difficulty arose on account of his submissive attitude toward boys and men, an attitude that was strongly encouraged when the double promotion made him the youngest member in all his groups. As puberty approached, situations began to arise that made him feel uneasy in the presence of his fellows. He remarked in an interview that "all through school the bigger fellows seemed to want to put their arm around me."

He was not aware of any answering erotic feeling, and he found nothing attractive in the more open homosexual advances to which he was occasionally exposed. Nevertheless, he acknowledged "a lot of effeminacy" in his nature, attested by his preference for female company even in the year or two before puberty. Masturbation was sensed as a blow to his still unproved masculinity.

Thus Kidd's self-consciousness and submissiveness conspired to make masturbation a deeply humiliating experience that propelled him to withdraw from social activity and to some extent from athletics. He was all the more profoundly shocked but at the same time fascinated when his older friend instructed him in a crude and somewhat sadistic conception of male sexuality. It took another year to muster up the courage to kiss a girl, and for a time he "didn't have the guts" to go beyond "necking"; but shortly after he was sixteen he picked up a "blonde derelict" known to be amenable, took her down a dark alley, and successfully asserted his manhood. This was the beginning of a series of closely spaced episodes; influenced by the way his college companions talked, he thought that sex was the main thing in life and the "epitome of social success."

Several weeks before the adventure in the alley Kidd had fallen in love. Shortly before he enrolled at college, he was introduced "very sudden like" to Mildred, who lived not far away from his home, and he began to take her out. This was "the best possible thing," he said, "to save me from softening." He described Mildred as "just the opposite" from himself, "clean, good humored, sweet personality, and extremely popular." In a later interview he characterized her by the following expressions:

> There is a real smile on her face all the time. She has a laugh that's real. There's a lot of life to her; she's very energetic. She is not backward in school but only slow; she didn't want to study. She suffers under no complexes. She will talk to anyone. She is not forward. She has an air of shyness but it doesn't cloud her personality, which is the same everywhere.

In further conversation he mentioned the strong likeness between the girl and his mother and remarked that he told her all his troubles in the first few days of their acquaintance.

He was soon deeply in love with Mildred, and this relationship worked a profound and not altogether constructive effect on his personality. The first effects, however, seemed to be beneficial.

By meeting this girl, I suddenly realized the condition I was in mentally and physically. I began to see life as it really was, from which I'd been hiding the past four years. I began to look up to this girl, and to respect and admire her; though this may sound dramatic, it's still the truth.

Since meeting this girl I've changed. I've tried to make the most of my school life by acting the age of my classmates in associating with them. I've lied about my age considerably since entering college. I am in reality ashamed of it, I don't want to be called a "kid" any more; on jobs, in conversation, at work or at play, I try to keep on a par with a twenty-year-old boy. I've lied about my age till I'm blue in the face, until now I almost believe myself that I'm over twenty since I've been telling people that day in and day out. Since meeting this girl I've lived for her and tried to make her look up to me. I've been in love with her for two years and I know she feels the same about me. I've never touched her and never will illegitimately.

Kidd plainly adhered to the idea that there are two kinds of women: the nice and the derelict, the former untouchable, the latter made for man's pleasure. Of sexual intercourse he wrote:

I think it should be respected to a certain degree and I think a fellow should be capable of making his own moral limits concerning girls. I dislike to have it referred to vulgarly. My attitude toward marriage is that it shouldn't be contemplated as anything but a sacrament. I personally wouldn't care much to marry anyone but a virgin girl.

In the meantime, events at home were beginning to take a difficult course for Kidd. He was fast losing his position as the favorite child. His father, who had but lately enjoyed taking him around and saying to people, "This is Joe, he's only fifteen but he's through high school," began to shift his interest to the other boys. Kidd became increasingly aware of his father's shortcomings: his laziness, his lack of self-assertion, his unwillingness to use his mind, his avoidance of responsibilities. When the mother, entering the menopause, began to have crying spells, Mr. Kidd would stalk out of the house, leaving Joseph to utter words of comfort. Yet Joseph's relation to his mother also took a turn for the worse, largely because of his own feeling. "I can't take her affection any more," he said, "it did too much harm." Life no longer seemed bright to him. Surpassed in social accomplishments by his older brother Mike, outdistanced in athletic achievement by his younger brother Tom, rejected by his father, unwilling to be babied by his mother, bored with his college studies, he turned with unnatural intensity to sex and to his love for Mildred.

The parents' moral attitudes were essentially hostile to adolescence. Kidd's father believed that the first twenty-five years should be a period of studious and obedient preparation, while his mother feared that a waitress might step in and thus spoil the plans for upward social mobility. The parents, moreover, could appreciate only what they understood, and this did not include the intellectual interests of a university. When Mike went around with the right people and when Tom won a place on the football team they were prepared to give their affectionate esteem, but when Joseph brought home the theory of evolution they angrily announced that the church did not accept such a doctrine. At sixteen Kidd suddenly reached a point where nothing in his conduct commended itself to his parents, yet he was quite unable to dispense with their interest and support. In his story completions two years later he made his heroes take the most roundabout courses rather than hurt or disappoint their parents.

The Lowest Point: A Person without a Personality

Our study began in the course of Kidd's junior year at college when he was eighteen years old. This was a peculiarly bad period in his life. In a supplement to his autobiography he described the situation as follows:

> About the beginning of school I began to think a lot about myself and my place in society. I've worried and fretted a lot since. It so happened that during the football season I became extremely upset over my past. This was due to the fact that my younger brother Tom, only a junior in high school, was making some headway in football, was gathering friends (who would call for him), was going to dances, and was becoming an all around swell fellow. But he began to rather ignore me than look up to me as I did with my older brother and I also began to look at myself and say "why." He began to become independent and express his own desires about his future. He seemed so independent "why wasn't I." He was a man, "why wasn't I." He was popular, "why wasn't I, his older brother." I began to look at the past to see what made me what I was and how. I was silly, childish, sexy, moody, temperamental, unpopular, considered conceited and had no independence or personality. For the love of my girl I wouldn't have cared a hang about the whole

world. I would have lived just for her and in fact I was. But she also was becoming ashamed of me in a modified way because I was not popular or at least a regular fellow since I was too much "for" her, not independent enough, too weak-kneed, and acted too much like a spoiled child, crying for my own way with threats that she realized would not be carried out.

She could see when we went to dances just how I fitted with the world: I couldn't mix, I couldn't have fun, I just couldn't stand other people around her. I was very jealous. She began to become bored with me and threw a sink-or-swim attitude at me unconsciously.

This was the last straw. Even his girl, on whom he had been leaning for emotional support, demanded that he grow up and behave like a man with a will of his own. Good looks and pleasing ways were no longer sufficient; he had to make himself worthy of love and respect. The role of the kid was completely played out, but he did not know just what to do next.

I began trying to fit a personality to my make-up. I began "acting" out personalities and tried observing people and copying them, but I realized what I was doing and so carried that "how'm I doing attitude," that is, continually looking at and thinking about what I'd said or done, what impression I had made. But these personalities were all short-lived because they pleased some and not others and because they didn't produce that underlying purpose of making people like me; and every time unconsciously I would resort to my childish attitude and to make myself noticeable. Examples of these "personalities" are independence (but I couldn't keep it up); arrogance (but people were only arrogant back at me); big shot in sex (but people weren't so much in love with it as I thought); hatefulness (people paid no attention to me); extreme niceness (people took advantage of it, kidded me about it because I did it to an ultra degree); humorous nature (but I was only being childish, silly); quiet and studious (but people were only passing me by and I kept feeling I was missing something). I became a daydreamer so intensively that up to the present I find I'm daydreaming almost all the time. I became conscious of a person's approach and would become fluttered, flustered, would try to make a friend of him no matter who he was but I overdid it.

It would be hard to improve upon this description of an intense need for love and attention. Kidd tried to make dramatic identifications with independent, assertive people, but he was everywhere betrayed by his need to be praised and admired. There seemed to be no core to his personality, no residue of pride or self-respect now that people no longer thought well of him. The sight of football players made him remember "how I spent my time masturbating while they were out forming a personality and building themselves up." Unwillingly he forced himself to go out with the fellows around him. Compulsively he stuck to his girl, "my only contact with the outside world"; without her he would have "retreated into a hide-away, to a hermit's life, to my mother's affection"; still more compulsively he sought derelicts.

> A fellow around school had a car, I'd provide the girls (tramps) and we'd go out once or twice a week with these different derelicts. I used this sex as a personal appeasement and also tried to flaunt it in front of fellows as if I was achieving success, but I found out quite a bit later that they were thinking less of me for it.

Between worrying about himself, worrying about his girl, debauching, studying feverishly for examinations, and "smoking an awful lot," he got quite worn out and retired to the infirmary with an attack of pneumonia.

> I was very sick for about a week and lost in all close to thirty pounds. This made matters worse because while in the hospital I was on my back all the time and could do nothing but think and all the time I fretted and worried myself sick. I became bitter, moody, and forceful in my determination to hurt people and make them sorry. At times I became so disgusted with all that I thought about suicide; this I can't deny as it was very true. I was very unhappy.

Emerging from the hospital four weeks later, he determined to throw himself into sports as a means of building up a personality. Four days after leaving the hospital he was playing hockey in subzero weather.

> Just after Christmas came a real blow when I found out that Mildred had gone to a prom with another fellow and had been playing around with him while I was in the hospital. This knocked me flat, and coupled with my disgust of the whole world in general, my family and all, I determined to pack up and leave. I wrote to everyone I knew outside the state asking for a job. My mind was aching and my nerves felt ready to snap; God only knows what kept me from hopping a freight when I couldn't find a job. I was desperate.

But I fought my way through midyears and came through with passing grades.

This put me at ease a little, but then the old routine continued. I made up with my girl, began going out, wasting time, thinking, daydreaming, and worrying.

And so matters rested at the end of his junior year. Kidd was to himself a man without a personality, helplessly pushed around by the strongest impressions of the moment. He experienced no stable governing forces in himself that might become the object of self-respect, and in consequence his mind was full of distressing tensions. Our knowledge of his more acute discomforts came from a supplementary autobiography written for us the following autumn. He was then feeling considerably better, so that an offer of therapeutic assistance, which would certainly have been appropriate the previous spring, no longer seemed indicated. In retrospect it is easy to see that Kidd's very interest in the study, his frankness, and what we might describe as his determination to put his worst foot foremost, gave evidence of a desire for help. The initial situation had not been defined, however, as one in which help was available; as a consequence he always gave us the story of his distresses in the past tense, as things he had suffered but now felt to lie safely behind him. In point of fact the chief interviewer responded to his need to the extent of discussing some of his problems with him, offering sympathy and encouragement, and being helpful with practical issues especially in relation to the college authorities. Nevertheless, the relationship hardly qualified as planned psychotherapy; Kidd's further development must be laid largely to events and to his own efforts.

Analysis of Imaginative Productions

Before we attempt to gather the threads of Kidd's story into a fully intelligible pattern, it will be profitable to examine his imaginative productions as represented by the stories he told in the Thematic Apperception Test. As noted before, this test is one in which the subject is asked to make up stories, prompted by a series of pictures usually susceptible to several interpretations. In performing such a task the storyteller draws on whatever resources he may possess, including stories he has heard and events in his own life; but the special value of the method lies in its power to reveal tendencies that are barely or not at all conscious and that could not otherwise be discovered except by long and searching analysis. A noticeable repetition of themes in the stories usually indicates some persistent emotional problem in the teller, and further inferences can be drawn from the behavior and competence of the heroes, the attitudes displayed toward parent-figures and love-objects, and the way the plots are brought to an outcome.

Three themes appeared so insistently in Kidd's fantasies that we can accept them as clues to important latent strivings. The first theme centers around the longing and loneliness engendered by loss of a loved person. There are five occurrences of this situation in the course of the twenty stories. Given a picture of an elderly woman peering from the threshold of a half-opened door, Kidd related the following unusual story:

> This picture, to me, depicts an old woman, about seventy years old, peering with longing in her eyes. She is alone in this house in which she lives, and has been alone there for the past ten years since her husband left—died, I mean. They were a devoted couple and loved each other dearly. His death shocked her and since they were childless, she was left positively alone. The past ten years haven't at all worn off his absence. At times the sense of loneliness so greatly overcomes her that she begins searching the house for him believing he is still there, sitting and reading. This idea which she holds that he is still alive and present in the house so overwhelms her as years go on, that eventually, one night, she imagines seeing him in a chair and goes over and speaks to him. The next morning some neighbors, missing her, search the house and find her seated in a chair very comfortably opposite an empty chair. She had died of a heart attack during the night.

In another story a young husband "by his constant nagging, jealousy and sureness of himself" kills his wife's love and drives her to leave him and marry again. He soon discovers, however, that he cannot bear her loss; he becomes "an outcast because of his eccentricities" and finally commits suicide. Here it is recognized that the hero, if he may be called that, by his selfishness sacrificed the treasure of love, but the value of this treasure in the storyteller's estimation seems all the greater from the tragic events that follow.

These stories, a sufficient sample of the five that turn on lost love and longing, give evidence that Kidd has experienced a deep feeling of bereavement. Since the chief characters in his life history were all still alive, this feeling probably came from the steady decline of his esteem-income, especially the gradual moderation of his parents' love and the growing indifference of Mildred. It is important that he several times made his heroes to blame for injuring a love relation, just as he blamed himself for having alienated Mildred's affections. In any event, the repetition of this theme in the stories gives evidence of an unusually intense craving for love, a craving that seems to contain strong elements of dependence.

The second outstanding theme occurred virtually unchanged in three of the twenty stories and with variations in four more. Perhaps the clearest expression was given in response to a picture that showed a gray-haired man looking at a young man who is sullenly staring into space. The younger man, according to Kidd, was a surgeon whose wealthy upbringing had given him an inhuman attitude.

> His operations were rash and sometimes without sympathy. Rather than spend precious time mending a mangled member he would take the easy way out and amputate. He sometimes unnecessarily operated because it was always quicker to learn the trouble that way than slowly studying the symptoms and this caused many of his patients to die. His career was on the brink of downfall when a kind old physician took him in hand, and for a whole year showed him the other side of life with its millions of people; its poverty; its sorrows; its love. The surgeon explained not from a lecture hall, but from an intimate standpoint, his duties toward these people. What arms or legs meant to them and what life and death meant to them, which must be included in our education towards profession. This, of course, caused this young doctor to realize he was dealing with people and not running a business, and then with this advice he succeeded.

The young man in this story is spoiled, thoughtless, cruel, and, judging from the phrase "running a business," greedy. These traits begin to spell disaster for his career, but he is taken in hand by an older man who is obviously interested in his success and who forwards it by educating him in kindness. The underlying theme of this story can be expressed as follows: *transformation of cruelty and greed by the sympathetic interest of an older man*. This theme occurred in another story with much less help from the picture, which showed only the silhouette of a man's figure against a bright window. Kidd told of a poet who had a grudge against the world and wrote spiteful poetry which nobody bought. When he was on the brink of starvation, an old man who had read all his work told him to climb a certain tower and find great wealth. Expecting to find money, he obeyed, but instead he encountered a vision of light and human happiness that set him on a successful literary career. The third occurrence of the theme was in response to a picture showing the dejected form of a boy huddled against a couch. Kidd saw a lad who had become vengeful "against his religion and his people" because of the death of his father. A priest, however, realized his frame of mind and comforted him so that he "braces up and goes ahead." All three of these stories make it clear that the principal character (the identification figure) is activated by hate, and two mention greed. The kindly intervention of the older man is completely successful in effecting a reformation and in setting the hero's feet on the road to success.

By "variations on the theme" we mean stories in which the hero is impelled by the same destructive motives but in which no older man comes to the rescue. In one such story aggression and acquisition reigned unchecked, so that the chief character committed what amounted to murder and was left in an agony of fear and horror before a punishment that fitted the crime. In another, an inventor used his ingenuity to get rich from the sale of explosive chemicals; he reformed and devoted himself to medical science only after an accidental explosion killed his beloved wife. From such stories we can infer that Kidd felt a profound helplessness to control the forces in himself. His villainous heroes, the victims of circumstance, were pushed on by destructive impulses only to be severely punished for the consequences. Only once did the hero try to change himself, influenced by love for a beautiful girl, and here he "finds the struggle hard" and was "tortured constantly by evil temptations," although he conquered in the end. In the main, Kidd did not borrow much strength from women. Perhaps they were too closely bound up with his aggressive problem to save him from it: two women were killed and a third alienated in his stories. His formula for strength was the affectionate interest of an older man, who alone could transform and socialize his impulses and save him from feelings of remorse. We learn from this how highly Kidd valued his father's love and how deep a loss he sustained by its withdrawal just as he reached an age when independence was expected of him and when father-substitutes were not easy to find.

The two themes so far discussed do not yield wholly new information. In his manifest behavior Kidd showed a longing for love, a certain helplessness to control impulses, and a desire for the affectionate interest of older men. But the stories indicate that these strivings are of unusual importance, so much so that they repeatedly polarize the field of fantasy.

Kidd's third theme, on the other hand, pointed to tendencies that were not overtly expressed. Several of his heroes betrayed deep feelings of bitterness and hate; they bore grudges against the world and seemed to feel that everyone was against them. Furthermore, Kidd seemed almost to enjoy enlarging on their cruel behavior and equally cruel punishments. A slum boy with a stolen car, for example, ran down the mother of seven children and was thereupon forced to view the mangled body. The inventor was gripped by a "lust for money and power," which included a willingness to blow up most of mankind and which actually resulted in the death of his beloved wife. The young surgeon used the scalpel with callous brutality. Most striking was a story about "the cruelest man in the Roman Empire" who constantly thought up new tortures for enemies of the state and who "loved to see them squirm, plead for mercy, and then slowly, very slowly, die in the worst possible way." Here we seem to be touching a deep well of resentment, a primitive desire to hurt and destroy, urges that Kidd never brought to expression in the submissive contacts of everyday life. In the safe realm of fiction he opened the gates to the bitterness engendered by his progressive deprivations of love and esteem. Perhaps the mother of seven children was killed because his own mother had hastened him into kindergarten in order to make room for younger siblings. Perhaps the grudges against life were expressions of feeling toward the playmates who deserted him, the father who lost interest in him, the girl who made impossible demands on his maturity. At all events Kidd's tendency to revel in aggressive scenes gives us insight into his tension and feelings of desperation. His dependence on parents and friends, and the strong feelings of guilt described in the autobiography, prevented him from working off the resentment he kept feeling as his frustrations increased. He could only seethe with feelings he hardly dared recognize as fury.

Interpretive Summary

From all that we can gather, Joseph Kidd started life with many assets: good looks, vigor, cleverness, and the admiring devotion of his parents. His early childhood, both at home and among his playmates, was healthy and happy. Something went wrong, however, so that by the time he reached his junior year in college hardly a vestige remained of his early promise. In order to understand him we must try to work out the reasons both for his earlier success and for his later failure. In explaining the failure we must be careful not to overdraw the picture, for it will presently be our task to understand his more or less spontaneous recovery.

Kidd's parents were strongly drawn to upward social mobility. When Joseph, their second son, proved to be an unusually attractive and clever child, their delight knew no bounds, and they could not resist the temptation to shower him with praise, show him off to their neighbors, and push him ahead in school. He was early accustomed to be the center of attention, and his economy of happiness was founded upon a very large income of loving admiration and acclaim. This childhood situation undoubtedly conferred an initial sense of security and well-being. But it may well have slowed his progress toward independence, and there seems little doubt that it enhanced self-display and self-consciousness, encouraging him to value himself as others visibly and audibly valued him.

At the outset Kidd had no difficulty in mingling with the neighborhood children. With his brother Mike, he belonged to a group of some fifteen or sixteen boys who regularly played and roamed together. Kidd recalled four who were his special companions, but none of these early friends stood out sharply as individuals. He emphasized their availability and familiarity when he described them as "just handy, well-known, healthy individuals." Group activities included a certain amount of vandalism, but Kidd emphasized the "goodness" of his particular crowd in contrast to others in the vicinity. Although they "hit the trash barrels" and occasionally broke windows, they made good use of the city playgrounds, where one summer Kidd was captain of a very successful softball team. They also showed themselves to be relatively stable elements in juvenile society by having paper routes and working on Saturdays in grocery stores. Kidd recalled that his earliest role in the group was "pretty active." He was capable of getting his way and convincing the others, and for a while was "pretty notorious" for vandalism. The last-named tendency was, he reported, "whipped out of me by the old man," and in later years he became a milder and less prominent group member. Group activity was a decidedly satisfying part of his childhood. "Life seemed cleaner and more enjoyable then than it does now," he said in retrospect; "we certainly were active and on the track I'd like to have stayed on." Apparently he achieved an excellent balance between home and playmates. Energies frustrated at home, including resentments, could be taken out in group activity, where he seems to have made good beginnings in the development of self-respect.

The zeal of the mother presently led to a double promotion in school, which put Joseph in the same class as his older brother. This started a very significant development in the younger boy's personality. Thrust into prominence because of his brightness, he began to experience the inevitable conflict between the role of bright child and the role of good fellow in the group. Even after his promotion he was brighter than the other members of the class, though at least a year younger. "I kind of lost the common bond," he commented, "which should exist between kids in the same class." It seems clear that Kidd yielded extensively to the temptations inherent in the role of bright scholar. Accustomed to praise and prominence at home, he could little resist their charm at school. Only gradually did he realize that his enjoyment of distinction was alienating him from his fellows. Even more slowly did he realize that their jealousy and hostility were responses to an attitude of superiority on his own part. Circumstances had placed him in two incompatible roles, and it was hard to learn that he could not have the benefits of both.

The difficulty increased when Kidd and his brother went to the distantly located Central High School. Few of their immediate neighbors were headed for college, and this step marked the final collapse of the local groups. For Kidd, twelve years old in a class where the average age was fourteen, the question of social membership took an acute turn. He had formerly been able to win respect by fighting or feats of strength, but now his only available role was to please and amuse his older companions by becoming a "clown" and a "stooge." As they all grew older, Kidd's attitude progressively failed in its purpose of winning esteem. He described this development in one of his story completions: the hero, good-natured and humorous, overhears one day a conversation from which he learns that "what he thought was being a good sport other people considered being a clown." This story runs closely parallel to its author's own experience. He gradually learned that the smiles of his comrades were counterfeit coin heavily alloyed with sneers at his "clinging vine nature," as he later learned to call it.

In consequence he began to stay at home, studying hard and going out scarcely at all. He spent more time with his father, hoping for support in his role of bright boy on the way to college. Evidently he hoped for more than the father could give. The role of bright child is most easily sustained when parents value it more highly than athletic or social prowess. Kidd's parents understood scholastic excellence only as a route to higher social status, and clearly expected Joseph, like his brothers, to win the athletic and social prominence which they understood so much better.

Kidd was thus not really satisfying parental expectations, yet now that he had lost his hold on companions of his own age his main motive had become to follow the path laid out by his parents. His mother, constantly busy running a "continuous kitchen" for her large family, satisfied his dependent tendencies yet disturbed him with a pressure toward achievements beyond her own understanding. His father was proud of him and gave him praise, but he himself displayed none of the energy and application that he expected of his favorite son. Joseph had the distinct impression that his father did not want his own indolent routine and simple pleasures disturbed too often by a boy who should be looking out for himself. It is not surprising that Kidd felt starved when he tried to draw his whole emotional support from his home. The result was a growing anger, a growing rebellion, which he dared not express at home and which therefore broke forth in the form of silliness and mischief at school. He did not dare to stop studying, but he could no longer take an interest in that hated obligation.

It was at this point that puberty multiplied his difficulties. His pangs of shame over masturbation were sharpened by the habitual self-consciousness, which made him feel that everybody knew what he was doing. Furthermore, he believed that his irresistable urge to masturbate came from studying too hard, thus being a miserable consequence of the very thing his parents were demanding of him; and he was sure that it interfered with his masculinity and put him at an additional disadvantage with boys of his own age. This was the frame of mind in which he received his sexual enlightenment from the older friend at camp. It is of interest that he perceived sexual conquests as a possible means of regaining not only self-respect but also the respect of his fellows. He was disappointed when he later found out that his college friends, in spite of their talk, had little admiration for a boastful "big shot in sex."

Kidd was floundering in all these difficulties when he met and fell in love with Mildred. He made it quite clear to us what he wanted in this relationship and how he constantly tended to spoil it. He wanted someone who would provide for him and love him as an ideal mother would love an only child. He wanted someone who would praise him and give him his own way. So strong were these cravings that he fell in love quickly and blindly, without much reference to Mildred's actual characteristics. Probably she too fell in love, impressed by the handsome neighborhood boy who seemed destined for a glamorous career. But Kidd soon found himself once more the object of demands. He felt that Mildred wanted him to be an heroic figure, whereas in fact he was shy and submissive with other boys. She grew tired of his dependence and was not inclined to restrict her interest entirely to him. Instead of contributing to his esteem-income, Mildred became an additional cause of bankruptcy.

One of the stories told by Kidd in the second Thematic Apperception Test, given three years after the first, surprisingly illuminates certain features of his development. The picture showed a young man lying face downward on a bed.

> The story of a youth who throughout life considered himself persecuted and unhappy because of others' attitude toward him. He never quite understood why people did not like him, taking any attitude people had towards him as being one of hate. And thus finally he turned away from outside activities altogether, remaining aloof from people whom he had come to fear, having no friends, living only by himself. He developed an attitude of animosity toward his fellow men and wanted to become a greater success so that he could in this way dominate and as a result satisfy his persecutory complexes. He never realized that perhaps the fault lay in himself. The people's attitude toward him depended on himself, not on other people, but for years he struggled under the impression that the trouble was on the outside, not that anything he would do was wrong; until the day he came to the realization, having met a girl he loved, that the world was right and he was wrong, that all his trouble, unhappiness, general lethargy was a result of his own imagination, and in an attempt to get on a normal footing with the outside world for the sake of this girl, he found it was too late—the little part of his life had come and gone, and that to start out again he would have to revert to a second childhood, and could in no way adjust his feelings of animosity to the outside world, with the final result being that it only led to greater introversion. The more he tried the more secluded became his life until he desperately committed suicide.

In this story Kidd gave a perfect account of a sequence of psychological events that is often found in cases of serious social maladjustment.[2]

---

[2] K. Horney, *The Neurotic Personality of Our Time* (New York: W. W. Norton & Co., 1937), especially Chapter 4.

The hero unwittingly displayed certain attitudes that caused others to lower their esteem. Angered by this loss, yet unwilling to perceive his own part in provoking it, he magnified the difficulty by ascribing more and more hostility to others. This could only result in his feeling weaker and more uncomfortable in their presence. Having thus through his own resentment poisoned his social relationships, he withdrew to solitude but built compensatory fantasies of power and success. Kidd even included the therapeutic process whereby insight is gained into the self-defeating character of one's own strivings, though this insight came too late to save the hero from despair. Kidd's story helps us to understand his own social difficulties during adolescence. There were plenty of external obstacles, but he revealed here the internal forces that helped push a previously active, friendly, energetic youngster completely out of athletic and social circulation.

Where was Kidd to look for a new source of esteem-income? His high hopes in Mildred were not altogether relinquished, but more often than not his companionship with her left him with an almost unendurable feeling of inferiority. He had a fleeting fancy that his younger brother Tom would look up to him and take him as a model, but Tom followed straight in Mike's footsteps. Both Mildred and his biological studies at college dammed the flow of parental esteem, and he arrived at a state of complete emotional bankruptcy. The word that he chose most often to describe the state was "self-consciousness." He represented himself as being painfully aware of other people's actions or words toward him and intensely concerned with their favor. Whereas in childhood, he said, "their eyes were on me all the time," in adolescence he began to have a desperate fear "of being insignificant, of being unknown, unheard." "I want people to talk about me," he continued, "whether bad or good. I'd just as soon have a bad reputation as a good one." In spite of this last defiance, it was doubtless true in the beginning that he wanted only good opinion. He was always acutely aware of what people thought about him, but this did not turn into a problem until he realized, particularly through the actions of his parents, his brothers, and his girl, that people were no longer inclined to think well of him. When this lesson was persistently pounded into him from all sides, he could see no value in life and even thought of suicide. But he was not really ready to give up the search for coveted esteem-income, even if at first he found no better plan than a frantic attempt to act out impossible roles.

Available Capacities and Existing Limitations

Physical Traits Kidd's physique was strong and solid, well-adapted for energetic and strenuous activity yet entirely free from strain and tenseness. His shoulders and chest were broad, his hips narrow, and the muscles of arms and legs large and well developed. Considering the social value attached to strength and energy in childhood, Kidd seems to have had a fortunate physical endowment. We have seen that he won the greater part of his fights, and he told us that his arm muscles were always especially good so that he was "able to beat the best of fellows in wrist contests." He took part successfully in numerous sports: football, baseball, hockey, tennis, and cross-country running. Kidd's physique was such as to be felt as an asset and reason for self-respect, the more so because his face and coloring caused him to be esteemed first as a pretty child and later as a good-looking young man.

In spite of his excellent build, however, Kidd spoke of a "sluggish, lethargic" feeling and pronounced himself less inclined toward athletics than the others of his school group. He may have misjudged his energy by comparing himself mostly with older playfellows, especially his brother, who was always a little taller, leaner, and more rugged. It is also possible that his motivation became sluggish and lethargic when, as the youngest of his group, he found it difficult to excel in sports.

Affective Qualities In striking contrast to Hartley Hale, Kidd was unhappy most of the time he was in college. Sometimes he merely felt discouraged and depressed; at other times he experienced great inner tension and a feeling of desperation. Success and elation had hardly come his way for a number of years. Although he could enjoy sports and especially a friendly and humorous social gathering, for the most part his happiest moments were characterized by relief from tension rather than by great joy. Even his sexual adventures, necessary as they were to his self-respect, yielded only a momentary satisfaction. Occurring mostly in the dark in the back of a car, they were quickly accomplished: "I just want to go ahead and get through with it," he told us; "I usually feel a little disgust afterwards anyway."

In an interview on the various emotions and their control Kidd represented himself as extremely impulsive. "I lose my temper easily," he said, "and do nothing to stop it." Arguing and being angry he found pleasant, but control of temper proved almost impossible. In spite of his general submissiveness, he often lost his temper quite violently with his friends and fellow students. It seemed that he had small power of control and could stop impulses only when he was truly afraid of their consequences. He declared that his feelings were easily aroused, that he gave them full vent when stirred, and that he often acted on the spur of the moment without stopping to think. Consistent with this were his self-ratings on a questionnaire, where he revealed himself as a changeable and disorganized person, unstable in his sentiments, erratic in his habits and in the pursuit of his goals. He gave himself a high rating on the statement, "I find that my likes and dislikes change quite frequently," but he dropped to a low mark when it came to the item, "I find that a well-ordered mode of life with regular hours and established routine is congenial to my temperament." For the statement, "I am on time for my appointments," he selected the lowest rating, a fair warning, one might say, of the long series of tardily kept or entirely forgotten appointments that marked his relation to the study. He also denied himself any efficiency in the matter of studying or in the matter of making his daily life run smoothly. All in all, he professed a degree of disorganization that seriously interfered with adaptation to the college world.

Intellectual Characteristics   In the Wechsler-Bellevue Adult Intelligence Test, Kidd scored an IQ of 118, putting him in the 90 percentile of the general population. He was much better on the verbal scale (IQ 126, 97 percentile) than on the performance tests (IQ 107, 68 percentile). Immediate recall was particularly good, and he spoke of good retention in everyday life, saying that "any situation is vividly pictured" even when he was not concentrating upon it. Although he loved arithmetic in grammar school and was successful with geometry in high school, the tests showed no great signs of mathematical ability. Reasoning and associative thinking were comparatively poor, a finding that was fortified by his inability to discuss general ideas clearly. He claimed deep thinking on philosophical subjects, believing that he could "stay in an argument with any priest" on the theme that man is only an animal; but from his exposition of this theme, one got the impression of a ruminating pictorial mind rather than one that made its way actively to clear concepts and rational synthesis.

Kidd's showing on the Wechsler-Bellevue Test would suggest that he might have some difficulty with his college studies, but another test (the Wells Alpha Examination) found him at the 99 percentile in the verbal exercises and at the 98 percentile on the performance items.

Both scores were higher than the average for Harvard College students. On the other hand, he fell far below his college mates on the Scholastic Aptitude Test of the College Entrance Examination Board, so low that there was at first some question whether he would be able to succeed with college work. Events proved that he could usually earn a passing grade by working hard at the last moment, thus utilizing to the fullest his good immediate recall. His college record, however, was a dreary succession of just-passing and just-not-passing grades, so that he was on probation most of the time.

Although Kidd seemed restricted in his grasp of general ideas and abstractions, he was not without gifts of imagination. He told stories of better than average originality in the Thematic Apperception Test. His use of language was frequently crude and awkward, but narrative seemed to bring out his best power of organization, as was shown by his reasonably conjunctive stories and especially by his account of his own life where the motive for understanding was intense. Such organization, however, seemed to be the spontaneous product of passive brooding rather than an active mastery of experience. Kidd rated himself as less than average as regards being logical and coherent in his thinking and admitted that he had spent little time trying to formulate his ideas clearly for communication. Outside of college work his reading was limited to newspapers and weekly news magazines.

Special Abilities Kidd proved to stand fairly high in two tests of manual dexterity. In the matter of fine motor coordination he claimed unusual excellence. According to his own account he made the best dissection of the dogfish brain that his instructor in biology had ever seen. Another manifestation of this skill was his ability at picking locks; at camp, he opened four trunks, the owners of which had forgotten their keys. Although he disclaimed mechanical insight, he had a good record in the rapid mastery of such skills as driving a car and running a motor boat. Kidd did not seem to be handicapped with respect to mechanical mastery, but he showed none of the interest in this subject that was so characteristic of Hartley Hale. One might almost have thought that he had been brought up in a different world, so small was his concern for mechanical objects and desire to construct material things.

In artistic appreciation he rated himself quite low, a judgment from which we could not dissent in view of his remarks:

I don't know one color from another. I can't tell a good piece of poetry from a bad. I can't see yet why they rave over Shakespeare. As for painting, I just see whether a picture looks natural. I have a good appreciation of music: classical, probably something soft and mellow.

Poetry and painting had scarcely appeared on his horizon, music was something he heard on the radio, and Shakespeare was one of the lessons he was obliged to study in school. He had received little encouragement for that flair for story-telling which appeared in the Thematic Apperception Test. His father played the piano, mostly for the purpose of accompanying songs at social gatherings, but while Kidd admired this piece of social skill he had received no encouragement to emulate it.

Social Skills and Attitudes In most of his social relationships Kidd was essentially passive and submissive. Occasionally he could be angry and argumentative; he told us that he was often irritable and impulsively critical, that his friends did not consider him compliant, and that he liked to carry on a verbal battle to the bitter end. It seemed likely that his submissiveness was the stronger of the two attitudes and that he tried to counteract it at times by putting up a bold argumentative front. When questioned about his leading and governing ability Kidd almost desperately disclaimed any such talent. "I can't have anyone depending on me to show them," he said, "I really can't, and I can't take the initiative at a supper table." He also questioned his capacity for friendship. Influenced perhaps by unfavorable comparisons with a very affiliative acquaintance, he found himself "not really interested" in friends, "not very dependable or trustworthy," and quite unable to keep confidences.

In view of the prominent place occupied by exhibition in his early memories, it is of interest to scrutinize the pattern of Kidd's self-ratings on this tendency. He gave himself high marks on all items that had to do with saying humorous things, acting the clown, talking about himself, boasting, showing off, and telling tales with dramatic exaggeration. These marks seemed to refer to what he did in congenial and familiar surroundings; under more exacting circumstances, especially when he was called upon to perform before a group, his behavior received a much lower rating, and he never took the lead in enlivening a dull evening. He very much liked to have people watch him do something that he did well, but with equal vehemence he disliked to feel that they were just looking at him or that their eyes were upon him. The need for exhibition appeared to be exceedingly strong, but it was associated with such a low frustration-tolerance that he did not always dare to express it openly. Deep preoccupation with the impression made on others was indicated by his maximal self-ratings on the following five items:

> I often think about how I look and what impression I am making upon others; my feelings are easily hurt by ridicule or by the slighting remarks of others; when I enter a room I often become self-conscious and feel that the eyes of others are upon me; I often interpret the remarks of others in a personal way; I pay a good deal of attention to my appearance: clothes, hats, shoes, neckties.

This preoccupation with himself and with the esteem of others doubtless prevented Kidd from utilizing his social potentialities. It was clear, for example, that he was capable of strong empathic feelings and of understanding the inner life of other people. Highly sensitive to inner problems and distresses, he was yet so bound up in his own sorrows that he almost never took action in behalf of others. His powers of sympathy, love, and lasting friendship seemed held in check by the more pressing urgency of finding himself and securing a stable basis for self-esteem.

From Eighteen to Twenty-one

In April of his junior year Kidd had just recovered from the shock of learning that Mildred had another boyfriend. After a quarrel with her, he made peace again and quickly slipped back into the unsatisfactory routine of the autumn term. His attempt to establish a place for himself among his college acquaintances by joining an intramural baseball team proved desultory, leaving him with the impression that he "just couldn't mix." His plans began to disintegrate.

> Just after midyears I began losing desire to go to medical school and I began looking around for easy prospects, business, teaching, but I couldn't put my heart into anything, it was all in this girl. I did nothing but work and plan for this girl and tried to make myself better for her. I was a terrific dreamer but wasn't much of an architect. My family was still rather looking askance at me for my actions, the way I was spending money.

As the term progressed, he became more and more bored with his school work. Aside from his evenings with Mildred his only interest was the lively company of a friend at college with whom he often went out in search of "derelicts." Presently his friend began to study for general examinations and another source of interest was cut off, for Kidd never made these expeditions alone.

With the approach of final examinations he became so upset that he passed only two of his courses.

> I had lost all ability to concentrate, remember, think, and correlate. I just couldn't study because when I did I became all nerved up and jumpy. I'd work, go out, go to a show, anything rather than open a book. I tried making up my mind to study but even this didn't help; I tried threatening myself and forecasting a wicked future in the event I failed at school, but my mind was continually going like a house on fire, nothing made sense.

During the summer he was employed as chauffeur at a summer estate in the Berkshires. Here his work was not supervised and he found himself dodging unpleasant tasks and doing things that he himself considered wrong. He daydreamed a lot and would occasionally "sit on a log and look into space for hours." It bothered him that he could not manage to make a positive impression on his employer. His brother Mike, he felt sure, would have used the opportunity to get himself a permanent job in the employer's business.

One more blow was still in store for him when he returned for his senior year. In September, Mildred took a position as a maid. She fell in with what Kidd described as a "fast crowd," threw him over in favor of new boyfriends, and fortified her rejection by having her employers forbid him to come to the house. Kidd was desperate. Night after night he could not sleep; day after day, secluding himself from others, he tried to reason his way out of a vicious circle of emotions. He could not help masturbating a great deal, and his imagination ran riot over Mildred's escapades with her new companions. It will be remembered that Kidd had never put Mildred in the class of girls with whom sexual intercourse was permitted; he maintained a celibate relation even when after a session of "heavy petting" his own inhibitions were the only obstacle. Now that she had rejected him and transferred herself to the class of "bad" girls he felt a burning desire for intercourse with her and for personal revenge, motives which do not seem to have been

clearly distinguished in his mind. "I almost committed some pretty das-
tardly incidents," he wrote; "only an overwhelming fear deeply im-
bedded since early days kept me settled. At one time I came very close,
but my inability to obtain a car at the last minute thwarted me."

It is interesting to work out the pattern of Kidd's conscience
insofar as it bore on sexual matters. Sexuality as a whole lay somewhat
under a cloud of guilt, but within the shaded area there were two distinct degrees of darkness. With "bad" girls, who in losing their virginity
had sacrificed their claim to respect, sexual intercourse was allowable.
Kidd held such girls in contempt not unmixed with fear. In one interview he announced that "society should nail bad girls to the cross," and
he admitted that he never went out with them alone, not wanting to
take the responsibility for "conducting the situation." Apparently by
leaving the initiative in the hands of another boy he reduced his own
anxiety connected with these escapades. All this, however, was very different from the clear pronouncements of his conscience on sexuality
with Mildred. Before her fall she was a good girl, a virgin, a future wife
who reminded him of his mother; with her, erotic activity must never
be consummated. From another incident we learn more of what Kidd's
conscience demanded. He met a "bad" girl in the Berkshires, but he
"couldn't touch her" and even found her "repulsive" because she was
three years older than he. His conscience drew its line so that good girls,
regardless of age, and older girls, regardless of virtue, were both strictly
prohibited.

The departure of Mildred, however painful at the time, marked
the turning point in Joseph Kidd's life. A few weeks later he met Grace,
with whom he formed a very close friendship.

> We talked for hours on end and had quite a few good times to-
> gether. She was very mature, of good broad character, the deepest
> sincerity. I've never met anyone quite like her. But our interpersonal
> feelings were far apart and had no emotional ties, at least I hadn't.
> She had money and a car and with me was very free with these
> assets. She in no way interfered with my time and tried to do a
> lot for my school work—she was always "on call."

During the autumn and winter Grace and her car were sources of much
comfort and entertainment. With other girls and fellows they went out
several times a week, driving far and wide. Kidd was particularly gratified that the girls, who had jobs, contributed their share of the expenses.

At the start of his senior year Kidd moved into one of the college dormitories. To save money he had been living in a dingy rooming house, but now he began to "meet a fine crowd of fellows" and have a really good time at college. It proved to be too late, however, to save his college record. He was still unable to study; when he sat down with a book he spent most of the time looking out of the window. He went to "few if any labs and less lectures" and prepared for each examination with one night of study. So bad was his record that he was required to leave college for the next three terms, and to establish a good job record as a condition for ultimate return.

> When I received the news from Harvard it didn't bother me very much. That which hurt me was my parents' disturbance: it broke their hearts. I left home for three or four days and lived with a friend. When I returned, nothing harsh was said. My father became rather easy about it and began to offer me an opportunity to go to some other college. But this I refused to consider and just said I'd rather take care of things myself.

Presently he found an agreeable position as a clerk in a Worcester business office.

> It was clean work and very interesting. . . . On the job one met a lot of people and since we had no responsible supervisor the job was comparatively easy. During my fourteen months in this position there were four other college undergraduates with us. When our nominal supervisor left in September, I was given the position with a raise in salary.

> On the whole I found my sojourn pretty amusing as to the people I met, the contacts I made, and the good times involved. It was a wonderful insight into business living routine and with me time seemed to pass very rapidly. It seems like yesterday that I began to work there. All employed in our department, above our job which was only considered as a part-time job, were college fellows and of the "regular" type.

It can be seen from this account that Kidd put emphasis on two features of the job not directly connected with the work itself: its easiness and its social status. Nevertheless, he did the work successfully and was promoted; furthermore, his job, imposing a certain order on his life as well as yielding an appreciable esteem-income, set in motion three more constructive strivings.

> From the first of the year on I began to read quite a bit and began to take piano instruction at a downtown studio. I joined the YMCA

around that time and began to take a different physical interest in myself. I struggled with the piano but found it hard to return to a routine. I kept it up until summer school opened. I gained something from time and money spent and would really like to return to it when the opportunity permits. . . .

I've gone in for exercise in rather a strenuous fashion, something which I never did before. Throughout the summer I did quite a bit of sculling and have lately been doing some running to improve my hockey. I also improved, through much practice, my tennis and swimming and have started to throw off smoking for financial reasons and otherwise. My athletics were always of a slack calibre but this I've modified by taking an active interest.

Meanwhile his erotic life began to fall into new patterns. The friendship with Grace gradually moved into physical intimacy, and for the first time in his life he was able to combine sex with respect and sincere feeling. This development was probably easier because his emotions were not deeply involved and because Grace offered encouragement: "it never could have been any more than friendship on my part and I talked her out of a crush on me." He admitted a little coolly that Grace was not good-looking and that he did not often take her out in public. Still he had broken down one of the barriers that blocked his capacity to love, and he had even encroached a little on the rules regarding age: Grace was six weeks older than Kidd.

Parallel with this development came a change in his activities with the "bad" girls. For a while after meeting Grace these continued with their usual frequency. He spoke of "five or ten" acquaintances and mentioned with a touch of pride "one young girl continually calling me and asking me to force her from her virtuous bonds—this I finally did."

But the more I engaged in it the less satisfied I was and when it did occur the reaction was one of disappointment shortly afterwards; for it didn't seem as though this was exactly what I wanted. In other words I judge it to have been another escape mechanism or shunt for my drives.

He began to rub out the line between good and bad girls; he came to like one of the latter, and treated her with something approaching a lover's tenderness. At last a situation arose, following Grace's departure for a distant job, in which all the old distinctions were obliterated. He met a "married girl," two years older than himself, whose husband was on the point of departing.

> She had a car and money to burn and wanted to fire it all on someone who would keep her emotions tepid. I took up with her at this point and with this girl my sex ambitions were satiated and really subsided. I spent a week with her down in Connecticut on our vacations. My relations with her were many and wholesome and from her I learned about all there was.

There was real friendship in this relation; in fact, the girl began to ask Kidd what he would do if she divorced her husband, to which he replied defensively, "Nothing; sit at home and listen to the radio." He took her to his home on one occasion, introducing her as a college girl and using only her first name. His mother was delighted and invited her to a family party. In spite of the coolness with which he gave these descriptions, Kidd felt a genuine interest in the "married girl" and could have imagined marrying her under circumstances less at odds with his parents' moral scruples.

As he began to bring sex and love closer together, he lost interest in sex without love. He was at last able to "quit browsing around," which made him feel a great deal better. As his energies were drawn away from the preoccupation with sex, he was able to distribute them into a more balanced array of interests. It was no doubt a matter of great importance that his later girl friends valued him so highly and took the initiative in declaring their interest. If Mildred took the last props from under his self-respect, Grace and the "married girl" put back a substantial foundation.

Kidd's year as a business clerk was on the whole a contented one. When he returned to repeat his senior year at college he was far more poised and self-possessed than we had ever seen him. His problems seemed to have reduced themselves to two. (1) Studying was still extremely difficult. "My mind," he said, "seemed to close up when I opened a book; I seemed to have formed some aversion to it." (2) He was still uneasy about his social relationships. Too submissive toward boys, too dependent on girls, too vain about himself, he continued to fall short of his own specifications for masculinity, especially in the matter of being respected by his own sex. He still missed in himself certain assertive, dominant qualities which he would have liked to find there. In spite of these unwelcome traces of the past, however, Kidd's general condition was greatly improved. He closed his supplementary autobiography with the following words:

> That's the story up to date just as it has come to me. . . . I took things rather easily and allowed certain relations to sink in. I have

striven to get away from over-worrying about myself and adjust myself so as to form my own way of living or personality as it is called. I am grateful for the opportunities afforded me but now it seems that everybody's dreams or ambitions are about to be interfered with. A lot of worrying and thinking about myself I am going to be able to do behind the butt of a gun. This sort of realization sort of snaps one out of it. At any rate here's to a successful future.

In retrospect it appears that Joseph Kidd reached his lowest point—a point of esteem-bankruptcy—at the end of the summer when he became nineteen. His credit with his parents, his brothers, his school and college companions, and his girl Mildred had steadily fallen away, and in the college environment he could not seem to find new sources of esteem-income. Two years later he had worked his way back to what might be called a subsistence level of esteem, though hardly an affluent one. He was more calm, more on the alert "for interests and a future," more able to "get out and act like a man." His statement of aspirations, which included "a comfortable future" and "enough means to send my children to college," showed that he was beginning to reject the ambitious pressure from home and accept a more modest step up the status ladder. But the gains were not yet securely won. He returned to college and did not renounce medical school in spite of a continuing violent distaste for studying. He had made a distinct advance, nevertheless, over his earlier outlook, which contained no middle points between being a doctor and being a total failure.

PART TWO: FROM TWENTY-ONE TO TWENTY-NINE

Our contacts with Joseph Kidd during the next eight years consisted of two exchanges of letters, one when he was overseas and one when he returned at the end of the war. When we proposed the second study, he responded with immediate willingness. Upon his arrival we were struck by his gain in confidence and maturity. Workers who met him for the first time thought that he looked young for his twenty-nine years, but he certainly looked much older than the round-faced, curly-haired, hesitant youth we had known before the war. One of the most marked changes was in his tone of voice. The soft, sometimes barely audible, speech of his college years had given place to a voice of normal firmness and assurance.

Four Years of Military Service

Some time after graduation Kidd applied for the U.S. Army Air Corps. He was attracted by the prospect of flying and also by the fact that "the money seemed good." This application failed, but with the approach of the draft he announced himself in favor of "getting everything you can while the getting is good, especially if you know someone or have the means to get it; they're all looking for something cozy." These sentiments seemed to guarantee that Kidd, whatever else might happen, would certainly not suffer from a shattering of fragile romantic ideals. His second application for the air corps was successful, but his training was not scheduled to begin for more than a year. He worked for several months in a war-connected job, but soon found himself feeling extremely restless and impatient. Accordingly, he secured release from the air corps and was inducted into service as a private. For some time he was signed up for the specialized training program in medicine, but when this failed to materialize he volunteered for a health survey unit. While he was in training for this work, a personnel officer, who took an interest in him and hated to see a man wasting his college education, encouraged him to apply for admittance to a medical school. Kidd's grades, however, had not been good and the application was rejected. In due time he went overseas with a unit consisting of fifteen men and a commanding officer. He sailed "with a laugh," completely carefree, feeling that he had found exactly what he wanted. His parents and brothers were sensitive to rank and commissions, but he himself felt wholly satisfied with his humble status in a small unit.

Throughout his years in military service Kidd found himself repeatedly selected for special attention. "Every place I went," he said, "I found older men or men better off than myself who seemed to become interested in me." The commanding officer of his unit had already singled him out for special jobs and special study. Kidd judged that this officer "had a lot of faith in me, lacked faith in himself, and needed somebody on whom to depend." Kidd found it extremely irksome to be singled out in this way, and he refused to become a model soldier. When the unit disembarked he led the men on an escapade; they were absent without leave for twenty-four hours, a thing that both infuriated the commanding officer and badly hurt his feelings. This incident was typical of many in which Kidd took a prominent part in raising Cain and dealing lightly with military regulations. After about a year of service with the health survey unit, however, his work was deemed satisfactory enough to warrant a commission, and he was transferred to a larger post. At once the colonel took a liking to him, invited him to table, spoke to him in mess hall, and tried to get special favors for him. "That I didn't like at all," Kidd related. "Perhaps he needed to depend on me, too. It was a bad deal, to be in with the boss and out with the outfit." Less than three months elapsed before the colonel, purely as "a personal thing," appointed Kidd detachment commander in charge of some eighty men recuperating at a convalescent hospital.

Elevated to this new post, Kidd was completely miserable. He had just been "getting in fine with the junior officers," but now he found them jealous and resentful, and the enlisted men furious. In particular he lost the friendship of a former college football star, "a rugged, good-looking fellow," who was the logical choice for the appointment. Kidd had several violent scenes with a sergeant who hated him and created every possible difficulty. He was able to hold his own in these scenes, but he found intolerable his duties of disciplining the men. The position really called for an older man, he believed, upon whom the enlisted men could legitimately look as a father.

> He would have to be hard, stiff. I never felt so bad as when sitting in judgment on some drunk, probably having a hangover myself, or on some man who had been caught with a native woman, as I had done myself. Sitting in judgment is what disturbed me. I had to mete out punishment, I had to be severe . . . I like to be *with* other fellows, not *over* them.

When the colonel was transferred to another command his successor lost no time in summoning Kidd, telling him that he was a misfit as detachment commander, and transferring him back to health survey work. If Kidd was unhappy at his demotion, this feeling was more than compensated by his enormous sense of relief. "I tried to fail," he said, and he was now free to resume work that he found interesting and that required little initiative.

In spite of his failure in leadership, Kidd looked back on his years in the army as the happiest time in his life. "I enjoyed the experience," he said; "I'll remember it all my life." He used the word "freedom" to describe one of the chief benefits of army life, then mentioned the provision that was made for one's comfort: three square meals a day, money in the pocket, only a few hours of work. Alcohol flowed freely, nurses provided feminine companionship, and there were occasional opportunities to take hunting trips and see the country. "It was a great life for a lot of people," he remarked; "when I came back I had a good deal of what I wanted under my belt." In another interview he attributed his contentment to "the fact that I got away from home, from school, got in with people, became less of an individual, more a part of a group." He contrasted himself with more settled men, generally married and with families, who wrote letters and wanted to get home. "I wanted to get up and go," he said; "I wanted to live, I wanted to get out with the guys," and there were enough men similarly disposed so that he did not feel out of place in having such feelings. He obtained some satisfaction out of having a commission to take home, but while he remained in the service he was content to remain in a subordinate position. Yet it was not entirely for its good times that Kidd looked back with satisfaction on his years in military service. Even more important was the gradual but permanent change that had taken place in his personality.

Kidd's own words were as usual very helpful in understanding this crucial development. In an hour devoted to free association he spoke as follows:

> I think I want to stay among people as much as possible because I understand them, I think I do, I can operate with people. I learned that very rapidly in the army, very quickly, and took to it very well, being able to work on people for what you want, bring them around to your way of thinking, but mainly to get what you want from them. That's what we call "corning" in the army.

He then described a small business which he and another soldier had set up for personal profit. Materials for the business, and knowledge of how to use them, were obtained from suggestible men in charge of stores by the misinformation that they were needed for the regular duties of the unit. This minor racket was interrupted when Kidd received his commission. His associations continued in the following vein:

> I wasn't wholly successful in the army, I didn't make a lot of friends, I didn't accomplish too much. I just feel as though I learned a lot of very useful things, and I think I got rid of a lot of the errors in my system where certain things have to be learned by trial and error, which is dealing with people. I made an awful lot of mistakes with people and lost their friendship or lost their respect,

and the like of that, but I don't mind thinking about that today because I accomplished something. With every experience I derived something of advantage to myself, put it away where it would do me some good in the future.

If Kidd's sentiments on getting what you want seem somewhat crudely self-centered, they nevertheless represent a certain progress over the blocked self-assertion and the whining demandingness he displayed as an undergraduate. One might say that in the army he had found belated opportunity to take up the thread of development broken off when he lost his contact with group life at the age of twelve. He returned at last to the track on which he would have liked to stay, that of group activity and group respect. In the army he created merriment as he had formerly done on the streets of Worcester, never carrying it quite far enough, however, to draw severe discipline. He restored his feeling of belongingness with companions of his own age, and he rejected the kind of ideals for which his parents had stood. Thus he canceled that surrender to parental ambitions which had only led him into deeper and deeper distress. Regaining contact with impulses more truly his own, he began to build a nucleus of self-confidence and self-respect by learning to get what he wanted through his own efforts. The pursuit of this necessary development required that he be placed *with* other fellows, not *over* them. To be competent among equals was more important than to be in a position of authority. Thus he felt as threats the attempts that were made to give him prominence and advancement —the very things that had ruined his life in school. No doubt he enjoyed the flattering attention of officers, but he had been too badly burned in that fire to let it come near him again. Perhaps the dependence he attributed to these officers was an externalization of dependent feelings which he did not want to experience in himself. At all events he "tried to fail" whenever he was pushed forward, and he refused to be deflected from a developmental task that at last began to feel right and natural.

Return to the Family Home

In view of the nature of his development in the army, Kidd's return to the home of his parents was nothing short of a crucial test. Would he feel once more the old familiar pressure, would he succumb to it, or would he find it possible to continue his growth toward independence and self-respect? In a letter Kidd likened separation from the service to a jump without a parachute. The "sorely missed heroes," he reported, had hardly more than walked through the door than they were "handed aprons and paint brushes." By this time Mike and Tom were married and were in their own homes, but Joseph had nowhere else to go. At first it looked as if he might succumb. He put out new applications to medical schools and enrolled in a summer session where he found a chemistry course painfully difficult. "The first year I was home," he said, "I didn't like it too well, didn't stay home much, didn't take any interest in it." In a desultory way he tried to help with his father's business while awaiting decisions on his applications to medical schools, but on the whole his life threatened to resume the disorganized pattern that had characterized it before he entered the service.

Before long, however, he discovered an opportunity for development right at home. His father's prosperous business began to decline. For years the business had been operated in the dingy old-fashioned shop originally purchased from the German floral decorator. In the meantime, rivals had come into the field, and Mr. Kidd found himself rapidly losing business to competitors equipped with air-conditioning, cooled show cases, and fluorescent lighting. It was clear that he needed to invest in a new establishment, but he showed no disposition to undertake such an enterprise. He wanted to continue in the old familiar way, especially now that his youngest boy Peter, handicapped in health and never successful in school, had joined him in the business and took some of the drudgery off his hands. Mrs. Kidd was again the chief source of initiative. As each of the older boys returned home she made him the object of a persistent campaign to secure a new flower studio. She poured forth her financial worries, her suspicion that the father was giving money to his improvident sisters, her despair because he kept no systematic accounts of his income and expenses.

Kidd rejected an interviewer's suggestion that his mother nagged the boys; he described her method as "harping," which seemed to him "a little bit different, but still just as disagreeable." "She'll stay on a subject," he said; "it becomes almost a maniacal fixation to her. She won't ask you to do something, but she'll stay on the subject of what's wrong, and of course you know the only logical solution." Again, "she's very jumpy and neurotic now; she complains and looks for sympathy, and she has a very clever way of playing one against the other." Her urgency was irritating, but Kidd judged her to be right, and he clearly saw the difficulty of forcing his indolent father to take the necessary steps.

Michael, a lawyer, and Tom, a bank clerk, were busy with their own occupations. Joseph alone had time at his disposal. With no help from his father, who resolutely turned his back on the whole enterprise, but with the strong support of his mother and the agreeable willingness of his brother Peter, he set out to reorganize the business and build the new shop. Mrs. Kidd, he said, was "wholly on my side, she leaned heavily on me to get done what she wanted done." Yet he did not feel driven by her pressure. He saw through her technique of "harping," kidded her continually for her irrational and stubborn ways, and criticized her with no little severity for her slurring remarks about her husband and his money. He confided to an interviewer that his mother had a very "dirty tongue," by which he meant that she tended to tell tales about people and knife them behind their backs. He considered this "the worst possible crime," and told his mother so.

Having taken on the project of rescuing the family business, Kidd began by trying to get an idea of his father's financial position. This was not easy, because his father often cashed large checks or made them over directly to creditors without keeping any record of the transaction. Kidd collected several bills his father had long given up. He then offered to make out the income tax and was able to reduce it substantially by claiming deductions his father had overlooked. Mr. Kidd expressed neither gratitude nor amazement; nevertheless, he was sufficiently impressed to allow Joseph to set up his books in such a way that all transactions appeared in the checking account. It was a moment of triumph when his father confided the combination of his safe, even though the contents proved to be of no great value. Kidd seemed to glow with pleasure when he related this symbol of paternal faith. But the father balked when it came to being involved in the new building; he gave his consent only on condition that he be not bothered by any of the details. This project therefore devolved almost wholly on Joseph, who had to secure the property that was to be rebuilt, engage the architect, contractor, and decorator, decide upon details as the work proceeded, investigate heating and ventilating systems, and procure enormous amounts of information for the family conferences at which vital decisions were made. After a year of work the new flower studio was ready for use. It won immediate acclaim, evoking spontaneous compliments from nearly everyone who saw it, and Kidd derived tremendous satisfaction from his achievement.

In making the many contacts with people that were required to carry out this project, Kidd was much helped by his experiences in the army. He was no longer a novice in getting what he wanted out of people, and he now had a chance to turn his training to good account. He was far from at ease, however, in his new and responsible role. He felt that everything in the studio had to be the latest and best of its kind. When ventilation had to be considered, for instance, he investigated every brand of equipment and collected stores of information about it. People told him he worried too much.

> I was very, very upset during that period. I smoked a lot, I moved around an awful lot, I talked excitedly to people, especially those from whom I was trying to get the information which would stop me from getting concerned and worried. And I would feel very, very relieved when I got the information authoritatively. I think it pays off to feel that way because you will tend to do more, you will tend to assure yourself you're right.

He had undertaken to do something for his family that involved expense and risk, something to which his father was opposed, something for which he himself lacked technical training. Obviously he had a high stake in being right.

Kidd mentioned in many interviews the satisfaction he derived from the success of the flower studio. He even intimated that he would have been loath to return for our second study if he had not had this solid accomplishment behind him. In an hour devoted to free association he kept returning to the theme. He said that he felt "a keen obligation" towards his parents and that "the purpose of repaying them was accomplished" by the project. This made him feel much better about leaving home and seeking out a life of his own. He knew that he had let his parents down—"turned their sacrifices for me into a joke, into a terrific loss"—by failing at college and by spending money running around with girls. "They were not only unhappy about it, they were very displeased." Certain of his associations suggested a feeling that the debt was even yet not fully paid. The business was on its feet again, but what if its apparent recovery proved only temporary? What if something happened to none-too-rugged Peter? Nevertheless Kidd's predominant feeling was one of tremendous satisfaction. "I gained peace of mind," he said; "I didn't have it when I came back." He also gained a real feeling of knowing what he wanted.

> I'm very happy because I accomplished that. I'm not getting all the credit at home, but it doesn't bother me. In myself I am very happy and satisfied.

I found myself becoming more definite on things, which I'd never been before. There were things I wanted a certain way; I was damned if they weren't going to be that way. I knew they were right and I wanted them done. And I don't remember ever having been so definite on anything before. It dawned on me after a while that I was knowing what I wanted. I was able to make up my mind.

These statements deserve comparison with his remark at the age of twenty-one: "I can't make a decision on my own and back it up; it's always guided by some factor outside my own intellect." Belatedly he was learning to respect himself and daring to act upon his own judgments.

The nature of the pressure that Kidd felt at home becomes clear from this chapter of his history. His failure to justify his parents' sacrifices and fulfill their high expectations had left him with a heavy burden of guilt. He had to repay them in some way and show them that he was good for something. When the army forcibly took him away from home, he was justified in postponing this obligation and leading his life as he really desired. On his return, however, he resumed his attempt to carry out the parental plan of going to medical school. Having found contentment in the comradeship and irresponsibility of military life, and having experienced again the old boredom and blocking when he tried to refresh his chemistry, he must have known that he was never going into medicine. But he could not announce this as a decision. He had to wait until the final failure of his last application made it clear to his parents that he could not take the course they had originally planned for him. Although this released him from a burdensome obligation, it did not set him free. But in the meantime he had begun to work off his debt by building the new flower shop. The project had to be a complete success in order to pay so vast a debt and prove him at last a worthy son; hence his anxiety while the work was in progress. When it *was* a complete success he was rewarded by "peace of mind"—relief from guilt—and a feeling that he was at last free to go away and seek life on his own terms.

Kidd had done more, however, than pay a debt and cancel his feelings of guilt. He had also caused his parents to respect him. Even if they did not acknowledge it, he knew that he had done a good job and earned the right to their respect. He had also found a way of rivaling, if not surpassing, his brothers. In contrast to Michael, who was receiving practically all of his law practice from his father's friends, he had carried through a successful project without paternal blessing. In contrast to Tom, the bank clerk, who had drawn plans that the contractor found impossible, he had taken pains to learn what he was about and to secure advice when it was needed. He had clearly shown himself to be a better man than his father, who was now highly dependent upon him. Strengthened by all these demonstrations of his own adequacy, Kidd could at last feel real affection for his father, recognizing all his severe limitations yet enjoying his humor, his piano-playing, and his ability to create hilarious good times. In a way, the relation between father and son became reversed, the son setting standards of initiative and business efficiency that the father was scarcely able to emulate. Certainly Kidd no longer felt constrained to live his life according to patterns emanating from his father.

Kidd's relation to his mother remained somewhat more complex. It revealed certain undertones that had barely been suggested in the earlier studies. All the Kidd boys had learned to tease and gently reprove their mother for monotonous harping and persistent curiosity. Joseph, as we saw, had taken her to task for slanderous gossip and had learned not to expect rational discussion on subjects close to her heart. Yet it was evident that he had great respect for his mother, whose drive and ambition had been solely responsible for the family's economic and social success. When first married she had wanted to take a job herself and she was contemptuous of her "lazy Irish" neighbors who had no thought of rising in the world. If she had actually remained somewhat like them, gossiping over her tea and never using her mind for serious thinking, it was because she had sacrificed her own life for her children. Kidd's attitude was compounded of respect, tolerance, and occasional outspoken criticism, but there was another element in the relationship. Somewhere along the way he had acquired a profound resentment, which came to expression mostly through indirect channels. Perhaps the original cause lay in her having other babies in close succession; perhaps it was her continual dominance and harping.

When Kidd was asked to associate to the phrase, *the worst crime*, he arrived finally at the subject of hit-and-run driving, which he characterized as "pretty cruel and heartless," a thing it would be impossible to forgive. It will be recalled that in an early story for the Thematic Apperception Test he caused a selfish and degraded young man to run down and kill the mother of seven children and to suffer torments of remorse afterwards. The earlier plot and the later associations began to seem like threads in a pattern when we observed the course of his thoughts upon being given the phrase, *what frightens me*. He spoke in part as follows:

> It doesn't bring anything to mind right off the bat. Very little frightens me. Ah . . . (long pause) . . . I couldn't say what outside of . . . ah . . . physical violence doesn't bother me . . . ah . . . perhaps anything happening to my mother. That doesn't frighten me, but that's always in my mind for fear that she'll step off the sidewalk to cross the street. Perhaps I fear a little bit that she might do it and get hit and killed some time. There are a lot of clowns driving in hopped-up junk-boxes. They likewise don't look or think where they are going. That's probably the only thing I fear, is her out on the street, is fear that she might be accidentally killed.
>
> If she should die a natural death tomorrow, I would feel bad but not so very broken up, but I think I would be very, very broken up if she were killed.

This curious fear that the mother would be accidentally run down by careless "clowns in junk-boxes" has several earmarks of an anxiety derived from early childhood. It can be interpreted as representing a hostile wish with respect to the mother, coupled with a fear that the wish might become a reality. If such a wish and its attached fear was still active enough in Kidd to create a definite uneasiness, we can see added reason for his feelings of guilt toward the family, his gratification at having maternal support, and his joy in the successful payment of his debt. We have now to consider whether a parallel problem has beset him in his relationships with women in general.

Relations with Women: Uneasy Bachelor

Great was our surprise to learn that Kidd's relation to Mildred had not ended during his twentieth year. He was quite sincere when he told us that it was over and done with, but he had not allowed for the possibility that Mildred would resume her interest in him and that he would find this interest irresistible. Shortly after the close of our earlier series of interviews he met Mildred at a party. He learned that she had sought an invitation because she knew he would be there. They began going out again together, but the relation was a stormy and tormenting one. Kidd was greatly bothered by Mildred's continuing interest in other fellows, and he felt that she was but little concerned with him personally; she never remembered, for instance, what he was doing in college or what medical school he might be hoping to attend. At Christmas he took her a present, only to find her receiving a call from another young man. One night he went to her house when quite drunk, thus losing the esteem he had enjoyed from her parents. Yet in spite of all these difficulties, Kidd felt that Mildred fulfilled his ideals, and he became increasingly sure that he wanted to marry her. He believed that his impatience to enter military service came partly from a desire to break through her coldness and draw expressions of her regret and affection. While he was in training he thought about her a great deal. On a three-day pass he saw her and had a nice time, but felt that something was on her mind. He mentioned his feelings to Mildred's mother, saying that he wanted to give her daughter a ring, and it was his impression that the mother acted disturbed and unhappy at this news.

Presently Kidd had a furlough, which led to a new development in the relationship. He and Mildred went to a bar together and drank more heavily than usual. Then they drove to a secluded lake where Kidd undertook to end the long-standing taboo on sexual intercourse with Mildred. "After all those years I went right ahead," he said, "took off almost all her clothes, and tried to have sexual relations with her," but although "she was cooperative, I couldn't have an erection; that was from the drinking. After all those years of wanting it, I couldn't have it." Some remarks made during this episode convinced him that Mildred was pregnant. Nevertheless Kidd dated her the following evening for the movies. The situation was awkward: "I felt guilty," he said, "and she felt pretty foolish about the whole thing." Kidd told us later that he had occasionally been impotent when extremely drunk; otherwise, he was a stranger to the experience.

They did not meet again before Kidd went overseas. Months later Mildred wrote that she was unhappy for him. He wrote back, saying that he loved her and wanted to marry her, but her subsequent letters were filled with news items and never touched a really serious note. Although after a time she stopped writing, he returned full of hope that she might be waiting for him. He learned, however, that she was engaged; she was married a few weeks later. "The day came and went," Kidd reported; "it didn't bother me too much. I don't like to talk about it." Sympathetic murmurings from the interviewer did not prevent him from continuing:

I wouldn't want to meet her husband. I'm glad I didn't do anything rash or ridiculous like dashing off and getting married or going to

California. If it had happened before the war I think I'd have gone
out of my mind. . . . If her husband died, I might play cat and
mouse with her, but I wouldn't get involved again. It's a killer of
romance when a girl has children by someone else. That should
close the gate.

Kidd may not have perceived all the possible difficulties in his
relationship with Mildred, but in retrospect he put his finger on one of
the most central problems. He was entirely sincere in wanting marriage,
he told an interviewer, yet there were times when he was visited by
doubt.

Sometimes when we made up and got together again I wasn't satisfied. I don't know, I wasn't at ease. I thought I was very sure it was
what I wanted, but a great many times I doubted what I wanted. I
guess I didn't have myself, so I wanted her. I wanted her life; I
didn't have my own life.

He had met Mildred when he was at low depths of unhappiness and disorganization. His strong attraction to her was heavily mixed with
dependence and a hunger for esteem. Mildred's coolness, her demands
upon him, her faithlessness did not wholly destroy feelings that were
rooted in such urgent needs. It is doubtful whether Kidd could ever
have cleared the relationship of these elements so inimical to a strong
free partnership, and it was probably best for his future development,
however painful the period of suffering, that he did not become per-
manently entangled in his first love. If he met Mildred today for the
first time, it would be a different Joseph Kidd who met her: one more
capable of knowing what he wanted.

In the meantime Kidd had continued to keep his eye open for
sexual opportunities. His experiences in the service carried forward the
development that had already begun after his first separation from Mildred. His most frequent companions were nurses, "older girls" whom
he could not consider "bad." "I found that the woman cared for me
when she did it," he reported, "so why should I think ill of her?" Sex
became a natural as well as a pleasurable thing. He recognized that his
earlier "hit-and-run affairs" had been heavily motivated by ideas of
conquest and achievement. "When it was a question of going steady
with a girl and sleeping with her, that was a new challenge. That gave
me an entirely different outlook on women in general." When he returned from the service he lost no time in establishing similar friendships. For more than a year he frequented the apartment of a "divorced

girl," often taking supper there and joining a congenial group of unmarried young people for whom the apartment served as a sort of social center. But he did not fall in love and he did not move closer to marriage, even though he began to feel embarrassingly conspicuous as a bachelor nearing thirty.

Kidd told us that he wanted to find an attractive, agreeable, intelligent girl with definite interests of her own. He wanted her to be distinctly different from his mother in respect to this matter of interests. The main function of the interests would be to prevent the girl from becoming dependent on him and interfering with his time. Kidd deplored the unfortunate state of one of his golfing companions, whose wife always seemed jealous about the golf games. "There's nothing worse than an idle woman," he said. He believed that a wife should "put up with what a man might do to annoy her" and "make very little demand on his time," not requiring to know "where he's going, what he's going to do, and the like of that." In one of his stories for the Thematic Apperception Test he represented a girl as "trying every means to hold" her man, "trying every ruse, every method to catch him. Most of these methods are pressure methods, wearing down, constantly chasing." Besides his fear of losing the freedom of his spare time, Kidd greatly dreaded being trapped in a monotonous job with no prospects. He cited the grim plight of one of his friends as a warning example. This man frankly hated his job, but with a wife and children on his hands he dared not sacrifice such security as it offered.

It was clear from his remarks that Kidd was not ready, even at twenty-nine, to settle down in marriage. He still needed to go ahead with a process of development generally accomplished earlier: testing out his own proclivities, becoming sure of himself, finding a vocation. Emotional difficulties had long hampered him in taking these developmental steps, but now that he was on the way he was acutely aware that he needed freedom. But there was more to the problem. He did not seem to fall in love with any girl. "I don't know, I don't love them," he said, and then, making a revealing slip of the tongue, "I think to get married *again* I would like to love somebody." Asked by the interviewer if Mildred had been the only girl he ever loved, he said: "That's right, I mean felt so deeply, but I wouldn't want that same strength of love, I mean something so overpowering and so overwhelming as to cut you off from all you . . . from all the range of living."

This was a real dilemma. He wanted deep love, but not the same kind of deep love that previously made him suffer and that seriously blocked his development. It was hard for him to feel this new deep love, free and self-respecting, because he still was not sure of himself, still felt betrayed by dependence, and in consequence, still experienced the hostility that went with his dependent love for his mother and for Mildred. He described as "cold and sarcastic" his general attitude toward women. He kidded them a lot, as his father kidded his mother. "I like to treat women," he said, "as a very odd class of individuals. I think it's for the sake of humor, but I guess at times I can get a little too sarcastic, a little too embittered, and with women who like me I am very cold." He was aware that he kept women "at arm's length," and for the time being he did not really want to do otherwise.

Relations with Men: Willing Listener

Kidd's self-consciousness and submissiveness in the presence of men continued to bother him when he entered military service. He still found it difficult not to "act like a son or kid brother" if a man showed him friendship. But he began to find a solution to this problem.

> During the service it began to disappear more or less. I found that in getting occupied, staying occupied, things worked out better. If I drove a truck all day, eight hours a day, I felt better that night. I wasn't thinking about myself, everything seemed to disappear, I could get out of the truck and talk to these fellows without suffering any complexes. That all seemed to disappear, and I just went ahead with what I had to do and what I had to say. It was plain work, it was activity, just keeping the mind occupied.

Work and the suppression of self-conscious thoughts made it possible for him to feel more like a man among men. As we have seen, his self-confidence and power of assertion increased rapidly while he was in the army, though he remained unable to accept the responsibilities of leadership.

Strengthened by these experiences, he became able, on his return, to improve his relation to his older brother Mike. He still perceived a wide difference between them—himself too sensitive and too fearful of giving offense, Mike too blunt, assertive, and inconsiderate —but he no longer judged this difference to be wholly in Mike's favor. With two men friends he and Mike made a foursome at golf nearly every Saturday morning, and Joseph played a basically better game than his brother, though he sometimes envied Mike's relaxed slam-bang methods. Joseph began to realize that Mike held him in real respect; he asked his advice, suggested that they might go into business together, and expressed disappointment at Joseph's plans to go elsewhere in search of his fortunes. A considerable burden of inferiority feelings was lifted from Joseph's shoulders by this development of the fraternal relation. His grief was painful and enduring when his brother's career was cut short by a fatal illness.

Alcohol was of some importance in helping Kidd's social adjustment. When he was in the service it played a part not unlike activity and hard work; it freed him from self-consciousness and allowed him to feel on equal terms with the other men. After the war he met alcohol wherever he went, and he often drank more than he wanted simply because everyone else was doing so. Although alcohol had contributed to his poise and self-confidence he viewed it as a possible danger. People told him that he drank too much, and he was sufficiently impressed to make a test of his power to restrict his drinking. He was pleased to discover that he could control it, that he was by no means in the grip of alcohol; but there remained a certain conflict between his desire to go along with any crowd and his desire to curtail alcohol "very definitely and, if possible, finally."

Kidd's relationships with men began to assume a characteristic pattern more rewarding than the old confused submissiveness. It was his particular pleasure to get them to talk, and he developed no little skill in the role of encouraging listener. He preferred to make them talk about their work, so that he could learn more about life without entering controversial realms. If political questions came up, he took part in the discussion, though he doubted whether people were much open to conviction on politics. He found it difficult to express and support consecutive opinions of his own. His technique of argument consisted rather in drawing out the opinions of others and then picking them to pieces. What he liked best, however, came to expression when he was asked to associate to the phrase, *I admire*:

> I admire intelligent people who can talk about their field, most especially if they are in a field involving people. I like to sit down and talk with somebody about their business, question them on it from different points of view and find out anything and everything I can.

Kidd then described a man in his middle thirties, a confirmed alcoholic, whom he sometimes met at the apartment of the "divorced girl."

I never enjoyed talking to anybody so much in my life, in spite of
the fact that he was always somewhat under the influence. He was
always very intelligent. He knows and understands people, a very
effective talker. Nobody else down there liked him too well, but I
would invite him in if he walked by the apartment and offer him a
drink and then talk to him. He wasn't interested in talking to me
too much; he was interested in the liquor and the food. He was a
very smart fellow, very enjoyable, worldly-wise. He had been around.

Further light was shed on this type of relationship by his associations
to the phrase, *when people meet me*:

I still have a tendency to a very small extent to exhibit some of those
traits of embarrassment or feeling of inferiority which plagued me
for as long as I can remember . . . I used to be very uneasy, then less
and less as time went on, and today I'm probably one-tenth as uneasy
as I was.

Asked if he experienced the uneasiness with any particular type of person he said:

People I would probably like to be, probably a well-built, good-
looking, clean-cut fellow, very personable and very easy. . . . Probably the easier he is with people in general, the uneasier I would
feel. . . . If he was sympathetic and kindly towards me, then I felt
very much easier and could get along with him. But it was lacking
probably the traits which I definitely lacked and saw in him that
made me uneasy, overanxious, or something like that.

In these excerpts Kidd made it clear that he was working on
the problem of identification. He wanted to be like these admired figures, to have their good looks and masculine self-confidence. The core
of his difficulty in their presence lay in the feeling that he compared
unfavorably with them. By getting them to relate their exploits and
exhibit their "know-how," he possibly felt a certain sharing of their
strength, and he was constantly storing up images of how he himself
would like to behave in future situations. Kidd's ideal image of himself had the earmarks of an overcompensation for past inferiorities. In
his actual behavior—his willing listening—he seemed inclined to settle
for vicarious satisfaction rather than copying his models. We know that
he had become much more capable of assertion than he used to be, and
it is therefore legitimate to assume that his relationship with men—a
compromise between an ideal image and his actual preference for easy-
going agreeableness—represented a stage of adjustment that is not incompatible with growth.

Plans for the Future

Kidd's life was easy but dull. For the most part, there was little to do in the morning. Almost every day he could sit down after breakfast to read the paper, or practice golf strokes, or do setting-up exercises. He resumed his piano lessons at a popular studio, and he spent several hours a day at the piano, partly practicing, mostly picking out tunes. His duties as business assistant were often discharged by half-an-hour's work when the mail came in, though sometimes he shared with Peter the more time-consuming work of preparing floral decorations for an important occasion. He no longer felt under pressure at home, but he got bored with that small world and generally left in the afternoon, taking his evening meal outside in the company of friends.

This routine was by no means satisfactory to him. "I don't like this life," he said, "I don't like it because it's too comfortable a racket. I hope I'll be able to do a day's work when I go out and get another job, which I plan to do in the very near future." He expressed the fear that if he did not get out soon he might never take that step. He did not in the least like the business.

> I think there's too much sham connected with this business. . . . The money is good, the hours are good. Another thing about it is that it calls for no ability and very little initiative, and you accomplish very little. You do a job, you make money. You've got nothing to show for it when the job is done. Your work is thrown away the next day.

He wanted to prove that he could work and make his own way rather than live off his father's business. But he had also developed, chiefly through the building of the flower studio, a need to exercise his growing power to deal with poeple and to have his efforts issue in substantial accomplishments.

At the time of our interviews Kidd had reached a definite decision to leave home within a few weeks. He thought he would start by taking any available job, but as soon as possible he would try to find the kind of thing he really wanted to pursue as a vocation. The thing that appealed to him most was the idea of owning and operating a public golf course. Although capital for the investment was lacking, he knew that certain ventures of this kind had proved profitable, and he liked the idea of building up a golf course into a "big, beautiful place, as much a credit to myself as it would be a money-making enterprise."

His visits to golf courses had given him ideas about improvements that he was eager to embody in a course of his own. He was impatient to set forth in search of his vocation, but at the same time he was prey to certain misgivings. Repeatedly in the interviews he returned to the subject, and we could see that it awakened deep conflict.

One element in this conflict was a hesitation to give up the pleasures and comforts that went with his present life. "I would always want to be able to enjoy life," he told us. "If I couldn't be more than a street-sweeper or laborer, where eight hours of your waking day is spent only in making money, I think I would go on the road as a hobo so as to enjoy life." He liked golf, bowling, playing the piano; he would someday "like to take up sketching and probably painting." "Those things are time-consuming," he well knew, "but I hope that I will always have the time." In the hour devoted to free association he discussed his music and golf as follows:

> I want to be able to play the piano well both because I enjoy it and I know what a useful social factor it is. But I do enjoy it myself. I can spend hours alone with it; some people may call it a waste of time, but it's an achievement, something I get my mind occupied with, doing something progressive.

> Golf is the first sport that I . . . first time I remember wanting to do well, to go out of my own way to achieve a knack, a degree of success, and I like the game. I can go out and play it by the hour, by myself, and I also know that it is a good and a useful social medium, and I would like to achieve a certain reputation. I would like to succeed in becoming a good golfer, putting a lot of time in it, and a lot of money in it, and a lot of patience in it. I want to continue that, too.

As business assistant to his father, making a comfortable living by working ten or twelve hours a week, he had plenty of time to pursue these interests. The privileges of his life thus offered stiff competition to his desire for independent achievement in a vocation of his own.

The difficulty of Kidd's decision was shown in the fact that he talked about it in almost every interview. It also appeared rather plainly in his imaginative productions. Two of his stories in the Thematic Apperception Test dealt symbolically with determinism and freedom, handled in such a way as to suggest that determinism meant the expectations of others and freedom meant the urges within himself. In both cases freedom was triumphant. One hero, for example, stood on a hill looking back on the foggy, dirty mills from which he had escaped. "He is free from a rigidly patterned, heavily pressured existence, where gradually his daily routine is more and more taken up by what he is required to do; all those demands on his time and physical and mental processes." The source of this imagery would seem to be Kidd's conflict with family ideals: on the one hand, the pressure to spend all his time studying so that he might fulfill parental aspirations; on the other, the freedom he felt with the neighborhood boys before puberty and with his comrades in military service. The mills meant home, school, homework; the hilltop meant escape from the home. Yet in the current situation his images had to be almost reversed. Staying at home guaranteed an extraordinary amount of freedom, whereas setting out to find a career carried grave risk of having to go down into the mills and submit to demands on his time and thought.

Equally confusing was the reversal that had taken place with respect to moral degeneration, a theme common in his earlier stories and not absent from the current set. One story, for example, told of a man going down hill to moral abandonment because he chose friends and performed acts "very much against what he had been taught, what he had been given, and what he was capable of." Reacting against these imposed ideals, "he wound up a drunkard, a criminal, and eventually died a very sick and broken man." This is the old familiar theme that we previously guessed to be a reflection of Kidd's inner struggle during the high school and college years, when his urge toward freedom became so entangled with hostile and sexual fantasies that he experienced it as dangerously degenerate. Now, however, the danger of degeneracy lay in remaining at home, where his evening rovings exposed him too often to the temptations of alcohol. Kidd's conflict could not be solved by reviving the imagery of his earlier ones; it could only be confused.

The truth of the matter would seem to be that Kidd, belatedly rejecting the pressure of parental aspirations, had begun to develop along two lines and had reached a point where the lines necessarily diverge. He had developed along the line of doing pleasant things, such as music, bowling, and golf, thus restoring contact with his own inclinations and following paths of natural interest. He had also developed along the line of assertiveness, gaining a certain assurance in knowing what he wanted and getting what he wanted from others. With the latter trait was associated an increased sense of the satisfaction to be derived from accomplishment and the leaving of creditable monuments. The pleasant side of life could best be served by remaining where he was, business assistant in an exceptionally easy and lucrative occupation. The goals of assertion and achievement could be reached only by breaking away, which meant taking chances, courting anxieties, and possibly not getting anywhere in the end. Kidd was unwilling to settle for the easier way without at least attempting the steeper path. This was partly because he had tasted the satisfaction of independent effort and achievement. It was partly for another reason: he could not wholly abandon the hope that he would some day justify his early promise and prove to be the outstanding member of his family. The character of this motive is well displayed in one of his associative sequences. When asked to associate to the phrase, *I secretly*, he responded with a candor that was exceptional even for him:

> I kind of secretly wish to be a renowned success. Probably more renowned than successful; in other words much like a movie star or politician or some other public figure whose reasons for renown aren't very concrete. I wish that perhaps to . . . well, to show the girl that I once loved and who since left me and married somebody else . . . try to make her regret . . . and perhaps to show the people and the public in my past that I am what they thought I was. . . . It's more of a revengeful success rather than a . . . a . . . so that they might say, I'm sorry, I'm sorry for what I did to him or . . . and I probably would like to see them regret very much what they did or what they said.

In this astonishing piece of insight we are shown an added reason for the importance of Kidd's conflict. No doubt the motive of revengeful success urged him forward; there had been much pain and humiliation that it would be pleasant to assuage. Perhaps this motive also added to his misgivings: only a quite dramatic success could truly accomplish the purpose. We must bear in mind that this "secret" fantasy of revengeful success was not unconscious. Kidd told us about it. That it held him in an irrational grip would be a decidedly arbitrary conclusion. It was one of the elements, nevertheless, in a very difficult conflict.

Opinions about Public Events

When we knew Kidd as an undergraduate, he was not in the least interested in public events. If pressed for an opinion he was likely to respond with a borrowed verbal sentiment, which often sounded strangely at odds with his actual behavior. Being at that time rebellious against religion, he nevertheless trotted out with approval all the conventional moral and religious precepts of his parents. He declared himself in favor of severe legal restrictions on the sexual behavior of unmarried people, and he opposed the idea that young people should have a knowledge of contraceptives. His mildly liberal views on the social order gave equal evidence of borrowing. He was clearly still working out his problems in a personal sphere and was unprepared to transform felt values into attitudes on public questions.

When we sought his opinions at the age of twenty-nine, we found them still to be less clearly formulated than was the case, for example, with Hartley Hale. Kidd continued to exhibit mental traits not highly favorable to building up a consistent political philosophy. Although good at detailed observation, he shied away from general ideas and preferred to operate in a factual, concrete fashion. He did not enjoy being questioned about his views. It was hard, he protested, to come right out cold with what you believed on a subject; he preferred to get the other person talking, reaching his own views in the form of criticisms as the conversation proceeded. Although he regularly read a paper and a weekly news magazine he seemed to have little knowledge that was quickly available for use in discussion.

Kidd's failure to reach consistent opinions was exemplified in his discussion of birth control. The state ballot in the last election had carried a referendum on this issue, and it was certain that he must have heard many hot arguments, yet his exposition was so full of contradictions that he himself finally admitted: "I haven't formulated any definite ideas on that subject." It became clear that he believed in the right of the Church to take an active stand on birth control. This enabled him to present several of the Church's arguments with respect to the referendum. What he had not worked out was his own relation to the Church; he therefore could not decide whether he stood ready to defend these arguments. Living at home, he sometimes went to Mass to please his parents, but he did not count himself a good Catholic. "I don't believe in the Church's strictest measures," he said; "I'm one of those guys who thinks that they don't apply to me but they should apply to certain other groups in society." A little later he declared flatly: "I don't believe in the commands of the Catholic Church." Yet his rejection of the Church had not inspired him to formulate an alternative philosophy.

I don't have many set principles that I live by. I mean I'm not too ethical in any morality or in regard to finances. I think that if I saw the chance to beat somebody for a large amount of money I probably would do it. I think if I found a wallet in the street, I doubt if I would return the money. I certainly believe in living and let live. I mean, I believe in the truth. I wouldn't perjure myself. Right now I wouldn't anyway perjure myself in order to obtain anything. I can't say what I don't mean. I find it a little difficult to sell somebody something which I don't believe in myself, no matter what the game might be.

Neither community activities nor politics held any appeal for Kidd. "I don't think the average fellow gives a darn about community activities," he said, and he expressed sharp distaste for the community in which he was living. His sole venture into politics consisted of helping the campaign of a man he considered dishonest, a man for whom he refused to vote when it came to marking his own secret ballot. This man held a city position that allowed him to dispense the favor of engaging Mr. Kidd as floral decorator for public banquets, and it thus qualified as good business to support his election campaign. "I've been hanging around politics enough to know it and appreciate it," said Kidd, "and I don't think I like it."

His views on wider political questions seemed to have swung in a conservative direction since the earlier studies. "I've become a staunch Republican," he said; "the Democratic party in power today has garnered most of its backing from Labor, and is very partial to anything Socialistic." One of his most stable opinions proved to be a violent antipathy toward labor unions, which he perceived as exploiting the economy without performing any genuine services. He was also against business monopolies, and thus emerged as the champion of the small independent businessman—the person he would like to become. For the next Republican party platform he proposed "definitely less government spending, and decrease in the income tax." He would hesitate to cut the Social Security program even though "many lazy, improvident derelicts" benefited by its provisions; but otherwise he favored the smallest possible government interference with free individual enterprise. In the international sphere he perceived Communism as the outstanding evil. He had once read a Communist book and found some of the doctrine appealing, but he felt that this doctrine was now being used as a cynical cover for power politics. Recognizing the need for "more teeth" in the United Nations, he balked at the thought of our surrendering more sovereignty. He also rejected the idea of building up the developing nations, a course that could only result in competition for markets and a lowering of our standards of living.

In his opinions Kidd thus stood a little to the right of Hartley Hale. His views were not out of line with those of many Americans around 1950 whose fears and angers were centered on Communism. His political outlook was heavily dominated by an imagery of exploitation. The groups he opposed were characterized as exploiting the average citizen, the small independent businessman, for the sake of profit and power. Kidd's sensitivity to exploitation may well have had personal roots. During adolescence he came to feel exploited by his parents, believing that they cared more for symbols of success than for him as a person. But he was also tolerant of his own exploitative tendencies as these emerged in sexual adventures and in minor rackets during military service. We must recognize that the outspoken theme of exploitation and easy money in Kidd's philosophy was not a personal invention. In considerable part he was shaped in this direction by the social class and ethnic environment in which he was reared.

Kidd grew up in a neighborhood of Irish Catholics, most of whom were not more than a generation removed from peasant life in the old country. His own parents were typical: the mother an immigrant, the father a child of immigrants. The neighborhood was not a disorganized one, by no means a slum, but it was more self-contained and less oriented toward upward mobility than would be the case in the average lower-middle-class community. The ambitions that prevailed in the Kidd family thus set them off from their neighbors; not one family in a hundred tried to send its children to college. Kidd described, almost in traditional stereotypes, the "lazy Irish" of his neighborhood: the women gossiping over their tea, the men content with a day's pay and a corncob pipe. Cohesiveness was provided by the common ethnic background and the common religion. Some of the more enterprising men, however, had established a virtual control over local politics. Everyone had a friend in the city government, and everyone expected that the bonds of friendship would be cemented by financial favors. Kidd's father by no means held himself aloof from this kind of activity and clearly prospered by it. Kidd's own outlook on the nature of success and the ways to achieve it thus did not markedly diverge from the one that prevailed in his early surroundings.

PART THREE: FROM TWENTY-NINE TO FORTY-THREE

Fourteen years after the second study Joseph Kidd was asked whether or not he would be willing to grant a long follow-up interview. It is easy to imagine that a man of forty-three, established in life and absorbed in a variety of enterprises, would be disinclined to resume even briefly the status of psychological subject and rake the ashes of personal history. Fortunately Kidd was not of this mind. He told the story of the intervening years in the painstaking and insightful manner that had made his earlier communications so useful to students of personality.

This new information is the more valuable because at twenty-nine his life history was decidedly in mid-air. Then an uneasy bachelor, he is now married and the father of four children. Then a temporary assistant in his father's business, in sharp conflict over his proper occupation, he is now well established in a line of work for which he took additional training. Then a willing listener seeking to form himself in the image of assertive men, he has now made himself a place in political life and found great satisfaction in public speaking. The transformations have been in some instances so large that it will tax us to detect their continuities with past history, but this makes them all the more useful in illuminating the natural growth of personality.

At the end of the second study Kidd had made a definite decision to leave his father's business and start a career of his own. His feelings over such a step were in such deep conflict that the outcome could not easily be predicted. Kidd acted upon his decision, however, and took a position as a salesman. In preparation he received two weeks of training in another city, learning about the product, which was a specialized one to be sold to business firms. The job was financially promising, but after two months he had had enough of it. Approaching prospective clients, developing an effective sales technique, explaining the uses of the product, and building confidence in it, all proved to be too much of a strain. He felt that the training offered by the company was not sufficient for so difficult a task of marketing, and he returned the materials and resigned his post.

This experience did not tip the scales in favor of staying in his father's shop. If anything, the initial optimism made him more aware of the force of his need for an independent life. Conscious of himself as a college graduate—"The public doesn't forget it, either"—he was oppressed by a feeling of shame over failing to establish himself in a manner worthy of his training. Of this feeling he said, "you conjure up a good percentage of it yourself," recognizing that his own pride was involved as well as the expectations of others. Accordingly the search for employment continued, including trips to other cities from which friends had written about possible openings. He now realized the importance of finding something with a future, where one could "see it from beginning to end" and thus start the construction of a permanent occupational identity. The opportunity came when a family friend with business connections steered him to a position in a large industrial organization located in Springfield, Massachusetts. It was not what he had expected or planned, and at first he felt himself a misfit; he even "suffered tortures" because of "the predicament of having gone to Harvard." But soon he found the work interesting, and he was attracted by the chances to move upward in the hierarchy of positions made relatively secure by promotion and tenure policies. Everything was sharply competitive at his level, but he prepared himself by hard evening study for a specialized type of appointment, passed his examinations very well, and rose to a position near the top of his section, with a salary that he described as "comfortable" and with virtually permanent tenure only months away.

In discussing the meaning of this career Kidd did not minimize his initial difficulties, nor did he overlook his good fortune in the fact that the organization was beginning a period of rapid growth. He believes that he might not have stayed on but for the influence of one man who was in charge of the section. This man represents "everything I would like in a father." Kidd described him as at times "rough" and "overbearing"; at first he did not like Joseph and was slow in procuring his advancement. But he is a "great man" who "sincerely has the company at heart," bringing new ideas into the office and making it "a living, breathing thing." Through this man's efforts the organization has not only grown but in Kidd's eyes has been upgraded: "There are ten or twelve Harvard graduates there now." Commenting on his own experience, Kidd mentioned the satisfaction of having a definite position or status, "of knowing where I stand" and of having others know it. Fortified by this status he believes that "I could get almost anything I want." He is glad to recall that he earned promotion in open competition with others, but his satisfaction in his work comes from a less crude source. "Gradually," he says, "I came to be looked for when there was trouble. . . . After you are known, they come to depend on you, lean on you, respect you."

Readers of the two previous studies may experience surprise that

Joseph Kidd, once so erratic, so driven by emotion, and so painfully uncertain of himself, should emerge as a man of conspicuous stability in
the eyes of others. But it is not incongruous that a person who has been
acutely dependent can become remarkably effective in supplying strength
once he has managed to achieve it in himself. Kidd's fear and hatred of
others, and his once prominent feelings of inferiority, have long since
dwindled, leaving him with the asset of readily understanding such feelings in other people. When he visits the company's branch offices, where
the central office is viewed as a sort of bully making irritating demands
for paper work, Kidd is aware that "you can't order them"; you have
to "get along," "bend, sway," "accommodate," "persuade." These
reassuring tactics change the atmosphere and allow the men to seek the
help that in fact can come only from the central office. Kidd feels that in
meeting new people he can tell quickly how to treat them. The promotional work that makes up part of his duties calls for "insight and respect for the reactions of your fellow men," and he enjoys the occasions
when he has accomplished some task with skill and good judgment.

How did Kidd succeed in developing the necessary strength in
himself? In his own account he fully recognized the influence of role
expectations. He goes to the outlying offices as a superior officer, secure
in the knowledge that he is so recognized, and this frees him to behave
in the friendly, helpful, yet gently authoritative way that is ideally suited
to the circumstances. But we must still take cognizance of a definite
advance over the time when, promoted to officer status in the army, he
found it intolerable to be "over" others rather than "with" them. Kidd
has discovered the way to be both. He has done so because this time
he has not been pushed into superior status by someone else's favor; he
has earned the position by the intelligent use of his own capabilities,
and he experiences it as part of his effective self. To the strong and necessary support of occupational status we must add, in order to understand his gains in confidence, that he is capable of delivering the goods.
He enacts the social role with ability and with his own creative touches
—he is far better than Hartley Hale in dealing with subordinates. It
was indeed a turning point in his life when he left his father's business
and started his own career in a large organization.

Recalling Kidd's earlier views on labor unions, it was something
of a surprise to hear that he had not only joined a union but served
two terms as its president. This testifies to an increase in his understanding of issues that were not plain in his father's highly individualistic
business. It also adds to the evidence that he inspires confidence and is

respected as a man of initiative and intelligence. But the most surprising testimony to these qualities in Kidd comes from his successful venture into local politics, which has given him the greatest satisfaction of anything he has done. In the small western Massachusetts city where he now resides he decided to run for the city council. He had met a good many influential citizens on the golf course, and he knew that there was a substantial Catholic vote which still lacked representation on the council. He put on a campaign, assembled a group to work for him, had telephone lines buzzing, got his name in the papers, and did everything to put himself before the public. "It parlayed, it worked out," he said: the morning after election showed that he had run high enough in the popular vote to give him a seat on the council.

The triumph was the greater because Kidd had run as a Catholic and a Democrat in a community where Republican Protestants had long been dominant, and he was thus regarded as a sort of maverick. Almost abashed by his victory at the polls, he went to the first meetings of the council prepared to "sit at the feet" of the more experienced older members. "I was probably too prone to hero worship," he said, and assumed that these must be great men who decided how to run the city, but he was "surprised to find them ordinary human beings," riven by rivalries and captured by cliques. Soon he was enjoying it all; in retrospect he could say, "I enjoy people who hate me and abuse me more than ones who like me"—a far cry from the irresistible need to be loved by which he was victimized during his college years. Before long he began to win respect as "determined, dedicated, and able." When he took initiative it was generally successful, and he takes pride in the fact that "some things are living and breathing now because I started them." "I have learned," he said, "how to react, meet the public, and above all get something done." The roughness of a political campaign, especially the criticisms of unfriendly newspapers, had on occasion sent him home "on the verge of tears"; but now, twice reelected, he is no longer sensitive in this way and has developed a "thick skin." He has the great satisfaction of knowing that he is "a person of note and prestige" in the city.

When asked what forms of activity had contributed most to the growth of confidence he replied without hesitation, "Public speaking; it's great therapy, I've recommended it to younger people." Recalling that Kidd was accustomed in early childhood to being shown off, that when self-respect declined he felt ashamed at notice from others, and that as a willing listener he greatly admired people who could talk with assurance, we can understand that being able to show himself off, so to speak, with a confident flow of words based on his own knowledge has a great deal of symbolic resonance. He has also gained a reputation as a skillful writer of reports, memoranda, and articles for the public press. He is frequently urged to do more of this and to help those who have trouble with writing.

In the second study we saw Kidd beginning to assume the role of the stable and responsible member of his family. When he supervised the building of the new flower studio he shouldered the family cares, and the success of his endeavors doubtless encouraged him to extend the responsible role into wider spheres. In the meantime he has become the family's Rock of Gibraltar: "Whenever anything happens they call me." If a brother or sister contemplates marriage, if the house needs repairs, if his mother is nervous about going to the doctor, if his cousin has another bout with alcohol, Joseph is promptly called to give counsel and lend support. The father continues to be useless in emergencies, and the son is called upon to fill his shoes.

Up to this point Kidd's story of fourteen years deals largely with success. When we turn to his marriage we discover that he is not intoxicated by success: he recognizes clearly the shortcomings of his family life and spares himself no blame. His interest in the girl he married began shortly after the second study. She came from a somewhat superior social background, and the friendship was not viewed with favor by her parents. As can easily be predicted in view of Kidd's strong prior conflicts between being in love and being free, the courtship was a stormy one with much passing back and forth of the ring. It was further complicated by her becoming involved in an affair with her married employer, who saw her merely as a "soft touch" and took advantage of her relative lack of sophistication. She soon regretted this episode, but it added to their strife, throwing Kidd into a state of turmoil and a renewed use of alcohol that caused him to lose whatever credit he had built with her parents. "I didn't have my own feelings," he said, "I had misgivings that I should give her up, but it was hard to think of living without her." So they were married, but it was "the worst type of lead-in" and a poor prelude to marital happiness.

The marriage has not been, Kidd admits, "particularly happy—idealistic would be a better word." He enumerates his wife's good qualities: she is a "good girl," "fine," a "comfortable companion" who has "no aggression," "keeps a nice house," and helps with his political activities. He describes her also as "withdrawn" and as having "no drive or zeal for accomplishment." In the previous study he specified that a wife should have strong interests of her own, but the function of these interests was to keep her from making demands on her husband's time, and it does not appear that his wife errs by making such demands. His political activities have persistently kept him out of the house and left few evenings for the family. Reflecting on his feelings, he says, "The specter of her affair still has a significant place in our relation; I can't honestly completely forgive her for it." But it seems to him that there is something more.

> Some guys can live for a woman. That I absolutely cannot do. It's been a good enough life. I can give her money, conversation, prestige, but I can't give the thing she most wants, which is me. I don't know, I just can't. It's not only a weakness, but a failing. I can't give it to the children, either. I don't know whether another type of girl could have changed that, but I don't regret it myself, but it's not a healthy climate for the family.

Kidd's difficulties with his children have clear roots in the less happy aspects of his own childhood. Particularly with the boys he is concerned that they should not be denied what he himself did not have—the role model of a good, capable, loving father. He wants the boys to "be the type to give this to," and is irritated that they seem not to be. He blames this on their having a feminine environment of mother and sisters, which has usurped the father's place and is "not conducive to male strengthening." But he is quick to recognize his own part. "I rebel at dependence on a father," he says, wishing in retrospect that he had been forced out to learn for himself. "I hate to see children around adults, probably because I was on show, so I generally shoo them out of the way." He shuns the Parent-Teacher Association and refused to intervene when one of the boys complained about his treatment by the Little League coach—there is to be no repetition of the double promotion which Kidd experienced as so disastrous in his own childhood.

This is the side of life that has not developed for Kidd in a natural and happy fashion. Because he was late both in marrying and in finding a vocation, his present position in life is in some respects comparable to that of Hartley Hale at thirty-three, and it is interesting that in both cases, though obviously for different reasons, the interests of career tend to take precedence over those of family. In Kidd's case it is not hard to appreciate the depth of personal meaning that is associated with his career. When one has passed through a childhood and adolescence beset by conflicting demands and devastated by feelings of inferiority, the discovery that one can be respected, effective, and to a degree self-directing is bound to produce profound satisfaction. Kidd comments on his "tremendous urge to experience, to succeed, a drive to be accepted," and he regards "suppressing self-expression" as something "horrendous, terrible, preventing you from doing what you want." If the last phrase sounds like an anticlimax, it is not so for Joseph Kidd. At twenty-one he felt himself driven hither and yon by imperious emotions and irresistible social expectations; at twenty-nine he had only a slight acquaintance with intentions and purposes proceeding from himself; only at forty-three has he attained confidence that "what you want," the plans and desires that emerge as truly your own, can be of real consequence in your life and your environment.

PART FOUR: FROM FORTY-THREE
TO FIFTY-FOUR

By any definition fifty-four years puts a person in the period of middle age. On meeting Joseph Kidd eleven years after the follow-up interview, however, it was not at once easy to think of him as a middle-aged man. His hair, still abundant and curly, was only slightly peppered with gray, his walk was springy, he had gained hardly any weight, and he thus continued, as earlier, to look younger than his years. Nevertheless it was soon apparent that the problems facing him were in many ways characteristic of later middle age in American life. In several respects his circumstances were unchanged. He was living in the same place, and his work and family life were continuing as before. But the children were growing up: the two eldest were already in college, and the two younger ones would soon reach that costly stage in education. For a man on a middle-range salary, putting four children through college is a formidable task. In addition, Kidd's political fortunes had ebbed, so that for the time being, at least, he saw no prospect of regaining that influence in the community which meant so much to him eleven years earlier.

After serving on the city council for several years, Kidd was defeated by a few votes for reelection. He was soon involved, however, in a heated community controversy over the public schools. The issue was whether to put up new, splendidly equipped school buildings, incurring many years of debt, or more economically to refurbish the buildings already in existence. Kidd became a prominent figure in the group that favored the latter course. He felt that those who wanted a lavish building program were careless of the future tax rate and heedless of statistical projections showing that the pupil population was unlikely to increase. A three-year battle was carried on, with proposals, counter-proposals, special meetings, and questions on the city ballot, all of which called for intense partisan activity. Under needling from Kidd's party the big spenders reduced their proposals by more than half, but the voters rejected even this in favor of economical rebuilding. The next year, however, the question was resubmitted and a somewhat larger plan was adopted, involving, in Kidd's view, considerable waste of money. Asked if this still might not be regarded as a partial victory, he said, "I hate partial victories." Furthermore, at the height of his success he had again run for the city council and again been defeated.

These setbacks undoubtedly reduced his chances for a further career in politics, but they also undermined his desire for one. Though he had some "good experiences" in public life, he thinks in retrospect that there is "very little to show for it." Personal satisfaction came from feeling trusted by his fellow citizens, yet he sometimes thought he was being stigmatized as a "sucker." Campaigns were always expensive, and although friends helped with modest contributions he wonders, in his disappointment over the results, whether they exerted themselves to go to the polls. At all events he is planning no further political activity. An invitation from the city librarian to write up his version of the school controversy affords him a little consolation, providing a chance to "leave something behind."

Freed from political obligations, Kidd has more time for his family, but "re-entry into family life" has proved difficult. For years he has been "just the guy who came home and raised hell at night," and it is not easy to achieve closer participation. Giving voice to what he recognizes as a far from novel thought, Kidd says that after a day's work "you need a few hours to yourself" with a chance to sit down and have some drinks. The tired businessman sinking into his chair is in no mood to share the excitements and hear the complaints of his children's day. If his wife joins him for drinks, this may only make matters worse. "No woman knows how to drink," he generalizes, and alcohol sometimes loosens in his wife "a sharp sarcastic tongue which I can't stand." Very likely he feels that his political failures have shrunk his prestige in the family circle. He himself "shed no tears" over lost elections, but "the kids took it to heart."

Kidd reproaches himself especially for not being around enough while his eldest son was growing up. Young Joseph had "emotional problems" in grammar and early high school, including "poor contact with other kids." These were problems that Kidd could well understand, but in his preoccupation with politics, which took up most of his evenings and most of his strength, he was able to be no more helpful than his father had been a generation earlier. Without paternal assistance the boy "achieved his identity" in congenial activities and groups at high school, after which he became "strong-willed" at home, so that there were scenes in which tempers were lost. A crisis came when the son wanted to leave home. Kidd and his wife wisely decided to let him live with friends for the summer. Having had this holiday from parental supervision, he returned to make home his base while attending college.

These descriptions do not signify that Kidd finds nothing but frustration in home life. When there are irritations they are often mentioned first, but further conversation discloses that Kidd has an enduring feeling of satisfaction about his family. He describes his children as "straight all the way through," and he gives his wife credit for being close to them. He reports with satisfaction that none of the four has been mixed up with drugs; he is pleased that they are such "good kids, acceptable, presentable." The parental regime has not been permissive—"they have to be in at sensible hours"—yet it is flexible and tempered by sympathy. When the girl at college had trouble with her roommates, Kidd gave her the money to come home for a short holiday, though he could ill afford the expense. Bothersome as his family may be, it evokes his caring and is a source of pride.

This is the more important because of a serious deterioration in Kidd's relations with his family of origin. At the time of the earlier follow-up he was continuing the role he had assumed by building the flower studio: he was a source of strength, consulted in time of trouble. But we must now assume that this role was made possible largely by his mother, for after her death there was a rapid disintegration into rivalry and strife. Especially galling was an episode in which Kidd found a bargain in a much desired domestic investment and needed a short-term loan which his father agreed to provide. His next brother, hearing of this, went to their father and persuaded him against the loan. Kidd was extremely angry, the more so, no doubt, because this felt like reduction to his earlier painful position as the out-of-favor son. "The act was deceitful and debasing," he declared, "to be expected only in the combat zone." At all events he has not seen this brother nor his father for ten years. Describing his relatives with such blunt words as "thief" and "drunk," he makes it clear that they have ceased to have value in his life. The situation is no better with his wife's parents. Never pleased with Kidd, they now rarely come to the house, and telephone conversations between mother-in-law and son-in-law quickly turn into quarrels.

Financial problems have done much to embitter these relationships. Kidd's father, having retired and sold his business, is "sitting on" a large sum of money which will go eventually to his children. Kidd's wife's father is sitting on a still larger sum while supporting a lavish life style, and he has refused to touch his capital for the benefit of any of his sons-in-law. Kidd wants money not for himself but for the children. His own tastes are simple: "Just give me a few drinks and some people to talk with and occasionally go some place." But he is committed, as were his parents, to the goal of giving each child a college education. Considering present costs and his current salary, this means saving, skimping, sacrificing, borrowing, and limiting the choice of colleges to those that are less expensive. "The need is now," he says; "money is to be used and moved." One can understand his resentment that money destined to come some day to him and his wife cannot be drawn upon at the time of greatest need.

His job continues to supply interest and security. The business is a stable one, modest salary increases can be expected, and if he stays with the company he will ultimately benefit from its good pension policy. In spite of boring paper work and in spite of occasional bureaucratic interferences the job is interesting, and he continues to enjoy especially his relations with his chief subordinates in the branch offices. He still finds opportunities for public speaking and for technical writing, his skills which are a source of pride. Evidently his knowledge and ability are respected in the company so that for the most part he works with relative independence. At this point, however, there are no glittering prospects. He has gone about as far as his training permits, and there is no reason to expect marked changes of status. Perhaps on this account he toys with the idea of joining some small business venture, where his interest in marketing and advertising might give some little known product a profitable sale. The novelty and excitement are appealing, but do not blind him to the risks. He is realistically aware of the responsibilities of the family provider. He wishes that things might break for him as they did for his sister's husband, whose father set him up in business and then helped him to make the business prosper. This is added reason to deplore the impounded capital of his own older generation.

The interviewer was surprised, though less so than before, to learn that Mildred had once more entered Kidd's life. Unhappily married, in her late forties she again reached out to her former boyfriend, and for the next eight months they met frequently at motels, "making up for the chastity we had sacrificed for in our six years of going together." During one of their trysts he said, "Mil, I should have laid you thirty years ago," to which she replied, "Joe, you'll never know how much I wish you had, and at that time wished you would." The affair ended amicably: in Kidd's words, "we are now the best of friends, meeting socially only two or three times a year."

When the interviewer reminded Kidd that his life history had been studied by many readers who may well have been helped to understand their own problems, his mind flew back to his troubled adolescence. In a recent discussion with friends, agreement had been reached that they would hate to live again through that tortured period of life which involves "coping with sex, social balance, peer achievement, and the disillusionment in testing taught values." After adolescence his own development, as we have seen, took a more favorable course, so that he presently discovered important capabilities in human understanding, speaking, writing, political campaigning, and business administration. But our lives are never independent of circumstances, and at fifty-four Kidd has lost access, at least for the time being, to the arena of politics and community service which had provided him with substantial satisfactions. His diminished scope, combined with his mounting financial pressures, makes this period of his life difficult. It is noteworthy, however, that under this stress he does not go to pieces as he did during adolescence. He can be discouraged and resentful, but there is no return to the indiscriminate self-blame, conviction of inferiority, and disorganized behavior that were so conspicuous at eighteen. His gains have been securely won, and he faces his current problems with a good measure of mature objectivity and fortitude. The natural growth of personality does not necessarily go into reverse because conditions are hard. Sometimes it even works the other way.

6

THE
BIOLOGICAL ROOTS
OF PERSONALITY

Our theme is Nature and man as part of Nature.

C. S. SHERRINGTON

Up to this point we have made no attempt to relate the study of lives to any basic theory of behavior. We have considered our cases as people rather than as organisms, which means that we have studied them in the complexities of everyday human life without trying to reduce their behavior to fundamental mechanisms. In this chapter it will be our purpose to bring personality into line with the *biological view of man*. We tried in the fourth chapter to see what could be learned from the social sciences; here we shall examine some of the leading ideas that come from research in biology and experimental psychology. The first impression will probably be that we have jumped to an entirely different realm of discourse. We were talking about lives; now we suddenly shift to the elementary mechanisms of behavior, abstracted from all those personal patterns that characterize human beings as we know them in daily life. If the climate seems to change, however, it is all the more important to trace the route by which the two realms are connected. Basic mechanisms somehow produce the behavior of physicians or businessmen, and it is one of our most vital tasks to understand how such things come about.

Central to any fundamental theory of behavior are the concepts of drive and of learning. The first concept is used for the active or energetic characteristics of an organism, the second for its plasticity in meeting the environment. These concepts carry us straight into the question of innate endowment. The biological view of man requires us to think about the essential structure and equipment with which each individual embarks upon his career of learning. It bids us consider that individuality arises not only from a unique history but also from the starting attributes of the person who lives that history. When we take this point of view, we cannot arbitrarily stop with drives and the capacity to learn. Other qualities, such as energy-level, mood, and temperament, play an important part in human life and require consideration as possible elements in natural endowment.

The Problem of Innate Endowments

It is a misfortune that the discussion of endowments has often strayed from the open fields of science and lost itself in the brambles of politics. Human nature has been made the scapegoat for many a program of exploitation. A martial instinct has been invented by those who wanted war. Competition and the profit motive have been declared inescapable human traits by the interested advocates of a cutthroat economy. The inherent stupidity of the average man has been used to justify seizure of power by dictators and cheap propaganda by demagogues. Innate racial inferiorities have been invoked to cloak political oppression and economic discrimination. In the nature–nurture controversy there has been a tendency for nature to keep bad company, while nurture has more often walked with those whose sentiments were humanitarian, democratic, and optimistic. The misuse of ideas about heredity has sometimes been so fantastic and savage that it is hard not to reject the whole notion with angry contempt, taking one's stand for a purely environmental theory and raising the flag for a doctrine of absolute innate equality.

It is our business here to draw the nature–nurture controversy firmly back into the realm of scientific discussion, where the taking of stands and raising of flags give precedence to a careful scrutiny of facts. Our task is to examine the character of innate variations for which there is acceptable evidence. Such variations should not be taken as an affront either to the humane spirit or to democratic principles. If there are real differences of tempo, style, and ability, they should be respected; each individual should be encouraged to learn and to live in ways he experiences as congenial. And a democratic society is better equipped than any other form of social organization to maintain respect for the individual, to help each member make the most of his endowments, to provide scope for different patterns of life, and thus to make beneficent and constructive use of human variation.

From what is known today about the mechanisms of heredity we would expect to find each individual uniquely endowed. When the germ cells of two parents unite, only a part of each parent's potentialities can be utilized in forming the new individual. The forty-six chromosomes initially contained in each germ cell become reduced by half, so that the new life receives only twenty-three from each side of the family. The selection depends on biochemical conditions that are very complex in character. There is scarcely a chance, however, that the resulting individual will be precisely like any individual who has ever before existed. The mechanism of heredity provides for a reshuffling of genes on each new occasion, and thus creates a degree of novelty every time a new life is begun. Two children of the same parents are apt to be more alike than two children of different parents, but they are never quite alike and often seem remarkably different even from the moment of birth. The babies in a maternity ward might be taken to the wrong mothers if an inattentive nurse shuffled the tags, but they would rarely be mixed because of a difficulty in telling them apart. Only identical twins enjoy the distinction of being hard to tell apart.

The mechanisms of heredity thus seem designed to produce unique individuals. Each person has his own profile of variations, some small and some great, from general averages. The next thing we would like to know is the precise nature and extent of these variations. Are they important enough to influence the course of individual development and to limit significantly the impact of environmental forces? Aware as we are today of the vast importance of learning, sensitized as we are to the influence of social forces, we have to approach this question with a wholly new sophistication. What is required is a conception that specifies the effects of any general trait on the lifelong process of learning. If innate peculiarities are important, it is because they consistently color the individual's response to his environment and thus produce significant slants in his life history. The understanding of such effects thus benefits from the study of individual lives.

Constitutional Traits

Human beings are adept at telling one another apart. Friends recognize each other promptly even after many years of separation, in spite of real changes of appearance that result from growing older. The cues to this striking power of recognition lie largely in stature, shape, facial features, coloring, vocal timbre, and other qualities that can be grouped under physical constitution. Some of our bodily characteristics are strictly individual and remain so throughout life.

Physique At the time when Hale and Kidd were first being studied, Sheldon had just developed a systematic method of measuring the components of *physique*.[1] This method involved photographing the body from three angles at a standard distance and using the photographs for a large number of precise measurements. On this basis Sheldon concluded that three main components account for the principal differences in physical structure. The first component contributes elements of softness and roundness to the body form; the second has to do with bone, muscle, and connective tissue; and the third favors lightness, slenderness of frame, and quick, alert motion. Each individual has something of each component, the minimal possible score being not zero but one. Each individual is likely to have a definite accent on one or another component, with a possible top score of seven. The three figures that represent the strength of each component are referred to as the *somatotype*. The perfect average, equality of the components with a somatotype of four-four-four, turned out in practice to be a relatively rare combination. With respect to physique there is great individuality.

Applied to our subjects, Sheldon's standard measures yielded for Hale a somatotype of 2–5–3½, for Kidd a somatotype of 4–5–1½. Both are highest, though not remarkably high, on the solid muscular component of physique, but Hale has a somewhat more wiry build whereas Kidd is a little more softly rounded. Sheldon believed it

[1] W. H. Sheldon, S. S. Stevens, and W. B. Tucker, *The Varieties of Human Physique* (New York: Harper & Row, Publishers, 1940).

possible to predict from somatotype a variety of behavioral and temperamental traits. According to his scheme, both subjects would be predominantly active, energetic, and assertive; but Kidd's display of these qualities would be tempered by a certain easy-going amiability and pleasure in human contact, while Hale's energy would be more nervously restless and tense. The description may seem to hit off Hale fairly well, but it gives the wrong impression of Kidd, especially during his college years when his tension and ineptitude in social relations sound more like a person high in the third component. The prediction from somatotype fails precisely at the point where it goes beyond organismic qualities to social and emotional behavior which lie open to environmental influences. Energy, strength, placidity, alert responsiveness, even initiative are believable expressions of constitutional endowment, but there are limits on what we should expect to predict from physique.[2] Our subjects, however, are not disembodied essences. Their physical characteristics had an influence on their lives.

Hale's physique was a crucial item in the dramatic "backbone incident" that set him on his way to self-confidence in physical competition. From this point onward he "grew stronger," as he himself put it, winning respect as a neighborhood athlete, finding bold friends whose example helped him conquer his anxieties, strengthening his social confidence by alliance with an ever-widening circle of acquaintances. Without athletic prowess he would probably not have become the most popular member of his high school class. Hale's physique thus permitted him to do certain things that would have been difficult if not impossible for a less robust youngster, and these things elicited a variety of social responses that further enhanced his feeling of confidence.

But Kidd also was physically robust. He rates as high as Hale on the muscular component, and at the outset he seems to have shown considerable assertiveness. In elementary school, before he began to feel the effects of his unfortunate double promotion, he could disturb the classroom by wild behavior; and with his playmates he was often ready to show himself a capable fighter, a notorious vandal, and a leader in adventurous enterprises. This pattern did not survive the miserable social situations and emotional problems in which he became involved in later childhood and early adolescence. Because he

[2] For a description and evaluation of Sheldon's work, see C. S. Hall and G. Lindzey, *Theories of Personality*, 2d ed. (New York: John Wiley & Sons, Inc., 1970), Chapter 9.

was so much with older boys, his natural physical prowess could not be used advantageously to win success and earn respect. It became a wasted asset, and the course of his social development was much more shaped by the roles of clown and stooge and by the force of his dependent love for Mildred. Yet we should not overlook his report that he still found relief in violent exercise like playing a fierce game of hockey in the biting cold. Such an outlet would probably not be sought by youths of comfortably plump or tensely fragile physique.

Activity Level Not unrelated to physique, though it has been studied in a different way, is the variable of activity level. Differences in the amount and force of motor activity can be measured even in newborn infants. These differences tend to remain stable. The quiet newborn turns into the quiet baby whose sucking is gentle, who may doze during feeding, who lies peacefully when put down, and who makes only small motor response when startled. The active newborn becomes the vigorous feeder, full of restless movement, who twists and squirms during diaper changes and kicks off the blankets when in the crib. Prediction from behavior in infancy to behavior at ages three to five have shown that the later activity level is correctly guessed for two-thirds of the children.[3] Using longitudinal studies made at the Fels Institute, Kagan and Moss comment on the stability of the trait of passivity throughout the childhood years. When the Fels subjects were restudied as adults, however, childhood differences in passivity were predictive for girls but no longer for boys.[4] This lack of continuity in the males may well result from social pressure toward activity as part of the masculine role. Activity level tends to be a somewhat stable, persisting trait, but it is not immune to social shaping forces.

The amount of activity displayed by an infant begins at once to affect social interaction. Mothers respond differently to active and passive babies. At the start the active ones may seem more responsive and appealing, but with the successive appearance of crawling, running about, and exploring the neighborhood, passivity may appear to be the

[3] S. K. Escalona and G. Heider, *Prediction and Outcome* (New York: Basic Books, Inc., 1959). The most detailed study of activity level is S. K. Escalona, *The Roots of Individuality: Normal Patterns of Development in Infancy* (Chicago: Aldine Publishing Co., 1968).

[4] J. Kagan and H. A. Moss, *Birth to Maturity* (New York: John Wiley & Sons, Inc., 1962), especially Chapters 3 and 9.

greater blessing.[5] Later social interactions continue to be colored by degree of initiative and assertiveness. During their school years Hale and Kidd provide a marked contrast in his respect. Hale's initiative contributed greatly to his social success, particularly in high school where his activities as an editor, stage manager, and general entertainer were at least as important as his athletic prowess. Kidd during the same period played a relatively passive part in social interactions; his roles in the group were those of clown and stooge. Then, as later, he seemed ready to let the other person fix the character of a relationship. Counteracting this submissive tendency and learning to get what he wants from other people has been for him a belated and difficult development, and in his fifties he is still more apt to be tactful and persuasive than bluntly assertive. Kidd describes himself as having been more assertive as a young child; his late childhood and adolescent social passivity bespeaks frustrations and anxieties rather than compelling natural endowment. But he well illustrates the difference, in contrast to Hale, between passive and active social experience.

The American cultural emphasis on competition and active mastery, applying with special force to males, tends to make high activity a virtue and passivity a deplorable vice. As we have seen, these cultural valuations have somewhat diminished, yet there is still a tendency to look upon social assertiveness like Hale's as healthy and commendable, while Kidd may be put down as unduly inhibited. We should therefore keep in view how well the moderate and gently persuasive social tactics ultimately developed by Kidd fit the important situations of his adult life. He can understand another person's point of view in a way that might always be closed to someone who placed unfailing confidence in his own point of view.

Control Versus Disruption Another important variable which may reflect natural endowment shows itself most obviously in situations of stress. There are large observable differences in people's capacity to maintain order and control under circumstances that threaten to disrupt behavior. To mark off the extremes we can compare astronauts, who coolly repair failing apparatus while hurtling through space,

[5] For a vivid description of highly active children and different parental ways of dealing with them, see S. Chess, A. Thomas, and H. Birch, *Your Child Is a Person* (New York: The Viking Press, 1965), pp. 41–43.

with short-fused commuters, who blow up when the percolator fails or when the car starts badly. Over longer periods of time the difference manifests itself in power to resist distractions, endure boredom and fatigue, and cope with discouragement; it is thus related to success in the pursuit of important plans and remote goals. The variable has been described in different ways, such as deliberation versus impulsion, stability versus emotionality, reflection versus impulsivity, ego strength versus ego weakness. Its exact nature is difficult to pin down and measure; furthermore, control of all kinds is acquired in the course of development and is therefore encouraged or discouraged by circumstances. Nevertheless, the differences have appeared in a large number of researches done by various methods, and they seem to be relatively stable.[6] Common observation certainly suggests that cool-headedness is a stable trait that looks as if it were at least partly born rather than made.

Hale's unusual power of control appears consistently throughout the stressful events of his life. In the "backbone incident" he learned not only that he could win a fight but also that he could force himself back to the battleground, preserve a brave front, "bore in with verve," use his fists effectively; in short, that he could control the inroads of anxiety. Earlier he had managed to control the guilt feelings that marked his rebellion against maternal interference. Later he was able to overcome his fears of moths and water. He controlled the emotions engendered by parental quarrels without becoming a model child. Almost always he controlled his anxiety before athletic contests and turned in a first-rate performance. He can control intense anxiety when a difficult piece of surgery threatens to go wrong, continuing to work with fine motor coordination and mental alertness. Hale is a man who does not easily go to pieces; neither motor nor mental control is readily disrupted by emotional stress.

In contrast, Kidd appears to have been more readily swayed by his emotions. This was conspicuously true at the time of the first study, when consecutive effort of any kind was disrupted by his accumulated feelings of inferiority and guilt. He described unhappiness, desperation, and states of mind in which all effort was immobilized so that he sat staring into space. A decade later he successfully managed the

---

[6] See especially H. J. Eysenck, *The Structure of Human Personality*, 3d ed. (London: Methuen & Company, Ltd., 1970) ; and R. B. Cattell, whose work is conveniently summarized in Hall and Lindzey, 1970, Chapter 10.

difficult project of building the new studio, but he was often upset and restless, sought advice excitedly, and felt "very, very relieved" when a knowledgeable person told him how to go ahead. Kidd has developed into a relatively stable middle-aged man, but control seems never to have come as naturally to him as it did to Hale.

This sampling of constitutional endowments by no means exhausts all possibilities, but it is sufficient to suggest that biological individuality makes a contribution to natural growth.

Abilities

Intelligence Of all human abilities intelligence is the most carefully studied. Unlike constitutional traits, which are essentially diffuse in their effects, intelligence can be brought to a focus in problem situations and subjected to. fairly precise measurement. The measuring of intelligence has been a major concern of psychology ever since the publication of Binet's first scale in 1905. Mental tests were originally devised to sort out school children who could not keep up with their classes. It was an obvious step from this to the sorting out of both duller and brighter men in military selection and assignment. The army group tests, developed in the United States during World War I and given to more than two million men, provided tremendous impetus for the further study of intelligence. At first it was supposed that intelligence was a unitary trait, so that a person could be assigned an overall score without further remark about individual peculiarities. Now it has become routine procedure for examiners to report the qualitative characteristics of each person's performance as well as the overall score. Each person uses his mind in a somewhat individual fashion. Why he does so sets a challenging problem for the student of lives.

Measurement is an important step in scientific advance, but what the measures mean is not always beyond controversy. During the heyday of intelligence testing, it was generally assumed that differences in intelligence were largely a matter of innate endowment. Furthermore, the tests with their many varieties of items were assumed to be broad enough to cover intelligence as a whole. Both assumptions have been severely challenged. Typical IQ tests turn out to be somewhat specialized measures of school aptitude; as McClelland has said, "the games people are required to play on aptitude tests are similar to the games teachers require in the classroom." Examining a good deal of recent evidence on the subject, McClelland concludes that intelligence tests are predictive only of school grades and that school grades are hardly at all predictive of success in later life.[7] Even this more limited aspect of intelligence, moreover, no longer looks like a simple expression of hereditary endowment. Experience has a good deal to do with the growth of intelligent behavior; and the circumstances of early life, especially the kinds of stimulation and opportunity they provide, undoubtedly contribute to later scholastic success.[8]

In view of these findings it is unfortunate that school grades and scholastic aptitude scores are respected so highly and used so heavily in personnel selection. They have this status partly because they are measured—the numbers are right there on paper—whereas other aspects of competent behavior have to be left more to inference or deduced from the life history. Dailey has advanced the argument that the choice of people for jobs should depend entirely on an examination of life histories; what a person has previously done provides the best-rounded information about what he will do next.[9] In the compound of qualities that leads to successful life performance, intelligence is only a part, and scholastic aptitude is only a part of intelligence.

Relatively neglected in the attempt to measure intelligence as a whole was the question of qualitative differences in intellectual functioning. People with equal IQ scores may use their minds habitually in quite different ways. Some do picture puzzles with effortless speed, while others simply do not see the shapes that will fit together. Many a gifted mental worker cannot replace a burned-out fuse or drive a car with real skill. Sometimes a person who readily grasps the complexities of party government will balk at fairly simple arithmetic, while an expert in mathematical physics will lapse into confusion when confronted by political issues. It has been repeatedly found that some people score much higher, others much lower, in the *verbal* part of an intelligence test as compared with the *performance* part. There is a

[7] D. C. McClelland, "Testing for Competence Rather than for 'Intelligence,'" *American Psychologist*, 28 (1973), 1–14.

[8] J. McV. Hunt, *Intelligence and Experience* (New York: The Ronald Press Company, 1961); *The Challenge of Incompetence and Poverty* (Urbana, Ill.: University of Illinois Press, 1969).

[9] C. A. Dailey, *Assessment of Lives: Personality Evaluation in a Bureaucratic Society* (San Francisco: Jossey-Bass, Inc., 1971).

similar tendency toward independent variation between the *verbal* items and the *numerical* items. These preferences may have an innate basis or they may be products of experience, but they exhibit stubborn persistence. Many young people have responded to the appeal of a career in medicine only to find that their minds, excellent in other directions, fumbled hopelessly with the peculiar intricacies of organic chemistry. Sometimes a change of vocation is required to provide relief from the frustration of having to use one's mind in an uncongenial way.

Individual Patterns of Intelligence Our understanding of these problems can be deepened by again consulting Hartley Hale and Joseph Kidd. Both men were given the Wechsler-Bellevue Adult Intelligence Test; Hale's IQ was 130, Kidd's 118. Closer inspection shows that Hale's advantage was largely in the performance part of the scale. His IQ on performance subtests was 126, compared to Kidd's 107, whereas his IQ on verbal items was 133, as against Kidd's 126. It is interesting to note that Hale's near equality between verbal and performance scores is more typical of engineers than of medical men, who on the average display a greater verbal predominance. He is, of course, something of an engineer—his attic workshop and his research testify to that—and he cares little for psychiatry with its predominantly verbal tools; but it will be recollected that his attainments include the writing of books. Hale's total score places him in the top one percent of the general population, and it is well in line with his successful academic career.

Kidd's score on the Wechsler-Bellevue Test raises more difficult problems. It suggests a level of ability that would make his college career a hard one, and it is thus consistent with his actual performance in college. But when we gave him the Wells Alpha Examination, a test better suited to discriminate at the upper levels of intelligence, he came out with scores that were higher than the average for Harvard College students. Which result is to be believed? Generally in such cases one credits the better performance; if the subject can do it at all he must have the capacity to do it. One would certainly assume from the Wells Alpha score that Kidd would be able to make a good record in college. We know, of course, about the emotional problems that stood in his way, that probably interfered grievously with his use of intellectual capacity, and that might even tend to depress some of his scores on tests of mental ability. But we have not yet fully explored the qualitative aspects of the two men's use of their minds. This leads to some interesting discoveries.

As an example of qualitative differences we shall first examine performance in the Vygotsky test. In this test the subject is offered a variety of small blocks and required to divide them into four consistent categories. The problem cannot be solved by using the more obvious principles; there are too many colors, for instance, and too many sizes and shapes for a fourfold classification. The correct solution is much more complex, and it is generally reached by college subjects only after much trial and error and a certain amount of prompting by the examiner.

Hale found the solution a little more quickly than Kidd, but our interest lies particularly in the way the two men worked at the problem. Requested to think aloud as he worked, Hale verbalized a series of clearly formulated hypotheses. Some of these he rejected merely by inspection; others he tried out by working with the blocks. His procedure can be described as *conceptual* in that he formulated principles and tested them out mentally before trying any random experiments with the blocks. Kidd's approach was very different. He seldom worked with a well-defined idea; rather, he placed the blocks in tentative arrangements, as if he felt that by fully exposing himself to their perceivable properties he would eventually see the solution. This procedure can be called *perceptual*. Although it sounds less efficient, the perceptual approach is just about as good as the conceptual in solving the Vygotsky problem, as it is in many of the problems of everyday life. Too stubborn an attempt to conceptualize, too little account of the properties of the blocks, can easily lead to failure in the test. Kidd reached the correct solution, but it is of interest that even when he did so he experienced great difficulty in formulating the general principle behind his classification. He described the four groups but fumbled badly when it came to stating the higher abstraction. Many subjects prefer the perceptual approach but can easily conceptualize the result once they have achieved it. Kidd found real difficulty in taking this final step.

The difference shown in the Vygotsky test is consistent with results from other procedures. Kidd's scores were well below Hale's in those subtests of the Wechsler-Bellevue that are most conceptual in character. The same difference is apparent in everyday life. In a political discussion, for example, Hale's views are clearly formulated, more or less fixed in advance, and pronounced confidently with little regard for what his listeners may feel or know. Kidd starts with no opinions, and he prefers to make other people talk so that he can reach his own conclusions from the material they put before him. Again, in procuring mechanical apparatus Hale decides what he wants and goes out to get it, if not to make it, while Kidd collects information from everyone and then decides what he wants. But the moment we start to follow this difference through its ramifications in everyday life, we become aware of its striking resemblance to the consistent trait difference we examined in the previous section. Kidd's intellectual approach to things is marked by a much greater passivity. He tends to open himself fully to the promptings of the material but hesitates to exert himself in the direction of active mastery through conceptualization and logic. Hale attempts from the start to dominate the material, trying to align it with preconceived ideas, highly conscious of the organization he is seeking to impose. But the very phrases we use to characterize intellectual procedure serve also to characterize the social procedure of the two men. Kidd's use of his mind reflects his more general trait of passivity; Hale's thinking shows the assertiveness that colors all the rest of his behavior.

These findings reopen the question of the origin of Kidd's passive tendencies. Is it plausible to suppose that the inhibition of social initiative by anxiety would spread so far as to produce passivity in intellectual operations? Should we infer that Kidd after all differs widely from Hale in temperamental endowment with respect to initiative and assertion? We have to be satisfied not with solving the problem but with seeing it. Qualitative differences in the use of intelligence need further study before their possible relation to variables of still greater generality can be discerned.

Other Types of Ability Of the many other kinds of ability in which people differ we shall mention only two. The first example is *manual dexterity*. Probably there are potential differences in the facility with which this asset is acquired, but the process of acquisition is an exceedingly long one. It starts with the baby's manipulation of the objects within reach. It receives practice in the nursery-school child's cutting with scissors and in the elementary-school activities of writing and drawing. Increasingly it becomes caught up in larger patterns of interest or of disinterest. Joseph Kidd did pretty well on dexterity tests, and his history showed isolated instances of skill, such as picking the trunk locks at camp and making good drawings in biology courses, but manual dexterity had very little significance in the main interests of his life. For Hartley Hale, in contrast, this kind of skill became increasingly important with the passage of time. He needed it for his mechanical interests, for building radio sets, for wiring the lights in school plays, then more and more in his biology courses and experimental work, until finally it became an essential element in his career as a surgeon. Hale constantly used his hands in finely coordinated work; a huge history of practice lies behind today's manual dexterity.

Even more complex is an attribute such as *mechanical ability*. Perhaps Hale had natural gifts for this kind of thing, but we have also noticed that he received, in contrast to Kidd, considerable encouragement during early childhood. When he started to build radios it was in the company of similar-minded friends; an overlap began between mechanical and social interests. This overlap increased during his career as a stage manager in high school. In the course of time mechanical ability became an integral part of his special attainments, his claim to distinction, and his ideal image of himself. It was inextricably caught up in his central interests and values. Meanwhile he had accumulated a tremendous amount of useful related information. He possessed a seasoned knowledge of electricity, for instance, long before he needed to use complex electrical devices in his medical research.

Most adult abilities, then, have to be conceived of as the end product of several conditions that have influenced the history of learnings. At the start there must be sufficient innate facility with the needed activities, and early circumstances must be such as to encourage them. Very important is the extent to which the activities then become incorporated in a larger pattern of interests. When their importance to the person becomes enhanced by such an association, they are almost certain to receive more than average further practice and to bring about the accumulation of stores of relevant knowledge. It is this end product of developed skill, interest, and "know-how" that constitutes the contemporary ability, whatever its biological roots in tissue endowment.

Motivation

The motivation of an adult human being is rarely simple, but there is often an obvious starting point for describing it. With Hartley Hale, for instance, we have no trouble in anchoring the account immediately in his powerful desire for a successful career in medicine and scientific research. His ambition, with its strong future orientation, supplies a key to understanding a great many of the actions that make up his daily and yearly life. His professional career has become, moreover, the largest channel for a variety of other needs, such as his dominance, his curiosity, and his pleasure in mastering mechanisms. If a description of adult motivation is even to approach adequacy, it must give full recognition to the *channels and personal pattern* of motives.

The trouble with this kind of description is that it seems to have almost no connection with biologically basic drives. Except for references to sexual life and to anxiety, our story of Hale's adult motivation appears to make no contact with the drives that are generally set forth as the fundamental springs of animal and human activity. Yet we are clearly not dealing with an abstraction. Hale's vision of career and of his developing professional roles are right at the operational level, affecting almost all of his major decisions and a good many minor ones as well. Indeed it is when we apply abstractions that we become separated from the operational level. The need for achievement, a valuable abstraction that has been the subject of abundant research, is certainly strongly developed in Hale; but his form of it does not prompt him to select patients according to their wealth, to start profit-making enterprises as a businessman might do, or to stand for elective public office as was done by Joseph Kidd. At the operating level Hale's need for achievement has to be given a description that specifies channels and pattern.

Basic Motivation: Drives If there is continuity between man and animals, however, the drives that are of such great importance in animal behavior must have relevance for human motivation. The concept of drive seems particularly appropriate when it is possible to specify bodily states of tension or deficit that produce marked heightening of activity, together with end-situations or supplies that restore a state of rest. Considerable agreement has been reached as to the list of these physiological determinants of animal behavior:

hunger and thirst, sex and lactation, the need for oxygen, elimina-
tive needs, and the avoiding of pain and extremes of temperature.[10] In
human beings the impact of these drives is to some extent mitigated by
socially organized, civilized arrangements for preventing their arousal
or providing ready means of satisfaction. But such arrangements can
never be complete, and the drives must be viewed with respect as
forces in the growth of personality.

This does not imply that they continue to act in their primitive
form, unaffected by the history of learning. Unusual hunger and thirst,
to be sure, can produce strong preoccupying images of food and drink
together with strenuous efforts to obtain these supplies. The sex drive
also has a way of entering imagination with relatively crude fantasies.
Freud's discoveries led him to conceptualize the sex drive as a continuing source of energy behind the dreams, daydreams, defense mechanisms, and neurotic symptoms revealed in his patients. But such
findings do not warrant a wholesale "nothing-but" conclusion: that
adult personality is nothing but a thicket of self-deceptions concealing
crude animal strivings. Learning produces not just a false front but a
real development of motivation. Motives can be learned, and the
learned ones can become the real forces that influence subsequent
behavior.

To take a relatively simple example, there is general agreement
that *dependence* is a strong motive in early childhood and often a
problematic one in later life when it becomes decreasingly appropriate.
But dependence is not a basic drive. It is an acquired motive, learned
in the situation of infantile helplessness when most of the basic drives
are being satisfied by human agency. Once acquired, it no longer depends upon high states of arousal of the basic drives. The disappear-
ance of the helping person, or even the absence of human company,
becomes highly unpleasant even if the child is not hungry or physically
distressed. In adult life, as we saw in Kidd's case, dependence has to
be considered a social motive with little relation to the basic needs that
caused it to be acquired. Kidd makes himself a willing listener and
seeks advice from others regardless of the state of his biological drives.

Basic Motivation: Other Forms Not all the biologically basic
forms of motivation fit the concept of drive. This becomes apparent

[10] S. P. Grossman, *Essentials of Physiological Psychology* (New York: John
Wiley & Sons, Inc., 1973).

when we reflect that the sensori-neuro-muscular system is composed of living tissues which have the particular function of maintaining effective contact with the environment. This system has often been described as if it were an inert mechanism that conducts the business of drives only on demand. Even so, its service lies in appraising the conditions that prevail in the environment so that drive satisfaction will be sought in timely and appropriate ways. It is a short step to suppose that the nervous system might have an interest, so to speak, in learning about the environment for its own sake. A clear advantage in terms of survival would appear to lie with a creature that spontaneously explored and manipulated things, building up out of sheer curiosity a certain knowledge and skill in dealing with the environment; this prior competence might well make the difference between life and death in a crisis provoked by hunger, thirst, or external danger. But we need not rely on speculation. Observation of young animals and children reveals a great deal of playful, manipulative, and exploratory activity that seems to go on without the instigation of drives. These activities are done for the fun of it, but they serve a serious biological purpose. Part of the fun can be described as a *feeling of efficacy*—or sense of mastery—and the biological purpose is clearly the attaining of *competence* in dealing with the environment.[11]

To conceive of this striving as a drive is apt to create confusion. It appears to originate in the nervous system itself rather than in other tissues. It does not follow typical patterns of drive arousal and reduction; it shows as a more or less continuous activity while the animal or child is at peace with his drives but still wide awake, and it subsides only with the gradual onset of fatigue. Nevertheless, the frequency and persistence of such activity in children entitles us to rate the need for efficacy as a fundamental motive that is highly important in the growth of personality. This need provides a broader basis for being interested in things than is implied in the concept of drive. The point can be illustrated by thinking of Hartley Hale reading a medical book. By radical reductive analysis we can interpret this act as an expression of drives for sustenance, sexual satisfaction, and protection from harm and anxiety; it is part of his career, and according to drive theory these are the biological roots of all careers. But such analysis hardly tells us

[11] R. W. White, "Motivation Reconsidered: The Concept of Competence," *Psychological Review*, 66 (1959), 297–333; R. S. Woodworth, *Dynamics of Behavior* (New York: Holt, Rinehart and Winston, Inc., 1958), Chapters 4 and 5.

why Hale reads the book if its contents are not needed for immediate application, nor does it show how he keeps his mind on his reading if the satisfaction of the drives is so indirect and remote. What keeps Hale interested is something much closer to the activity itself; he enjoys the feeling of efficacy that comes from increasing one's mastery of an area of knowledge. This is, of course, not all that is involved in human interests, but it greatly improves our power to understand what keeps people absorbed in enterprises for their own sake. There are ways of being quite directly interested in things even when drive satisfaction is a remote contingency.

Another form of basic motivation that fits with difficulty into the drive concept is the propensity toward aggression. We all recognize this propensity as our most serious liability in civilized living, and its effective control confronts us as a never-ending social problem. Surveying aggression throughout the animal kingdom, Johnson comments on the human "difficulty in living harmoniously with nature and with our fellow men," and on episodes in human history that manifest "unspeakable violence and brutality."[12] In comparison with other animals, he shows, the human animal seems more rather than less given to violence, and technological progress increases the power to destroy. The evolutionary role of aggression—its survival value for its possessors under primitive conditions—is not hard to imagine. In the presence of frustration, the aggressive response consists basically of a mounting output of energy against the frustrating obstacle, accompanied by anger and physiological mobilizing for strong action. Some observers believe—and Freud with his "death instinct" was among them—that the extent of human malignity implies deep springs of aggressiveness which overflow without external provocation. Whether or not this is true, the large part played by frustration is not open to doubt.[13] One might speculate that natural selection has left us with a lot more aggression than we know what to do with when trying to lead civilized lives under conditions that are no longer primitive.

In individual behavior, frustration is likely to start as a challenge to competence. What is directly obstructed is some sequence of acts in progress, and the first threat is to one's feeling of efficacy in

[12] R. N. Johnson, *Aggression in Man and Animals* (Philadelphia: W. B. Saunders Co., 1972).

[13] J. D. Carthy and F. J. Ebling (eds.), *The Natural History of Aggression* (New York: Academic Press, Inc., 1964).

carrying out these acts. This suggests one way in which aggressive behavior can be reduced through learning. In the treatment of children given to tantrums and senseless violence it is valuable to show alternative ways of dealing with frustration, ways which are more effective and increase the child's sense of competence without being socially disruptive.[14] But the control and channeling of aggression in individual behavior is inevitably a difficult problem. Growing up in a family where another child is the permanent favorite, or growing up in a subgroup that is subject to lasting discrimination, leaves little room for efficacious action and creates chronic resentment that may be destructive to other aspects of development. If anger is too heavily suppressed by early intimidation, all forms of assertiveness may be inhibited, leaving submissiveness and conformity as the only safe alternatives. These and other problems in hitting the right balance are discussed in the light of experimental evidence in a thoughtful paper by Staub.[15] Great as is the human tendency toward violence, there are other propensities in human nature that can be enlisted to promote altruism, goodwill, and forms of social organization that enhance justice and human rights.

Social Motives As development proceeds in its human environment, the individual acquires a variety of motives with respect to other people. As in the case of dependence, these motives are not rooted in any one biological tendency; they arise because the response of the human environment is important for all biological tendencies. People have properties in their own right, ranging from loving and stimulating to aggressive and intimidating, and one's dealing with them becomes a matter of great personal significance. In a systematic description of needs, Murray listed a variety of social motives such as affiliation, recognition, dominance, nurturance, exhibition, deference, and abasement.[16] While there are large individual differences in the strength and pattern of these needs, there can be no doubt about their

[14] A. E. Trieschman, J. K. Whittaker, and L. K. Brendtro, *The Other 23 Hours* (Chicago: Aldine Publishing Co., 1969).

[15] E. Staub, "The Learning and Unlearning of Aggression: The Role of Anxiety, Empathy, Efficacy, and Prosocial Values," in J. L. Singer (ed.), *The Control of Aggression and Violence* (New York: Academic Press, Inc., 1971), Chapter 4.

[16] H. A. Murray, *Explorations in Personality* (New York: Oxford University Press, 1938), Chapter 2.

importance. To win praise and acclaim, to receive a high income of esteem, may yield vast satisfaction and may even become the chief goals of a person's life. To be rejected as a failure or a disgrace may come to be felt as a fate worse than death. How one stands in relation to other people, how secure one is able to feel in one's human environment, has been given the central place in at least one theory of the development of personality.[17]

Channels and Personal Patterns When we try to describe an individual case and understand what is "really there"—what effective forces are actually operating—it proves necessary to specify motives in great detail. True as it may be that Hartley Hale and Joseph Kidd both strive for recognition, we cannot properly understand the history of this striving or its present mode of operation until we describe the specific interests through which it seeks expression. Hale early ceased to seek recognition for his athletic ability; Kidd continued for some time wanting to be recognized for his golf. Hale specifically strives for recognition as a physician and scientist, and he wants that recognition to come from fellow physicians and fellow scientists. Whatever spread his need for recognition may enjoy in fantasy, it gives a strong push to behavior only along specific lines. Kidd's need became channeled into his business role and particularly into acceptance by the voters of his community.

This specifying of individual motives leads us to important insights. In the course of life, urges become increasingly channeled into particular kinds of action and interest. As these channels develop, energy is withdrawn from other kinds of action and interest that originally seemed perhaps equally alluring. An analogy can be suggested to what happens when water is poured on sloping sandy ground: small streams push out in several directions, but when one of these finds the best downward route its channel is quickly deepened and the water drains out of the other streamlets. But this process of finding and discarding channels is not the only thing that happens. Simultaneously there is a gathering of different motives into more inclusive spheres of action and interest. Almost all important human concerns represent an integration of numerous motives, which come to a focus on a specific interest or work together in an available social role.

Kidd's former interest in operating a public golf course can be taken as a case in point. It was to be a way of making money. It was a "white-collar" job, or, more accurately, a "sports-shirt" job, which fitted his status aspirations. It would make room for his interest in playing golf and attaining distinction along that line. It would allow relative freedom with his time. It would provide opportunities for pleasant sociability and for the willing listening which he then found so satisfactory. In picturing such an occupation Kidd sensed that it would provide channels not for one main motive but for nearly all his important strivings. Needs become channeled in the course of development, but they also become absorbed in larger patterns of interest and concern.

These ideas about motives do not make for simplicity of conceptualization. The constant crisscrossing of drives, interests, and sentiments has suggested to Cattell the concept of a dynamic lattice.[18] Probably nothing less simple can be of any assistance in studying motivation as it occurs in the individual case. We shall not pursue this concept in detail; rather, we shall use a single example to illustrate what difference it makes to conceive of motives as being involved in a dynamic lattice.

To raise the issue sharply we can take the relation between Kidd's sexual and his social behavior. A strong basic drive is involved, and according to Freud's theorizing this drive determines the character of social relations. We have noticed that Kidd, who felt a strong barrier to sexual gratification with the object of his affections, was powerfully driven to find casual partners for hit-and-run escapades. Does this represent a straightforward expression of the sex drive? Kidd himself held a less naive theory. When he called sex a "shunt for my drives" he was recognizing, in principle, that his evening adventures were part of a dynamic lattice. He was saying that more than the sex drive was involved. The pattern included proving masculinity, demonstrating bold assertiveness, and thus shoring up his shaky self-esteem. It included, we can infer, a way of forgetting irksome school work, family pressure, and the difficulties of social adjustment. It provided an agreeable if temporary anaesthetic for chronic distress. Many motivational channels fed into Kidd's adolescent sexual pattern.

Freud's way of thinking can also be applied to another aspect

[18] R. B. Cattell, *Personality: A Systematic Theoretical and Factual Study* (New York: McGraw-Hill, Inc., 1950), pp. 157–162.

of Kidd's social behavior: his submissiveness and passivity in relation to men. Assuming that social attitudes are heavily determined by the sex drive, the hypothesis would be that Kidd's way of relating to other males depended upon passive homosexual inclinations. Certain of his remarks can be taken to indicate an erotic coloring to his submissiveness. His masturbation at puberty seems to have begun with a passive attitude of both body and mind, and he did not at once associate this pleasure with an active sex role. He reported that older boys sometimes liked to put their arms around him; reciprocally, he felt a strong admiration for clean-cut, good-looking fellows, and he was particularly likely to become flustered, uneasy, and self-conscious in their presence. On the other hand, Kidd was aware of no erotic interest in boys or men, and he had rejected with mild distaste, yet with no apparent anxiety, the homosexual advances that occasionally came his way. Thus he was not overtly homosexual, and the hypothesis has to be that the urges were unconscious. This is possible, but it hardly argues for a simple drive explanation. From earliest years Kidd was shown off for his good looks and encouraged to take pleasure in being admired by others. The development of his own assertiveness was blocked when his double promotion put him in the company of bigger boys, with whom only submissive roles such as stooge and clown seemed possible. Whatever else was involved, it seems clear that Kidd's submissiveness served to avoid the anxieties of competition and to draw such trickles of esteem-income as the situation permitted.

The study of human motivation is rarely a question of matching current behavior with biologically basic drives. The long process of learning lays a complicated trail. Needs are drawn into particular channels of expression, and they are combined into patterns according to personal interest and social role. The importance of primary drives should never be overlooked; as Krutch once said, "whenever man forgets that man is an animal, the result is always to make him less humane."[19] We can add that when he forgets he is a human animal he is also likely to make himself less humane. Being a human animal implies precisely the complications, the channels, the social needs, and the personal patterns of motivation that have been described and illustrated in our two subjects. In the human animal the end products of learning are unlikely to fit a convenient scheme of abstractions; they

[19] J. W. Krutch, *The Twelve Seasons* (New York: William Sloane Associates, 1949), p. 186.

are forever stamped with the impress of individual histories. So we cannot escape the task of describing adult motives as contemporary systems of interest, desire, and intention.[20]

The Central Position of Learning

Everything that we have studied thus far testifies to the importance of learning. Social influences such as cultural values, social class outlooks, group sanctions, and role expectations exert their shaping force through channels of learning. Constitutional traits and innate aptitudes enter the growth of personality because they facilitate certain kinds of learning and make other kinds more difficult. Drives and other basic urges become woven into the lattice of adult motivation through long sequences of learning through experience. In the study of personality, learning seems clearly cast in the star part.

But this stardom does not necessarily make for easy explanations. In trying to understand individual lives we have constantly been pushed away from convenient abstractions about human behavior. It was misleading, for example, to place Hale's ambitions, without qualification, in the category of upward mobility, just as it was misleading to identify his parents' values with average ones for the upper middle class. Similar trouble arose in the attempt to compare Hale and Kidd with respect to such variables as intelligence and a need for recognition. For many kinds of research it is useful to put people in categories, disregarding the finer details, but for understanding an individual life we have to work for more exact description. Each person's history of learnings is his own, resulting in a unique personal pattern. This is the pattern that actually operates to guide his life and determine his responses to future events.

Reinforcement One of the most elementary principles of learning is conveyed by the word *reinforcement*. This principle has its most eloquent modern advocate in Skinner, whose experiments have shown that the behavior of birds and animals can be extensively shaped by judicious application of food rewards.[21] Thorndike's historical ex-

[20] G. W. Allport, *Pattern and Growth in Personality* (New York: Holt, Rinehart and Winston, Inc., 1961) discussed in Chapter 10 the theoretical problems involved in the transformation of motives.

[21] B. F. Skinner, *Science and Human Behavior* (New York: The Macmillan Company, 1953).

periments with cats, in which the animals learned to escape from puzzle boxes provided an initial model. Cats do not naturally unhook tricky latches, but if in their random clawings and bitings they cause the door to open and thus reach the food reward, their most recent actions are reinforced and become more likely to occur again in subsequent trials. Skinner taught pigeons to peck at a certain spot on the wall by rewarding each spontaneous move in that direction. In the case of children, the concept of reward can be extended to include parental affection and approval, which gives reinforcement an important position in the process of socialization. In adulthood, the range of social motives becomes still wider, and a great deal of the learned behavior that constitutes personality may owe its existence at least in part to the principle of reinforcement.

This concept is valuable for understanding not only the *acquisition* but also the *maintenance* of behavior. In the contrived situations of the learning laboratory it is easy to show that behavior which goes unrewarded tends to lose strength and may be wholly extinguished. If it is desired to maintain certain behavior at full strength, continued reward is necessary. There is thus a presumption that when more complex forms of human behavior persist they may be receiving some kind of current reward. The value of looking for contemporary reinforcements has been shown in the study of behavior disorders. Delinquency, emotional outbursts, and anxiety attacks, which on the surface do not seem rewarding to anyone, sometimes prove to be sustained by unintended reinforcements. Only through such behavior, perhaps, can a child capture attention and elicit expressions of concern from otherwise preoccupied parents or teachers.[22] Continuing reinforcement may be important also in the maintenance of stable behavior. Implicit in Hale's success as a physician is the enduring presence of sick people and the constant need for his evolving skills. When the reinforcement pattern fails, as it did in Kidd's adolescent loss of esteem-income, behavior can be seriously disrupted.

Although reinforcement is a sound principle, it must be applied with careful discrimination. In discussions of child development the mother is often pictured as exerting nearly total control over the child's behavior by manipulating rewards and punishments, thus reinforcing what she desires and suppressing the rest. There are two faults

---

[22] D. E. Peterson, *The Clinical Study of Social Behavior* (New York: Appleton-Century-Crofts, 1968).

in this reasoning. In the first place, it rests on too literal a cause-effect, stimulus-response model—the mother's rewards as cause, the child's behavior as effect—and thus falsifies the interactive nature of all human relations. The child's behavior should be viewed as a cause in its own right which has a variety of reinforcing effects on the mother. In the second place, the model implies that all rewards come from other people, chiefly from their approval or disapproval. As we saw, children's exploratory and playful behavior carries its own rewards apart from parental approval, sometimes even in spite of it, as when a child risks punishment to pursue some interesting adventure of his own.

Imitation In view of all that has to be learned, growing up would be interminable if children always had to follow the slow piece-meal process used by rats in mazes and cats in puzzle boxes. Fortunately there are more economical ways of acquiring new patterns of behavior. One of these is imitation, whereby it is possible to copy all at once whole blocks of another person's behavior. The imitative tendencies of children are so familiar that we take them for granted, but copying is not a simple process. Bandura, who has made a long series of experiments on what he calls modeling behavior, makes two interesting points in this connection.[23] In the first place, copying involves more than simply matching the behavior of a model. The child cannot perceive his own behavior in the same way—from the outside—as he perceives the behavior of the model. Copying involves, in other words, a transformation of external perceptions into motor and expressive behavior. In the second place, imitation often occurs not just at the moment when a model's behavior has been observed, but some time later. Both of these facts point to internal registering and transforming activities—*representational* processes—that make for great economies in human learning. Simple notions of reinforcement obviously do not account for these more complex events. Imitation often occurs without any external reward of praise or approval. Apparently it gives satisfaction in its own right, perhaps in the form of feelings of efficacy.

One variety of imitation, *identification*, was assigned great importance in development by Freud. Using as examples the small boy's

[23] A. Bandura and R. H. Walters, *Social Learning and Personality Development* (New York: Holt, Rinehart and Winston, Inc., 1963), Chapter 2; A. Bandura, "Modeling Theory," in R. D. Parke (ed.), *Recent Trends in Social Learning Theory* (New York: Academic Press, Inc., 1972), Chapter 3.

attempts to be like his father and the small girl's attempts to emulate her mother, Freud believed that these early identifications persisted into adult life and continued to influence behavior in ways that might or might not be realistic. In the case of Hartley Hale we had reason to assume a considerable identification with his father, and persistence into later life was indicated by his striving to emulate his father's decisive clear-mindedness even when most people rated him high in this quality. Identifications are not confined, of course, to parents; brothers and sisters, teachers, athletic coaches, admirable peers like Hale's bold friend Dan, and the heroes and heroines of history and fiction may participate in the modeling of behavior. The individual does not have to learn his social behavior by laborious trial and error. He grows up in a world of models who provide a variety of patterns for copying.

Observational Learning Internal activities or representation are by no means confined to imitative behavior. We learn a great deal about the environment simply by observation. This is not a passive process; it is one that necessarily entails selection and organization. Present views of human cognition start from the fact that we are constantly overloaded with sensory input and are obliged to reduce it to manageable proportions. Cognitive activity can thus be interpreted as a series of strategies designed to simplify, codify, and conceptualize the flood of information so that we can respond effectively to such of it as is useful for living.[24] Our acquired knowledge of the environment presently becomes an organized representation of our surroundings and of ourselves in our surroundings. Tolman referred to this representation as a *cognitive map*; incoming information, he said, is "worked over and elaborated into a tentative map indicating routes and paths and environmental relationships."[25] The construction and continual improvement of such a map does not depend entirely on acts performed and reinforced. Cognitive learning can occur through observation or through information obtained from others. It depends upon "the perception of relations between one part of the external world and another, between one action and another, or between one's

[24] J. S. Bruner, *Beyond the Information Given: Studies in the Psychology of Knowing* (New York: W. W. Norton & Co., 1972) ; H. C. Ellis, *Fundamentals of Human Learning and Cognition* (Dubuque, Iowa: William C. Brown, 1972).

[25] E. C. Tolman, "Cognitive Maps in Rats and Men," *Psychological Review*, 55 (1948), 189–208.

own action and its effects."[26] Very likely the chief difference between human and animal mentality lies in the human capacity for elaborating such representational processes and thus living in a vastly more extended and complex world.[27] It is hard to think of a true animal analogue for Joseph Kidd's extensive gathering of information and weighing of alternatives when directing the construction of the new flower studio, or for his desire to see a career "from beginning to end" before committing himself to a vocational choice. Even in the matter of learning a social role, in which trial-and-error through attempted role enactments can certainly play a part, there is need for the idea of cognitive learning. Much can be found out about the expectations that go with different roles simply by listening to ordinary conversation and gossip, watching television, or reading books. We live and learn, but we also learn and live.

Plans Human learning is still seen in too simple a guise if we slide over the problem of how cognitive maps become effective in the guidance of behavior. Knowledge does not automatically lead to action; the action has to be guided not only by the map but by where the person intends to travel—what he sets out to accomplish. It has been proposed that we reserve the word *plan* to accommodate these intentions.[28] In a technical sense a plan is a process that acts like a set of instructions for carrying out successive stages of action leading to some intended result. The concept of plan provides a way of including what Murray calls the proactive aspects of behavior, as contrasted with the reactive: those aspects that point to the future and move us in a persistent, organized fashion toward distant goals. We have only to remember Hartley Hale's progress from the decision to become a doctor to actually becoming one, or Joseph Kidd's outside study and persisting performance in the business hierarchy, to realize how grotesquely we would misunderstand personality if we omitted proactive concepts like plan.

With this enlargement of our thinking about learning we can

[26] A. L. Baldwin, *Behavior and Development in Childhood* (New York: Holt, Rinehart and Winston, Inc., 1955), p. 434.

[27] R. W. Leeper, "Learning and the Fields of Perception, Motivation and Personality," in S. Koch (ed.), *Psychology: A Study of a Science* (New York: McGraw-Hill, Inc., Vol. 5, 1963), pp. 366–487.

[28] G. A. Miller, E. Galanter, and K. H. Pribram, *Plans and the Structure of Behavior* (New York: Holt, Rinehart and Winston, Inc., 1960).

come nearer to encompassing the operations and products of experience in adult life. Although there is value in the idea that behavior is acquired and maintained by external reinforcement, this formula cannot correctly represent all that enters into adult behavior. We can understand Hale and Kidd much better if we recognize, with Bandura, that "most human behavior is not controlled by immediate external reinforcement"; rather, people to some extent "regulate their own actions" and "set themselves certain performance standards," responding to their own behavior "in self-rewarding or self-punishing ways depending upon whether their performances fall short of, match, or exceed their self-imposed demands."[29] Moving along such lines, it becomes easier to grasp that central and highly significant product of experience, the self-concept, with all its import for the organization of personality. If this product seems to lie a long way from the biological roots of behavior, and to be much influenced by surrounding social forces, it is nevertheless a product of learning, an achievement of the nervous system, the outcome of processes that affirm man's kinship with animals and his position "as part of Nature."

SUGGESTIONS FOR FURTHER READING

A consistent attempt to use the ideas of constitutional differences and temperamental traits in the study of personality will be found in Solomon Diamond's book, *Personality and Temperament* (New York: Harper & Row, Publishers, 1957). Valuable on the genetic background is J. L. Fuller, "Genotype and Social Behavior," in D. G. Glass, ed., *Biology and Behavior: Genetics* (New York: Rockefeller University Press and Russell Sage Foundation, 1968), pp. 111–117, and W. R. Thompson, "Genetics and Social Behavior," in the same volume, pp. 79–101. The relation of biological individuality to the growth of personality is discussed by R. W. White, *The Enterprise of Living: Growth and Organization in Personality* (New York: Holt, Rinehart and Winston, Inc. 1972), Chapter 7.

A good work on the nature of intelligence and the extent to which it is open to environmental influence is J. McV. Hunt's *Intelligence and Experience* (New York: The Ronald Press Company, 1961).

Assistance in placing the topic of motivation in its physiological setting can be obtained from S. P. Grossman, *Essentials of Physiological Psychology* (New York: John Wiley & Sons, Inc., 1973). A discriminating

[29] Bandura, 1972, p. 48.

analysis of social motives will be found in H. A. Murray's *Explorations in Personality* (New York: Oxford University Press, 1938). Motivation connected with attaining competence in dealing with the environment is discussed by R. W. White, "Motivation Reconsidered: The Concept of Competence," *Psychological Review*, Vol. 66, 1959, pp. 297–333.

Two recent books among many on aggression can be especially recommended: Roger N. Johnson's *Aggression in Man and Animals* (Philadelphia: W. B. Saunders Co., 1972) and Jerome L. Singer, ed., *The Control of Aggression and Violence* (New York: Academic Press, Inc., 1971).

An excellent introduction to the problems of learning is Henry C. Ellis's *Fundamentals of Human Learning and Cognition* (Dubuque, Iowa: William C. Brown, 1972). The value of certain types of learning theory for the understanding of personality is set forth by A. Bandura and R. H. Walters in *Social Learning and Personality Development* (New York: Holt, Rinehart and Winston, Inc., 1963). An account of personality with an orientation toward cognitive learning is to be found in Robert W. Leeper and Peter Madison's *Toward Understanding Human Personalities* (New York, Appleton-Century-Crofts, 1959). The significance of the concept of "plan" is developed in *Plans and the Structure of Behavior* by G. A. Miller, E. Galanter, and K. H. Pribram (New York: Holt, Rinehart and Winston, Inc., 1960). The relation of learning and anxiety to the development of abnormal behavior is discussed by R. W. White and N. F. Watt in *The Abnormal Personality* (New York: The Ronald Press Company, 4th ed., 1973), Chapter 3.

7

JOYCE KINGSLEY, HOUSEWIFE AND SOCIAL WORKER

I have been very lucky to have the kind of family I have. They have given me a good foundation, and now it's up to me.

JOYCE KINGSLEY

Joyce Kingsley was first studied when she was a senior in college. She was one of several students invited to take part in a study designed to bring out the relationships between opinions and other aspects of personality. Invitations were issued in such a way as to secure a group that represented a diversity of opinions; beyond this, selection was determined by the subject's willingness to give the time, at a fee based on current rates for student employment. Joyce responded to the invitation with enthusiasm. She needed spending money, she was interested in social problems, and she enjoyed the prospect of possibly contributing to research in a field closely related to her own. No doubt she was also interested in what she might learn about herself, but at no point did she give signs of desiring our guidance or advice. She took her duties seriously, doing her best to provide whatever information we seemed to require. Like many subjects, she clearly enjoyed being the object of so much personal interest by so many workers, and this bonus seems to have increased her willingness to tell everything she could about herself.

Five years later Joyce, by this time married and living in a midwestern city, came to Boston for a brief visit to her parents. This visit was made the occasion for our second study. Fourteen years then passed, bringing her to the age of forty, at which point we were able to extend the history by means of a long follow-up interview, and she was interviewed again when she reached fifty.

PART ONE: THROUGH COLLEGE

Family Background

The Kingsley grandparents, beneficiaries of a fairly successful business venture in the previous generation, lived comfortably and sent their children to college, but their granddaughter was firm in placing them well down in the middle class. In spirit, she declared, they preserved the smugness and narrow interests of their New England small-town forebears. The grandmother annoyed Joyce by attempting to pry into her affairs, by gossiping, and by having no serious interest in life beyond disposing of personal effects. The family fortunes had long since dwindled, but the grandmother was still able to maintain, with occasional help from Joyce's father, her own small separate establishment. Joyce more than hinted that her constant presence in her son's household would not have been welcome.

Joyce's father had been destined for business, but after four years at a college of business administration he rebelled against the parental design and, much against his father's wishes, entered the ministry. After three years in a nearby theological school, he made what his daughter referred to as "the big break" by accepting the call of a parish in Indiana and establishing there his first independent home. Subsequent calls took him to larger parishes, first in Michigan, then in New Jersey. He became known especially for his success with administration, so that after twelve years as a pastor he was summoned to a full-time executive post in the regional organization of his denomination, with headquarters in Boston. At the time of the second study he still occupied this post, from which he retired several years later.

The Kingsley grandparents hoped that their son would marry a "nice Boston girl," but again he kicked over the traces by choosing a wife who came from the West. Joyce's mother was a college graduate and a teacher. She had attained this status largely by individual effort, receiving neither help nor understanding from her parents, whose resources were limited and whose marriage eventually disintegrated. Joyce was not well acquainted with her maternal grandparents. The grandmother suffered a "mental snap" in middle life; on the single occasion after this when Joyce saw her she appeared "old, frail, bewildered by the noise of the family," and her thoughts were constantly occupied by spiritualism. Joyce had not seen her grandfather since she was six, but he, too, had left an unpleasant impression: he was anxious to be affectionate, and Joyce did not care to be fondled. The maternal grandparents were assigned definitely lower middle-class status by their sociologically educated grandchild. They had both been brought up in German-speaking immigrant homes and had only partly assimilated American middle-class values. Joyce mentioned an incident to illustrate their lack of proper standards. As a year-and-a-half-old baby she had been left with them for the evening while her father and mother attended a meeting. They wanted to be nice to her, so they took her to the movies. "Mother was furious at such poor judgment," said Joyce, adding that she never went to the movies again until she was at least nine or ten.

Joyce's mother, fighting her way up the educational ladder, had clearly rejected her parents and their social status. There was little contact between her and her parents even when, during the Michigan years, the two families lived no great distance apart. Mrs. Kingsley's rebellion extended into the sphere of political opinions; her study of American history had given her a "terrific reaction" against the staunch Republicanism of her childhood home. Her religious affiliation was also of her own choosing, and it was in consequence of this act of independence that she met her future husband. That the friendship progressed to marriage may have been partly due to a sense of alliance in the common cause of achieving independence. Both the young theological student and his future wife had rejected the materialism, the narrow interests, the cultural barrenness, and the unreflective political conservatism of their childhood homes. Both had turned to religion as an integral part of the quest for a better and nobler way of life.

In determining the social status of Joyce Kingsley's family it is necessary to specify quite a number of details. In the first place, both parents had become professional people in their own right; therefore, as we saw in studying the family of Hartley Hale, they occupied a curious position somewhat to one side of that central status ladder which is determined largely by wealth. Joyce was fully aware of this dilemma. "We have to entertain and make a small salary stretch," she said; "we have many obligations to fill"; and this placed the family definitely in middle-class financial status. On the other hand, many of the social contacts were upper-class or were with other professional families. In discussing status, Joyce made the common professional distinction between two kinds of upperness. She said:

> This distinguishes the upper and lower: using your mind to the greatest possible extent. My family is upper in this sense. Money is a side issue; in that sense I have no particular ambition toward the upper.

It must also be mentioned that the social status of a minister has to be defined somewhat differently from that of other professionals whose contact with their clients is more restricted and less personal. In carrying out the duties of his office a parish minister is expected to enter even the wealthiest homes and to be treated at least as an equal. His uppermost social status is thus in a sense determined by the range that is represented in his parish. Mr. Kingsley's parishes included members who were upper-class in the social-financial sense, so that when his daughter disclaimed an interest in that kind of status it was not because of a feeling of hopeless exclusion.

In Joyce's case we can perceive with particular sharpness the collision between democratic ideals and the subtle directives of social class. During her later childhood, in a crowded New Jersey industrial city, she was not allowed to play indiscriminately with the neighboring children. When the family moved to Boston, sacrifices were made so that she could attend a private college-preparatory school and seek friendships among her schoolmates. Earlier she had gone to public school, and when questioned about her contacts with lower-class children she said, "I wasn't part of it, but not an outsider either or a snob." Then she added, "My ambition is to put people at their ease, including those below you socially." Yet Joyce's considered values were based on the Christian democratic ideal, and her response to class and ethnic differences had indeed been much softened by her parents' explicit attitudes toward these questions. The Children of Israel figured as wonderful people in her early education, and when in New Jersey she first saw mysterious Yiddish signs and was told that this was the neighborhood of the Children of Israel she felt at once that it must be a "most special" place. Occasionally the family had a black maid, who was always treated with respectful consideration. She remembered being furiously indignant at tales of injustice and cruelty weepingly related by one of these helpers. Joyce's convictions with regard to ethnic groups were entirely free from prejudice, and she was prepared to act according to her convictions. But she had been exposed to so much status conditioning that her feelings did not always keep in step with the equalitarian ideal. Often the best that she could attain was a condescending tolerance. Speaking of black classmates at college, she said, "I'm not overly close, but I talk to them when I get a chance." We must count it to her credit that she then added, "That sounds smug, doesn't it? I don't mean it to be."

If the social status of the Kingsley family cannot be written off with a single phrase, the same is true for Mr. Kingsley's occupational role. We must be careful to avoid stereotypes. Contemporary life histories show many cases of rebellion against the spiritual claims of religion in favor of an occupation at once more materialistic and considered to be more practical. In view of this trend, we become inclined to think of ministers as being also ministers' sons and as continuing, perhaps rather unadventurously, to tread in paternal footsteps. The idea of a courageous young man flouting the materialism of his parents and going into the Christian ministry with a chip on his shoulder, so to speak, does not fit with our common preconceptions. Yet Mr. Kingsley had to defy his parents in order to become a minister; in the beginning, at least, there was a rebellious freshness in his desire to exert a spiritual influence and to create a happy, cooperative, Christian home. Let us now consider how his life enterprise appeared to the eyes of his daughter after it had been going on for twenty-three years.

The Kingsley Family

When Joyce handed in her autobiography we found that she had elected to give a title to the story of her life. She called it *Joyous Adventure*. She had not had time to complete the proffered list of topics, promising to supply the rest at a later date. The break came between *major positive experiences* (defined in our outline as "events accompanied by great elation: success and joy") and *major negative experiences* ("events accompanied by great depression and discomfort: frights, humiliations, failures, transgressions"). At the end of the interviews we reminded her that the written autobiography was incomplete. In due time we received a detailed account of what she considered to be her major negative experience, together with a full discussion of the remaining topics in the outline.

Joyce's positive and negative experiences are highly significant in understanding her personality, but we must revert for the present to the earlier part of *Joyous Adventure* in order to appreciate the formative influence of the family circle. Of her father Joyce wrote as follows:

> He is a very remarkable man. Some people think of him as always smiling, others talk of the kind and thoughtful things he is always doing; no one has ever seen him get angry, and almost everyone thinks of him as a very busy man (and he is). . . . Wherever Daddy has gone he has been particularly successful in the administration end of Church work. He devotes most of his time, of course, to the Church. He has been particularly active in Sunday School work. He is also very much interested in the cooperative movement and is an active member here in Boston. He is very skillful at doing many things—I think he would make a competent gardener, plumber, cook, or carpenter, or almost anything else you could think of. He is very observant. I imagine that's why he can do so many and varied things.

Joyce's praise is unqualified, but we are entitled to wonder how she felt about this admirable figure when she was younger and could not appreciate his public importance and service to the community. She has drawn us her father in profile, intent on the many things he can do so well, rather than as a person bending his gaze upon herself. Although she mentions repeatedly the happy atmosphere of the home and the many things they all enjoyed doing together, there is an undertone of frustration that her relationship with her father was not more warm and demonstrative. She remembered that at the age of five, during a time when her mother was away, she was greatly grieved because her father left her for the evening with her godmother. Another memory, presumably a little later, was introduced with the remark: "Neither of my parents was overly affectionate; Daddy was busy, but we had tremendous fun with him." Then followed this recollection: "I loved going into Daddy's study and tracing writings. I went there after I was supposed to go to bed, turned on the light and traced writings." When we examine the stories Joyce told for the Thematic Apperception Test we find that she has portrayed two kinds of fathers. One is quite cold and authoritative; he "dominates his children to such an extent that he expects them to feel just as he does," and he is further characterized as "self-conscious," "self-righteous," "crabbed," "priggish," "thrusting all emotion aside." In describing this character Joyce was reminded of Father Barrett in *The Barretts of Wimpole Street*, an identification that leaves room for considerable hidden emotional interest in a talented daughter. The other kind of father appears in two stories, both involving the circumstance that the mother is dead. This father is devoted to his daughter, around whom his life revolves; he grieves deeply in the story in which she is killed in an accident, and he yields gracefully in the tale that ends with her meeting and being wooed by a handsome young artist. But we need not rely on inference, for in a later interview Joyce told us how she felt. Asked what she considered to be bad or missing in her upbringing, she replied:

> I only regret that—well, it goes back to Dad's childhood when he wasn't close to his father, and his mother didn't help him to get close to his father. Dad is helpful but he is not very close. He hasn't many close friends. I take after him. I didn't have any close contacts with friends, that is, family close friends.

In the autobiography Joyce characterized her mother as follows:

> Mother's interests have been many and varied. She is an excellent teacher. When we were little she had a nursery school. Later on, when I was in college-preparatory school, she taught seventh and eighth grades. She has a very eager and logical mind and has turned it to many uses. Everything from writing Sunday School lessons to devising quick and efficient methods of cooking and doing dishes has benefited from her logical approach. She has remarkable insight into human situations, and has helped many people to solve their problems through her kind and understanding approach.

Again Joyce has used the profile method, and again we must look further if we are to discover the mother's role in the daughter's emotional development. The mother's influence was so constant that Joyce could not separate it out into particular incidents. Mother read to the children, she taught them the Bible, she took them on trips, she participated in some of their games, but from none of this can we gather much about the daughter's feelings. When we look at the Thematic Apperception Test stories we find Joyce prone to eliminate the mother: the heroine's mother was dead in four stories, and older women in the pictures were sometimes made into aunts or foster parents rather than mothers. It appears that the heroines achieved greater freedom of action through this handling of mother figures. In one remarkable story we were told that as a little girl the pictured heroine was dominated by the pictured old woman: "I'm not sure if it was her mother or if this woman is an entirely different critter." At all events the old woman, a gossipy and scheming person, still continued her attempt at domination, while the heroine successfully asserted her own personality and rejected the interference. This struggle, Joyce predicted, is destined to continue, and the heroine's efforts will not be quite fully successful because "she's tied to the woman in some way— it isn't a case where she can get away from her even if she goes to the far ends of the earth." The full import of this story will become clearer when we examine Joyce's account of her moral training. It is clear, however, that the mother's influence was strong and pervasive, that it was somehow sensed to be an interference, but that outright resistance could not be openly contemplated. Moreover, it seems justifiable to assume that Joyce found the bargain of submission a hard one, insufficiently rewarded by maternal appreciation. She said in a later interview, "I minded Mother's being taken up with work perhaps more than I should have minded it."

Joyce was the eldest child and only daughter of the family. She was followed within two years by Albert, then a few years later by Henry. "I adore both my brothers," Joyce told us, and in the autobiography she did their profiles as follows:

> Albert, who is eighteen, is already an expert on everything concerning electricity; Henry, who is fourteen, has a lively sense of humor and a keen mind which he can turn to anything.

These profiles were considerably amplified in later interviews, and it is important to examine the effects of the two brothers on Joyce's development.

Her earliest memory has to do with Albert. The episode is given as follows in *Joyous Adventure*:

> I have faint memories of a party there. I think it was a children's party and I'm pretty sure it was a birthday party given for me. Albert was old enough to sit in a high chair and to know very much that he wanted to come to that party. I remember that he screamed and had to be taken out into the other room, and that he sat in his high chair howling away because he wasn't included in the festivities.

This incident sets the theme for everything she had to say about Albert. It seems that Albert was "bad"; at least he always had a "bad temper." He got into a great deal of mischief, such as locking his sister and himself in the bathroom so that firemen had to be called to the rescue. Joyce recollects that he tried to climb into her crib, a thing that her mother says could not have happened. But Albert's badness was especially remembered in situations like that of the birthday party, when he was excluded from something that Joyce was allowed to do. Thus when the Kingsleys went next door to inspect a radio, leaving him behind because he was too small, he was found on their return to have swallowed a quantity of pills from the medicine cabinet. Again, when he was still too young for church, which Joyce in her best frock was allowed to attend with her mother, he appeared suddenly in the chancel, unkempt and dirty, while his father was conducting the service. Joyce confessed to having "violent disagreements" with Albert, though in retrospect she called them "very childish and remote." His badness did not preclude "wonderful times" together, and lately she has come to consider him a "wonderful guy." In an interview she said:

> We have had lovely times together. We're not really close; there's no demonstrative affection, it's just esteem for each other. He sort of idealizes me and is proud of me. He expects girls to be like me. But he considers me dumb on things scientific.

Albert's badness seems to have had a drastic effect on the course of Joyce's early development. His behavior was a shock to his parents. Joyce noted that she herself always "followed the baby books," was "docile and willing," and "never did anything to offend Mother or Father." After this happy introduction to parenthood the Kingsleys were utterly unprepared for Albert's rambunctious ways. In many a drastic scene "Mother and Father didn't know what to do"; indeed, they were so upset that they asked their friends for advice, and at one point Mrs. Kingsley retired for several weeks to a rest home. It can be sensed that to a certain extent Joyce admired and envied her brother's rebellious assertiveness, but the effect of his actions on the parents must have strengthened her inclination to play the well-behaved part she had begun in her days as an only child. Being good now acquired the meaning of a strategy in the competitive struggle for parental favor. The only trouble was that the parents seemed unable to give Albert the punishments he deserved. There was danger that they would play the game unfairly by failing to make him a proper outcast. Joyce told us that at some point in these early years she developed a fantasy of an imaginary companion. Far from being a playmate, this companion, Myra, was a woman who had had a great many children and who therefore knew exactly how to deal with them.

> I objected to going to bed one night and I discussed it with Myra. She was on my side; it was not right for me to have to go to bed. I must have doubted that Mother and Daddy were right. Perhaps I sensed their hesitation in knowing what to do with Albert.

We judged that Myra was both more appreciative of the wishes of a good child and more severe in punishing a bad one.

Brother Henry exerted a less marked effect on Joyce's development. "We welcomed him when he was born," she oddly remarked; "we were excited about him." Like Albert he passed through a stage when he "couldn't be even remotely civilized" without discipline; but if she is sometimes still angry at his noise and disorderliness, she has come to admire his brilliant mind and practical skills. "He's such a good cook," she wrote, "that he can make substitutions in recipes and have his things turn out to be delicious, whereas I'm still at the follow-the-directions-very-carefully stage." Henry's health is not of the best, so that he is sometimes moody and difficult. This causes Joyce to feel concern about him, and she sometimes wonders whether her mother is not taking his troubles too lightly in calling them just a phase of growth. She even wonders on occasion whether Henry is not punished unfairly, but although she has once or twice expressed this thought she usually checks it with the reflection that her mother is tired. There are times when she and Henry become real pals, though for the most part she is "pretty much an older sister." It is evident that Joyce's attitude toward Henry changes under different circumstances. She can be annoyed and somewhat punitive, but she can also sympathize when he seems unhappy and misunderstood.

Joyce Kingsley's history exhibits with unusual clarity the effect of the family group on later social development and group memberships. It also shows, more explicitly than our two previous cases, the impact of moral constraints and the internal evolution of conscience. We are therefore justified in examining at considerable length what Joyce wrote about the family atmosphere.

> Our home has always been a very happy one. Our family has been quite close together—in our own kind of way. It's not a family

where there is a great deal of affection shown overtly, but we do have strong ties and mutual interests and enjoy doing things together. No one of us had a lot of attention as an individual—so that none of us feel that we, or any of the others, are the "favorite" with our parents. I guess I have never been much of a worry to Mother and Daddy. Neither of them is dominating or possessive but they are fond of all of us. I can't quite describe their attitude: they leave us pretty free, but they are always concerned with the way things are going for us. Perhaps it can be summed up by saying that they realize that we aren't possessions of theirs, but they are nevertheless vitally interested in our welfare. This means that they can be quite close to us and very fond of us, but not use that feeling in a way that would be harmful for our development. Our family responsibilities as well as our privileges as members of the family have always been made important. I, as the oldest, and a girl, have perhaps had quite a large share in the responsibilities, but I do not feel that it has been a disproportionately large share. Our servants have been few and far between, but I think they were all fond of me.

It is odd that Joyce selected this particular point to remember about the servants. Perhaps her wondering about love should be taken as referring unintentionally to the whole preceding paragraph. An undemonstrative regime, no matter how fair and devoted, can create an air of uncertainty about love, especially when more than one child is involved. Again we feel that Joyce is a little dubious about the bargain of conformity: was she asked for too much, was she given too many responsibilities, in return for a restrained and evenly divided show of parental affection? The heart is not always satisfied by what the head considers fair. But Joyce was not prepared to object, and she still does not openly object, as we see from her remarks on discipline.

Looking back, it doesn't seem as if we've ever had much discipline. Or maybe I'd better say that I never had much. It isn't a case of always having done everything I should do, but rather one of being punished more by the conscience pangs I have afterwards than by Mother and Daddy. Punishment, whenever it has been given to any of us, has been perfectly fair—which is perhaps why I don't remember it. This situation makes me completely unable to determine just what our most serious offense could have been (or is). I think that perhaps it's obstructing the family harmony and progress by putting considerations of ourselves before those of the welfare of the whole group when they have not deserved that importance.

The last sentence reminds us that Mr. Kingsley was interested in the cooperative movement and makes it plain that cooperation occupied a high and explicit place in the moral code of the Kingsley household. Cooperation is a mature concept not easily grasped by young children. Indeed it is scarcely possible to create a domestic cooperative movement: inevitably the parents function as final arbiters when it comes to deciding what obstructs "family harmony and progress." We should not be surprised that the glad cooperation desired by the parents sometimes felt like an irksome yoke to the daughter. It is clear from the following paragraph, however, that the cooperative ideal was applied for the most part to understandable necessities, and that the Kingsley parents played with their children and shared happy times as well as requiring contributions.

> I have already spoken of the amount of work around the house which the family has done together. This has been true ever since we have been old enough to help. It has never been more than we could handle. When Al and I were five or six years old we had duties like setting the table for breakfast or drying the supper dishes, and we did these for our weekly allowance of five cents. By the time Henry was two he had requested to stand up on a high stool and wash the dishes! Mother and Daddy used to play games with us and they also read aloud to us. We all planted gardens together and did things like raking leaves and shingling and painting floors, too. One summer we fixed up a car trailer and took our tents and supplies and camped west as far as Montana. During the last few summers we have all worked hard on a cottage at the beach. We have had a lot of fun doing things together, and planning things together.

Returning to the question of moral training, Joyce characterized it as "largely unspoken."

> By that I mean that Mother and Daddy have not been primarily concerned with it—or, rather, they have never given us "lectures" on the subject of our morals. We have always talked to them freely about our impressions of what is going on around us, and I think we have benefited from those discussions in that our moral education has not been imposed on us, as it were, but has gradually and normally developed as we were ready for it. In the last year or two Mother has been utterly amazed to find that Albert and I, in talking to her, have voiced almost identical opinions about subjects which

we have never discussed before. We feel very strongly about some things. The only possible source of moral training seems to be in what Mother and Daddy have lived, and in what we have done together as a family. I ask myself how this can possibly be. And my answer is that I don't know. It really doesn't seem logical that indirect influence could be so strong. Our conduct at home has had to measure up to certain standards, but it has never been a case of "you do this, or else . . ." Mother and Daddy have been consistent in their own behavior. I imagine that there has been strength for us in that very consistency—for if we ever doubted the rightness of anything we did, that certainty was there anyway, acting as a sort of support to us. Our religious training has not been so indirect. I imagine that it is quite possible that much of our moral training has come from this. . . . Here again, Mother and Daddy were always consistent in living their religious principles. This was a far more effective teacher than all the spoken words, whether meaningful or unmeaningful to us, could ever have been.

Joyce's description of the way in which moral values got into her behavior must be a classic of its kind. The Kingsley parents evidently took seriously their obligation to exemplify, as well as to preach, high standards of Christian conduct. They did not argue or quarrel, they did not criticize people, they were contained and long-suffering when a disaffected faction in their church placed them under sharp criticism. They also stood for the cooperation and the personal freedom that formed part of the ideals of their church. As Joyce paradoxically put it, they had "a sense of leading people to freedom of choice"; they even tried to "do this with each other." It is clear that Joyce early adopted the path of conformity. She became a firm ally of her parents and their values, as one can see from her constant use of "we" in talking about her family. When younger brothers began to compete for parental love she became all the more firmly cast in the role of docile, responsible child. Unquestionably there was strain, but Joyce sustained her alliance through all the vicissitudes of childhood and adolescence, reaffirming it on the final page of her autobiography with the words, "I have been very lucky to have the kind of home and family I have." If it had been hard to live up to her responsibilities, she had never openly rebelled against them, and as she reached her twenty-first birthday her life was firmly established on the religious and moral values of her home. One can guess that Albert and Henry, never able to equal Joyce in her chosen role, experienced greater difficulty in becoming cooperative members of the family group. Albert, in particular, found the role of rebel more rewarding. At eighteen he had definitely broken with the church, and he was more or less constantly at odds with the family. There were in fact several points of serious friction developing in the Kingsley household, but we did not learn of these until the second study.

Childhood: Golden Years

Joyce was puzzled about the paucity of her memories. "I don't know why my memory is so hazy about my early experiences," she wrote; "I just remember little snatches of events, and all my memories are happy ones."

Actually her early memories were about as numerous as those of other subjects, and they were not always completely happy. We begin to sense that Joyce has a stake in believing that her life's adventure has been joyous, unmarred by major negative experiences. Yet what she recalled about childhood, especially what she recalled about the years in Michigan where she lived until the age of seven, suggested many grounds for happy contentment. The minister's daughter was considered a charming and lovely child—"Sweet Joyce," she was called—so that she was the recipient of much attention and many gifts. She took a great interest in flowers, recalling the time at Michigan as one long brightly colored summer. Christmas pageants, Easter hunts, birthday parties crowded her recollections. There were a good many animals: dogs, rabbits, chickens, and a cat, the latter having to live under the porch because Mrs. Kingsley did not like cats in the house. Joyce was also fascinated by wild birds, thrilled when she saw a "special" bird like a bluebird or noticed a robin perching on the window sill. She was fond of dolls. For a while all dolls, regardless of sex, were named Samuel because she was fascinated by the Biblical story of the boy who was called by the voice of God. There was a time—a short time—when with Albert's help she sometimes gave a doll rough treatment; but soon people began to give her dolls with nice clothes, and in the end she had about twenty-five dolls, most of them too nice to be played with. Joyce seems to have been from the start sensitive to beautiful things, responding with real joy to colors and sounds, to nature and to lovely objects, and her childhood environment seems to have provided her richly with these sources of pleasure.

A favorite playtime activity, shared with Albert, was a game called "waterworks." The children often made their mother take them to see the town waterworks; afterwards they would build models with blocks, realistically continuing to wear their rubber boots in the play room. One game was played by Joyce alone. "I early aspired to be a lexicographer," she wrote; "I remember copying lists of words in the back of primers, and trying to include all the words I knew, arranged alphabetically, almost as soon as I could write." But most games were shared: with Albert she played store and church, with the boys of the neighborhood she hunted for "very special" marbles and buried tin boxes containing "very special" treasures to be dug up again later. When she began school, at five, her circle of acquaintances enlarged and included, for the first time, girls as well as boys. She wrote: "There were quite a few other children and I enjoyed them." As far as she could recall, her social behavior was always "cooperative," her disposition "sunny and cheerful," her reception by others uniformly friendly. "I wasn't much interested in competition," she said; "perhaps I never needed to be."

However much Joyce may have forgotten unpleasant happenings, the tone of her early childhood seems to have been predominantly happy. The strongest evidence for this judgment lies in the pained astonishment she recalled having felt when suddenly confronted by evil. With regard to Albert's swallowing of the pills she remembered being "quite astonished that he would do that." She described with similar words how she felt when her kindly meant attempt to pat a strange rabbit resulted in her being bitten: "I was shocked that he would do that; I was angry at first, but then I reasoned that he didn't know I was going to pat him." The most dramatic instance was the occasion when she was stung by a bee. This event occurred on the steps of the school, and its import was probably heightened by the fact that her mother was busy helping one of the teachers. At all events Joyce, who had come on roller skates, fell down and landed on the bee. "It stung me," she said; "that was a bitter blow, I didn't expect to be treated that way."

Joyce herself recognized that her cooperation abruptly vanished on the occasion when she went to the hospital. She was six years old and was suffering from a mastoid infection. Resisting all the blandishments of the doctor and nurses, she refused to eat, drink, take medicine, or submit to examination unless her mother were present. It finally became necessary to provide a cot so that her mother could stay at the hospital practically all the time. The child's anxiety is sufficiently explained by circumstances, but it is perhaps not without significance that conformity and cooperation should be the things that collapsed when she was sent away from the family circle. One is led to infer that at this period Joyce's conformity was sustained by a feeling that she stood closer to her mother than did the outrageous Albert.

While the family remained in Michigan, Joyce's education was in the hands of her mother, who ran a school for her daughter and a few neighborhood children. This venture seems to have sprung from the mother's desire to be active rather than from any disapproval of the local schools. When Mr. Kinglsey was called to a city parish in New Jersey, Joyce entered the second grade in the public school. "It was very different from the kind of school I had known," she commented; "I didn't really get well settled until I was in the third grade, but from then on I was very much a part of things that went on." She remembered her teachers quite clearly, almost always with affection. Along with three or four other pupils she was regularly accused of being the teacher's pet. One teacher, an elderly woman whose hands were tremulous, appointed Joyce to write for her on the blackboard. Another encouraged the children to write letters and send presents to Joyce when she was at home with an illness. It was during this period in the New Jersey public school that Joyce decided to make teaching her life work. But in spite of her tendency to identify with her teachers and to become the object of their special interest she took an active part in the affairs of her contemporaries. In addition to the more organized activities, such as dramatics, Girl Scouts, and young people's groups at the church, she was a member of a couple of clubs in the sixth and seventh grades that degenerated pleasantly into "rowdy clubs."

Preparatory School: Adventures in Self-Discovery

When the Kingsleys moved to Boston, Joyce was entered at the Walter School, a small private school for girls. She was "bewildered at first," but soon she became acquainted with her new schoolmates and found herself "getting adjusted again." It was not long before she emerged in the eyes of the teachers as a well-behaved, reliable girl who worked hard and did well in her studies. Joyce touched lightly on the effort she had to make to win her way at Walter, but a period of uneasy strain is suggested by the fact that she had occasional attacks of day-time enuresis during her "early teens," her first years in the new environment.

I got it under control in after years. I've often wondered about what it was. Being with older and younger people a lot and being a little silly, I would laugh very hard about things and then I'd have a little trouble controlling my bladder. I rather imagine I took things a little more foolishly than they were meant. When I was with older people there was pressure to measure up to their standards. To live up to them meant being noisy about things and laughing a lot.

As she achieved a happier and more secure position Joyce began to be troubled by the difficulty of managing different roles with different groups. She also began to feel a marked conflict between family ideals and the values of her adolescent friends. In *Joyous Adventure* she discussed these problems as follows:

I have always had a great many friends, but most of the friendships have been quite casual. Usually I can "handle" only two or three good friends at once. My friends are not all the same kind of people, and I sometimes find it difficult to mix those who are interested in music, for instance, with those who will have nothing to do with music. I haven't had quarrels with any of them. I have usually been a leader in groups, but have often felt not as much a part of the gang as I would have liked. This has been partly, I think, because I don't share most girls' attitudes toward boys . . . I do not feel that I have been left out of groups, although I do not feel that I have been an integral part of some groups with which I have associated. . . .

I have usually been regarded as quite an idealistic person, although possibly that's because I have had ideas and ideals and have not been hesitant about expressing them.

It is easy to see that Joyce, strongly identified with parental values and inclined to extend the identification so as to include teachers and school authorities, would have difficulty with adolescent peer groups. She was soon typed as a minister's daughter, a Victorian, and a goody-goody in her own right. "I hated it," she said; "they don't know the half of it." She kept holding class offices, but this only caused her to be "regarded more as a class officer than as an individual." She found this "hard to take," yet her efforts to break down the reputation were often not successful, leaving a barrier between her and girls whose affection she desired. "Can you be a member and leader at the same time?" she asked.

Joyce was unaccustomed to rejection. Just as she had been

shocked by the rabbit that bit her and the bee that stung her, so now she was upset to find that her well-intentioned behavior made her the object of criticism. It was impossible for her to go over suddenly to the rebellious independence of adolescence, yet this meant that she could not meet the demands for conformity which are so imperious within adolescent groups. At times she was extremely unhappy. When she wrote her autobiography, these particular troubles were four or five years past, but they had been sufficiently grave to alter her vocational plans. She wrote as follows:

> For the last several years I have realized more and more that I do not want to teach, although I am intensely interested in education. I want very much some day to make it possible for people to enjoy their schooling and their lives more than many of them do now. I have known some very unhappy people. Usually I have not been in a position to make them really happy (they really have to do it for themselves, anyway). But they may benefit by having some "tools" which will help them to become more happy, and thus to be more useful and productive members of society. The ambition to do something about this has been growing for the last four or five years. The best approach would probably be through schools. Many people go through school being perfectly miserable because they had some problem which they could not solve for themselves, and so often they wanted help but didn't know where to turn for it. One or another form of this ambition has existed during the last few years, and it has always seemed perfectly attainable, although I do not know yet just what I am going to be able to do about it.

Two of the events that Joyce rated as her major positive experiences took place during her last year at Walter School. The first of these, which she considered "most major," was meeting Rennie. The occasion was a young people's convention sponsored by the church, and Rennie was one of the delegates from Indianapolis. Joyce told us that she had always enjoyed boys as playmates, but when she came to Boston and entered a school where the emphasis was on "men for dances and for dates" she felt at first decidedly lost. Before long she was being dated, and she enjoyed especially boys who could "discuss things, especially politics, economics, social problems, religion, and philosophical problems." "I really enjoy them as *people*," she wrote, but she soon found that she did not enjoy them as cavemen. Holding hands and kissing did not please her; as for necking, "that was the surest way for a boy to get himself vetoed." Rennie, however, did not hastily insist on these privileges, and Joyce soon began to discover in herself a whole new range of emotions. During the convention she and Rennie had wonderful times together, including planning "the farm we both wanted to have some day." Separated again, they "kept the mailman very busy," and occasionally Rennie came for a weekend.

> As we grew older we grew more and more certain that we were the people for each other. It's hard to be objective in telling what kind of a person Rennie is. He has had as happy a childhood as I have. He is much the same kind of person I am, only he is more gentle and kind and understanding. He has been a leader all through school, too, and he has been more of a success scholastically than I. We share the same interests, except that he is intensely interested in group sports, especially in baseball.

Evidently Joyce took comfort in the similarities of background and interests, the sharing of religious and other basic values. With fundamental solidarity assured, she felt no threat in their disagreement on politics: they could "get quite heated" when she espoused Roosevelt and the New Deal against his "midwestern Republicanism." In due time they considered themselves engaged, and a public announcement to this effect was made during Joyce's senior year at college, a little more than four years after their first meeting.

In writing about Rennie, Joyce told us how she felt without reference to the particular time when she felt it. It is probably safe to assume, however, that both the joy and the idealism expressed in the following paragraphs were active elements in the relationship from the very beginning.

> We are both looking forward to being married, although we are not sure yet when we can be. We want to create the kind of home we have longed for, and we want especially to do many things together which we have not been able to do before. Here again our ideals are pretty high. We believe that there is just one person created for everyone, and we do not regard marriage as a thing to be tried and abandoned if things don't go smoothly. We think that things can go smoothly if we consider each other.

> Through Rennie and with him I have found more satisfaction and joy than I have ever found in any other way. The most wonderful thing about it is that it continually grows and develops and I sometimes wonder if I can hold any more without bursting.

The second major event in Joyce's last year at the Walter School was her election as president of the Student Government Association. This association had only just been started; its organization and its policies all had to be built up as new creations. Joyce proved to be a hard-driving president. She wrote as follows about the year's accomplishment:

> I expected quite a bit from the girls in building it up, and I got a good deal of it. The major part of the experience was working with them—and working with the teachers. At the end of the year the organization was really established and the girls had a good deal of power to run their own affairs, and although the faculty was included in making decisions they seldom gave any advice unless we asked for it.

Let us pause to examine these two major events: student government and Rennie. Why were they major? Why do they stand out as landmarks in Joyce's history? When we undertake to study the natural growth of personality we are committed to explaining the positive developments, the forward strides, as well as the problems and frustrations and defeats. We find Joyce troubled, uneasy, inwardly quite unhappy during her first years at the Walter School; then happen two major events, and she begins to function with great freedom and energy, almost bursting with happiness. Any psychotherapist would be delighted if he could produce so large a change in so short a time. We are entitled to suppose that the two events were felt to be "major" because they opened paths through an existing dilemma, gave Joyce a chance to go forward without too sharp a change in direction, and provided expanding opportunities for the expression of her main needs and interests.

Taking first her work in student government, it is clear that Joyce had solved the problem of the respected but unloved officeholder. She had cast her lot with student officialdom, and she was fully prepared to accept whatever isolation from the youth culture this might entail. Having taken this step, she was free to advance into a more dominating role than she had ever assumed before, expecting much of the girls and getting it from them. She was free to affirm her ideals, to side with law and order, to create an organization designed to govern the more unruly tendencies of the adolescent group. She could develop her identification with parental values as against the disruptive tendencies exemplified in Albert and Henry. Many of her oldest needs were thus caught up in a new pattern of constructive activity. Yet there was an important difference between her new position and the one she had occupied in the family circle. She was now the elected president, the legitimate authority, not merely the eldest daughter who was uncertain of her standing and bound to a firm code of cooperation. She could at last really run things the way she wanted them run. Furthermore, it was part of her job to make the students maximally independent of faculty control. It was easy for her to keep peace with the teachers because she shared most of their ideals, but she did not have to be their mouthpiece. She could symbolize her right to be independent of parental control without tumbling into the disruptive rebellion of the youth culture.

Thus Joyce won her way through the formidable social problem of adolescence. But how, we must ask, had she accomplished the first step? How had she overcome her fear of isolation from the peer group, her seemingly urgent need for the affection and approval of the other girls? This is where her meeting with Rennie was crucial. When she returned to school for her senior year and assumed her presidential duties she had met Rennie, enjoyed his company, fantasied the future farm with all that it implied. She was in love and her love was returned; though only sixteen, she had met the man she was going to marry. Thus she had jumped clean over the rating-and-dating problems of adolescence. From being the prim and backward girl who evoked the sneers of her more sophisticated companions she had gone at one bound into the position of an engaged young woman, leaving adolescence behind her. She did not need the esteem of the still-experimenting girls once she had swept past them and reached the stage toward which they were groping; all the more she did not need it from the girls when she was receiving it from Rennie. Thus she freed herself from meeting the requirements of the youth culture and regained her capacity to work for the ideals she had taken from parents and teachers, ideals upon which she and Rennie were in essential agreement.

It is not to be assumed, of course, that Joyce's development really advanced at a magical pace. Her love for Rennie was at first undoubtedly that of a starry-eyed schoolgirl. Subjectively, however, her relationship to Rennie gave her a tremendous increase of happy confidence and security, thus opening the way for further development in several directions. She could even allow herself more feeling in response to boys, secure in the knowledge that she could afford to reject a boy if he insisted upon too much sex or in some other way displeased her. This was illustrated in the incident of Carlos. Joyce described Carlos as "the only other man in whom I have ever been seriously interested." He was a Latin American who had come to Boston to study music. He was unable to find a place to live, and when his plight came to the ears of the ever-helpful Mr. Kingsley, he was promptly installed in the Kingsley household. Almost as promptly Carlos began to take an interest in his host's seventeen-year-old daughter. Joyce described what happened as follows:

> As I have said, I am very interested in music, and was especially much interested at that time (when I was a senior in preparatory school). Carlos knew of no other relation to have with a girl except an amorous one. I regarded him as an interesting person who danced well, and with whom I could play duets. I was so interested in Rennie that I didn't think of Carlos as anything but a friend, as so many other boys had been. He had always gone around with rather "fast" girls whom I didn't enjoy. Naturally I saw a lot of him and became more and more fond of him. For a while he convinced me that I was in love with him. It didn't last very long, because I soon realized what kind of a person he really was. Carlos is really very sweet, and very dependent on other people. He's lively and gay, and I especially fell for his good dancing. But he can (usually) wheedle anything he wants out of people, and he isn't honest with himself or with others. So that put an end to that.

Carlos was not classified as a major positive event, but in spite of his indignant dismissal he seems to have had a considerable influence on Joyce. She experienced a quickening and deepening of her esthetic interests, which thenceforth occupied an increasingly important position in her economy of happiness.

College Years: Living with Enthusiasm

It was during her first year at college that Joyce encountered her major negative experience. Perhaps under no circumstances could her recent happiness have continued at its exalted level, but the actual situation let her down with a bad bump. "I look back on it as a perfect nightmare," she wrote; then, becoming scientifically analytical, she considered under five headings the "several forces" that produced her misery. Her first two paragraphs described the difficulties so commonly met in making the transition from a small school to a large college:

(1) I had come from a school situation where I was one of the "big shots." I don't think that ever went to my head, but I was used to being in the middle of things, having the lead often, and having people look up to me and respect what I said (sometimes). I had also been very successful academically, never getting a mark below a "B."

(2) I didn't know anyone else who was going to Radcliffe, and most everyone else did. I was living at home, and that made getting acquainted even harder.

Joyce's next point is given a coloring somewhat more peculiar to herself. Having lost her distinguished position, she found it more difficult to dispense with the approval of her age-peers.

(3) At school I had always stood out against the mores of the crowd. I wouldn't chase after boys at the dances, nor would I discuss my dates as much as the other girls did. I found that this approach didn't work as well at college; not that one had to broadcast dates, but several times after I had taken very attractive boys to dances and had had good times with them I was rather automatically "admitted" to friendship with many girls. In prep school I would have scorned those people, but I soon learned that I should not in college.

In her next point she returned to a common complaint of freshmen, especially those who cannot live at college.

(4) Also I think I was unaware of much that was going on around me. I had to study hard and help at home and didn't get to Forum or the League for Democracy or the Outing Club meetings I would have liked to have gone to sometimes. I was timid about talking to professors and instructors. In other words I wasn't outgoing enough.

Joyce did not weight her "several forces," but it is probably justifiable to assume that the fifth one was the most shattering of all. The keystone seemed about to drop from the arch.

(5) And to make matters worse, I went down to Princeton for the first time to visit Rennie in November. Rennie was going through a time when he wanted to be very much "one of the gang." He had a roommate who was facing the same difficulty and who couldn't understand anyone who wasn't just like him (and I wasn't). I was thoroughly bewildered at college, and looked to Rennie for help. I didn't hear from him for three months or so after that visit. I didn't know what had happened. And that just added to my bewilderment.

Rennie was young, too; he was disappointed when Joyce, deep in the throes of her other problems, seemed unresponsive to a weekend of jollity. It began to look as if the idealistic romance would not survive the college years.

After a while Rennie broke his silence, but Joyce was no longer so confident about the future. Her pattern of life began to change:

> Toward the end of the year I began going out a lot, got more into things, made many friends, and stopped worrying about my marks. I decided to go to school that summer, and became thoroughly adjusted to the whole situation more or less automatically, so it all turned out all right after that.

She made herself more "outgoing," even to the extent of having two or three dates a week. Joyce was pretty and lively; it was not her fate to be a wallflower. She enjoyed going out, especially with boys who could talk about serious things, and it was doubtless reassuring to her to find that she need not be without partners. Her new friendships were not, however, marked by "serious interest," even of the sort evoked by Carlos, much less of the kind she had felt, and still felt, toward Rennie. They were also not marked by any forward steps in sexual experimentation. She had decided that this realm should be explored only after marriage. Even in an interview with the woman who had earlier been her tutor, for whom she felt warm admiration, she dealt with the topic of sex in somewhat distant fashion. "I regard sex as a sacred thing," she said; "I've always objected to anything else." And she confessed to a "sort of repulsion against the dirty side of it, as it were." Joyce had experienced "no tendency" toward masturbation, which she felt would probably disturb her. She was not accustomed to discuss sex with her friends; such knowledge as she possessed came from her mother, largely in answer to questions, and from courses in biology and psychology. Her store of information she considered rather limited, but about this she was cheerfully unconcerned. "I think I know the things I need to know," she said; "if there are more things that I need to know I will know them, by finding out or by intuition."

Joyce's real feeling remained attached to Rennie, and before long her affection was again reciprocated. Within a year of the ill-starred trip to Princeton they became secretly engaged. The reason for secrecy can be inferred from the reaction of Joyce's parents when, nearly two years later, she consulted them with a view to announcing the engagement. They both approved highly of Rennie, and were probably not startled at the news, but they were reluctant to believe that the time for marriage had really arrived. Although they agreed to issue the announcement, they counseled that the engagement should be a long one so that both youngsters would have time to become more settled and mature.

Once her engagement became a fact, even though a secret one, Joyce found herself again released from dependence on the approval of her girl friends. She began to resume her role as an official. Several elective offices came her way, including a rather prominent one in which she felt that she was able to make an important contribution. The "feeling of separation" that had characterized her freshman year was replaced by a welcome sense of belongingness. In an interview she listed "having a great many friends" as one of the three best things in life, "being ostracized" as one of the worst. She learned that officeholding at college did not entail the same estrangement from the group that accompanied it during her schoolgirl years. She took increasing pleasure in meeting people and talking with them, sharing enthusiasms and serious interests. "I love to talk and discuss public affairs," she told us, and although she did not choose friends on this basis she found particular pleasure in the company of those who shared her interest in public events.

With regard to closer friendships, however, she remained unsatisfied. No longer fearful of rejection as a teacher's pet and "goody-goody," she still felt that her relationships lacked intimacy and depth. She noted that her best friends were either older or younger, that she tended—like her father—to be somewhat distant, and that she didn't know how to set about deepening a friendship. Replying to a question about her intuitive ability, she said that her intuition was "pretty good, mostly in the sense of understanding rather than in the sense of being empathic." Clearly she craved intimate friendship, but it was difficult for her to experience the feelings that nourish such a relationship. It was difficult to give confidences and to exhibit the quality of sincerity that she several times mentioned as the essence of true friendship. Joyce's problem is not the less interesting for being extremely common among college students and for exemplifying a marked characteristic of the American culture. Diffuse sociability and close personal friendships are two very different things. Our contemporary culture encourages the former but strews various obstacles in the way of the latter.

Before we analyze this problem in Joyce, however, it will be well to complete our description of her college years.

A wide range of interests and enthusiasms kept her happily busy during her last two years at college. There was never enough time for all the things she wanted to do. Discussing politics, meeting people, taking part in student activities took up part of her energies, but she was also interested in pottery, sewing, and cooking. Her early fascination by flowers and birds continued, exposing her to a bad annual attack of spring fever, and she was often "ecstatic" over beautiful views and glorious sunsets. She loved the colorful, the cheerful, and the gay in objects as well as in people. Positions of special importance in her life were occupied by music and dancing. She loved the music that went with dancing, but she also loved choral music and experienced some of her deepest rapture in connection with the great religious choral works. Starting at nine, she had taken piano lessons for several years and had become fairly proficient in reading music at sight. The system used by her piano teacher did not emphasize sight-reading, but Joyce shunned the difficult exercises, "never practiced properly," and developed her piano technique more or less in her own way. She found in sight-reading not only musical pleasure but also a challenge to work the piece out, similar to the challenge of solving a problem in mathematics. She considered music the greatest of her enjoyments.

Joyce's use of her mind in intellectual pursuits afforded an interesting comparison with Hale and Kidd. Even in artificial test situations there were fundamental differences. With the Rorschach ink-blots, for instance, she showed none of Hale's precision or preference for mechanical objects, nor did she display Kidd's laborious search for details and leaning toward drab interpretations. She was inclined to take in the whole blot at a glance, giving it an overall interpretation that made up in enthusiasm for what it lacked in point of detail. Her main responses suggested a proclivity for vague, rosy-hued philosophizing, and something of this sort could be detected in her approach to serious intellectual problems. In conversation her ideas flowed with fluent ease, but they took the form of generalities sometimes none too well backed by detailed information; her arguments proceeded not so much by strict logic as by an almost esthetic combination of concrete examples and strongly affirmed values. In the Vygotsky experiment her classifying of the blocks was almost entirely a perceptual process, in contrast to the highly logical Hale. Like Kidd she manipulated the blocks as if waiting for them to announce their properties, but she did not have Kidd's difficulty in formulating the principle once she had discovered the correct solution. Logic was available to her, but she preferred to work in a more colorful, esthetic fashion.

In spite of this quality in her thinking, Joyce's general ideas were formed into a working philosophy that in a very real sense acted as a guide to behavior. She was far more explicit concerning values than either Hale or Kidd. This was because she was heir to her parents' explicit system of values, an inheritance she showed no disposition to reject. Both parents, it will be recalled, had rebelled against rigidly Republican backgrounds and sought the position of independents in politics. On the national scene they supported the New Deal and were warm admirers of President Roosevelt. When Joyce was asked for her views with regard to people who had recently run for state office, she came out with precisely the same slate that had been favored by her parents. It was noteworthy that when she discussed political figures she often reported that "we" feel thus-and-so, "we" think this-and-that, as if opinions were a matter of unanimous decision around the Kingsley dining table. "We admire Mr. and Mrs. Roosevelt greatly," she said in an interview; then she called attention to a parallel "greatness" in the way the Roosevelts and her parents had taken public criticism.

It goes without saying that Joyce was religious. "Religion has been a lifelong thing for me," she wrote; she accepted it because "it has the most plausible explanations of how the world came to be and why man is what he is." We were not vouchsafed an account of the more personal side of her religion. "The religious experiences I have had are too intensely personal to write or to relate." But it was plain that religion was the cornerstone of her thinking about social problems. "I don't believe that men will ever be completely happy," she wrote, "until their lives are on a religious basis; by that I mean they will acknowledge God as the Supreme Being and the source of their lives and proceed to try to live up to that." She recognized that such a development could not be forced; it must come about as a slow growth through education in the broadest sense of the word. Essentially she held the view that social betterment comes about by improving the quality of individual lives. Her own role was "to live as well as I can, to build the characteristics I say others should have in myself, and to try to help my children to have them also."

It is interesting to note that Joyce's personal philosophy was a shade more individualistic than that of her father, who was, as we have seen, deeply interested in the cooperative movement. The following excerpt, given in answer to a question about cooperation, is hardly a model of clarity, but its confusion becomes meaningful when we recall her position as eldest daughter in a cooperative home, pledged not to put personal interests ahead of those of the group.

> Cooperation is a wonderful thing, but for its strength it depends on people realizing their own value. It's important, but I value my own privacy a lot; so I'm not sure that it's valuable in all fields. But cooperation in any economic endeavor is the best thing; potentially every man has a chance. Though it often takes a long time. We're tied down by the past. If it were left that each individual were left in freedom to the greatest extent and could still fulfill his obligations, it would be a good thing. When one is tied to a thing like that you have to do it all day and all night, and it suppresses individual wishes—which might be a good thing. But anyhow it would be difficult.

Joyce herself recognized in these remarks a lapse from her usual standard of coherence. "Oh, I guess I'm rambling," she said, "but I do get so enthusiastic and excited!" She probably did not recognize, however, the precise nature of the personal problem that was here invading her public sentiment. Privacy and independence had suffered a bit in her development; service to the group figured as a somewhat bleak duty, in contrast to the lively enthusiasm that characterized most of her behavior.

The story of Joyce's last two years at college would be incomplete without mention of her baby cousin Philip. In fact, Joyce listed Philip, along with Rennie and her presidency of student government, as one of the three major positive events in her life. Philip came to live with the Kingsleys because his mother became mentally deranged shortly after his birth. He was soon "the center of everything," and his mother's continued ill health made it seem likely that he would be a permanent member of the family. Joyce wrote:

> He is now a year and a half old, and one of the most delightful babies there has ever been. I have had a grand time taking care of him and playing with him. He is quite cooperative most of the time, and a joy to be with.

Elsewhere, comparing him with her two brothers, she made the remark, "I'm freer to shower my affection on Philip." Apparently she found in Philip a sudden, unexpected, welcome outlet for a flood of tender cherishing that had previously been impounded within her. Her maternal feelings found a channel agreeably free from obstacles. With characteristic enthusiasm she took on the mothering of her parents' "adopted" child.

Writing about her plans for the immediate future Joyce gave her chief aim as that of finding a job on the West Coast. Rennie's training in the sciences placed him in a highly specialized section of the military program, and he expected to stay on the West Coast for the duration of the war. She continued:

> Another chief aim is to be married. I think that emotionally we're ready to be married now. We have other problems to face, though: mostly finances, and parents who think we should see more of the "big wide world" first. The parents can and will take care of themselves when the time comes, but the finances aren't as easy as all that. There just plain aren't any at this point. I have enough money to take me to the West Coast and hold me over until pay checks start coming in. Rennie has a private's pay, most of which he puts into war bonds. We think now that it will be better to wait a while for these reasons. But that doesn't stop us from planning and working hard toward this, our main aspiration, all the time.

Joyce was stepping forth into a troubled world and an uncertain future, but she was doing so without dismay. She looked forward with cheerful confidence to whatever might happen next in life's joyous adventure.

Beneath the Surface: Analysis of Free Associations

It should not be laid down as a dogma that no one can have a happy childhood. We have reason to believe that Joyce's childhood was, in the main, a happy one, and that her adolescence was in a good many respects a joyous adventure. Yet we were led to suspect that she had a special interest in painting a sunny picture of her life, as if her emotional economy depended upon seeing things in their most cheerful light. Her own surprise that her early memories were so uniformly happy can be taken as evidence of a dim sense of incompleteness. Furthermore, it became increasingly apparent that certain tendencies —independence, rebelliousness, aggression—played almost no part in

her self-picture but betrayed their presence in side remarks or in statements quickly dismissed as of no importance. Was she fully satisfied
that her duties as eldest child and only daughter were no more than
fair? Was she content when she came to recognize the silent infiltration
of parental moral values? Had she been able to accept without rebellion the whole high code which her parents preached and sought to
exemplify? Did she resent the tie to her mother? Did she herself have
certain qualities which defeated her search for close friends? On all
these points there were scraps of evidence suggesting that beneath the
surface Joyce was not without her resentments and aggressions. Her
psychological development had not been as easy as she seemed inclined to believe.

It will be remembered that Joyce characterized Rennie as
"more gentle, kind, and understanding" than herself. Interesting in this
connection is a story she told in the Thematic Apperception Test. A
young couple was happily married, but the wife destroyed the initial
happiness by "making selfish demands" on the husband, stubbornly
persisting even when she saw that he did not like it. When the husband
was called to military service, she weepingly realized her loneliness and
loss, and during the three years of his absence "just concentrated in
everything she did on overcoming interest in herself and making herself more and more outgoing and thoughtful of other people." Because
of this strenuous moral development on the part of the heroine, the
story came to a happy ending. It may well be that this tale recapitu-
lated her own temporary estrangement from Rennie; at all events, it
suggests that Joyce was to some extent aware of a streak in herself that
was very different from her professed ideals, a streak of selfish demandingness and resentment that could be subdued only with a definite struggle. It is not surprising that if being "thoughtful of other
people" required such formidable self-discipline it would not be readily
available in the spontaneous form needed for intimate friendship. We
can think of Joyce as one who, because of a need for alliance with
parents against brothers, had tried to be too good too soon. She had
tried to suppress her selfish needs faster than they could really be
suppressed, especially in view of occasional doubt about the sufficiency
of parental rewards. As a result her selfish needs had given her a real
tussle, and she was still made uneasy by their undercover activity.

Our clearest insight into how Joyce carried on the battle for
goodness came from an hour devoted to free association. The session
was conducted by a woman graduate student who put questions only

when Joyce fell spontaneously silent. As often happens in free association, Joyce chose her first topic by looking around the room, but
almost at once she arrived at an emotionally charged problem—her
mother.

> The first thing that comes to my mind is seeing the curtains. I like
> to plan dresses and things. I like to sew. I'm thinking, worrying—
> no, thinking of dresses I need. I want to try to make some block
> prints to put on the bottom of a skirt. Pretty little birds with crowns
> on their heads. Mother thinks that maybe flowers would be good.
> Big spring flowers. Umm. (Pause) This is difficult. I don't feel like
> thinking any particular thing at this point.

Pages could be spent analyzing this utterance, so simple and banal yet
thematically so rich. The most significant item is the decorations on
the dress. Will it be birds or flowers? Will it be what Joyce wants or
what Mother thinks is good? Here the associations block and the
outcome is enigmatic. The resolution of this conflict is also obscured in
the Thematic Apperception Test. The story has already been mentioned in which a young woman finds herself bound by a mysterious
and inescapable tie to an older one. In contrast, there are two stories
in which the heroine rebels against parental expectations and successfully goes her own way. The first story finds her leaving the farm with
its round of domestic duties in order to become a music teacher. In the
second story a girl of eighteen falls violently in love, and there is
nothing her mother can do to prevent her from going ahead with
marriage. It is interesting, however, that Joyce gave a certain distance
to these two plots: she specified that the farm parents were European
immigrants preserving foreign ideals, and that the love-smitten girl of
eighteen was only the adopted child of the worried mother. Thus both
in her stories and in her initial free association Joyce avoided a definitive decision on the mother-daughter problem.

Pursuing the free associations further, Joyce devoted a substantial part of the hour to thinking about the Parkins family. Mr.
Parkins was a close friend of the family, and the one child, an adopted
daughter Mabel, was one of Joyce's friends and schoolmates. Joyce
had been talking about her brother Henry, incidentally criticizing her
mother's insufficient concern about the boy's health; then came a long
silence which was broken as follows:

> I can't help wondering about Mabel. Her mother seems to be awfully
> happy about letting her go away. I wonder if Mabel can sustain

that and pull through it without getting sick. She doesn't know how to cook and isn't interested in learning. It's most cruel to children to protect them like that, to indulge them in everything and give them what they want—whether they're adopted children or not. After all, in later life they are not going to have such privileges. Lack of discrimination in buying things and . . . I think Mabel would be much happier if her mother hadn't let her dress up so in school . . . with high heels, carrying a big load of books, all stoop-shouldered. It was unnatural. She's never been very happy. She's always had to think how her mother would react. She seems to have had the right approach, though. She just lets things ride and her mother comes around, like she did about Fritz.

Then followed some remarks about Fritz, Mabel's fiancé, a foreign-born young man with various undesirable traits, which, however, Joyce was inclined to excuse on the ground of a difficult economic and family situation. She was soon back at Mabel.

Maybe Mabel will do a lot for him. What a situation it would be, though, to start out and not know how to cook and take care of a house. Nor to use money. Plenty of people start out knowing very little, but they are more practical than Mabel is. Maybe she has it in her and we've just never seen it. (Pause) She certainly has developed a method for getting around her mother. I wonder if it's a conscious method or Mabel just is that way.

It seemed like a change of subject when Joyce, again pausing, began to talk about Mabel's father, but she did not stray far from her underlying theme. Mr. Parkins was a saintly man, never known to criticize, but always "the prey of his wife's will." Two or three episodes were mentioned to exemplify his wife's selfish, nagging demandingness and his own distress at her behavior. Then Joyce said:

Mother said he was very embarrassed that Mrs. Parkins hadn't gone to the meeting after Mother had called her up and told her of my engagement. It was hard for her to take. She felt it very keenly that Rennie is a college graduate and Fritz isn't. It is also a little tough on her that Fritz is a foreigner and Rennie isn't. Still, I can't imagine Mabel settling down with any of the people her mother would have chosen.

It appeared that Mabel had taken no chances of incurring parental objection to her engagement. Unlike Joyce, she had made the announcement herself.

It must have been a little hard for both of them, to just suddenly have her get a ring and take it to church and show it around and let people know that way. When Mabel showed the ring herself it was as if her parents weren't backing her up. Mrs. Brown said at the time, "Wasn't it a shame!" We were kind of flabbergasted that anyone would say that about any kind of engagement.

Possibly Joyce received a silent inner warning at this point that her sympathy for Mabel's independence needed a touch of discipline. Had not her own parents given her great benefits yet at the same time left her free?

It certainly makes you appreciate parents who are aware of things and particularly who are eager to leave you free to make your own choices and accept the responsibility you are going to take. I think if we'd been very wealthy I still would have learned to cook, sew, and so forth.

Having said this much, however, she received another prompting from a tendency not quite so docile:

I often wonder just what it is that made them the way they are. . . .

It certainly helps the parents out to have older children to accept some of the responsibility, so that they are left a little freer to take care of the others.

This was dangerous ground, and she did not tarry longer. After dealing with several other matters she went into a long discussion of memory, which eventually led her to the following observation:

Seems kind of strange when all your childhood memories are happy ones and you wonder why there aren't some unhappy ones. You don't think there would be, or the happy ones would bring them up if there were any. I wonder just how much there is to the idea of repression. Seems as if sometimes it must be exploited a bit.

And these remarks on memory, which brought the free association hour to a close, could by no means be regarded as chance driftwood on the surface of Joyce's consciousness. In the very last interview of our series, which we call the "worm turns interview" because of the encouragement that is given the subject to criticize both the procedures and the investigators, she offered as her sole serious criticism the failure of the interviewers to appreciate the importance of her having had a happy childhood.

Joyce's free associations clearly disclosed the residual tension left by her full acceptance of the parental ideals of conduct. She had been obliged to give up a little too much of her independence and the pursuit of her own desires. She had accepted a little too much of her mother's domination. Beneath the surface there was resentment and rebellion. Nevertheless, her adoption of an approved life pattern had been far from a sullen and mechanical conformity. She had thrown her whole soul into it, she had lived it with enthusiasm, and it had brought her great rewards, such as her presidency of student government, her place in college activities, and Rennie. Within its requirements she had fallen in love and was planning her own home, and her life was rich with a wide variety of interests. Rebellious aggression was probably linked with childhood anxieties, but it was also out of harmony with her current self-picture and could be sensed only as a disruptive force in the program of her ongoing concerns. The free associations show how she dealt with it. She could be very critical of, not her own mother, but Mrs. Parkins, who selfishly ruled the household. She obviously envied Mabel's independence, but she could be indignant about Mabel's crudeness in announcing her engagement and about her ignorance of household duties. Throughout the free associations her comments about people were decidedly acid, and as she voiced her criticisms she did nothing to avoid the implication that her own way of doing things was morally superior. She thus gave herself constant doses of reassurance while at the same time making outlets for no small amounts of righteous aggression. Her treasonable impulses seemed well controlled by this procedure, but at the cost of the tolerance and humility that would have helped her to make intimate friendships.

PART TWO: FROM TWENTY-ONE TO TWENTY-SIX

Immediately after graduation Joyce departed for the West Coast, where she secured a job in the large military research unit to which Rennie had been assigned. She and Rennie were married the following spring. Rennie's educational plans after his release from military service brought them back to Boston for a two-year period, during which they occupied an apartment in the Kingsley home. Then Rennie obtained a position with a large manufacturing company, and he and

Joyce moved to Detroit to set up a home of their own. It was from there that they came, two years later, for the brief summer visit which gave us the opportunity to make the second study.

Out into the World

Joyce was excited by what she found awaiting her on the West Coast. The scenery was enchanting, the people in the vast unit were endlessly interesting, the work kept her happily occupied; in short, it was "just the most fascinating place that anyone could possibly be in." She continued to live with enthusiasm, and she soon became aware of considerable changes taking place in herself. Questioned about these changes, she gave us the following piece of self-analysis:

> I think that getting away from home did a lot for me, as far as change goes. I think that just being away did a lot, though I'm not quite sure how. Maybe making my own decisions without any . . . oh, there hadn't been parental interference, but there were attitudes about what I did, and without those around, I think that accounts for a good deal of starting independence, my foundation for it, anyhow.

Continuing her discussion of change, Joyce reminded us that she had never had many close friends and did not know how to make them. The new situation helped her a great deal with this problem. Rennie had found a highly congenial group of friends, many of whom had either wives or girl friends, so that Joyce was immersed in a pleasant social whirl. "I just sort of got a beginning there," she said; then she added, laughing at her own way of putting it, "I could see the possibilities and get some techniques for being a friend to somebody." Her relationship with Rennie "grew a great deal," and she believed that this had a lot to do "with changing attitudes and gaining independence." Joyce was not in a competitive situation as regards men, nor was she too starvingly in need of the approbation of other young people; this made it easier for her to enter on the path of establishing warmer friendships.

Joyce expressed astonishment that the strict standards under which she had been reared did not interfere with her social growth on the West Coast. She described the situation as follows:

> One thing that amazed me out there was my quick adjustment to a change of standards. As was probably evident before, standards at

home were pretty high and pretty strict, in a way. And . . . well, in the unit there were just no holds barred in conversation; anything went. And I didn't have any trouble adjusting to it, which amazed me, because I would have thought I would have. But it was the pattern, it was a completely new place, completely different, and it just came all right. Fortunately!

By way of illustration she mentioned a girl who had "*quite* a reputation" with the boys. "I discovered that she was a very charming girl and I thoroughly enjoyed her."

The theme of adjusting to different standards was developed further in another interview during which Joyce was asked what she wished had been done differently in her own upbringing. She wished that she had gone to college far away from home, feeling that she would thus have learned earlier to be more tolerant of other people and their standards. Her words fully corroborated the inferences we previously made concerning self-righteousness and its effects on friendship.

I think that being away at college would have been awfully fine because I would have had a chance to establish myself separately and to really test what I thought I believed. As it was, I didn't have that until I went out to the West Coast, and fortunately it came smoothly then. But I had a sort of sense of being different from everybody, which isn't conducive to establishing good relationships with new people at all. I mean, I don't think it was being different in the sense of being better, although there are some implications of that in the sense of "this is the way for me to behave; you don't behave that way"—you know. You can't help feeling that what you think is right is the best thing. But I think that the social adjustment eased a good deal when I got away from those standards. And it wasn't so much a question of not accepting the standards any longer as it was of being freer to see and understand other standards.

The last sentence in Joyce's reflections is of particular interest. Pleased as she was to find herself growing more tolerant and friendly, irked as she was by the memory of her former prudish subjugation to the parental value system, she nevertheless claimed that her new understanding had not made it impossible for her to act upon standards of her own. It is often difficult for a person to achieve independence of parental ideals without swinging to an opposite extreme and becoming an enemy of all fixed values. Joyce implied that she had avoided this swing of the pendulum. From an incident described in another connection we concluded that she might well have judged herself correctly on this point. Her job was at the young people's recreation center, and she found herself increasingly at variance with official policy. One or two of the employees seemed to her unsuitable to be in charge of adolescents, and several parents had become unwilling to have their children go to the center merely to dance, drink Cokes, play cards, and do a little necking. Joyce's desire to be a friendly person and a cooperative member of her society had not obliterated her antipathy toward the youth culture of early adolescence. She was outraged, moreover, by the failure of the recreation center to offer its young clients sufficient opportunities for the development of serious interests. Her anger was further aroused by a series of orders issued in peremptory military fashion though intended only for the civilian personnel; one such order required her to work overtime on evenings when Rennie was at liberty. She was already meditating a letter of protest when another order arrived which affected one of the few remaining serious enterprises at the center. Some strange bureaucratic whim dictated that the paper published every Wednesday by an enthusiastic group of youthful editors should thereafter be published on Friday. Joyce undertook to voice the editors' objections, only to find herself on an endless chain of official "buck-passing." So she composed her letter to the higher authorities, detailing her grievances and outlining a program of what she believed could and should be done at the recreation center; at the same time she resigned from her job. She distributed the letter widely to interested parents and to the military hierarchy, including the commanding officer of the post. "And something did get done," she told us:

> They used the blueprint that I'd started on as a basis for working it up again, so I think it was a useful thing to do. But, again, I think it was another step toward independence, because here I was, thinking something out completely for myself without going to talk to Mother about it, which was really something when you get right down to it. And having confidence in my ability to do it.

During her year on the West Coast Joyce thus made rapid strides toward independence. To a considerable extent she extricated herself from hitherto unquestioned parental influences and acquired the confidence to feel and act in her own right. Being away from home was a highly successful venture. At no time, however, had she really been an insecure stranger without a point of anchorage in the new community. She was engaged to Rennie, and presently she became his wife.

Marriage

When Joyce first arrived at the military post she elected to live inexpensively by taking her meals at the mess hall. Soon the fare began to pall, so she started cooking the evening meal in her dormitory room and inviting Rennie to eat it with her. "It was just superb," she said; "we spent all our evenings together and went hiking practically every weekend." Rennie was due for a furlough in December, but Joyce's parents vetoed a plan to have the wedding so soon. This was disappointing, but "the winter flew by in a hurry," and by May the Kingsleys were able to have their house redecorated and their preparations made for a large wedding. "I made my own wedding gown and some of my trousseau," said Joyce, but then she added truthfully, "Mother made most of it because I didn't have very much time." After the wedding she and Rennie returned to the West Coast until his military service was completed, at which point they took a honeymoon camping trip in the mountains. Then they returned to Boston and settled down in the apartment, a more or less separate suite of rooms in the Kingsley house, which they were to occupy until Rennie completed his specialized training.

When questioned about the sexual side of marriage Joyce reported, after a little hesitation, that she had experienced some difficulty in achieving a relaxed attitude. That she was able eventually to attain orgasm and a feeling of satisfaction was due in part to her husband's understanding.

> Fortunately Renn is one of the most patient people on the face of the earth, and I think he understood how it does take a while to get to the point where you really are free and warm. Having strict standards makes it a very difficult break. I think that Renn did . . . while I don't know that he realized the problems, I think he did everything he could to make it easier. And when you're very much in love it's easier anyhow, I suppose, than when you have doubts. I think also that it's a process that goes on and on.

In response to another question Joyce said that it had taken "about a year" to reach good sexual adjustment. When the interviewer remarked that this was not an unusually long period, she said, "It seemed long to me." One can hardly escape the conclusion that for a while she experienced the sexual relationship as an irksome obligation, a frustratingly difficult task rather than a pleasure. She has made progress, but she is not unaware that learning to be "free and warm" is a process that "goes on and on."

Joyce was more concerned, however, about a problem in marital adjustment that arose where she least expected it. Shortly after the marriage Renn reached the conclusion that he no longer believed in religion. Joyce was deeply upset; "it was especially difficult for me," she said, "because I had grown up in a home where there was strong religious influence and I had expected certain elements of that to carry over into our own life together." What bothered her most was the discovery that she could not do anything to change Renn's views. At first she was much concerned about "helping him to see the light," but she soon realized that her efforts only made matters worse.

> I eventually got to the point where I saw that there wasn't anything I could do except sit back and see what happened. He sort of wanted to work things out for himself and wanted to take his own time doing it. It's sort of hard to get to the point where you can realize that the best thing for you to do is just plain not to push it. It took me a year or two to really be able to do it.

The problem was aggravated by the move to Boston, where Joyce felt that Renn "had to keep up certain appearances." She kept hoping that events would hasten his return to religious faith. When his mother died she thought, "Now maybe this will help." She encouraged herself by practicing silent psychological diagnosis: his agnosticism was part of his need to achieve independence from his parents. All of this was not very comforting, for Renn seemed to be making little progress back toward religion. When questioned, Joyce admitted that her disappointment about his religious views had hindered the process of sexual adjustment. "It made me overly critical," she said, "and I don't think it helped me in the relaxing problem."

The move out to Detroit proved helpful in reaching a compromise on the question of religion. Away from the parental atmosphere Joyce found it easier to make fewer demands. Furthermore, the minister of her church in Detroit turned out to be an uncongenial person having a different shade of views from those to which she was accustomed; and she herself preferred to attend, at least temporarily, a church of another denomination that had an active program for young married people. "There are so many other things to do on weekends," she admitted with a laugh, "that we've become rather lax about church-going." Renn agreed to accompany Joyce to church, but she found it expedient not to press for too frequent attendance, and she decided not to insist on the custom of saying grace before meals.

There was another problem which likewise reached its height during the stay in Boston and improved after the move to Detroit. Joyce discovered that she could not help behaving somewhat like the demanding wife of her story in the earlier Thematic Apperception Test.

> I found it awfully hard to leave Renn as free as he wanted to be left, for quite a while. Of course the transition from courtship to marriage is quite something. I think that I expected some of those same attentions to hold over and found it a little difficult when at times they didn't. And I made demands on Renn which he didn't want to have made on him because of that, demands for time and attention. . . . I had sort of a picture of a glorious future when we did everything together, which is really very silly, because I don't think it does anybody that much good. You've got to have independent things so that you bring something new into the relationship all the time.

Joyce was shrewdly aware that this problem was mixed up with that of becoming independent of her mother. Renn told her that she was a different person when she was near her mother.

> I think I realized that in coming back there would be a problem, that Mother had never realized the influence she had on me, and that I knew it but didn't know what to do about it, how to handle it. She never wanted to influence her children in terms of deciding what they would do, or think, or feel, but she has a very strong personality herself, and she just inevitably *does*. I don't think she can help it. And I think that I sort of depended extra much on Renn because of that, to sort of tide me over. And that's pretty difficult for a new husband to take, really.

Things began to look different when Renn received an excellent appointment in Detroit and moved his wife away from the Kingsley home. He and Joyce bought an old house cheaply and worked together to repair it. Having more of her husband's time and attention, Joyce could afford to be more tolerant of his occasional independent activities with men friends and associates at the shop. Hearing her description of Renn we were reminded of some of the things she said earlier about her father, but Renn's exploits were even more numerous than Mr. Kingsley's:

> He has great skills in mechanical things and in carpentry and in gardening and masonry, and any other direction you want to turn, practically. . . . He has great facility in ironing out human relations problems; he's just so creative in human relations. . . . And then he plays on a baseball team. He's pretty terrific. Boy, can that guy hit? Golly! Wonderful! I have to go to every game. I don't have to; I go by choice. We form an active rooting group for our division team. ... . They're getting him in the Young Republican Club—over my dead body!

Joyce has learned painfully that she cannot dominate her husband nor direct the course of his life. He is no longer Rennie; he has proved to be Renn. But perhaps he has served all the better in disengaging her from her mother's influence, and perhaps she is more rather than less fond of him now than she was in the days of courtship and honeymoon. At all events she is happier. "Looking back," she told us, "I think there was never a time when I was really unhappy, and yet it seems to me that I'm so much more happy now than I was then. It quite amazes me!"

Joyce was well aware, however, that she would be still more happy if she had a baby. Thus far she had failed to conceive, and she was greatly distressed about it. She had sought medical aid and been given a clean bill of health, but the advice to "go to it" had not served to solve the problem. At first she worried too much, counting days and keeping temperature charts, but this seriously interfered with relaxing at times when conception was most likely to occur. Then her physician suggested that she forget about it and take up some line of work or study that would absorb her interests. In consequence of this advice she entered the school for social work, but when spring came she "got to one of those times when it is *very* hard not to have children" and appeared again at the physician's office. She was found to have an elevated basal metabolic rate and other evidences of tension. The school year had been strenuous, so she was advised this time to take the summer off and vegetate for a while. She was in process of vegetating at the time of the second study.

In discussing this major frustration, Joyce agreed that there were certain advantages in not having children too early in one's married life. She realized that she and Renn had had a chance to do more things together and to build a strong relationship, and she felt that he would probably be a better father and she a better mother because of having to wait for a baby. But her perception of the silver lining did not detract from her feeling about the cloud. Asked if she were using school work to keep her mind off the problem, she replied:

> You can't. I mean, it's just impossible to forget it. I wonder how anybody does, if anybody does. It's just always with you, and there are times when it's more pressing than other times, like this spring when my sister-in-law and one of my best friends both had babies at about the same time, and that was just awful. . . . You think you've gotten control of it, then whamo! You haven't after all. And it just keeps cropping up.

It is significant that Joyce here made no use of the device we suspected her of practicing when she wrote *Joyous Adventure*: that of putting things in a rosy light and repressing the disagreeable aspects of experience. She was in close touch with her maternal desires and was not in the least inclined to find anything joyous in their frustration. If she harbored repressed feelings that made her resist becoming a mother these feelings were operating in a very circumscribed channel—that of producing tension in the sexual relationship—and they were distinctly not creating a falsified picture of the blessings of childlessness.

The Kingsley Family Revisited

Five years had wrought a dramatic change in the Kingsley household. The stable serenity portrayed by Joyce in the year of her graduation from college had given place to decided storm and stress. Mr. Kingsley had passed through a serious crisis with regard to his work. Mrs. Kingsley had suffered a bout of ill health from which she had emerged to resume on a larger scale her independent career as a teacher. Joyce was revisiting her parents when she came for the second study, so we chose them as a topic on which to open the new interviews. We found that we were in for some surprises.

In his position as regional executive officer for his denomination, Mr. Kingsley was under the control of a board of governors. He had always had a certain amount of trouble with the board, but recently there had grown up a strong movement to oust him. For a time it seemed that his office might be abolished. Finally the board decided to extend it temporarily but to give Mr. Kingsley a less flattering title. Joyce considered that the situation was not good and probably never would be. "The effect in the family," she told us, "was felt most by Mother who has had a terribly hard time adjusting to the attacks—the very vehement personal attacks—that have been made on Daddy." Mrs. Kingsley was struck down simultaneously by arthritis and colitis. Her physician told her, in effect, that she could regain and keep her health only if she broke out of the frustrations of her present way of life and embarked upon the kind of career she really wanted. This advice, based on the supposition that the physical ailments were rooted in psychological problems, proved to be thoroughly sound. Mrs. Kingsley resumed her study of education and was soon appointed to an important post in a well-known school. According to Joyce this gave her "a completely new lease on life; it's just lifted her out of all the petty little mirey sorts of things." What things did Joyce have in mind?

> It took her out of home and it gave her people whom she enjoyed to associate with. Before, she'd been rebelling like fury against associating with the traditional church-woman sort of activity where you go and sew once a week or knit. One time she was program chairman of a reading club, and she was quite ecstatic about the prospect of presenting modern poetry, Rilke and so forth. And the good ladies didn't like that. She was just completely ill at ease in that sort of life. And going back to school just helped a great deal to give her people that she really could enjoy and intellectual stimulation for the very brilliant mind that she has.

Happy as she was over her mother's new buoyancy, Joyce could see "ways in which it isn't so good." Mrs. Kinglsey was so determined to stay out of church affairs that she would not even attend a convention in which her husband was much interested. "That is going too far to extremes," Joyce declared; "people kept asking where she was, and she told me something about Daddy saying that he couldn't invent any more excuses." Mrs. Kinglsey had hoped that as a consequence of the friction in the regional office her husband would leave the church altogether "so that they could go off and start afresh," and for a while Mr. Kingsley actually entertained this idea. But, as his daughter expressed it, "when a man has put his whole life into the church you just can't change it that way." When the worst of the clouds cleared away, Mr. Kingsley decided to stay on; he felt that his work was important, and he resisted his wife's urgings to make a break while it was still possible.

When we asked Joyce more about her father and his work we received an account that corresponded scarcely at all to the picture drawn in her earlier autobiography. Her description included the following:

> When he's really in a pinch he pulls himself out of it. But his main trouble is that he lets himself be bogged down by a myriad of petty details, and because of that he gets so busy with them that he can't do the big things. And much of the stuff he does is really not necessary.

Apparently Mr. Kingsley did many things around the office that could readily have been delegated to others. He charged himself with details that properly belonged to individual parishes and their ministers. In addition he managed his mother's finances and made out her income tax, and he did a great many things around his own home. Joyce concluded:

> I don't know how to account for the rest of it. I mean, it's just bad organization. And he's so mired down in it and has been at it for so many years that it's just come to the point where he's running himself ragged. It's crazy, but he can't get himself out of the rut apparently. He's that way and I guess you have to take him that way. It seems very silly, a lot of it, to me.

The drastic change in Joyce's attitude toward her parents, especially toward her father, deserves careful consideration. She exhibits a trend, quite common in the twenties, toward detachment and frank appraisal. We have already described a similar progression in Joseph Kidd's outlook on his parents. On the whole she is not unduly caustic, and there is certainly no little admiration for her mother's achievement in independence. The thing that is unusual in Joyce's case is not her objectivity at twenty-six but rather the gilded picture she created at twenty-one. Granting that things were better at that time, we must still ask why she needed to believe that her parents were so perfect, her home life so harmonious, as she portrayed them in the first study.

In attempting to answer this question it is necessary to bear in mind that identification with parental values played a vital part in her plan for living. It had served her in early childhood as a means of keeping Albert from crowding her out of parental favor. It had served at puberty as a weapon against the youth culture and as a platform for action and leadership. There had been little occasion to repudiate these values, which had not prevented her from finding a husband, which shielded her from things like sex of which she was afraid, and which frustrated her only to the extent of limiting her capacity for friendship. She had not really attempted to set up an identity of her own or to accept full responsibility for decisions and opinions. She was further exempted from perceiving the conflict between dependence and adult autonomy by the fact that her avenue of escape from the family was guaranteed by her engagement. Renn's values were like those of her home, and she knew that her parents could offer no permanent obstacle to her marrying such an admirable man. In the meantime, she found comfort in believing that her upbringing had been perfect, laying a "good foundation" for what lay ahead.

As we saw, she was much upset after marriage when Renn's religious values proved to be different, so that her own religious interests had to be the subject of compromise. She was again upset when renewed proximity to her mother reanimated the old dependence, and she then blamed Renn for failing in the function she had counted on him to perform. But once she found out that with Renn's help she could take her own stands and find the security of friends, she had little further need to lean on an idealized picture of her family.

Joyce brought us up to date concerning her brother Albert, of whose development during five years she sharply disapproved. Albert's passion for electronics had increased during military service and he had afterwards gone directly to work in an industrial laboratory without attempting to complete his education. Toward the family he was more surly and rebellious than ever. After displaying interest in a girl much admired by the Kingsleys ("We were pretty thrilled about it," said Joyce, reverting to the "we" of her undergraduate opinions), he perversely drifted off and married a girl as unkempt and careless as himself. As Joyce described it, "They both go around wearing jeans and shirts and tousled hair and practically look like twins." Joyce admitted that they "seemed pretty happy together," and she wondered if their coming baby might help them to be less rebellious. Throughout her conversation about Albert one could sense the working of her old childhood grievance. Albert was bad, but he did not receive enough punishment. He neglected his appearance and his education, he was boorish, he did just what he wanted, he did not marry the right kind of girl, and he was rewarded by having a baby, which both he and his wife would probably neglect. Joyce could hardly be blamed for having a continued sense of injustice.

Among Albert's sins was his undue influence over Henry, whom he indoctrinated with rebellious and bohemian ideas. Apart from this, however, Henry was developing nicely, and Joyce found him altogether charming. But it was when we inquired about Philip, now six, that Joyce really warmed to her subject. "Oh, he's a honey," she said with a laugh; "he's just delightful." We learned that she had helped take care of Philip during the stay in Boston and that for the past two summers Philip had lived with her and Renn in Detroit while Mrs. Kingsley took summer courses. "We have a lot of fun," she said, "and so does he." Joyce rejected our suggestion that Mrs. Kingsley could not have had much time to take care of her adopted child. "Her freedom from the general situation," Joyce declared, "has not meant that she has ignored Philip in any way. I mean, he's had mothering all right. He's had more variety of people around him and it's been good for him, because he's a very social little guy." Joyce believed that the visits to Detroit had been decidedly helpful to Philip. Renn was an eager mentor in sports; he had already inducted his youthful cousin into baseball, football, and tennis. And Joyce was sure that the atmosphere of their home would make things "a good deal less confining" for Philip "than they were for Albert and me, for instance. I think it will be a lot easier for him to adjust to the general mores than it was for us."

Some of Joyce's views on child rearing emerged from an incident she told us about with some pride. Philip was being constantly annoyed by the teasing of a girl playmate, which often drove him into a tearful rage. The little girl's mother told him to hit his tormentor as the only possible way to make her understand. Philip consulted Joyce concerning this heroic prescription.

> I presented him with another way to do it, thinking that that could very quickly get out of control. How would he know when to stop? That's expecting a good deal from a six-year-old. I suggested that he run off and do something else interesting when he wanted to do what she was doing, and first thing he knew she'd get interested in that. He was very intrigued and found that it worked, and he could get back to the swing before she got through with the tractor, and so forth. He would pretend that he didn't even hear her when she was saying something that bothered him.

If Joyce has in some respects diverged from parental ideals, it is not in the direction of tolerating overt aggression. One wonders whether she

invented the technique used on Philip or whether she merely remembered it.

It seems probable that Joyce's large share in taking care of
Philip gave her a certain consolation for having no baby of her own.
Philip was available, however, only in the summer time; for the rest of
the year her substitute activity was to attend the school for social
work.

Preparing for Social Work

When Joyce was advised by her physician to take up some work that
would occupy her interest she was at first completely at a loss. "What
on earth do I want to do?" she asked herself; then, consulting her
experience on the West Coast at the recreation center and her more
recent Girl Scout work in Detroit, she decided that the greatest promise lay in social group work.

> The social work part can just go hang, as far as I'm concerned, but
> you have to take the other stuff along with group work. And it just
> seemed like practically the only thing that I was really interested in
> and fitted for and could get into. . . . As far as the actual work of
> group work goes, it's the spot for me, because it combines a very
> intensive understanding of the individual personality, the psychology
> of the individual, with a just developing understanding of what goes
> on in a group. . . . But getting that darned old degree is just plain
> drudgery. I don't know if it's worth it, I really don't.

Joyce believed that her studies at the school, and the field
training that went with them, had helped her to become more tolerant
of diverse standards. One feature of her family's value system carried
over very nicely into social-work philosophy: the emphasis on "leaving
people free to make their own choices." "That is something that falls
right in with what I've always had," she reminded us; "practically a
family standby, or at least a standby of our church." To illustrate her
remarks she chose the subject on which she herself had previously
been most intolerant.

> The place where the standards come in is the question of "Now
> here's a bunch of teen-agers; what about their petting?" That sort
> of thing. And do I try to impose my standards on them or do I
> accept what they've got? And in working on something, do I work
> toward my standards or do I work toward something they choose?

That sort of thing. And that's the only place where there has been any conflict, and that isn't conflict, really, because emphasis in group work is on the use of the worker's personality as a tool in working with the group. And in doing that you have to generate warmth, if you haven't got it—and we hope you have—for all sorts and conditions of people, as they happen to be. And you have to accept their standards for what they are, which is part and parcel of this question of leaving a person free, really.

It is indeed difficult to effect a reconciliation between fighting for one's standards and working with people in that peculiarly tolerant and disarming fashion that is characteristic of social work. Joyce's problem at this point is more than a personal one.

It was obvious, of course, that Joyce had not entered social group work because of urgent need for a career. For the present, her whole heart was set upon having children. She had often, however, weighed the claims of homemaker and career woman, and her mother's example made it impossible for her to overlook the difficulties of a decision. "I still feel that the combination of some form of career with children is a good idea," she said, "but I don't quite know how it will work, or how to carry it out." Then she offered some wise reflections on the needs of young children and concluded that only some sort of part-time volunteer work would be compatible with these needs. Yet it was hard to make any solution retain a permanent shape. "I haven't solved for myself yet the conflict between getting educated and having children, and I don't know that I will. I keep trying. But you think you've got it under control and sometimes it just blows up in your face, and you gradually work it out again." The forces on either side of the conflict seemed too strong to remain long bound by a rational solution. But of course it was impossible for Joyce to reach a stable attitude when she did not know one of the most essential facts. She had to face the possibility that a career would be forced upon her or that the homemaker's role could be chosen only by adopting children. With this issue unsettled it is hardly surprising that she should close with the comment, "It's awfully hard to relax about the whole thing."

On the question of warmth in personal relationships Joyce did not, when pressed, make excessive claims to progress. When asked whether she had some close friends in Detroit she answered, "Yes, we do," and it required a further question to learn anything about friends whom she did not share with Renn. She then mentioned a number of people encountered at the school or in her Scout work. "I feel much more able to handle relationships on my own," she said. "That took a while, I don't know just why." Speculating on the reason, she mentioned that being a minister's daughter makes you "see yourself in a different role from what is the normal role." She was not wholly clear about it, but she had an inkling that a "superior" role, such as minister's daughter, president of student government, or leader of a Scout troop, might obstruct a warm response, especially from people who were either awestruck or irritated by that role. Yet it was in such roles that she felt most comfortable, and in spite of her gains on the West Coast and in Detroit she still had a lot to learn. "I think," she said, "that I have good hostessing skills but am just developing the more basic make-this-a-warm-and-lasting-relationship sort of skill. It is a long process, too. Got a long way to go yet."

Joyce's trouble with this problem sheds light on the psychological requisites for warm personal relationships. It is essential to intimacy that a person reveal what he is and how he feels regardless of desirability. He must be able to talk about faults, discouragements, and anxieties as well as valued feelings and cherished aspirations. Reassurance and closeness can result from the discovery that one's weaknesses are shared or at least understood by another person. It is here that Joyce runs into trouble. She learned long ago to suppress the kinds of impulse that flowered so disgracefully in Albert. From parental example she learned to express no resentments and to permit overt criticism only of what was morally inferior. So there is a feeling of risk about candor, an uneasy sensation of letting go a whole system of accustomed controls. Although there is a long way to go, she has at least made a start. She mentioned two friends who were often outspokenly critical, toward whom in return she was sometimes critical; then she went on to say that she had found these relationships particularly satisfactory and helpful. She was thus discovering a place where her defenses could be safely loosened.

PART THREE: FROM TWENTY-SIX TO FORTY

There is no better way to illustrate the evolving nature of personality than to break off the story of a life at an arbitrary point in time. The reader is left in suspense, feeling that the person under study may be significantly changed by what happens next. It is therefore a cause of satisfaction that Joyce Kingsley's attachments in the East occasionally brought her back from her present home in San Francisco and that she was willing to keep us informed about the progress of her life. She had sent a long letter covering another year when she received the typescript of the first two parts of this chapter, and there had been a conversation midway between then and the time when we asked for a long follow-up interview. On the latter occasion a worker who had known her before remarked that she "looked very lovely," and a colleague who did not know her described her as a strikingly attractive woman. Her good humor and radiant vitality might have suggested that everything in her life had turned out happily. The actual story teaches that these qualities are not so closely dependent on fortune's bounty, for Joyce had preserved and developed them through years that bore some of the somber colorings of tragedy.

The question that is likely to be raised first by students of Joyce's life is whether or not she eventually had children of her own. She did not, but she had a family by adoption consisting of a boy and a girl sixteen and fifteen respectively at the time of the third study. As her family is the central concern of her life, it is here that we shall look for the main theme of her history. At the age of twenty-six, however, the decision to adopt had not been made, and it is at that point that we take up the narrative.

We did not know at the time of the second study that the marriage was approaching its most serious trial. She believed that she had made progress in allowing Renn to be independent, but she had not made progress enough. She wrote of realizing bitterly that "one cannot hide one's head in the sand and play *Joyous Adventure* all the time." Events forced her to see that in the marriage relation she had substantially continued to deny difficulties: "by last spring the rut was dug pretty deep." Her letter continues:

> In order to keep reassuring myself that it was all right to stay in the rut, I had built up elaborate stereotypes about the way young husbands and wives should act—for instance, they should never go to sleep without kissing each other goodnight. Somehow I had amalgamated all the ideas from the movies and the magazines and goodness knows where else about what a marriage should be, and was trying to act by them rather than to follow my own good sense. Needless to say, this got too stuffy for Renn, and he rebelled. If this was marriage, he wasn't sure that he was fitted for it or that he wanted any. A contributing factor to his rebellion was the near-collapse of the marriage of some good friends of ours. Renn allied

himself with Sandra in her unhappiness, feeling that perhaps he was more interested in her than he was in me. This was a great blow to my pride, sense of morality, self-confidence and everything else. I have never felt so unhappy, miserable, and completely lonely.

Joyce tried to cope with her feelings by plugging away at her social-work studies, but sometimes she could not force herself to go out and stayed at home with her sorrows. Then she swallowed her pride—"it went down hard"—and sought the help of a counseling agency. The best therapy, however, seemed to come from a ten-day trip with a group of her classmates to a conference in a distant place.

I had a good time and forgot about Renn and home most of the time. I rediscovered faith in myself in associating with our group of five congenial girls and three boys. By the time I came back home Renn and Sandra had stopped seeing each other, but I still had to convince him that he wanted to stay married to me. The long slow process of rebuilding began, with both of us much freer individuals.

Joyce characterized this experience as "the most devastating I can imagine happening," but she saw that nothing less would have pulled her out of the rut she was "so complacently making deeper all the time."

I hadn't dared to be an independent person, having always leaned on either my mother or on Renn for support. I don't mean to indicate that I don't want or need support now, for that is certainly far from the case. But at least I have greater freedom of judgment and more ability to stand on my own two feet and look at what *I* really think and feel. My job contributes to this independence far more than staying home would.

Joyce's account of these painful events must be considered striking testimony to her fair-mindedness and self-understanding. It would have been easy to make Renn to blame for spoiling their relation, charging him with irresponsibility and unwillingness to accept the necessary restraints of marriage. Many a marital tangle is a tangle precisely because each party fails to recognize his own contribution. Joyce reserves the sharper criticism for herself, saying that she complacently persisted in conduct that was unworthy of a mature relation. In view of the close parallel between these events and the story she told in the Thematic Apperception Test six years before,[1] we are en-

[1] See p. 263.

titled to suppose that she was in some sense aware all along, though dimly, of her tendency toward selfish demandingness; perhaps her stubborn deeper digging of the rut was the only way she could prevent herself from painfully confronting this dangerous trait. The real events brought to light one point that had not been clear in the story. She saw now the force of her dependence and need for support; she encountered the anxiety that had prompted her to demand such constant proofs of closeness. The enemy that betrayed her own good sense came at last into the open, and the struggle to achieve true independence could finally be entered on fair terms.

In a period of history when the marriage bond is often dissolved, even when there are children, opinions will probably differ about undertaking "the long slow process of rebuilding." Would it not have been easier to end the marriage and solve the problem of independence by each taking a separate course? Joyce could undoubtedly have found another husband, if that were all that mattered; but what she could not have found was someone able to fill the place Renn occupied in her life and, we can almost say, in her personality. Their relation had started when they were teen-agers still in preparatory school. It had continued with almost no interruption for ten years, nearly all their lives since they ceased to be children. Many of Joyce's strongest and deepest feelings throughout this period had centered upon Renn. The vital part he had played in her development, the happiness he had given and the security he had conferred, gave to his loss the meaning of utter disaster. To some extent the two lives had been woven together as the warp and woof of one fabric; separation would have been almost equivalent to disintegration. One of the difficult aspects of a bereavement is the sudden block to all that part of one's existence that has been carried on in meaningful relation to the lost person. No doubt the therapeutic benefit of Joyce's trip to the conference lay in her seeing that some part of her life did not depend upon Renn, but at this point it certainly did not feel like enough to carry her. We do not know whether Renn felt this sort of thing as strongly as Joyce, but he was open to persuasion that the marriage should be rebuilt, and together they went to work on it. Writing within a year of the crisis, Joyce reported progress: "What we have found is a new relationship to each other, one which allows for and encourages our individual development." Not only could she see that Renn was happier in the new relation, but she could begin to sense that for herself it would mean greater freedom, maturity, and self-respect.

An early step in the reconstruction was the decision to adopt a child. "I think I'll settle down more," Joyce wrote, "when we have adopted our baby, although I know that there will be adjustments to make then, too." The decision may have been precipitous, influenced by the expectable side-effect of cementing the marriage and strengthening the motives to rebuild it. Evidently it appeared in some such light to the private adoption agency to which they turned: their application was refused. Joyce was disappointed, Renn was incensed that they were not considered adequate parents, and their friends consoled them with a display of outrage. So they made application to a public agency which, after the usual protracted interviews and long delays, provided them with a charming four-year-old boy.

To have your first baby arrive suddenly four years old is a rather different experience from bearing your own, but the new member of the family proved skillful in minimizing the shock to his parents. Raised thus far by relatives and by only one set of foster parents, the child was secure and adaptable and "settled right in." Renn, perhaps as much as Joyce, found it difficult to accept not having children who were biologically their own, but he was somewhat mollified when young Richard developed into an active, muscular boy with a taste for sports. Plans to enlarge the family a few years later were taking their slow course when Renn was unexpectedly transferred to Texas with the job of opening a new branch of the company. Suddenly faced by the necessity to move and by the unwelcome prospect of starting all over again with adoption proceedings in a new state, they put pressure on the Detroit agency and rather hastily accepted a girl of seven, barely a year younger than Richard. Betty came from a home that had been broken up by court order following repeated desertions by the mother and alcoholism and sexual molesting of the children by the father. Living in this environment and a succession of foster homes, she had developed a bitter mistrust and a violent antipathy to restraint. She arrived in her new home to find a sibling already comfortably established in parental affection. Richard was cooperative and easily disciplined, and Betty was thrown more violently into the rebellious role that at this point already came natural to her. Joyce hoped that "tender loving care" would redeem even this seared soul, but it seemed to pour ineffectively through a bottomless pit. Furiously jealous of Richard, more than once expressing the wish to kill him, Betty fought all attempts to restrain her wildness and responded to discipline with screams of abuse. Joyce sometimes found herself regretting more than ever that she had not had children of her own.

The move to Texas was not a violent disruption of Joyce's life. For several years she had been happy and successful in group work, eventually being put in charge of a community program, but she had given this up in order to devote herself to the children. Her husband's assignment was important, carrying the promise of becoming permanent head of the new branch, which seemed likely to develop into a large operation. She spoke with admiration about his skill in public relations, his sure hand in making the new plant acceptable to the community. But for Renn there soon came a time of serious reappraisal and the facing of crucial decisions about his occupational future. He had never intended to be merely an industrialist. When he went to work for his firm in Detroit it had been with the idea of getting a start financially and building up skill and experience with the various aspects of business. He had mentioned five years as the likely duration of this phase of his career. So conspicuous was his success that he could now look forward to splendid prospects in the company, but this made him see all the more clearly that it was not what he wanted. After considering many alternatives, he finally decided to join an educational foundation located in San Francisco. Joyce has heard him tell friends that she did not influence his decision in any way except finally to ask why he was making it so hard for himself and to indicate her willingness to take whatever might be involved in the way of moving and lowered income. She saw that this was "part of his self-realization" and she wanted to put no obstacles in his way. Comparing this with her troubled reaction to his loss of religious belief some years before, we see evidence that the rebuilding of their relation had become a good deal more than a wish and a hope.

In the long follow-up interview Joyce devoted a great deal of time to her children. After eight years Betty was no less a problem. Joyce described her as "strong-willed," "incredibly self-centered," and impulsive—"what she wants at the moment is what should happen." Unsure of herself and of "who she is," unable to guide her behavior according to future needs, she seemed to be consistent only in her love of dancing and in "a built-in striving to conquer." In the end she responded a little to the atmosphere of her home, where Joyce tried to be permissive without sacrificing a necessary basis of standards and values, but this only developed a conflict between good and bad selves in which the bad usually prevailed. In Betty's mind Joyce was the enbodiment of good, and her biological mother of evil. At moments she would try to live up to the good image and would, for instance, shun the television set and play only classical records. "Our standards are not really that high," said Joyce; "she has an utterly unrealistic concept of what I am and want and expect." Naturally Betty could not long sustain such virtue, and when the bad self took command it carried her far in the opposite direction. Sent to a coeducational boarding school, she was almost expelled for "overcoedding," and her friendships with boys, pushed on by her hunger for affection, were intense and indiscriminate to a degree that mobilized constant parental worry. Joyce found the parental role bewilderingly difficult. She valued independence for itself, and she found it hard to cope with those scenes in which Betty renounced the past and vowed to make a fresh start, even though she well recognized the low sustaining power of the girl's vows. Betty's "independence" was a different article from the kind Joyce had slowly won for herself.

It can be assumed that Joyce, because of her own earlier relation with her brother Albert, would respond with strong predispositions to the situation of having a "good" child and a "bad" child. It is hard to imagine that she could avoid identifying Richard with herself and Betty with Albert, despite the reversal of sexes. Yet it is true that Joyce had gained greatly in self-understanding, partly through everyday experience and partly through her social work training, and we are entitled to wonder what she would have done if given a reasonable chance. Fate was indeed unkind to give her a daughter already too seriously hurt to trust and accept kindness, especially if it had to be shared with a sibling rival who had gotten in ahead of her.

When Joyce turned in the interview to the subject of Richard, we expected that the story would take on a happier tone. In fact it did so; the bringing up of Richard had been in many respects a highly gratifying experience. The boy had easily become a member of the family, returning his parents' affection, accepting their values, and sharing their interests. Joyce described him at various points as "a nice boy," "a honey of a boy," "a man's boy" who also had an artistic bent. Richard was proud of his strength, which he diligently increased by weight lifting, and athletics early "became his meat." He was also sociable and showed considerable ability to take the lead in enterprises with his friends. But even with Richard parenthood was not without its trials. He had turned out to be no scholar. He had to repeat the second grade, and a considerable reading difficulty dogged his progress in school. Lately he had been "acting up at school." His social and athletic skills and his capacity for leadership made him "cock of the walk" amongst his contemporaries, sharpening the contrast between his competence in these spheres and the painful chore of trying to master lessons; so he "decided not to try any more in school work." "We vacillated," Joyce continued, "between no pressure and encouraging more effort. It's kind of frustrating when you know he is capable of delivering the goods more than he will." As Richard attempted to form an adult sense of ego-identity, he reflected more about his own origins, became aware of differences between his father's feelings and his own, and evidently felt a little estranged in picturing what direction to give to his life. Joyce regretted that at this point, when even in the favored field of sports Richard often expected too much of himself and as often gave up in disgust, Renn was several times absent on business trips. The boy needed a man, she was sure, to guide him in these realms which were clearly not a woman's province—she was aware of asking him the most stupid questions about football. No doubt Richard was in a normal process of establishing his independence, but it was frustrating that his course of life did not seem to point in directions in which his parents through their own experience would most naturally give him understanding and support.

Describing the present outcome of the rebuilding of the marriage, Joyce said that she and Renn "don't have a closely interdependent relation." "It's all right by me," she went on, "but he's a very independent person who doesn't like demands made on him, though he makes them himself." She described do-it-yourself projects that "seemed to go on forever" even when results were much needed. "If there is consistent discipline of the children it comes from me, and he is merely the arbiter of what I do." There are "many areas of friction" between them, but "we rarely erupt—we tacitly agree to accept each other as we are." On the credit side she records that "we have more and more fun together as the years go on." Renn continues to be "tremendously patient, accepting, and forgiving," and these qualities remind her that she was "darned lucky" to have married such a man.

Both Joyce and Renn are much interested in the community in which they live. Both are active in a newly founded church that undertakes, under the leadership of a dynamic young minister, to "slough off the unnecessary elements" in historical Christianity and create a truly contemporary expression. This church, virtually nondenominational, has no connection at all with the faith in which they were both reared, but it is interesting that Renn now regards that faith as in some sense truly "their own" and is on the board of trustees of one of its colleges. He has been taking part, moreover, in religious discussion groups; and although he is "a person who approaches things with questions," it seems evident to Joyce that he has been "working through his views" on religion. As a man of initiative and judgment Renn has been elected to several community boards. Joyce, too, plays an active part in community affairs, including the League of Women Voters and work connected with the foundation that employs her husband. Time never hangs heavy on her hands. She finds great satisfaction in forwarding the purposes of these organizations and in the company of her fellow workers. In addition she has "a host of friends and acquaintances" and has found everywhere congenial groups of people with whom she experiences solidarity of values. Reminded of her former difficulty with respect to ease and warmth in human relations, she laughed and said, "I'd forgotten. It's no problem now."

That she had forgotten what was once a fairly harassing personal problem is eloquent testimony to natural growth. When a difficulty has been overcome we enjoy the psychological prosperity that results, and cease to dwell on the outgrown time of troubles. In terms of the growth of personality there is a great distance between Joyce as a college senior and Joyce at the doorway of her forties. Gone is the inhibition of feeling that stood in the way of warm friendships. Gone is the need to dress life in the costume of joyous adventure, with sorrow, egotism, and resentment banished beneath the surface. Even the deeply rooted dependence, first on her mother and then on Renn, has been outgrown to the point of accepting her husband's considerable requirements in the way of autonomy. To be sure, the long job of rebuilding the marriage has come out somewhat imperfectly. Fate has not regularly smiled upon it; the circumstances have been more difficult than one might reasonably have expected. But we should not judge family life at this age according to romantic standards of ideal marriage. There are many frustrations in Joyce's home life, frustrations in her desire to give love and receive it, frustrations to her sense of competence as a mother nurturing the growth of her children. The list is long enough to look plausible in a textbook as precipitating causes of nervous breakdown. Joyce is sometimes discouraged, but by and large she meets the frustrations with spirit and when necessary bears them with fortitude. Her developing of strong outside interests is entirely adaptive now that the children will soon be leaving home.

PART FOUR: FROM FORTY TO FIFTY-ONE

Joyce Kingsley's history during her forties takes its shape from two major developments: her children grew up and moved out into lives of their own, and she herself, after a brief return to work, decided to prepare for a new vocation.

Although she is no longer responsible for bringing up the children, Joyce's interest in them has not waned. Richard, originally the easy child, is still seeking the right path for himself and has by no means settled down. At high school he was sociable and likable, but stumbled badly in his studies; "a wonderful boy," as one teacher put it, "but hopeless in academic work." Presently he became deeply and alarmingly involved in the drug scene, then at its height at his high school. Joyce believes that this chapter has closed, but she is not perfectly sure. She interprets his academic limitations as an emotional block, and there is indeed a sharp contrast between his practical intelligence, as shown, for instance, in building and in the mastery of machinery, and his incapacity whenever figuring and mental work are involved. She thinks that identity problems still plague him: aware that he cannot be like Renn but unacquainted with his biological father, "he doesn't know who he is to be." Recently he made a pilgrimage to the city of his birth but made no attempt to locate his parents, whose identities are locked away in the files of the adoption agency. Joyce mentions again his artistic proclivities and regrets that because of high self-imposed standards he "cannot let himself be an artist." At twenty-six he is not ready for commitment to either vocation or marriage. His girl friends are numerous, but he shows no enthusiasm for the married state; and his present job, working for a building contractor, still has the character of an exploration.

Unexpectedly Betty, the difficult child, has blossomed into a happy wife and mother. During the high school years she had continued to be restless and easily upset, a stormy influence in the home. At the beginning of senior year she clearly "didn't want to be in the family," so Joyce and Renn decided to let her live away. As a boarder she moved from one family to another, never able to settle comfortably. For the most part she kept in touch with her parents, except during an interval when she was living with a man. Finishing high school, she held a succession of secretarial jobs. In the last of these, at an animal hospital, she was happy in being allowed to help with the care of the animals. Then she met the man who became her husband: a young garage mechanic who treated her with confident assertiveness. According to Joyce, she liked his dominance at first, then had doubts, but finally decided in his favor. Presently she had a baby and gives every evidence of happiness in motherhood. Joyce takes no credit for this successful outcome. When Betty was adopted she had demanded a new first name; now she has returned to the original one, thus symbolizing the temporary nature of her role as Joyce's and Renn's daughter. But Joyce has a large heart. She is made happy by Betty's happiness, continues to see her and the baby, and expresses admiration for Betty's considerable insight into herself and others.

In contrast to Joseph Kidd, now so much at odds with his family of origin, Joyce speaks affectionately of her relatives. Her brothers Albert and Henry have both been successful in lines of forward-looking technology that she does not pretend to understand. Her cousin Philip, so important in her life before she adopted her own children, has grown up to be a university teacher. Her father, long retired, continues to make occasional visits during which he helpfully makes repairs around the house. Her mother died recently, but left an unforgettable model of determination to complete her life work. When first incapacitated, she was planning to write several papers. As her strength failed so that she could no longer write, she continued to work out her ideas and dictated them to Joyce or to her husband. Since her mother's death Joyce has met or heard from many people to whom she meant much, especially students in whom she recognized and encouraged special talents.

As we saw in the previous section, Joyce continued in various outside activities even while her children were small. When the children needed her less, she returned more seriously to social work. But she soon became aware of a gnawing dissatisfaction with this work, which she now felt lacked sound theory and a tested knowledge of effects. It took time to identify the source of her discontent, but she experienced a variety of "messages bursting through" which all indicated that she "wanted to use her mind more" and that it was "legitimate to do so." She wanted to learn more and think more; this meant further education in an academic program. She was aware of the similarity between this change of direction and her mother's return to an academic career at a like point in life. Her decision, however, looks like more than a copy; it was a response to a similar course of experience. Throughout Joyce's childhood her mother faithfully filled the role of minister's wife, which allowed her to carry out her own commitment to the ideals of the church. Joyce lived in this tradition, assuming that her own role must be supportive. Against these culturally backed expectations it is no easy matter for a woman to decide to undertake a career which is demanding in its own right. Joyce took the daring step more easily than did her mother who, it will be remembered, had a breakdown of health and required her doctor's encouragement to resume her teaching career. But it still took repeated signals from within to convince Joyce that her interests were serious enough to merit the necessary priority.

In her academic program Joyce took a course in family relations, and this moved her to reexamine her own childhood experience. She felt a need to understand more fully her long-continued dependence on her parents and their values—the "joyous adventure" outlook of the first study—which became such a hazard to her marriage and perhaps only now has been finally mastered in the decision to pursue her own intellectual career. Why was she so powerfully attached to home and parents?

Her answers, set down in two essays, do not conflict with the interpretations made in the previous sections of this chapter, but they provide deeper insight into the forces behind her attachment. She draws a vivid picture of her mother's miserable childhood as one of the many children in a disorganized German-speaking family. After the father's desertion and the mother's mental breakdown, the young girl was left to the care of older siblings to whom she was a burden. Sent away at fourteen to a denominational school, she discovered happiness in the serene and comfortable academic community. One teacher in particular, whose name was Joyce and who later came to be called "Aunt Joy," befriended the promising young student and became a substitute mother. In this benign atmosphere she flourished and prepared herself for a teaching career, but she counted herself unattractive to men and did not expect to marry. After a short period of teaching, however, she met Mr. Kingsley, newly graduated from theological school, and discovered in this idealistic and considerate man the unexpected possibility of being loved and cherished as a wife and mother. Joyce's birth eleven months later was part of the miracle. Mrs. Kingsley now had a chance to right the wrongs of her own childhood, to surround Joyce with the love that was the central value of her religion, and thus to create for her daughter the ideal environment for growth to perfect womanhood. Joyce grew up amidst high expectations which she simply took for granted. When she was old enough to perceive other possible ways of living, she was "also old enough to sense how vulnerable my mother felt and how crushed she would be if I were to default." Thus "not hurting my mother took precedence over very natural desires to be myself."

The path laid out by her mother's expectations was further reinforced by her father. "I was often told as a child that I looked like him," Joyce writes, "and I was also identified from early babyhood as having my father's temperament—sunny disposition, even temper, energetic style." As early as age four and five she was taken by her father on trips which combined religious meetings and visits to his parents. Sometimes she accompanied him on parish calls, and as she grew older and took more part in church activities she was "naturally and spontaneously involved with my father's work." In her recollections, she observes, home and church are closely blended. When a parsonage is close to the church, the minister's family readily becomes involved in his professional life. This is a circumstance of which families sometimes complain, but Joyce took it for granted. Her participation evidently gave her father much pleasure, and it earned her the approval of everyone else connected with the church. "The way of life I knew as a child," she writes, "was determined by my father's work." Because she lived at home while attending college, she was still close to this life when we made her acquaintance during her senior year.

These descriptions forward our understanding of the force behind Joyce's dependent tie. She perceives correctly that she was not identifying with her father; "I knew that the ministry was 'men's work' and that little girls did not grow up to be ministers." Rather, she saw her father's work "as including and involving me; I was part of the action." But she also perceived her father as being involved in their domestic life. He did most of the family shopping and was always ready to take on disagreeable chores. Joyce looked for like helpfulness, consideration, and closely knit activities in her marriage, but in these respects Renn was unlike Mr. Kingsley. She had to get used to the more secular atmosphere, the readier expression of criticism, and the expectations of independence that Renn had learned from his own childhood experience. Renn's was the more typical upbringing; but it is easy to see that Joyce would experience a sharp sense of loss in trying to accommodate to the cooler climate.

Joyce is now more than halfway through her program of graduate training. Although "pretty fed up with the grind"—a normal phenomenon among graduate students of any age—she is sure that her decision to return to school was wise and is taking her where she wants to go. This means teaching and research, with emphasis on the latter; the desire to make more use of her mind implies thinking out problems and developing ways to investigate them. Now that she has dared to try such a career, the prospects look decidedly attractive.

Home life proves to be "more fun" now that the children are gone. Joyce and Renn are not an unsociable couple, but more than before they value being together and arrange their lives to make this privacy possible. Renn has been conspicuously successful in the work to which he shifted fifteen years ago, and the circumstances of their life have become stable and secure. Joyce says that he seems better able to understand and support her needs, but she hesitates over a suggestion that they communicate better; perhaps it is just that she more easily gives voice to what she wants. If one reads this remark to mean that she has done more of the changing, it still seems possible to conclude that the marriage has been successfully rebuilt. Compared to other couples of their age, they stand high in the sharing of home life and recreations.

At the beginning of this chapter stands a statement made by Joyce at the end of her senior year. How would she express herself today? She has modified in various discriminating ways the influence of her family background, but she still has a good deal of respect for the values that prevailed in her childhood home. The closing words, "and now it's up to me," with their recognition of personal responsibility and their implicit charge to confront life with energy and initiative, she would have no reason to change.

8

THE COURSE
OF DEVELOPMENT

To be healthy means to overcome the past.

W. STEKEL

Biological and social ways of thinking sometimes seem to be miles apart. Moving from animal learning to the learning of social roles, passing from basic drives to desires for higher social status or a professional career, can easily feel like crossing a wide intellectual chasm. In this chapter we undertake to bridge the gap by examining the course of development. This means looking at the intervening steps whereby a small child becomes transformed into an adult social being. The relevant information lies properly in the domains of developmental and social psychology, but influential ideas about personal growth have come also from psychoanalysis. In describing our three cases we have necessarily utilized an array of psychoanalytic and developmental concepts; understanding would scarcely be possible without them. Here we shall consider these ideas in more orderly fashion. Following the plan used when describing social shaping forces and biological roots, we shall select for discussion certain leading ideas, then illustrate them in the three lives with which we are now familiar.

The course of development consists of a long series of transactions between a growing individual and his environment, especially his human environment. Through these transactions he eventually passes from the simple needs and satisfactions of infancy to those highly complex intentions and equally complex conditions of reward that characterize the adult personality. Whatever theory of learning one chooses to apply, these events cannot be adequately described without reference to progressive patterning and organization. Human beings exhibit a striving toward competence which prompts curiosity, sustained investigation, and the forming of patterns of mastery. Human beings are likewise subject to fear; in the course of time they develop organized ways of protecting themselves from anxiety. Far more extensively than animals, human beings engage in continuous cognitive organization whereby separate experiences become shaped into useful knowledge about the environment, knowledge which serves to guide planning and future action. There is also progressive selection and organization of social experience; people obviously differ in the value they come to attach to different kinds of social interaction. Another significant strand of growth is the developing of internal controls and the forming of values which influence one's responses to current situations. Finally there is the evolution of a sense of self: substantial parts of adult behavior are intelligible only when seen as attempts to protect, maintain, or expand a satisfying conception of oneself. These are the chief lines of development that lead us from biological to social man.

The Development of Competence

The picture of a father holding his infant son provides us, if we stop to think of it, with an astounding commentary on human growth. Twenty-seven years ago, let us say, the father was an infant of just this size. In the course of those years he has turned into a rising young executive respected for his confidence, initiative, poise, social skill, sense of responsibility—in short, for an array of behaviors that bespeak a competent adult. Being competent is not the only goal of development, nor is it even necessarily a virtue. But for a creature who starts life helpless, and whose way is strewn with causes for anxiety, the growth of competence is a centrally important theme. Competence and anxiety stand in a reciprocal relation. We are subject to fear when we are helpless; fear is avoided to the extent that we feel competent to deal with what is before us.

Initial Security: Attachment and Dependence Establishing independence from one's family eventually becomes such a vital issue that it may be hard to think of attachment and dependence as desirable conditions in infancy. For the helpless infant, however, security can lie only in provisions made by others which satisfy needs and produce states of comfort. Research indicates that neglectful upbringing, impersonal care in institutions, and even a cool efficient household, are all detrimental to later development. Becoming warmly attached to the mother and her ministrations may well be the strongest basis for security and trust. Very likely this initial tie may also be the best preparation for later affectionate relations. At all events, the infant's chief resource for influencing the environment is to give signals of distress, and the most competent way to live—odd as the expression sounds—is to use these signals to elicit effective action from the caretakers.

Attitudes of dependence, however, become decreasingly appropriate as the infant grows older. In the course of time they must be largely outgrown, and their persistence can present obstacles to growth. In later life we are apt to have short patience with people who wait helplessly for us to do everything for them, who expect us to make their decisions and relieve them of all disagreeable effort. We are not pleased with those who persistently demand service or more subtly try to maneuver us into positions where a refusal to help would seem rude. The course of development calls for advancing first toward a relative equality in human relations, then toward becoming a giver of nurture rather than a receiver. Entrenched dependent tendencies interfere with this progress and sometimes crop out unexpectedly to spoil an important forward step. Joseph Kidd, it will be remembered, gave up a sales job because he was not provided with sufficient guidance and training to help him make the sales. And Joyce Kingsley, who was in many respects highly responsible and capable of giving love, as to her young cousin Philip, discovered a degree of dependence on her husband that almost brought the relation to an end. There is room, of course, for reasonable degrees of dependence in adult life; it should not be looked upon as a sin requiring perfect purification. People who are ill, burdened by handicaps, or just plain overworked can make nuisances of themselves by refusing available help. On the whole, however, outgrowing dependence stands as one of the major developmental tasks.

Although dependence is at its height in infancy, we cannot be certain that its later strength comes wholly from the first year of life. Early fixation is the concept favored, though never fully clarified, in psychoanalytic theory. Dependence was overlearned, it is assumed, because of conditions prevailing in infancy, and this caused resistance to relearning. An alternative explanation would be that the trait persisted because of continued reinforcement through the childhood years. In this view, dependence would remain prominent if it continued to serve as a successful strategy in a household inclined toward spoiling. The issue cannot easily be settled, but in the case of Joyce Kingsley's problem of dependence the second explanation seems more suitable. Although a golden infancy can be inferred, it seems indisputable that Joyce's marked dependence, as late as her last college year, on family solidarity and an explicit set of family values had served her well up to that point. She was happy at home and in church activities, and she had developed a relation with peers which was both safe and satisfying. When she left home and committed her life to Renn, whose expectations were different, her dependent pattern had received twenty years of reinforcement. Perhaps we should be surprised not that it persisted but that it did ultimately change.

Anxiety and Defensive Operations Anxiety is an unavoidable feature of existence both in childhood and in adult years. It is a painful and disruptive emotion, a signal that life itself may be in danger, and it thus evokes the most strenuous efforts toward coping with the difficulty. Its disruptiveness is likely to interfere with rationality, all the more so in childhood when the child's grasp of the situation may be inadequate in any event. The *defense mechanisms* disclosed by psychoanalytic study are for the most part primitive ways of coping with danger. They are not ideal solutions; they all imply that the true state of affairs has been falsified in the interests of safety. This is most evident in what is probably the most primitive of the mechanisms: *denial*, as when a baby persistently looks away from a source of danger, an angry man declares that he is not in the least upset, or an ostrich hides his head in the sand. The situation is not much different with *repression*, which signifies the ejection from consciousness of frightening memories and of impulses in oneself that might lead to dangerous consequences. In fact all the mechanisms—projection, reaction-formation, isolation, undoing, intellectualization, and so forth—imply a certain failure to take full account of reality, whether it be the reality of the outside world or the reality of one's inner experience.[1]

The effects of anxiety and defense on development have been most fully studied in connection with the neuroses. The crucial point seems to be that early defensive measures are likely to interfere with the progress of further learning. They represent ways of responding in which the child dares not take full account of reality. To the extent that they become fixed, they prevent him from making a new and more hopeful appraisal of reality. The tactics of the ostrich never permit him to find out that the danger may be less great than he supposed, which is very often true with respect to things that seemed frightening in early childhood but could easily be dealt with a little later in life. In the neuroses it is a regular finding that the patient is still afraid of childhood threats; he still repeats defenses against them which cripple his adult behavior and which do not permit him to revise his earlier estimate of the danger. A patient feels uneasy in the presence of his employers, for example; he tends to placate them by ingratiating submission, and this actually hinders his chances of advancement because his employers really want him to show initiative and bring new ideas into the business. It turns out that the patient behaves in this self-defeating way because he still feels the excessive fear that he used to feel when scolded and disciplined by his father. In those earlier crises he applied defenses against his own resentment, repressed his wish to assert himself in return, accomplished the reaction-formation of being extremely submissive, and thus protected himself from further anxiety; but at the cost of never again asserting himself in the presence of older men and never learning that it was safe for him to do so. Conceived of in this way, neurotic behavior is the consequence of an early block in the learning process. Defense against childhood anxiety has taken so large a toll as to wall off important areas of development.[2]

Undoubtedly these blockages are more severe in neurotic than in normal development. No one, however, can get through childhood without anxiety, and no one is likely to be wholly free from the patterns of defense that served him in his early crises. People who have

---

[1] The continuing classic work on defense mechanisms is Anna Freud, *The Ego and the Mechanisms of Defense* (London: Hogarth Press, Ltd., 1937).

[2] This view of neurosis is fully described in R. W. White and N. F. Watt, *The Abnormal Personality* (New York: The Ronald Press Company, 4th ed., 1973), Chapter 3.

occasion to study themselves often discover that there are certain situations they regularly try to avoid and certain actions they are chroni-
cally reluctant to perform even when circumstances require them.
Take the instance of a highly gregarious student who loves to be in the
company of other people, hates to study by himself, and prefers to
carry his books to a place where he will have people around him. This
is a not uncommon preference, but it may go further: the student forces
his company on a honeymoon couple, converses on the bus with a
passenger who obviously wants to sleep, and wears out his welcome
with friends by talking far into the night. If we then discover that he
becomes extremely uneasy when he returns to his room, the picture is
complete of an irrational striving to avoid being alone, a situation that
is not currently dangerous but feels so because of an earlier association
with anxiety. For a second example, take a young man who suffered
early intimidation on the subject of expressing aggression. The idea of
getting angry and speaking strongly may be so repugnant to him that
he cannot expostulate, criticize, or protest even when other people
treat him outrageously. Problems of anxiety and defense are part of
the universal stuff of development, and their traces can be found in
almost any life history.

Undoubtedly there are times when a person's behavior can be
correctly understood as concealing a true motive behind a false façade,
but this is not typical of the strategies of everyday life. More characteristic is a pattern in which there is a fusion of adaptive and protective
goals. Joyce Kingsley found true satisfaction in her alliance with
teachers and her position in student government, through which she
developed confidence and poise; at the same time, this adaptive pattern
kept her aloof from adolescent high spirits, dating, and sexual involvements, of which she was a little afraid. Most adaptive patterns require
us to sacrifice something for the sake of something else, and we may
gladly choose to sacrifice what in any event makes us uneasy.

Such balancing of adaptation and defense can be clearly seen
in a trait like humor. A person with a gift for humor can use it as a
technique for preventing serious contact with others and avoiding
commitment to causes and values. If conversation starts to get personal, the threat can be parried by producing a laugh. If serious topics
come under discussion, a well-timed joke can cover up one's ignorance
or lack of reflection. When humor is serving an important defensive
purpose it is likely to be employed out of season, sometimes even to
the point of creating annoyance. Yet on the whole it is highly adap-

tive: We owe a great deal to the people who can make us laugh. They often give us a good time and put us in a happy frame of mind. They perform a useful service in relaxing tensions and smoothing awkward social situations. They sometimes achieve real dignity as social critics, puncturing pretensions and directing the deadly shaft of ridicule against vicious self-seeking and ill will. Humor brings satisfaction to author and audience alike; it can be a highly constructive strategy of adaptation. The extent to which it serves a simultaneous defensive purpose in a given person can be established only by careful individual study. Humor is a trait that can stand on its own adaptive merits.

Evolution of Competence Past theories of personality have not always made it clear that human beings have intrinsic urges which make them want to grow up. When a child seizes the spoon from his mother and tries to feed himself, a motive emerges that acts contrary to dependence and that does not at first increase the intake of nourishment. The satisfaction can be described as a feeling of efficacy, which implies making something happen and producing an effect on the environment through one's own effort. This is a simple instance of the many-sided striving for competence. Great as are the charms of dependence, there are decided attractions in discovering how to manage by oneself. Self-sufficiency as a real need becomes unmistakable a little later when children try to attain difficult goals like climbing on a wall and show angry frustration if an adult lifts them up. Being autonomous presently opens the pleasing possibility of explorations and experiments when parents are not looking and cannot spoil the enterprise. Some parents admire independence and intend not to thwart it in their children, but they are ever mindful of possible dangers. We miss the point of the striving for competence if we attribute it to parental reinforcement or even to parental tolerance. It has its own reward, as anyone who has climbed a steep bank or a tall tree can testify. The satisfaction is in the experience of being efficacious, and this is more important than the social feedback, which in such cases is almost certain to be negative.

Both motor and mental development are strongly forwarded by the urge for competence. This goes on throughout life, with crises of various kinds appropriate to each stage of growth. Successive skills have to be mastered, including those that form part of school work and those that are of service on the playground and in the world at large.

Adolescence brings on the expectation that one must display grown-up competences, among which driving a car is a powerful contemporary symbol. Among our three cases Hartley Hale most conspicuously illustrated mastery of inanimate objects, all the way from the boat in the bathtub through radio sets to the highly technical equipment needed in medical research. Skilled mastery of this sort becomes a source of confidence, interest, and pride, and it may play a significant part in the evolution of the sense of self.

It is legitimate to speak of interpersonal competence provided we limit the definition to influencing others and do not include other aspects of human relations. Social objects present the same question as inanimate ones: to what extent is it possible to have an influence on other people through one's own action? There is a wide range of individual differences with respect to the sense of interpersonal competence. Schizophrenic patients have been known to rate their influence at zero, describing other people as locked doors to which there seems to be no key. At the opposite extreme stands the arrogant, overbearing person who confidently expects everyone to do his bidding and jump to his command. Fortunately most people are somewhere in between, having discovered who will be responsive in what ways and recognizing limits to their own power of social influence. Here again there is a long developmental history. Often mentioned in the literature is a phase of negativism at around age two-and-a-half, which on closer examination proves to be a testing of the power to resist adult commands and to issue commands of one's own. These tests are apt to be unwelcome to parents, who may react strongly to such direct confrontation and feel it necessary to suppress rebellion and arrogance before they get out of hand. The path to interpersonal competence may run smoothly, but often there are difficulties which can be overcome only with effort. Joseph Kidd describes with unusual clearness his belated emergence from a humiliating social submissiveness. In what was to him, paradoxically, the free and irresponsible life of the Army, he began to recover his much earlier assertiveness, asking for things he wanted, engaging in manipulative tactics, even setting up some minor rackets. If his first steps were not on a lofty plane, they greatly increased his self-respect, and he presently turned his improved social initiative to the more useful task of rebuilding his father's business. Thus he moved toward a better ratio between helplessness and effectiveness in dealing with other people, a ratio more consistent with self-esteem.

Inferiority and Compensation The importance of inferiority feelings and of attempted compensations was first pointed out in convincing detail by Alfred Adler. Led by his psychoanalytic work to search for the childhood origins of neurotic problems, he drew attention to the countless ways in which children can come to feel incompetent and inferior in comparison with others. They are small, they are awkward, and they are surrounded by larger and more competent people. If they have parents who are impatient or rejecting, if they have rivalrous siblings, if they are too much exposed to the untempered competitive zeal of assertive playmates, they are likely to be victims of serious belittlement. If they are handicapped by disfigurement or by marked ineptitude along lines that children value, they can hardly escape becoming objects of derision and contempt. Adler was fond of drawing a parallel between injured organs and injured self-esteem. An injured organ, in the attempt to compensate for its reduced efficiency, may grow to unusual size and strength, producing in the end an overcompensation. Injured self-esteem, with its resulting feelings of inferiority, may similarly set off a push toward competitive success that may not stop short of desires for unbounded superiority.

The desire to stand well in relation to others is clearly a natural consequence of being brought up in a social environment. Feelings of inferiority and strivings to be superior are more or less universal in human experience. Adler spoke of an *inferiority complex* when this commonplace sequence was elevated to singular intensity as a result of severe belittlement that had left deep wounds. Inferiority feelings assume the proportions of a complex when they become generalized and prompt unfavorable comparisons with almost any excellence shown by others, when they become acutely painful so that anyone's success causes despair and bitterness, and when they occupy so much space in the personality, so to speak, that they come to dominate the course of growth. Sometimes a person tries to forestall further belittlement, and perhaps secure crumbs of encouragement, by constantly apologizing for his lack of ability or charm. Sometimes he directs strong compensatory effort straight at the spot where he has been most humiliated; for instance, by employing strenuous practice to become a successful athlete after early failure in sports. Sometimes superiority is sought in a different region: the child who has been shamed in physical activity may set himself the goal of dominating school politics or of getting the highest marks. A compensatory striving for superiority can sometimes lead to brilliant achievement, but only if it is backed by uncommon abilities and smiled upon by circumstances. Usually an uncompromising desire to be outstanding leads to the setting of impossible goals and to despair and misery if they are missed, even to the small extent of winning only the vice-presidency of the class or standing second on the dean's list. Furthermore, a single-minded struggle for superiority is not likely to endear a person to others; it can be pursued only with a damaging sacrifice of what Adlerians have come to call *social interest*, signifying friendship, affection, and kindly concern for others. Ultimate triumph can be lonely and hollow.[3]

Among our three cases we find the clearest example of inferiority feelings in Joseph Kidd. These feelings do not seem to have had the early origin that Adler found characteristic of neurotic patients. Kidd began his life with a high income of esteem from others and a good deal of confidence in himself. In later childhood, however, there was a disastrous drop in his level of self-esteem, due to his double promotion and forced association with boys a little older than himself. In order to stay in these boys' good graces he was forced to make himself an amusing and obliging companion rather than a forceful competitor; even so, he somehow lost them when they passed into puberty ahead of him. As a college student at the time of the first study he had not recovered satisfactory status with young men or in his family, nor had he established it with his girl, and his feelings of inferiority were painful and indiscriminate. He described with memorable detail his attempts to "try out" different "personalities," such as the self-reliant strong man, the arrogant autocrat, or the dedicated student. He wanted to be good at everything, but nothing yielded quick returns and he could not persist along any particular line of excellence. At that point he exemplified Adler's concept of the inferiority complex, but as usual in the individual case there was a shade of difference. Kidd would not settle for respect without love; his "personalities" failed "because they didn't produce that underlying purpose of making people like me." As we have seen, in his adult supervisory and promotional work there is no trace of the compulsive dominance that would testify to an overcompensation for inferiority. He does not tell subordinates what to do until he has won their friendship so that they will do it without disliking him.

---

[3] A. Adler, *Superiority and Social Interest*, ed. by H. L. Ansbacher and R. R. Ansbacher (Evanston, Ill.: Northwestern University Press, 1964).

The Family Circle as Environment for Growth

Exclusively at first and importantly for many years, the immediate family is the environment in which the child's development takes place. Here occur a large part of the encounters and interactions, the rewards and punishments, the loves and jealousies and hates and fears, that are crucial for growth. Here the young individual is exposed to the family version of the culture. Unfortunately for simplicity of thought, families come in all sizes. To be raised as the only child of a widowed or deserted mother is obviously different from growing up in a household crammed with children and adult relatives. There is currently general agreement that the family should be conceptualized as a social system involving interactions among all the members, perhaps with subsystems created by alliances and rivalries. But it is vexing for research that there is no universal pattern, like two parents with a boy and a girl, so that one could hope for a limited number of generalizations about interaction in the family. We have to deal with a large range of differences, and the differences are important. The human family seems not to have been designed for the convenience of scientific thought.

One line of research that has been pursued for many years has to do with the effects of parental attitudes on children's growth. An early attempt to organize the problem was made by Symonds, who suggested that parental attitudes be classified to lie on two dimensions, one extending from acceptance to rejection, the other from dominance to submission.[4] *Acceptance* meant that the child was loved and that he received kind care and consideration. *Rejection* implied that the parents either overtly or covertly did not want the child and were inconsiderate of his interests. *Dominance* referred to an attitude in which authority and discipline were emphasized, the child's wishes being subordinated to patterns of conduct and goals desired by the parents. *Submission* designated the reverse of this: indulgent subordination of parental wishes to the desires and whims of the child. According to this scheme the attitudes of any given parents could be characterized by indicating their place on each of the two dimensions. Subsequent

[4] P. M. Symonds, *The Psychology of Parent-Child Relationships* (New York: Appleton-Century-Crofts, 1939), pp. 18–28.

research has in general followed Symonds' suggestion, and the results can be expressed in his terms.[5]

Experimental and clinical evidence show pretty clearly that parental *rejection* has an unfavorable effect on development. If a child's first experiences in human relationships make him feel that he is not wanted, he is given little basis on which to build self-confidence or a warm feeling toward others. When parents have an affectionate interest in their children they are more likely to notice them, take pleasure in what they do, and add to the inherent rewards of accomplishment the bonus of their loving esteem. Under such circumstances growing up can be a source of gratification and pride, and such frustrations as go with relinquishing childish ways can easily be endured. Parents who lack affection are in a weaker position to encourage growth. They are less alert to the child's spontaneous moves toward self-help and may even be annoyed by them; self-feeding and self-dressing are at first neither neat nor rapid. Such parents may try to use pressure to hasten a developmental step, but this is likely to produce either sullen compliance or evasive rebellion, if not both. They may resort to intimidation, but this produces anxiety and a deadening paralysis of the child's own urges. If they fail to enforce any discipline, they merely pass along the problem of socialization to other authorities, the teachers and church workers and police, who will be fortunate indeed if they can win the second round after the first round has been lost.

Clinical workers have been impressed by the special difficulties that arise when parental rejection is present in a covert form. It sometimes happens that parents attempt to suppress their rejective feelings by exaggerated overt attitudes of kindly interest and concern. It is difficult, however, to make a complete success of this maneuver; under the constant pressure of childish demands and irritations the intended attitudes collapse and the child learns that in certain crucial respects his interests are not considered important. Karen Horney attached great significance to this pattern in the family histories of neurotic patients. "The basic evil," according to her view, "is invariably a lack

[5] W. C. Becker, "Consequences of Different Kinds of Parental Discipline," in *Review of Child Development Research*, Vol. I, ed. by M. L. Hoffman and L. W. Hoffman (New York: Russell Sage Foundation, 1964), especially pp. 189–199.

of genuine warmth and affection."[6] When a child is for the most part well treated, when his parents tell him that they have only his interests at heart, his response to occasional evidences of rejection is apt to be peculiarly disastrous. He senses all too clearly the underlying threat to his security, but he dares not express his resentment lest he shake further the feeble foundations of parental love. Anger and anxiety must both be controlled; self-confidence and self-respect are almost certain to suffer.

The effects of parental *dominance* are of a somewhat different nature. The child's attitudes toward authority and his power of initiative are likely to be chiefly affected. When dominance is associated with acceptance, the child is likely to become a fairly docile vehicle for parental intentions. He accepts parental values, attempts to realize parental hopes, and adapts himself to the requirements of authority in the school and in the community. The danger in this pattern of development lies in its possible effect on self-confidence. Dominated children sometimes have difficulty with new and free situations in which they must rely on what they can improvise rather than on what they have been taught. They may be unhappy on the playground, uneasy in the creative art class, bewildered by new and unfamiliar schoolwork. Parental *submission*, on the other hand, is liable to produce faults of an opposite kind. Overconfident conceit and a blithe disregard for the rights and interests of others are characteristic of the "spoiled child" whose parents have made his wishes their guides.

The differential effects of parental dominance and submission are clearly shown in Levy's well-known study of maternal overprotection.[7] The mothers selected for this study were all strongly acceptant, but they carried this to a fault by overprotecting their children. They attempted to keep their children safely at home, preventing them from developing friendships or finding independent interests on the outside. They offered help with homework, excused their children from irksome household tasks, and generally tried to make the home so attractive that there would be no incentive to leave. With respect to dominance and submission these mothers fell into two rather extreme groups. The dominant group had diligent, docile, neat, polite children

[6] K. Horney, *The Neurotic Personality of Our Time* (New York: W. W. Norton & Co., 1937), p. 80.

[7] D. M. Levy, *Maternal Overprotection* (New York: Columbia University Press, 1943).

who were hopelessly timid on the playground and awkward with other children. The submissive mothers, highly indulgent, found their children increasingly impudent, tyrannical, and violent around the house, and at school full of bossiness and self-display.

Some years ago *permissiveness* came into vogue as an ideal of child rearing. Its popularity can be understood as a reaction against the dominance that was considered natural in earlier generations. At its best, permissive child rearing is designed to maximize initiative, curiosity, and a sense of competence. The permissive parent is willing to sacrifice docility and conventional good behavior rather than risk intimidation and the impairment of self-confidence. This implies letting the child do what he wants within limits of safety and the rights of others. Unfortunately the permissive philosophy became popular at the more educated levels of American society just at a time when traditional standards were being questioned and reappraised. Permissiveness became an easy refuge for parents whose values were shaken but not reconstructed and who from personal insecurity could not decide what they wanted to ask of their children. Jokes about child savages and parental doormats were justified when permissiveness was practiced in this caricatured form. Research and observation have since made it apparent that children who are taught no standards of social conduct, who are thus given no guidance for social living, tend to flounder and become anxiously insecure rather than confident.[8] To produce its intended good results, permissiveness must be practiced with discrimination by parents who have reached some certainty about their own values.

Complications in the Individual Case When we try to apply these ideas to the study of individual lives we are at once struck by the difficulty of making a proper diagnosis. How close can we come to placing the Hales, the Kidds, and the Kingsleys on the acceptance-rejection axis? On the whole, these three pairs of parents probably stood pretty well on the side of acceptance. Their children all had something good to say about their devotion. Yet none of our three subjects spared their parents a certain amount of criticism for failure

[8] See for example D. M. Baumrind, "Child Care Practices Anteceding Three Patterns of Preschool Behavior," *Genetic Psychology Monographs*, 75 (1967), 43–88; and a summary in L. E. Longstreth, *Psychological Development of the Child* (New York: The Ronald Press Company, 2d ed., 1974), pp. 423–438.

to understand them and appreciate their needs. Kidd complained specifically about parental pushing, which obstructed an appreciation of his own real wishes and problems. Hale was deeply upset when his parents appeared to forget him in the course of their quarrels. Joyce Kingsley was not satisfied with her father's distance, her mother's preoccupation with work, or the burden of household duties that fell to her lot in the name of family cooperation. Each child put a finger on certain rejective elements in the parents' behavior. We can rightly judge that these elements were substantial only in Kidd's case; and even there the parents exhibited, within their views, a large and sacrificial concern for their children's welfare.

Each individual instance of an abstraction like acceptance-rejection has to be seen as a variation on the general theme. Each instance has its own peculiar form that produces an individual pattern of effects. This can be vividly illustrated by comparing two examples of dominance. Both Joyce Kingsley and Joseph Kidd felt the weight of parental dominance, but there was a subtle difference in its quality. In the Kidd household it took the form of dressing Joseph in fine clothes, showing him off, pushing him into the limelight, forcing him ahead in school, and putting pressure upon him to enter the medical profession. He was not given the chance to voice his own preferences in these matters; in fact, it took quite a little persuading to enlist his interest in what proved to be the disastrous double promotion. Kidd was hurried into activities before his own motives were fully aroused. His parents took initiative for him, with the result that they took it away from him and robbed him of the satisfaction of doing things on his own account. This encouraged a feeling of helplessness together with a kind of passive resistance that operated to prevent him from fulfilling parental expectations. The Kingsley parents, in contrast, were rather sharply aware that they should not be too directly dominant. Their religion emphasized freedom of choice; they realized that their children were not to be regarded as possessions, and they tried to encourage a proper amount of initiative. But they stood for a firm and explicit set of moral values that they did not hesitate to enforce. Joyce's mother, moreover, unintentionally dominated others simply because of high energy and positive opinions. Joyce's initiative was less injured than Joseph Kidd's, but it was not easy for her during childhood to take steps of which her parents might disapprove.

In working out the effects of parental attitudes, we have to bear in mind that the two parents may not present a united front. The

Kingsleys apparently did so, but the Kidd boys learned to appeal differently to their father and mother. Conflicting parental attitudes can be a source of confusion to a child, and severe quarrels may force an unwelcome taking of sides. But a constructive outcome seems not to be impossible. Hartley Hale managed to benefit from the differences between his parents, even though at times they caused him anxiety. His mother was overprotective, telling him to wear rubbers and not to fight, but his father often forgot to wear rubbers and arranged for him to have boxing lessons. Hale exhibited practically none of the tendencies found in Levy's study of overprotected children. He rebelled against overprotection, and it is quite possible that his father's attitude gave considerable aid in this enterprise.

Brothers and sisters, when present, can play an important part in the family system and thus in the environment of growth. Sometimes they function as allies, sometimes as friendly companions, sometimes as models; they can be sources of harassment and ridicule; and they may be bitter competitors for parental favor. Adler introduced the idea that one child, most readily the eldest, might make himself the "parents' foreman," siding with parental values and bossing and punishing the other children with a sense of assured righteousness. If one child slips into this role it becomes closed to others, who may thereby be pushed toward rebelliousness and the less oppressive company of peers. This division of roles was characteristic, as we saw, of Joyce Kingsley and her brother Albert. It was important for Joyce's development that docile conformity carried the added benefit of beating out Albert in the struggle for parental affection, just as it must have been important in Albert's development that he could never hope to compete with his sister in virtuous conduct. In Kidd's case the two brothers, one a year older, one a year younger, likewise played a crucial part though of a somewhat different nature. The older boy's presence was often a support, though his jealousy could be a threat while Joseph was still the parents' favorite. The younger one's athletic and social success was a definite factor in precipitating Joseph's most serious crisis. When he realized that his younger brother held him in contempt rather than admiration, his self-esteem took a disastrous plunge.

If it is necessary to consider the parents and siblings as constituting a total pattern of influence, it is also necessary to bear in mind that the attitudes of all members of the circle change in the course of time. When we characterize a parent as dominating we must realize that he does not necessarily dominate all the time or with respect to everything, and we must allow for the possibility that he changes as he grows older. Joyce Kingsley told us in some detail how her parents had changed in their methods of child training as a result of experience with each successive child. Sometimes parents change attitudes because of events happening in their own careers; they are not immune to wars, economic depressions, political problems, and marital crises. Often they change because of their own special reactions to different phases of the child's growth: a mother may adore her child while he is relatively helpless, for example, but react angrily when he is big enough to break things and launch out on independent adventures. Change of parental and sibling attitudes played a drastic part in Joseph Kidd's career. When he disappointed his parents and lost his position as the favorite son, he was placed under many of the pressures that are the lot of a rejected child.

In a variety of ways the child's membership in the social system of the family affects the course of development. Difficult as it may be to isolate any one influence from others operating at the same time, we can hope to understand individual development only if we learn a great deal about the family environment in which so much of it takes place.

The Growth of Affection

There can hardly be doubt that the growth of affection is an important strand in the course of personal development. Yet it is often not treated as a strand; discussions of the infant's love of the mother, of children's friendships, of chum relations, and of sexual development are often taken up as separate topics as if they had nothing in common and yielded no cumulative consequences. Actually there are several aspects to what is sometimes called the capacity to love. The differences should not be overlooked, but neither should the common theme. The dramatized conception of falling in love that is so conspicuous in American culture tends to obscure the claims of development. In the worlds of film and fiction, love descends like a bolt from the blue, transforming two people whose human interactions up to that point in life have been uninspired. For the student of personality, however, the bolt-from-the-blue hypothesis must be considered improbable, and affection must be treated as having a developmental history.

Affection in Family Relations The attachment of the infant to the caretaker is the starting point of this history. At first the relation is hardly personal—any competent caretaker will do—but by the middle of the first year the mother has been discriminated as someone special and her absence can be seriously upsetting. Under favorable circumstances the child's love for the mother grows strong, and this relation, with its rewards and security, leaves a deep imprint for the rest of life. So lasting can be the tie that even when the mother becomes very old, and the child middle-aged, her death may occasion shock, deep grief, and a feeling of emptiness. The experience is different, of course, if the affectionate tie was only weakly established or was destroyed by negative feelings. Love for the mother, a dependent and unequal relation, cannot be carried over without modification to the loves of later life; it may even hinder them because of its one-sided expectations. It seems clear, however, that this love is better than no love at all as a starting point for affectionate relations.

One of the heresies with which Freud shocked the Victorian world was his theory that a child's love of parents soon took on a sexual coloring. At four or five, in Freud's view, sexual excitability increased to such an extent that the child experienced feelings much like those of adult sexual love. What ensued was a version of the eternal triangle of fiction. Citing Sophocles' drama of Oedipus, Freud attributed to the boy child a desire to possess the mother and kill the rival father; to the girl child, the same feelings with a reversal of characters. Such wishes inevitably produced fears, and Freud believed that the manner in which the child coped with this complex of feelings was of large consequence for all future development. It appears unlikely that the Oedipus complex is such a pivot of development as Freud made it. But we should recognize that children of four and five express their affections with increased vigor and initiative, that they have developed a sharper sense of themselves as persons, and that they have begun to grasp the idea of roles in the family. Jealousy and rivalry are obvious among siblings. There is no reason why they cannot have an important place in relations with parents.

Brothers and sisters might seem to provide ideal objects for affection, especially if there are younger ones who might arouse nurturant feelings. But here the situation is so complicated by competition and rivalry that affection can easily be smothered from the start. Older siblings often recall with resentment how they were obliged to watch over younger ones; younger ones often recall with resentment how they were watched over by older ones, Siblingship is not an ideal situation for developing uncomplicated warmth. Many siblings treat each other with resigned detachment as inescapable but not necessarily welcome presences. But the opportunity for affection may not be wholly lost. Between some siblings there is warm and lively companionship, sharing of confidences, support in times of trouble, and a sense of lasting mutual trust that may endure to the ends of their lives. Joyce Kingsley and her brothers, in spite of earlier rivalries, have preserved a deep devotion, differing in this respect from the Kidds, whose lives have drifted emotionally far apart.

Friendship Outside the family, affection has a chance to develop in the relation of friendship. For serious study, the term *friendship* must be reserved for pairs, not used indiscriminately to refer to acquaintances and members of groups. The distinction is important because the developmental consequences of friendship pairs are different from those of more diffuse social interactions. Being in groups and crowds, even being in small cliques, does little to foster really close human relations or to deepen affection. The peculiar property of friendship is that protective barriers can be let down, making possible an exchange of intimate experiences. In the recent past, American culture placed heavy emphasis on social adjustment, meaning the ability to be comfortable and effective with people in the plural—groups, neighbors, work associates. So strong was this cultural obsession that teachers and guidance workers sometimes tried to separate pairs and get them back into healthy group activities. Recently the developmental possibilities of friendship have received more respect. Warmth, openness, trust, love, capacity for enduring devotion are best grown, it is now recognized, between members of a pair.

Friendships of a sort appear early in a child's experience outside the home. Another child becomes a preferred playmate and even a constant companion. For some time, however, the emphasis lies on doing things together rather than on feelings of affection. One of the services performed by friendship is to facilitate separation from parents and their requirements. In a study of preadolescent girls Deutsch describes pairs who share secrets in a locked room, discuss with giggles everything of which their parents disapprove, and gain strength from alliance with each other.[9] At this age affection may play a minor part, but the building of confidence that results from sharing secrets and realizing one's increased autonomy tends to fill the relation with good feeling.

A critical advance takes place when, as Sullivan expressed it, there begins to be "a real sensitivity to what matters to another person." At some point, probably ten years old or later, the child begins to wonder what he can do "to contribute to the happiness or to support the prestige and feeling of worthwhileness of my chum."[10] This represents, in the first place, a cognitive development: the egocentric perspective of childhood is giving way to the possibility of understanding another person's outlook and experience. But it represents also an affective development: the wish to make things better for the friend and enhance his self-esteem is an expression of love. Because friends usually stand in a relation of equality, this can be regarded as the first experience of love in its adult form.

Exchanging confidences in a relation of trust can have important consequences for development. To discover that someone else has guilty secrets, self-doubts, and anxieties like one's own, or to find that another person engages in self-flattering fantasies and glorious plans such as fill one's own daydreams, is to overcome a sense of isolation and to feel oneself, faults and all, more a member of the human race. Of value also is the free criticism that often flows between close young friends. As Wenar says, a friend's criticism "provides a mirror which enables the adolescent to see himself from a different perspective. Being confronted with himself by someone he values is a priceless growth experience."[11] Wenar adds that friendship by no means excludes aggression; in fact, quarreling and making up are fairly common. But when the relation embodies a strong bond of affection, anger and hurt feelings will be endured rather than lose the friendship.

At its best, friendship can bring about important advances both in affection and in understanding. But it is not always at its best. Like parental upbringing or like socialization by peer groups, friendship can

[9] H. Deutsch, *The Psychology of Women: A Psychoanalytic Interpretation*, Vol. I (New York: Grune & Stratton, Inc., 1944), Chapter 1.

[10] H. S. Sullivan, *The Interpersonal Theory of Psychiatry* (New York: W. W. Norton & Co., 1953), Chapter 16.

[11] C. Wenar, *Personality Development from Infancy to Adulthood* (Boston: Houghton Mifflin Company, 1971), p. 275.

have damaging consequences. A friend who turns out to be fickle, unsympathetic, or exploitative can be a source of much pain and sorrow, which in turn may discourage further seeking for affectionate relations. It is a piece of good fortune for development when the right friend is discovered at the right time.

Sexuality and Affection Affection between friends is not in itself a manifestation of sexual interest. The pairings of middle childhood, like many of the friendships of later life, typically do not depend on physical attraction and can be sufficiently understood without invoking a hypothetical latent sexuality. As puberty approaches, however, sexual attraction becomes a new ground for taking an interest in another person. Adolescents who have not previously had the luck or initiative to find a real friend may have their first experience of friendship under the promptings of sexuality. Sometimes the need for friendship takes first place, so that the time spent together is filled with talk, exchange of experiences, and attempts at self-definition; as Erikson expresses it, "many a youth would rather converse, and settle matters of mutual identification, than embrace."[12] As we found illustrated in the case of Joseph Kidd, sexuality may have nothing to do with affection. It can be pursued as a separate enterprise as though its only possible dimension were physical satisfaction. But even when it starts in this impersonal way it is capable, as we also saw in Kidd, of being joined to affectionate feelings, and increasing their depth. The shared love of a happily married couple, where friendship and sexuality are fully united, can be considered a peak achievement in the growth of affection.

Love for the Young There is another aspect of affection which is best represented in caring for the young. The nurturing kind of love in women presumably springs from a biological root, but it is probably stronger in men than is allowed for in cultural stereotypes of the masculine role. Nurturing love has mixed opportunities during the course of development. Taking care of younger siblings can be, as we saw, a frustrating experience. Age-grading in schools, which becomes more rigid as schools grow larger, tends to reduce contact with younger children; it becomes natural to say, "I never met him, he

---

[12] E. H. Erikson, *Childhood and Society* (New York: W. W. Norton & Co., 2d ed., 1963), p. 228.

was in the class below me." Among adolescents there is preoccupation with establishing self-sufficiency, and this tends to suppress impulses to take care of one another. Thus it can happen that parents approach the birth of their first child with an extraordinarily thin experience of nurturant love. This event is less of a shock if the parents' histories include caring for animal pets, babysitting, jobs as a mother's helper, volunteer work with younger people, serving as an aide to the handicapped, and other experiences with those who are in need of help. Schools which have the requisite resources are increasingly being designed to diminish age segregation and create an environment with natural opportunities for interaction with younger and older children. An adolescent boy who can comfortably pick up, hug, and comfort a baby may have to fight off charges of being a sissy, but he can be credited with rare progress in the growth of affection.

Moral Development

During the normal course of development there is a trend toward more effective internal control and organization. Experience is utilized to meet the demands of living in a more discriminating fashion. The requirements of living together in society have traditionally been referred to as *moral*. The strand of growth which we shall select here for examination has to do with the moral aspects of behavior, represented in concepts such as superego, self-control, conscience, and guiding values.

Superego We are indebted to Freud for the useful concept of the superego. The concept was evolved in order to explain the appearance of seemingly irrational guilt feelings in the free associations of neurotic patients. It appeared that the patients were troubled not only by the wayward and perverse impulses that seethed beneath the surface of awareness, but also by a persistent tendency to feel guilty and miserable, as if someone were about to visit punishment upon them. These guilt feelings often seemed oddly foreign to the patients' conscious standards, and Freud therefore believed that they were carried over from early childhood. He traced their origin to the child's collisions with parental moral authority. After a certain number of experiences with parental displeasure, the child learned to forestall punishment by inhibiting the behavior that would evoke it. Freud described this process as an introjection of parental standards, and he envisaged the superego as governing the child, much as the parents themselves had originally done, by chidings, threatenings, and exhortations to perfection.[13]

The superego can be regarded as the child's form of conscience. As such it is subject to all the limitations of childish understanding. For the most part the meaning of rules and the purpose of prohibitions exceed the comprehension of a four- or five-year-old child. In a series of investigations on moral judgments, Piaget has shown that young children think of a rule as something that simply exists, almost like a physical object; only in middle or later childhood do they grasp the idea that rules are created by men for a distinct social purpose and can be changed by mutual agreement.[14] In his early years a child is likely to assign absolute status to the rules that emanate from his parents, and his application of these rules will be literal and indiscriminate. Thus if the parents scold him for a boisterous outbreak he may conclude that all active assertiveness is bad, rather than making the more precise deduction that the noise disturbed his parents. Furthermore, a child may react to a frustrating prohibition by attributing either more or less anger to the parents than they actually felt. In this way his superego may become either more violent or more lenient than the pattern from which it was copied. Clearly the young child is handicapped in grasping the implications of a moral code. It is small wonder that the action of the superego appears irrational if it continues to govern his thoughts and behavior in adult life.

Although it was discovered in the course of studying neurotic patients, the superego is an important concept for the understanding of any life history. It is upon the foundation of the superego that later moral values will be constructed. Freud was skeptical about the possibility of changing this foundation, except through the long process of psychoanalysis. He conceived that a mature moral code might be reached through later experience and reflection, but he doubted whether these accretions had much effect on the original moral nucleus. This is not an easy point to prove, but we would certainly be neglecting an important insight into the development of personality if we failed to

[13] Freud summarized his views on the superego in *New Introductory Lectures on Psychoanalysis* (New York: W. W. Norton & Co., 1933), pp. 82–98.

[14] J. Piaget, *The Moral Judgment of the Child* (New York: Harcourt Brace Jovanovich, Inc., 1932).

search carefully, even in a healthy life history, for evidences of an archaic conscience and for signs that it has not wholly surrendered its power over conduct. Many forces tend to fixate the superego. In the early years, displeasing one's parents may create powerful feelings of anxiety and guilt. Social conditions are often unfriendly to the outgrowing of childhood conscience. Few people are really encouraged to think for themselves on moral matters; irrational guilt feelings provide an easy means of keeping people in line.

In studying Joseph Kidd's account of his sexual life we had reason to assume that a childlike conscience was governing his behavior. The sharp distinction between touchable and untouchable girls, the prohibition against older girls, and the strikingly effective inhibition of sex with the girl he loved, even when circumstances were favorable, testify at once to a childlike primitiveness of logic and an enduring power of control. While it is impossible to be certain about the origin of this pattern, we are justified in assuming that it expressed in some way what Kidd had grasped about sex from his training in early childhood. Kidd's further learning had all the earmarks of a persistent attempt to broaden the range of permissable sexual experience in accord with his changing ideas. Sometimes the superego is hard to put down. We infer that it retained enough force to govern the situation on the night when he took Mildred to the lake, and it may have delayed his progress in developing lasting love.

How does moral development go forward after its unpromising start in crude superego? We shall look first at the cognitive aspects, then at the types of experience that are conducive to growth.

Cognitive Aspects Piaget's historic studies of moral judgment stimulated research on the cognitive side of the problem. A mature understanding of moral issues which takes everything into account is a cognitive achievement of a high order. Children move toward it by slow degrees and adults may stop short of attaining real moral sophistication. Piaget's own view was that the child advances from *moral realism*, a belief that rules exist in a literal concrete form that permits no change, to *moral relativism*, in which precepts are perceived in relation to the intentions behind them and the social purposes they are designed to serve. For younger children a lie is a lie, punishable in proportion to how far it departs from the truth; it is twice as bad to say you saw six rabbits than to say you saw three, when in fact you did not see any. Only later is such crude arithmetic modified to consider whether or not there was intention to deceive and to allow for the possibility that an untruth might have been designed to protect someone's feelings. Piaget investigated moral judgment by talking over with children of different ages the rules of games and discussing incidents that contained moral dilemmas. Using similar methods, Kohlberg has enlarged upon the developmental sequence.[15] At a level which he calls *premoral*, rules are obeyed simply to avoid punishment. This is characteristic of the great majority of seven-year-olds but declines to 10 percent at the age of sixteen. At a level called *conformity*, rules are obeyed in order to avoid the guilt feelings that result from censure by parents or other authorities. The proportion of children with this outlook rises steadily between seven years and sixteen. At the level of *principles*, rules are obeyed as an expression of the person's own conscience, representing the values in which he has come to believe. In Kohlberg's study, which stopped at sixteen, not quite 20 percent of the oldest group had attained this degree of sophistication; certainly at age nineteen in a college population we would expect it to prevail more widely. Moral understanding requires well-developed cognitive resources. We cannot expect children to grasp everything that a reflective adult might consider essential to a truly moral outlook.

Conducive Experiences Understanding moral principles by no means guarantees that they will be followed. There is a motivational aspect to moral development that produces results all the way from a determination always to be good to a determination never to be good. The superego originates from parents; its force is related to how much the child fears the parents, how much he loves them, how great is the fear of loss of love. An early idea that parental severity led to a strongly introjected superego—as if fear were the crucial variable —gave place to the realization that loss of love might be more effective. Research and clinical observation alike now support the view that early conformity is strongest when parents are predominantly loving— high on acceptance—establishing a warm relation which the child does not want to imperil. When parents are rejecting so that there is no love to lose, the child is likely to stick at the lowest level and follow parental constraints only when there is danger of being caught.

[15] L. Kohlberg, "Development of Moral Character and Moral Ideology," in *Review of Child Development Research*, Vol. 1, ed. by M. L. Hoffman and L. W. Hoffman (New York: Russell Sage Foundation, 1964), pp. 383–431.

Among our three subjects Joyce Kingsley was the most enthusiastic ally of parental values. As we saw, she felt much loved and secure, and she was strongly motivated not to hurt or disappoint her parents, all the more so because this emphasized her superiority to the ill-behaved Albert. Joyce likewise contributes evidence for one of the most important processes in the learning of moral behavior: *identification*. Puzzled by the paucity in her memories of explicitly stated precepts and moral chidings, she concluded that her "moral training seems to be in what Mother and Daddy have lived." She described her parents as "always consistent in living their religious principles," and she considered this "a far more effective teacher than all the spoken words could ever have been." Admiring her parents, Joyce copied them, and for the sake of family solidarity gladly put up with the necessary sacrifices. There is no one among our subjects to represent the opposite extreme. It is best typified by those juvenile delinquents who are motivated by resentment against parents and all other authorities. Their loyalty is to their own impulses and desires, and they fight to protect these from adult interference. Their skill in carrying on this battle can be the despair of well-intentioned professional workers bent on helpful intervention.[16]

Moral development is often stimulated by peer groups and by friendships. Through these contacts a child may learn for the first time that there are precepts and points of view that differ from those of his family. This may be confusing, but it sets in motion a process of comparison, and the child may find welcome support for some of the youthful inclinations toward which peers are likely to be more tolerant. Wanting to be a friend or an accepted group member provides inducement to accept these variant values, and the process of identification can again be of service in enacting new patterns. Substituting new conformities for old is not in itself a dramatic moral advance, but the almost inevitable conflict of values sets the stage for choice and opens the way for deciding what one will affirm as one's own. In adolescence, with increased capacity for abstract thinking, the scope of comparison is greatly enlarged and ethical systems may become a topic of long-lasting debate.

[16] F. Redl and D. Wineman, *Children Who Hate: The Disorganization and Breakdown of Behavior Controls* (New York: The Free Press, Inc., 1951); A. Bandura and R. H. Walters, *Adolescent Aggression* (New York: The Ronald Press Company, 1959).

Especially conducive to moral growth is to be the sufferer from another person's violation. The nature of cheating is never driven home more forcefully than when someone cheats in a game at your expense. Rights to property are never more sharply appreciated than when someone makes off with your favorite plaything. The tiresome rule that you receive privileges only when old enough suddenly wins your support when your younger sister clamors for the lipstick and later hours for which you have just qualified. Continued injustice is destructive, but children can learn a great deal from occasional instances. To be sinned against gives one a personal reason for valuing a precept which until then may have felt like an arbitrary restriction.

Self and Identity

At the end of the chapter on social shaping forces we met the concept of self. The right of this concept to a place in that chapter lay in the fact that social scientists, notably Cooley and Mead, have argued persuasively that the self is a social product. The conception each of us comes to form of himself is strongly influenced by the way other people treat us and the words they use to describe us. Hardly anyone will question the large measure of truth in this way of thinking. Yet after a chapter on biological roots and another on the course of development we again come inevitably to the concept of self. We are now in possession of more material for studying the self, but we meet it again for the same reason as before. It is the key to organization, and it corresponds to a central feature of personal experience: that each of us is one person and remains the same person, in spite of numerous changes, throughout the course of life.

Approaching the self from the side of biology and development means thinking of the person as an organism. It is characteristic of living systems that they grow. They do so in constant interaction and exchange with the environment, yet without losing essential form and identity. The feeling of being the same person from day to day and from year to year comes partly from the constant presence of the familiar body. A further contribution is made by the continuity of personal memories. We wake up in the morning inside the same skin in which we went to sleep, and as drowsiness passes we hook up with the memories of our personal past. The organismic outlook, moreover, requires us to recognize the activity that is inherent in living systems.

My self includes not only "me," my perception of myself as object, but also "I," my experience of myself as active agent capable of reflecting, choosing, and intending. Through this inner activity and through the production of effects upon the environment we affirm the fact that we are alive.

We perceive ourselves as objects, we experience ourselves as agents, and we have feelings about ourselves. These feelings can be put under the heading of *self-esteem*, and they are of tremendous importance in our lives.

Self-Esteem Because it is easy to think of the self as a higher order organization, and of self-esteem as a superordinate motive, we may make the mistake of regarding them as abstractions standing far from the operating forces of everyday life. In fact they are constantly on the front line, exerting a direct influence on behavior. Self-esteem, we correctly say, is a touchy matter, and it tends to be frequently touched in everyday life. This is obvious during arguments, when suggestions creep in that one is reasoning from greater experience, knowledge, and wisdom, and when denials ensue that one's logic and information are inferior. It is apparent even in trivial talk: if a listener disagrees with a carelessly made remark, it is hard to resist trying to prove that the remark was really a pearl of wisdom. Everyday behavior gives evidence of a more or less constant preoccupation with the maintenance, defense, and enhancement of self-esteem. We may be secure, well fed, comfortable in a material sense, happy with our lives, and therefore relatively free from the more primitive causes of anxiety. But we must still maintain vigilance against belittlement and make sure that no disasters befall our self-esteem.

That self-esteem is a touchy matter is apparent also in daydreams. Illustrative, though extreme, was the fantasy set off in a student when reprimanded for a blunder in translating German: he imagined himself years later an authority on German literature, invited to give a lecture at his old school, with the teacher as an appreciative member of his audience. Daydreams may not approach the vividness of the secret life of Walter Mitty as portrayed by James Thurber, but honest examination will show that they have a great deal to do with self-esteem. But daydreams, pleasant as they may be, are relatively ineffective in bolstering actual self-esteem. What they cannot provide is a firmer sense of competence to reach the desired goals.

Sense of Competence In the course of development competence is likely to become sharply diversified. Viewing a person
objectively we could give ratings on dozens of different capabilities:
better at science than literature, more esthetic than athletic, stupid
with machinery but gifted in crafts, socially confident with peers but
constrained with older people and obtuse with younger ones, and so on
through a detailed inventory. But it is possible to speak of a person's
general sense of competence without meaning simply the sum of all
specific capabilities. The self is the product not of arithmetic but of
organization. There is real meaning in William James's contention that
self-feeling depends "on what we *back* ourselves to be and do."[17] The
esthete does not back himself to be an athlete, the craftsman to be
a mechanic, the practical person to be a great brain. Typically a person
puts together a pattern of qualities that are important to him and
becomes more or less indifferent to the rest. The overall sense of
competence is strong to the extent that the person feels efficacious with
respect to this pattern.

In some of the earlier theorizing there was a tendency to
equate self-esteem with praise and approval received from other people. Self-esteem was thus represented as being pumped in from the
outside. Young children are indeed highly responsive to their parents'
appreciation and may not always recognize the worth of their own
accomplishments without this ratification. Before long, however, children begin to recognize when praise is undeserved, a thing they could
not possibly grasp if there were no internal criterion of success. When
a child intends to build a dog kennel but cannot make it come out to
his satisfaction, his pride cannot be artificially restored by praising his
hard work or the botched job. As soon as acts begin to be clearly
intended, competence is experienced by realizing the intention, not by
eliciting praise. Increasingly the sense of competence becomes the
foundation of self-esteem. Confidence derives from proving able to
deal with the world in the ways one has backed oneself to deal with
it.

Identification and Self-Dramatization The construction of the
self is much assisted by *identification*. New patterns of behavior can
emerge suddenly through the copying of models. In studying life

[17] W. James, *The Principles of Psychology*, Vol. 1 (New York: Henry
Holt and Company, 1890), p. 310.

histories it is usually difficult to recover the history of identifications because many of them occur unconsciously. The imitation of parents has been most studied and may be best remembered. Other models can be important, as was Hartley Hale's friend Dan, to whose boldness Hale attributed the overcoming of several of his own fears. A reasonable guess about identification seems to be that it plays a large part in the growth of self, but not a simple part. Evidently there is nothing compulsory, so to speak, about identification. We do not copy everyone, we do not necessarily copy parents, and when we do imitate a model it is only in those respects that appeal to our own needs. A timid adolescent boy may copy a peer's confident conversations with girls but not his belligerence with boys or his disruptiveness in the classroom. There is, in short, much selectivity in the copying of models, a picking out of what is needed at a given moment for the person's own development. What typically occurs, according to Erikson, is an accumulation of fragmentary or partial identifications which have to be synthesized into a working whole.[18] Once again it becomes evident that the self is a consequence of extensive organization.

To picture the developmental course more clearly there is need for the additional concept of *self-dramatization*. Perhaps the term at first suggests shallow histrionics, showing off, or a deliberate attempt to manipulate one's image. These are unpleasant variants of a process that has a much wider significance for personal growth. Self-dramatization implies imagining oneself in future situations, picturing how one will behave, rehearsing what one will say. Children can imitate but they can also improvise, imagining things beyond what they actually experience. This creativeness is the beginning of the serious self-dramatizations that form an essential part of planning for the future. When a person looks ahead, he tries to take account not only of the facts he knows but also of how he will feel in various future circumstances. He sets a stage in his mind and puts himself upon it as an actor, trying to anticipate the congeniality of the part. The metaphor of the theater keeps us reminded that imagination enters creatively into the process of personal growth.

Self-dramatization is illustrated in the episode during which Hartley Hale reached his decision to become a doctor. He was greatly helped in reaching this decision by his perceptive and outspoken friend, but he did not accept any of his friend's judgments at face

18 E. H. Erikson, 1963, pp. 277–284.

value, arguing far into the night that the whole proposal was poppy-cock. He utilized his friend's observations, nevertheless, and the long-drawn-out nocturnal session amounted in fact to a profound attempt on Hale's part to imagine himself alternately in the roles of advertising man and physician, in order to see which role could absorb the greater portion of his preferences and interests. Medicine won the battle be-cause it took in his interest in biology and because it appealed to his desire to be taken seriously as the giver of profoundly needed services. Hale found that he could imagine himself more satisfyingly in the role of doctor, and he made his choice on this basis even though it meant a more difficult education and a longer postponement of financial re-turns. Thus he selected the drama in which he preferred to act.

Ego Identity A valuable broadening of ideas about the self has been offered by Erikson, who attaches importance to *ego identity*—the sense of being a distinct individual within a social frame-work. This concept adds a social dimension that is often neglected in writings about the self. A person's identity does not depend entirely on who he is, but on how he fits into that part of the world which he has come to accept and take seriously. This statement should not be misread to imply uncritical conformity; the part of the world that a person chooses may be strictly nonconformist. But a complete sense of identity requires feeling that one's life has a place among other lives, that one is meaningful in a circle of meaningful people, that one is taken seriously by a significant group of which one is a part. Introduc-ing the concept in 1950, Erikson wrote that the study of identity is "as strategic in our time as the study of sexuality was in Freud's time." This judgment was fully borne out during the ensuing years when young people, progressively liberated with respect to sex, experienced mounting difficulties of commitment in a forbiddingly impersonal world of runaway technology. During adolescence there is a critical time when ego identity becomes heavily dependent on the judgments of one's peers. "The danger of this stage," says Erikson, "is role diffu-sion. It is primarily the inability to settle on an occupational identity which disturbs young people. To keep themselves together they tem-porarily overidentify, to the point of apparent complete loss of iden-tity, with the heroes of cliques and crowds."[19] The search for identity comes into better focus as progress is made in understanding one's

[19] E. H. Erikson, 1963, p. 262.

own capacities and finding a place among other people where these capacities can be used to advantage.

In a study of college students, Marcia has described four different states or patterns in the development of ego identity.[20] Marcia applies the term *identity foreclosure* to those subjects who seem to have arrived without struggle at a firm commitment to some way of life. This may imply an unimaginative acceptance of parental values and of things as they are, but it can signify early choice of a congenial and socially valuable life pattern, and it can mean unusual maturity in thinking about one's place in the world. *Identity diffusion* means the searching state described by Erikson as typical of adolescence. The subjects can be characterized as adrift and uncommitted. This is different from the status to which Marcia gives the title of *moratorium*. Subjects placed in this category are still vague about their plans and preferences but are actively struggling to achieve serious commitments in the near future. They are on the way to what others have already attained, *identity achievement*, in which a person looks ahead to a pattern of life and values worthy of full commitment, arrived at after much searching.

Whatever else may be true of personality, it is certainly a consequence of growth. By examining the course of development we have been able to discover what lies behind several of the most important features of mature personal organization. We cannot suppose, however, that development stops, its work finished, at some early point in life. Our three subjects, studied between twenty and thirty and in two cases into middle age, can assist us in attempting a preliminary sketch of continuing natural growth during young adulthood.

SUGGESTIONS FOR FURTHER READING

The topics covered in this chapter are described at greater length in R. W. White, *The Enterprise of Living: Growth and Organization in Personality* (New York: Holt, Rinehart and Winston, Inc., 1972), Chapters 8–11, 13, and 16. Likewise organized around the course of growth is Charles Wenar's *Personality Development from Infancy to Adulthood* (Boston: Houghton Mifflin Company, 1971).

The nature and consequences of dependency are discussed by five

[20] J. E. Marcia, "Development and Validation of Ego Identity Status," *Journal of Personality and Social Psychology*, 3 (1966), 551–559.

distinguished researchers in *Attachment and Dependency*, edited by J. L. Gewirtz (New York: V. H. Winston & Sons, Inc., 1972). Anna Freud in *The Ego and the Mechanisms of Defense* (London: Hogarth Press, Ltd., 1937) gives the psychoanalytic view of defense mechanisms. The best way to make the acquaintance of Alfred Adler is through the excerpts from his writings collected with explanatory comments by H. L. and R. R. Ansbacher in *The Individual Psychology of Alfred Adler* (New York: Basic Books, 1956).

The conclusions of research on parental attitudes toward children are summarized by W. C. Becker, "Consequences of Different Kinds of Parental Discipline," in *Review of Child Development Research*, Vol. I, ed. by M. L. Hoffman and L. W. Hoffman (New York: Russell Sage Foundation, 1964); see especially pp. 189–199. Searching studies of the family as a social system are contained in John Spiegel's *Transactions: The Interplay between Individual, Family, and Society* (J. Papajohn, ed., New York: Science House, 1971). Brian Sutton-Smith and B. J. Rosenberg discuss the parts played by brothers and sisters in *The Sibling* (New York: Holt, Rinehart and Winston, Inc., 1970).

A lively survey of many of the problems connected with the growth of affection is given by Zick Rubin, *Liking and Loving: An Invitation to Social Psychology* (New York: Holt, Rinehart and Winston, Inc., 1973). Oriented especially to theory is the volume edited by B. I. Murstein, *Theories of Attraction and Love* (New York: Springer Publishing Co., 1971). H. S. Sullivan's influential view of intimacy is in *The Interpersonal Theory of Psychiatry* (New York: W. W. Norton & Co., 1953), Chapter 16.

On moral development there is an excellent paperback by Derek Wright, *The Psychology of Moral Behavior* (Baltimore: Penguin Books, Inc., 1971). The topic is briefly but clearly reviewed in Chapter 14 of L. E. Longstreth's *Psychological Development of the Child*, 2d ed. (New York: The Ronald Press Company, 1974).

Erik H. Erikson's views on ego identity, introduced in *Childhood and Society* in 1950 (New York: W. W. Norton & Co., 2d ed., 1963), are further developed in *Identity: Youth and Crisis* (also published by Norton, 1968).

9

NATURAL GROWTH
DURING
YOUNG ADULTHOOD

> Organic growth and repair have their counterpart in
> the personality in the process of renewal: a con-
> tinued making over of ideas and attitudes, of senti-
> ments and plans, so that the person will overcome
> the animal tendency to repetition, fixation, automa-
> tism.

LEWIS MUMFORD

Up to this point we have been conducting two parallel investigations.
On the one hand we have made a painstaking attempt to understand in
detail the lives of Hartley Hale, Joseph Kidd, and Joyce Kingsley. On
the other hand we have tried to evaluate some of the leading ideas
about personality that have issued from the social sciences, biological
research, and the developmental study of man. Our findings fully con-
firm the value of a threefold approach to the understanding of lives. Our
three subjects would have been strangely misinterpreted if we had
failed to consider the shaping influence of the culture, social class,
group experiences, and occupational and other roles. They would have
been curiously disembodied if we had omitted all reference to drive,
the learning process, temperament, and the nature of their abilities.
They would have been peculiarly depersonalized if we had left out the
special impact of the family circle and the course of their growth
toward competence, affection, moral values, and self-respecting iden-

tity. All three sources provide us with indispensable information. One can take a narrower view only at the risk of talking plain nonsense about human nature.

Although our understanding has been greatly benefited by a combined social, biological, and developmental approach, we have experienced certain frustrations. It is confusing to realize that so many forces operate at once in a given personality, producing an elaborate system of interconnected events rather than a simple model of cause and effect. Bothersome also is the constant finding that general concepts, such as social class and occupation, drive and motive, parental attitude and developmental stage, require so many qualifications in order to fit the individual case, and that change has to be described with reference to so many particulars. But perhaps the most recurrent difficulty is accounting for natural growth. It always seems easier to explain the more rigid, crippled, and irrational features of our subjects' personalities than to understand the constructive side of their development. Clearly we must devote more attention to what happens *when lives are in progress*. Our task in this chapter is to think specifically about the conditions under which natural growth takes place, using as our chief material the growth trends that are characteristic of young adulthood.

Directions and Conditions of Adult Growth

Growth implies both a process of change and a direction of change. It is easy to think about the direction if we confine ourselves to children and to obvious ways in which they develop. We expect them to get larger, stronger, smarter, better controlled, and more responsible. We expect them to grow up. By the time they are five or six they should have attained fairly complete locomotor control, being able to walk, run, hop, skip, jump, and climb. At about the same age they should have mastered the structure of language so that they can talk in relatively adult fashion. When they are ten they should be capable of applying themselves somewhat steadily to tasks and of managing a certain amount of social interaction without constant supervision. When they are sixteen or so they should be able to hold regular jobs and take part in various other adult activities. When they are eighteen they should be able to assume the further responsibilities of the ballot box and of financial self-management. But now they are "of age"— they have become legal adults—and while we do not suppose that personal development ceases at this point, it is now more difficult to define the directions of further growth. Historically, directions of growth after the point at which biological development is complete have been defined in ethical terms. In recent years, with the rise of psychological and social science, attempts are being made to work later growth trends into a naturalistic system.

Maturity Obviously suitable for describing earlier growth trends, the concept of maturity has commonly been extended to cover the later ones. It has come to occupy a prominent and influential place in our thinking. In part this comes from the prestige that is currently accorded to science. In part it comes from the weakening of religion and ethics as guides to personal conduct. In part it comes from confusion in secular values other than those derived from science. This means that the idea of maturity is being drawn upon to fill a large ideological vacuum. "The maturity concept," said Overstreet, "is central to our whole enterprise of living. This is what our past wisdoms have been leading up to."[1] To be the culmination of past wisdoms, to take over defining the good life in the good society, is indeed a mighty burden, and we should not expect the concept of maturity to bear the whole weight. At the same time we cannot overlook its widespread practical influence. It has a direct point of application in child training, guidance, teaching, and psychotherapy, and it is being used every day to influence the development of personality.

When it is the fate of ideas to fill an ideological vacuum, taking the place of values that have crumbled, there is danger that they will be misused. Such has been the case with two ideas, *mental health* and *adjustment*, that originated in the study of mental disorders. Instead of standing as first rough attempts to define directions of growth, they were seized upon as scientifically ratified guides to conduct and paths to perfection. Mental health was soon presented in the distorted form of a list of traits all of which one should possess, regardless of temperament, aptitude, and the circumstances of life. Adjustment quickly degenerated into a doctrine of conformity, twisted to mean that everyone should adjust themselves to things as they are.[2] One can fear that

---

[1] H. A. Overstreet, *The Mature Mind* (New York; W. W. Norton & Co., 1949), p. 14.

[2] R. W. White, "The Dangers of Social Adjustment," *Teachers College Record*, 62 (1961), 288–297; "The Concept of Healthy Personality: What Do We Really Mean?" *The Counseling Psychologist*, 4 (1973), 3–12.

the ideas of mental health and adjustment, inflated into sweeping precepts, may have done a good deal of harm.

The concept of maturity is exposed to the same danger of inflated and indiscriminate use. Because it is inherently set in a framework of development, however, it can be more easily protected from this fate. It can be founded on the study of lives in progress, on the examination of events and experiences that have enabled people to cope more successfully with problems, increase the effectiveness of strategies, deepen their appreciation of their surroundings, and expand their resources for happiness. In Saul's book on the subject we find several "criteria of maturity" that are expressed as growth trends, with more or less specific directions of change: for example, "from parasitic dependence to independence of parents," "freedom from the constellation of inferiority, egotism, and competitiveness," "construction of own conscience," "attaining a firm sense of reality."[3] The concepts that we shall use in attempting a sketch of natural growth during young adulthood are of a similar type and are harmonious with the idea of maturity. Having three actual lives freshly in mind will be a help to us in describing growth trends. Each person presents us with a particular version of general processes; and it is these versions, taken together, that lead us to an understanding of individuality.

Situational Changes in Young Adulthood The chief happenings that generally mark the decade of the twenties are the finding of an occupation and the establishing of a new family. Although neither commitment is necessarily permanent, they are intended to last as long as possible. A number of changes in the circumstances of life are likely to result. Entering an occupation usually implies staying in one place and engaging continuously in one line of activity. Marriage means bringing one's affections to a focus on one person with whom the daily details of life are shared. Having a family means assuming responsibility for offspring whose care is a continuous operation. Young adulthood thus brings about certain restrictions and continuities not previously experienced. There is less room for variety, novelty, and impulsive adventure, but more challenge to develop depth in both feeling and understanding.

[3] L. J. Saul, *Emotional Maturity*, 2d ed. (Philadelphia: J. B. Lippincott Company, 1962).

We should take note that this description fits the lives of two of our subjects but not the third. Joseph Kidd was well into the thirties before committing himself to occupation, marriage, and family. For him, late adolescence was stretched out over a decade, partly by circumstances such as his long military service, partly because of his own need to catch up after a prolonged slowdown in early adolescence. Kidd's example serves as a reminder that people develop at different rates. Schemes that divide the course of life into developmental stages have to be formulated loosely beyond adolescence.[4] Young adulthood, as described here, should not be attached too firmly to chronology. It is the stage people are in when they make decisive commitments to vocation and marriage, whenever this may be. Keniston points out that the pursuit of graduate education changes the average chronology for a great many contemporary young people. Extended education postpones full entry into an adult vocational role, though it often does not postpone marriage. To emphasize the paradoxical position of being no longer adolescent but still not quite adult, Keniston suggests calling this period *youth*, but he adds that it "obviously cannot be equated with any particular age range."[5] Kidd at thirty still fitted the psychological picture of youth, whereas Hale edged into young adulthood shortly after entering medical school at twenty-two.

The conditions brought about by vocational and marital commitment are likely to favor a deepening knowledge of the real conditions of life. One is placed in a better position to find out how things work in detail. Staying at least for a time with one job, a person discovers how the organization works, how interests clash and compromises are made, how the whole enterprise stumbles along rather than moving straight to rational goals. Struggling to make both ends meet, a couple may join the taxpayers' association, only to discover that this group bitterly opposes any improvements in the public schools their children will attend. Wanting to elect a congressman with congenial views, young voters may learn at firsthand that they cannot avoid dealing with an entrenched local political organization. Learning how things work in detail is regarded by Rappaport as so significant

---

[4] For a survey of such schemes see L. Rappaport, *Personality Development: The Chronology of Experience* (Glenview, Ill.: Scott, Foresman and Company, 1972), Chapter 4.

[5] K. Keniston, "Youth: A 'New' Stage of Life," *The American Scholar*, 39 (1970), 631–654.

that he adds it to occupational and marital choice as "a third factor which seems critical for personality development" during young adulthood.[6] He gives it the title of *disillusionment*, but in the sense of outgrowing youthful illusions rather than becoming a discouraged cynic. "Entry into adulthood," he writes, is not "inevitably accompanied by cynicism, or the loss of all ideals, but typical experience in this period does inevitably force young people to reevaluate and change most of their ideas about themselves and the world." If it seems regrettable to lose illusions and glowing ideals, solid satisfaction can be found in the growth of wisdom and competence.

A Study of General Trends Highly relevant to our theme is a massive longitudinal study recently reported by Jack Block.[7] This study deals with adults in the age range from thirty to thirty-seven, but they were adults who had been extensively studied before as children and as adolescents. The subjects were 171 men and women who had grown up in Berkeley or Oakland, California. Lower-class members were underrepresented but not absent, and the predominant middle-class membership assured that the group would not represent an intellectual elite. The available information, though not perfect, was unusually abundant, and a carefully devised system of ratings by a corps of judges insured that it was used advantageously. The comparisons that are of the most interest here are those between ratings in senior high school and ratings during the subjects' early thirties. All statements of change were derived from differences in judges' independent ratings between the two periods.

Findings were reported separately for men and women, but certain growth trends were common to both sexes. There was a general increase in the clarity and consistency of personality, a stabilization of self and identity. The subjects had gained in coping capacity, were less defensive, and were less given to fantasy, impulsiveness, and sensual gratification. Since high school they had come to assume greater responsibility for themselves and others. They had moved in the direction of giving rather than taking. One could say that they had settled down to the serious business of adult living and were mostly making a go of it, though not without some sacrifice of freedom and spontaneity.

[6] L. Rappaport, 1972, p. 335.
[7] J. Block, *Lives through Time* (Berkeley, Calif.: Bancroft Books, 1971), especially Chapters 2, 3, and 5.

The ways in which male and female development differed reflected the social roles of breadwinners and homemakers. The men changed toward qualities appropriate to achievement in the outside world. They had become more confident and assured, more dependable and controlled, more goal-oriented, better satisfied with themselves. These gains, however, were not without cost: the necessities of work had pushed them toward detachment and compulsiveness, making them less relaxed, less responsive to humor, less sensitive esthetically, and in a way less interesting. "The experience of becoming an adult," Block remarks, "is not entirely beneficent, but is more a matter of driving a bargain between the self and the world." Qualities of personal expressiveness and playfulness had to be traded off for greater competence in dealing with widening responsibilities.

Changes peculiar to women were influenced by the occupations of homemaking and child rearing. Most of the women in the sample were engaged primarily in these occupations, and the changes indicated greater coping capacity. There was movement in the direction of security and comfort in interpersonal relations. The impulsive selfishness and easily hurt feelings of adolescence had declined, while psychological mindedness and understanding of human relations had improved. Gains were apparent in warmth, giving, nurturance, tender attachments, and cheerfulness, and these affective enlargements did not require the constrictions observed in the men. But the women had become more inclined to worry and feel guilty. Perhaps their guilt feelings were related to their having moved toward what Block describes as "a culturally conventional deferent femininity." Such feelings might arise in interaction with culturally conventional males who coolly exert the privilege of being master of the house.

In the following discussion of growth trends during young adulthood we shall concentrate, as in previous chapters, on selected ideas rather than attempting an exhaustive account. Episodes of growth drawn from our case studies will serve to illustrate general trends and will direct attention not only to the *direction* but also to the *process* of change. Growth in a given direction takes place under certain conditions and through certain kinds of experience. It is not something that just happens because we grow older. If in addition to designating trends we can identify the conducive conditions under which development occurs, we shall have made a step forward in the understanding of natural growth.

Growth Trends: 1. The Stabilizing of Ego Identity

As we saw in the last chapter, there are great individual differences during the college years in the extent to which ego identity is achieved. Some students are still in the throes of identity diffusion with little sense, as they put it, of who they are. Others, either through early foreclosure or recent struggle, seem to be able to answer this question with clarity and certainty. Yet even those with a firm sense of identity at graduation still have a long way to go. Identity becomes a finally fixed achievement only much later in life, if at all. We shall concentrate here on one important aspect of its growth, a trend toward stabilization, which seems to be prominent during young adulthood.

Direction of Growth There are many vicissitudes in the development of ego identity, but the overall trend is toward an increase of stability. When one takes a long enough span of time, continuing well into adulthood as we have done with the cases presented here, ego identity can be seen to become not only more sharp and clear but also more consistent and free from transient influences. It becomes increasingly determined by accumulated personal experience. In this way it progressively gains autonomy from the daily impact of social judgments and experiences of success and failure. To be called a coward by a kindergarten playmate may be an extremely upsetting experience; one is not sure to what extent the epithet may be deserved. To be called a coward at the age of thirty is quite another matter. It may be upsetting if the person feels that others have discovered a weakness he was trying to hide, but it will not be upsetting at all if the person knows that it is not true. The point is that at thirty a person pretty much knows whether or not he is a coward; he can make a self-judgment on the basis of his accumulated experience, and he knows that this judgment is sounder than the one arriving from outside. Even praise is not accepted, as we saw in Hale's case, when inner judgment cannot agree that it was deserved. A similar trend can be observed with respect to the evaluation of successes and failures. The single incident progressively loses its power to send self-esteem into the sky or into the depths. Accumulated experience, organized as an increasingly stable set of self-feelings and self-estimates, more and more outweighs the impact of new events.

It is not an objection to this view to say that with some people ego identity does not seem to grow more stable over the years. Any theory about growth makes the allowance that fixation and regression can occur. It makes the further allowance that conditions may not always be favorable for extensive growth. Nevitt Sanford has shown in a study of college women that ego identity becomes less stable during the senior year. This happens because of real uncertainty about the position in life that is to replace being a student. Many of the young women looked forward to early marriage and were not prepared to commit themselves to an independent occupation, but because the future husband's personality, occupation, and social position were still unknown they had no way of picturing the circumstances in which their lives would be led.[8] Conditions of uncertainty are inimical to stability of any kind. In giving the *stabilizing of ego identity* its status as a growth trend, we are suggesting that change in this direction represents an increasingly full realization of capacities for development. It results, moreover, in a greater capacity to exert an influence on the surrounding world. As ego identity grows more stably autonomous, the person becomes capable of having a more consistent and lasting effect upon his environment. The more sure he becomes about his own nature and competence, the more solid is the nucleus from which his activity proceeds.

Of our three subjects, Joseph Kidd ranks as the greatest authority on the earlier growth of ego identity. Because this aspect of growth was peculiarly difficult for him, and because of a serious setback during his later school and college years, Kidd became sharply conscious of the whole process and was able to give us an unusually vivid firsthand account. His description of himself at eighteen as "acting out personalities," "observing people and copying them," then falling back to a "childish attitude to make myself noticeable," deserves to be considered a classic account of a frustrated search for ego identity. Kidd staked out the ensuing trend of his development in two neat summaries given a decade apart. At nineteen he said, "I can't make a decision on my own and back it up; it's always guided by some factor outside my own intellect." At twenty-nine he expressed himself as follows: "It dawned on me after a while that I was knowing what I wanted. I was able to make up my mind." It is worth while to sketch again his progress between these two points.

[8] N. Sanford (ed.), "Personality Development during the College Years," *Journal of Social Issues*, 12 (1956), No. 4.

Kidd's growth was aided by the temporary suspension of parental demands that resulted from his entrance into military service. He was able to drop a whole series of goals and pretensions that had never been invested with a substantial amount of self-feeling. Freed from pressure to study at college and prepare for medical school, permitted to leave all major decisions in other hands, he regressed for a while to the happy atmosphere of adventurous and irresponsible companionship he had once enjoyed with neighborhood boys. In this way he recovered contact with true interests of his own and began testing his initiative with a great deal more persistence than had characterized his early trying out of "personalities." When he could carry through a hard day's work on a common task, he became aware of an increase of poise and confidence in his relationships with the other men, a thing he deeply wanted to achieve. Presently he ventured on experiments in "corning" and found that it was not impossible for him to be effective in getting what he wanted from other people. When he was commissioned an officer, however, his growing self-confidence went out from under him; he found it impossible to muster the decisiveness needed to direct and discipline the men under his command. He had again been placed in a position that did not "feel right" in the sense of freely enlisting his own desires, which were, after all, "to be *with* other fellows, not *over* them." When reassigned he was able to pick up his own development once more, so that by the time he undertook to manage the building of his father's new business establishment he was able, albeit a little nervously, to seek out information, choose and reject propositions, and require that things be done to suit him.

It was while building the flower studio that Kidd became clearly aware of knowing what he wanted and making up his own mind. The building stood in his mind as the payment of a debt owed by a son to parents whom he had in some respects disappointed. By paying the debt he freed himself from their lingering expectations, thus removing the chief remaining obstacle to the stabilizing of his own ego identity. He had managed to lay a sufficient basis of assertiveness so that he did not feel wholly unable to go after the things he really wanted. He had managed also to clarify an image of himself as a businessman and a friendly, likeable fellow. The flower studio stood as an enduring monument to his ideas and his labors. It represented the longest and biggest attempt he had ever made to exert an influence on his environment, and its success was of great value in further stabilizing his identity.

Process of Growth When we turn from the *direction* of change to the *process* of change, our focus of attention shifts to the single steps that cumulatively make up a growth trend. We become interested in the conditions under which the stability of ego identity receives an increment of natural growth. We shall not engage ourselves with such vaguely defined conditions as an atmosphere of parental acceptance, which could probably be reduced, after all, through sufficient study to a set of specific incidents. Rather, our concern will be to consider the steps in learning that appear to be most crucial with respect to the growth trend in question. Although we speak of continuous change and cumulative development, it would certainly be arbitrary to interpret these expressions literally as meaning an unbroken growth through time. Growth trends occur through specific incidents that are sometimes well separated in time. Some incidents, moreover, are much more important than others, even to the extent of producing an astonishing transformation. Hartley Hale gave us an example in the famous "backbone incident," and Joyce Kingsley assigned rather special importance to her single-handed rebellion at the western army post.

One type of event that often contributes to the stabilizing of ego identity is placement in an occupational status or in some other socially recognized position. Social roles provide us with a means of establishing identity. They also provide us with opportunities for action whereby we further define and stabilize ourselves. Hale's sense of identity began to assume a more definite form as soon as he decided to go to medical school, and his identification with his occupational role proceeded at a rapid pace when he had a chance to enjoy the privileges and utilize the opportunities provided by his profession. Similarly, Joyce Kingsley used her position as president of student government as a means of defining part of her identity and as a platform for effective action. But it was again Joseph Kidd who provided the most striking illustration. He described vividly the manner in which his old self-doubts and uncertainties receded when he came to occupy a clearly defined position in a hierarchical business organization. In general it can be said that the stabilizing process owes much to those enduring roles which are characteristic of adult life. As a person shapes his behavior into his occupational role, his marital role, and his parental role, for example, his experience begins to accumulate more and more selectively. The stored-up sources of his stability come increasingly out of behavior within roles. Under stable social conditions much strength can thus be borrowed from the environment through consistent playing of consistently defined roles.

It is not possible, however, to understand the stabilizing process without taking into account the interest and initiative that a person brings to any proffered role. We can take as an example Kidd's history as an army officer. Here we witness the failure of a well-defined and generally much coveted position to stabilize the behavior of its occupant. Kidd was not interested in being an officer. He made little attempt to overcome his distaste for issuing commands and administering discipline. It was impossible for him to adopt the proffered identity or to behave in such a way as to strengthen it. His interests were slowly moving him toward an entirely different ego identity, and the role of officer, which would have deflected this development, had no more than a transient negative effect on his stabilization.

It must be remembered, furthermore, that social roles do not define individual identities in a precise or sufficient sense. If a person's sense of identity consisted of nothing except that he was a doctor it could hardly be called well stabilized. Within any one social role there is room for a great deal of individuality. Three vice-presidents in a bank, for example, might bring different skills and interests into the company, each making his own special contribution. This point is well illustrated in the case of Hartley Hale, whose ego identity went far beyond what was implied by his role. Within the general framework of being a doctor, he had preferred orthopedic surgery, come to favor a radical attitude toward surgical intervention, taken a stand for rapid and efficient ward rounds, devoted a good share of his time to research, selected one particular field of research, and so forth. All of these represent options within the physician's role, and Hale made the choices because of preferences he discovered in himself. Using one's preferences to fill in the details of a role, sometimes even to transform the role, gives one's sense of identity a firmness that could never be wholly borrowed from social expectations.

Consideration of the part played by interest, preference, and sense of competence leads us to perceive the types of experience that are most conducive to stabilizing one's ego identity. Stated schematically, any episode has this effect which serves to heighten the efficacy of accumulated personal experience as against new outside judgments, fresh experiences of success and failure, or new objects of possible identification. This heightened efficacy results most readily from a situation of choice in which there are immediate pressures on either side. Decision necessarily turns on becoming more aware of personal preference and of the things for which one really wants one's life to stand. Perhaps our best illustration is to be found in Joyce's collision with the authorities at the military post on the West Coast. When the youthful magazine editors asked her to present their grievances, she was faced with a considerable challenge. If she kept still, she would preserve her job, save a great deal of unpleasantness, and spare herself the criticism of her friends for being too zealously righteous. But she had strong convictions about leaders who let a mixed group of adolescents run wild and who carelessly interfered with the only activity that embodied serious responsibility toward young people. Joyce was forced back to her basic values. She found out what was more important to her and she proceeded to take a stand for it. She learned that she was competent to do this: she could bear the anxiety over possible rejection and ridicule, and her protest appeared to have favorable consequences in the environment. The result was a permanent sharpening and stabilizing of her ego identity.

Obviously no single growth trend can do justice to everything that happens to the self. The trend we have described in this section resembles in certain respects, though not entirely, McClelland's concept of a trend toward *self-consistency*, a trend that has been given central importance in Lecky's theory of personality.[9] A somewhat different aspect of growth has been described by Allport under the heading of *self-objectification*. This refers to "that peculiar detachment of the mature person when he surveys his own pretensions in relation to his abilities, his present objectives in relation to possible objectives for himself, his own equipment in comparison with the equipment of others, and his opinion of himself in relation to the opinions others hold of him."[10] These trends are discernible in our subjects and are important in understanding them. The stabilizing of ego identity is but one of several ways in which the self proceeds toward full development.

[9] D. W. McClelland, *Personality* (New York: Holt, Rinehart and Winston, Inc., 1951), pp. 542–559; P. Lecky, *Self-Consistency: A Theory of Personality* (New York: Island Press, 1945.)

[10] G. W. Allport, *Personality: A Psychological Interpretation* (New York: Holt, Rinehart and Winston, Inc., 1937), Chapter 8.

Growth Trends: 2. The Freeing of Personal Relationships

The second growth trend to be selected for discussion lies in the sphere of personal relationships. Like many other aspects of human behavior, personal relationships are deeply colored by their history. The circumstances in which they develop are not always auspicious for ultimate maturity. Especially in the family circle, with so many cross-currents of emotion and so much at stake, patterns may be acquired which have more to do with defense and enhancement of the self than with real interaction. Personal history does not reliably teach us to respond to people in their own right. Our social behavior is thus often poorly fitted to new circumstances.

Responding to people in their own right as new individuals is not easy even for the most socially seasoned adult. It is a difficult human achievement. Our social learning is forever lagging behind the demands put upon it, and our most alert and sensitive responses are apt to reveal bits of inappropriate historical coloring. To some extent this lag results from the inherent difficulties that attend learning in a social situation. When we learn something like the multiplication table, or the way an internal combustion motor is put together, we can at least concentrate on what we are trying to learn. In a social situation, on the other hand, several things are likely to be going on at once. Social interactions have a content as well as an emotional undertone. We are apt to be doing something with the other person, or talking about something, so that our learning is by no means confined to the process of interaction. When someone talks about a trip he has taken, for instance, we respond simultaneously to the contents of his description and to the attitude he displays toward us. Perhaps a very "subjective" listener will respond wholly to the attitude, searching the narrator's manner and tone of voice for proof of affection, condescension, or distaste, and recall nothing about the geography of the trip. Perhaps a very "objective" listener will come away with a full knowledge of the itinerary but no impression whatever of the person who took the trip. These extremes serve to point up the dilemma of social learning. Most of our social interacting is learned under conditions of high distraction. We do not fully perceive either the other person or ourselves, and this circumstance tends to favor the persistence of old attitudes rather than the learning of new ones.

In view of this weakness in the typical learning situation, and in view of the high emotional stakes that are often involved, it is no wonder that personal relationships are easily injured by anxiety and defenses. Anxiety adds to the distraction; defenses freeze the repertory of safe social behavior and block the attempting of new responses. Suppose that a person has learned to cover social discomfort by fast, superficial chattering, thus avoiding both the silences that would make him anxious and the serious discussions that would challenge his competence. His discomfort forbids him to stop chattering; thus he never learns how people would respond to him, or how he would respond to them, in any other kind of interaction. Social learning is peculiarly vulnerable to the workings of anxiety and defense.

Many of the troubles for which people seek psychological help turn out to be disturbances in interpersonal relations. The counselor's task in such cases is to bring about new social learning. Information relevant to our second growth trend can be gained by briefly examining the well-studied process of psychotherapy.

Social Growth in Psychotherapy   When defensive blocks have occurred in learning to interact with others, psychotherapy is a matter of removing these blocks so that learning can be resumed. The growth that goes on during and after a period of psychotherapy is therefore no different in principle from the normal course of development when important blocks have not been present. The essence of psychotherapy is to provide a situation in which the patient will feel progressively less anxious, less defensive, more able to put out new feelers in social behavior and thus to enlarge his capacity for personal relationships. The process has been studied intensively, especially since Freud developed the technique of psychoanalysis, and it is now fairly well understood. It can be translated, as Dollard and Miller and others have shown, into the concepts of a theory of learning originally derived from much simpler facts.[11]

The central feature of the therapeutic situation is the attitude taken by the therapist. He accepts with composure and interest whatever the patient has to say. He shows that he considers it important, and he receives it without disapproval, criticism, or censure. He encourages the patient to talk freely even about embarrassing and fright-

[11] J. Dollard and N. E. Miller, *Personality and Psychotherapy: An Analysis in Terms of Learning, Thinking, and Culture* (New York: McGraw-Hill, Inc., 1950), Chapters 14–20; A. Bandura, and R. H. Walters, *Social Learning and Personality Development* (New York: Holt, Rinehart and Winston, Inc., 1963), Chapter 5.

ening things, which he does not treat as if they betokened inferiority or wickedness. This is new and surprising; probably the patient has never before encountered such tolerance for his personal problems. As a result he becomes able to talk of more and more things, including experiences long forgotten and feelings long banished from awareness. The individual steps of psychotherapy can all be conceived of as acts of social learning. The feelings expressed by the patient, whether of love, dependence, jealousy, hate, or fear, find an unexpectedly permissive reception. The therapist may point them out and interpret them, thus showing their inappropriateness in the current situation, but he does not respond in such a way as to create new cause for anxiety. This makes it possible for the patient to try out an increasing range of social initiatives that feel dangerous but that prove not to have alarming results.

The essential changes do not take place, however, entirely during the therapeutic hours. The patient's improvement would indeed be fragile if it depended upon a permissiveness that is almost never found elsewhere in life. As he begins to feel greater freedom in his personal relationship with the therapist, the patient tries out his new behavior on other people and becomes able to increase his range even when the reception is not permissive. Except for the fact that the therapist stands ready to offer encouragement when these experiments receive a setback, the outside learning that accompanies psychotherapy is simply a natural course of growth. The patient belatedly makes the kind of growth that would have gone on through childhood and young adulthood if anxiety and defense had not effected a block. The therapist has provided the rare permissive atmosphere necessary to break the block, but the really vital learning must eventually be accomplished in the patient's own social orbit.

During the last thirty years there has been an impressive development of group psychotherapy. One of the virtues of this method is to assist the process of social learning with people other than the therapist. The other patients in the group provide what might be called a test environment for social interaction. It is not as exacting as the outside world because the therapist is ever present to soften and interpret the exchanges and because the patients themselves are all trying to change. Such a situation makes it easier for patients to learn the effects their behavior has on other people. From signs of resentment and from direct comments they may learn that their habitual way of talking is unwittingly bossy, condescending, or marred by undertones of spite.

They may also learn what kinds of behavior by others make them unduly anxious or angry. Thus group psychotherapy embodies a sort of apprenticeship in social interaction which may forward a learning process likely to move more slowly in the world at large.[12]

Direction of Growth The second of our growth trends moves in a direction we shall now describe as the freeing of personal relationships. Under reasonably favorable circumstances during young adulthood the natural growth of personality moves toward increasing responsiveness to the other person's real nature. In early adolescence social interaction is still apt to be marred by impulsive inconsiderateness and egocentricity even if it is not burdened by anxiety. Immersed in his own behavior, intent on the impression he is making or the point he is trying to put across, the youngster fails to perceive clearly the people around him. Progress during the college years seems to be an irregular phenomenon; studies of the college experience yield conflicting reports.[13] During young adulthood there usually proves to be still a good deal to learn before one truly interacts with others in their own right as individuals. As a person moves in this direction he develops a greater range and flexibility of responses. He notices more things in the people with whom he interacts and becomes more ready to make allowance for their characteristics in his own behavior. Human relations become less anxious, less defensive, less burdened by inappropriate past reactions. They become more friendly, warm, and respectful. There may even be greater room for assertiveness and criticism. In short, the person moves in the direction of increased capacity to live in real relationship with the people immediately around him.

Joyce Kingsley proved to be our most lucid informant concerning the freeing of personal relationships. In the first study she described in great detail, though not with much insight, her strong identification with her parents and their values. Indirectly, she gave evidence of marked dependence on her mother and of covert resentment against certain features of the parental regime. She also reported her difficulties in achieving real friendships with people of her own age,

---

[12] A representative account is I. D. Yalom, *The Theory and Practice of Group Psychotherapy* (New York: Basic Books, Inc., 1970).

[13] D. H. Heath, *Growing Up in College* (San Francisco: Jossey-Bass, Inc., 1968); P. Madison, *Personality Development in College* (Reading, Mass.: Addison-Wesley Publishing Co., 1969); S. H. King, *Five Lives at Harvard: Personality Change during College* (Cambridge, Mass.: Harvard University Press, 1973).

and she gave us reason, in her free associations, to suspect that these difficulties were occasioned by feelings of superiority and hostility. Five years later Joyce had become much more aware of what went on in her personal relationships. Through returning to the family home after a period of absence she had come to realize the force of her dependence on her mother, though she was not able to do very much to change it. She saw her parents in a new objective light and could be critical both of their behavior and of their values. With fine shrewdness she had sensed the poisoning of her social relationships by anxiety-based feelings of moral superiority. Here she had found it possible to venture a wider range of social behavior which had distinctly increased her capacity for interaction. Joyce's history clearly exhibits the trend toward the freeing of personal relationships, even though, as she herself put it, she still had at that time "a long way to go." Fourteen years later the long way was so fully traversed that she had forgotten about the problem.

Process of Growth In general, the situation that is most conducive to change is one in which the other person responds unexpectedly, thus disrupting one's own habituated way of behaving. Children learn that other children are not mere assistants in their games when the assistants rebel and prove to have desires of their own. Children learn that other children are not enemies when the supposed enemies show friendly interest and kindness. Similarly, in the course of psychotherapy the patient learns to be unafraid because his behavior is greeted with boundless permissiveness and understanding. When faced with such surprises one learns to observe the other person, to understand and respect him, and one becomes more aware of one's own action. The next attempt at interaction will be a little different, and differences may accumulate in such a way as to constitute a decided trend toward the freeing of personal relationships.

An example of the first step is provided by Joyce Kingsley's difficulties over her husband's departure from religion. Joyce attempted to meet this astounding development by utilizing her well-practiced argumentative and dominating modes of behavior. These efforts came to naught, and she was forced to observe Renn more closely. She discovered his strong trait of independence, his determination to work out the problem for himself, and his unwillingness to be hurried. Because she cared deeply about Renn, she was obliged to respect these wishes and hold in check her own desire to argue him back into the fold. This particular experience upset her for quite a while, but her patient waiting was a completely new response which represented a broadening of her capacity for personal relationship. She had learned to respect another person's convictions in the way that she wanted her own convictions to be respected. The next study showed that Renn had later behaved still more unexpectedly even to the point that the marriage was threatened. Still further learning was necessary before they established a relation with real mutual respect for each other's characteristics.

If a person's social behavior is not too heavily bound by defenses against anxiety, it tends to become more varied as experience accumulates. Each occasion on which the other person's behavior has to be observed adds an increment of knowledge about human diversity. It also adds an increment of variation to the repertory of social behavior. This sort of growth by increments is well shown in Joyce's account of her increasing tolerance and friendliness toward others. She described her growth as proceeding steadily though slowly, a little at a time, without sharp or striking incidents.

There are times, however, when a growth trend moves ahead by sudden jumps. Such occasions correspond to the "learning by insight" first emphasized by the Gestalt school of psychologists, a good example of cognitive learning.[14] The other person is perceived first in one way, then in an entirely different way, the change representing a sudden reorganization of the perceptual field. Hartley Hale's attitude toward his eldest daughter seems to have undergone one of these abrupt reorganizations. He felt nothing but irritation at the child's disobedience until he suddenly realized how much she resembled his own stubborn independence at a like age. He thenceforth grasped the inner meaning of the little girl's behavior and became much better able to treat her with an appropriate amount of patience. Hale's learning exhibited *empathy*, which in this connection means experiencing the same feelings as another person through having been in the same situation oneself. He realized why his daughter rebelled because he had "been there" himself. In a study of nursery school children, Lois Murphy showed that empathy was very much influenced by personal past experience. A child who had once had a broken arm, for instance, would display special solicitude when another child arrived with an

---

[14] First described by W. Köhler in the classical work, *The Mentality of Apes* (New York: Harcourt Brace Jovanovich, Inc., 1927).

arm in a sling.[15] The capacity to produce new behavior in social situations is thus favorably affected by having a large *empathic range*, a rich store of experiences which can be used as a basis for understanding the meaning of another person's behavior. Sometimes a person can use the tragedies in his own life as a means of understanding other people's tragedies.

The two growth trends thus far described prove to be not unrelated. One of the things that contributes to the freeing of personal relationships is the stabilizing of ego identity. This is nowhere better exemplified than in our subjects' attitudes toward their parents. Joseph Kidd was always a child in his father's presence until he went away to military service and began to construct a more definite identity of his own. Upon his return he gradually was able to treat his father in the new way that was more appropriate to their respective ages. He began to collect bad debts, manage accounts, figure taxes, and generally take over initiative in the business, until at last he assumed full responsibility for the new shop that his father needed but lacked the energy to procure. Instead of asking for pocket money, Kidd found himself giving his father pocket money out of the funds now subjected to orderly bookkeeping. To some extent Kidd freed this relationship from past distortions by actually working with his father and finding that in the end his father responded favorably when things were done for him. But it is doubtful whether Kidd would have advanced so rapidly if he had not been away for four years building a personality of his own. Interactions between parents and children rarely change as fast as would be warranted by the children's growth. A period of absence is therefore often of great benefit in putting things on a new footing. As the children become adults and stabilize their own identities, they are apt to view their parents more objectively, with more dispassionate criticism and at the same time with a warmer and more empathic appreciation.

Growth Trends: 3. The Deepening of Interests

Interests play a curiously small part in current thinking about personality. They have often been crudely "measured" for purposes of vocational guidance, but little attempt has been made to formulate their place in the growth of personality. Interests do not present themselves as clinical problems, and they are hard to describe in a systematic way.

[15] L. B. Murphy, *Social Behavior and Child Personality* (New York: Columbia University Press, 1937), Chapter 9.

Perhaps they have also suffered from our frequent habit of describing personality at a fixed point in time. Interests are not static; it is of their very essence that they constantly move forward and almost never reach final goals. Thus it happens that the scientist, typically a person of the strongest interests, has found few ways to study this elusive topic. Yet interests are often of tremendous importance in the personal economy of happiness. The loss of opportunities to pursue them can sometimes be an irreparable catastrophe.

The nature of interests was well set forth in one of John Dewey's notable contributions to education. An interest, he said, was always connected with an activity that engaged a person in a wholehearted fashion.

> Interest is not some one thing; it is a name for the fact that a course of action, an occupation, or pursuit absorbs the powers of an individual in a thorough-going way. But an activity cannot go on in a void. It requires material, subject-matter, conditions upon which to operate. On the other hand, it requires certain tendencies, habits, powers on the part of the self. Wherever there is genuine interest, there is an identification of these two things. The person acting finds his own well-being bound up with the development of an object to its own issue. If the activity goes a certain way, then a subject-matter is carried to a certain result, and a person achieves a certain satisfaction.[16]

Direction of Growth The growth trend with which we are now concerned may be said to take a direction toward the state of affairs described by Dewey. It is a trend toward increasing identification of one's own satisfaction with "development of an object to its own issue." Stated another way, it is a movement toward fuller engagement with objects of interest so that "their own issue," their inherent nature and possibilities for development, increasingly guide the person's activity and become a part of the satisfaction. As with the freeing of personal relationships, we are dealing here with the young adult segment of a growth trend that is lifelong. Interests develop very early; in the first grade children already show distinct and apparently lasting individual differences in this respect. During childhood and adolescence interests may be diffuse and transient, but on the other hand they may be stable and highly important, influencing the course

---

[16] J. Dewey, *Interest and Effort in Education* (Boston: Houghton Mifflin Company, 1913), p. 65.

of development and contributing heavily to feelings of worth and happiness. "Interests, as an aspect of personality," writes Anne Roe, "have a place in any significant personality theory and must be subject to the same developmental principles as any other aspect of personality."[17] This is true at any age from the first to the last years of life, but the term *deepening* seems particularly appropriate for the kind of growth undergone by interests during young adulthood.

Little is known about the origins of interests. In some manner yet to be fully fathomed, certain objects, places, classes of people, or types of action come to have a special attractiveness that captures the child's attention. They engage him and even fascinate him in a way that distinguishes them from the common run of experiences. It is easier to attach theories to this process than to prove that the theories really work. One possibility is the early conditioning of strong positive affects to objects, people, or actions that were somehow connected with gratifying situations. Or one could suppose that interest would attach particularly to activities which had received parental encouragement and reward, although any such hypothesis would have to be kept flexible enough to account for interests that persisted in the face of discouragement and punishment. Freud's contribution to the topic took the form of a doctrine that all such early interests expressed, either directly or symbolically, the child's preoccupations with libidinal pleasures and problems. Thus an interest in painting might have roots in the forbidden pleasure of smearing feces, while scientific curiosity might spring from the child's wish to understand the sexual facts of life.

None of these explanations can be set up as a model of precision, but if origins remain somewhat baffling it is not so difficult to discern what happens after an interest has started. In Allport's words: "As an interest grows it creates a lasting tensional condition that leads to congruent conduct and also acts as a silent agent for selecting and directing whatever is related to the interest."[18] Sticking to Dewey's idea that interest is always connected with wholehearted activity, one can readily grasp the significance of this selecting and directing. We come to live and act upon our interests more fully, and as we do so we increase both our knowledge and our capacity to influence what per-

[17] A. Roe and M. Siegelman, *The Origin of Interests* (Washington: APGA Inquiry Studies, No. 1, 1964), p. 4.

[18] G. W. Allport, *Pattern and Growth in Personality* (New York: Holt, Rinehart and Winston, Inc., 1961), p. 237.

tains to the interests. Interest, in short, becomes strengthened by feelings of efficacy, and a growing command over the sphere of interest may contribute importantly to one's sense of competence.

Problems of the origin and growth of interests are well illustrated in the case of Hartley Hale. Two things were impressive in his early childhood: an eagerness to master physical objects and a strong curiosity about sex. We found reason to relate his curiosity to the problem of his parents' sexual relationships, and thus possibly to the frustrations of the Oedipus situation. No clues could be found to the origin of his strong interest in mastery; we noticed, however, that the interest was present in his earliest memories and that it received considerable encouragement from his parents. From these childhood beginnings it proved possible to trace a more or less continuous course of development that finally culminated in biology and medical research. Mechanical interests and sexual curiosity took separate courses through his high school years, but it seems not unlikely that the profound interest awakened by his first biology course came from a combining of the hitherto separate strands. Hale learned quite early to subordinate his immediate desires to the requirements of his objects. He abandoned the vision of a perpetual motion machine and settled for a boat that would go twice around the bath tub. He kept at the building of radios until he made a set that would work. Although in most respects he tended to be quick and impatient, his research career was marked by willingness to wait for years, if necessary, in order to develop the apparatus and strategy required to answer a single question. It was a crowning stroke of good fortune for Hale that his developing interests lent themselves so readily to the demands of the profession of medicine.

Anne Roe has made studies of artists, physicists, biologists, and several other groups of professional workers. If one examines the findings of psychological tests there proves to be a good deal of variation within each professional group and only a small number of marked differences between groups. The distinctive thing about these people seems to be that quite early in life they got interested in the subject matter they later pursued as a vocation. The cumulative deepening of interest was the thing that guided them to their careers and that largely determined their success.[19]

[19] A. Roe, "A Psychological Study of Eminent Psychologists and Anthropologists and a Comparison with Biological and Physical Scientists," *Psychological Monographs*, 67 (1953), No. 2; "Artists and Their Work," *Journal of Personality*, 15 (1946), 1–40.

In speaking of a trend toward the *deepening* of interests we have in mind the progressive mastery of the knowledge and skill that is relevant to a sphere of interest. Interests often enough grow broader as well as deeper, but our concern here is with one particular quality rather than with quantity or extensiveness. We are also not referring to the amount of time a person devotes to his interests; a trend toward deepening does not imply that he spends more and more of his hours in a state of absorption until at last everything else is excluded. The trend we have in mind is away from a state in which interests are casual, quickly dropped, pursued only from motives that do not become identified with advancement of the object. It is toward a state in which the sense of reward comes from doing something for its own sake. Adolescent interests may be strong, but they are not typically deep in the sense intended here. An adolescent may be greatly interested in national politics but indifferent to the local political scene from which national careers are actually launched. He may be fascinated by the image of himself as a great composer but uninvolved in taking up the study of harmony and counterpoint. He may work hard for the honor of being chosen editor of the school magazine but perform the editor's routine duties with careless indifference. Interest deepens when it reaches down into the whole operation, so to speak, when day-to-day activity is performed wholeheartedly, and when satisfaction is no longer limited to social rewards and distant visions. This is the kind of development that becomes particularly important in young adulthood, when commitment must be made to specific and realistic paths of life.

The careers of distinguished people could provide striking examples, but let us take a perfectly prosaic illustration. A man allows himself to be nominated for the water board in a small town. At first he is motivated by a desire to participate in a necessary public service, to see his name in the town report, and to feel that he has the esteem of the citizens. Ten years later he may have become greatly interested in precipitation and watersheds, location of reservoirs, piping and pumping systems, filters and purifiers, and the economic side of a water supply. He has built up a store of knowledge and expertness. He is interested in making the town water system a better water system, and he might not care too much if through a printer's error his name was left out of the town report.

Process of Growth There are no doubt many circumstances that favor the deepening of interests. Hale called attention to one of these when telling about the teachers who had encouraged his scientific pursuits. When a teacher disregarded his outward cockiness and expressed faith in his serious abilities, he became aware of a sudden increase in his capacity to become absorbed in scientific studies. Others have reported similar experiences, especially during adolescence: the encouraging interest of an older person seemed to give them needed assurance to pursue activities requiring detachment from the daily round of life. Adolescence is a period of intense loyalty to groups, intense conformity to the prevailing youth culture. Anyone who chooses to pursue an individual interest might therefore be expected to feel a need for special outside support. It seems likely, however, that something more is involved. Hale emphasized the fact that his favorite teachers disregarded his competitive aggressiveness.

Another of our subjects, not reported in this book, made the matter even clearer both through his behavior and through his responses on the Thematic Apperception Test. He indicated that creative interest always suffered when he felt competitive, hostile, or under the necessity to prove that he was not inferior. When the self was threatened and required defense, there was no energy left over to be expended on creative tasks. This man also responded very well to the interest of one of his teachers. Apparently the teacher's acceptance of him as a promising equal released him from the necessity of defense and allowed him to let his energies flow forth in new directions. We are entitled to suggest that the deepening of interests is favored by circumstances that abrogate anxiety and cancel expensive defenses. The peace of mind that goes with security and the rewards that come from encouragement are important aids to constructive growth.

The process of deepening, however, cannot be sufficiently explained by favorable social influences. The critical type of experience is one in which action is undertaken and satisfying consequences follow. Among these satisfying consequences an important place is occupied by feelings of efficacy. Hale during medical training was allowed to take part in surgery and found he could do it well; it became his central medical interest. Kidd discovered that he was a good extemporaneous speaker and could persuade people to work together; exercise of these powers found him interested in union policies and in city management in their own right. Joyce found satisfaction in being an officer in student government; when training as a social worker she came to specialize in group work with adolescents. It is characteristic of interesting objects that they offer an endless series of problems and challenges. One can never exhaust the things to be learned in a field of science or the obstacles to be overcome in research. One can never run through the possibilities of enjoyment and expression in art, literature, or music. People whose hobbies have grown to well-nigh professional proportions give ample testimony to the inexhaustibility of interesting things. Thus it is possible for satisfying transactions to go on and on, and this tends to build up funds of knowledge and expertness that make the person equal to still more difficult transactions.

Occasionally the deepening of an interest occurs quite suddenly. In a way that almost resembles a religious conversion, a person "discovers his field" and goes forward with exuberant enthusiasm. Hartley Hale had an experience of this kind when he shifted his vocational plan from advertising to medicine. We can offer the guess that these sudden bursts of interest occur when several separate lines of previous interest become merged in a new unified activity, or when frustrated lines find their first real opportunity for free development.[20]

The deepening of interests has a great deal to do with effectiveness and happiness in one's occupation. A person may want to become a doctor for many reasons: prestige, social status, money, identification with the white-coated heroes of the moving picture screen, a zeal to banish suffering, perhaps even a private mission to conquer the disease that has prematurely taken away a beloved relative. These can be powerful motives, but in themselves they do not make a good doctor. Granted a sufficient level of ability, the crucial thing is the possibility of becoming more and more deeply interested in the detailed subject matter and daily activities of medicine. Whatever the initial motives, they will not produce a good doctor unless they can be channeled to support a deepening interest in the details of a doctor's arduous life. There were people who shook their heads dubiously over the idea that Hartley Hale, hellion of his high school, was going to be a physician. Yet he became a very good physician because there was no limit to his capacity for interest in medicine.

[20] R. W. White, "Critical Events in Life Histories," *Annals of the New York Academy of Sciences*, 193 (1972), 248–252.

Growth Trends: 4. The Humanizing of Values

The line of development next to be considered is a continuation of the moral growth described in the last chapter. Values surround a child even in the early years, but, as we learned from Freud's reflections on the superego and Piaget's on moral realism, they are grasped only in the most primitive fashion. All in all, values get a bad start in early life. They are accepted under a certain duress, they are misunderstood, they are taken over wholesale by identification, they are rejected wholesale in a phase of negativism, and they may well become a bone of contention in contests between parents and children. Out of such beginnings must we fashion a system of values that is worthy to be considered adult.

Direction of Growth The growth trend observed in the study of young adults is in a sense a continuation of Piaget's trend toward relativism. We prefer to call it a *humanizing* of values in order to emphasize the following facts: (1) the person increasingly discovers the human meaning of values and their relation to the achievement of social purposes, and (2) he increasingly brings to bear his own experiences and his own motives in affirming and promoting a value system. The overall trend, starting from childhood, might be described as a trend from absolute received values to a personally wrought value system. This does not mean that the person creates his value system without benefit of historical tradition. It does not necessarily mean that he substantially changes the content of his received values. The growth trend implies that his values, whatever their content, become increasingly his own, increasingly a reflection of his own experiences and purposes.

Hartley Hale as an undergraduate did not believe in socialized medicine because the midwestern Republicans amongst whom he had grown up were generally opposed to socialization. At thirty-three he did not believe in socialized medicine because he had experienced great benefit under a system of individual freedom and believed on highly specific grounds that medical progress would eventually be crippled by state control. Whether or not one agrees with Hale, it is clear that his values became more humanized. They were more closely in touch both with his own ongoing interests and with the needs of sick people as he perceived them.

As we have already indicated, Joyce Kingsley proved to be an unusually illuminating authority on the humanizing of values. As a college senior she was a staunch advocate of the whole parental value system, even down to the details of national and local politics. She discussed values in the first person plural, as if she felt no need to discriminate her own views from those that emanated from the two ends of the family dining room table. Her value system was the "good foundation," built for her by her parents, on which she expected to construct her life. Five years later she made it clear that she had been inspecting the "good foundation." Her personal relationships had been marred by difficulties that seemed traceable to defects in the received value system. She had begun to think of improvements which she hoped to practice in the bringing up of her own children, and she had begun to find new meaning, through her personal experience in social work training, for the doctrine of freedom of choice that formed part of her religious tradition.

Process of Growth   The general situation that leads to the humanizing of values is one in which existing values become an occasion for conflicts. Perhaps a value that has been automatically accepted is challenged by a competing value. The person then faces the choice of espousing the new value or affirming the old one; and even if he chooses the latter course, as Hale did when challenged by socialized medicine, his affirming represents a new perception of what is involved and a new enlisting of motives that are really his own. Sometimes in such a conflict the person finds that the new value captures his personal loyalty. He then shifts to it, realizing more clearly than before what is implied both by the new value and by the old one. Joyce seems to have taken some such step when she changed from wanting to be a teacher to wanting to be a counselor of misunderstood adolescents. Sometimes growth comes about when a person in the course of acting upon his usual values produces an unexpected and unwelcome result. Intending to be upright he finds that he has been cruel, or supposing that he is friendly and obliging he learns that he has been taken for a financial ride. This kind of thing happened to Joyce when she realized that her righteous administration of student government prevented her from having intimate friends.

In the humanizing of values, as in the freeing of personal relationships, an important place is occupied by the concept of *empathic range*. Often a marked growth occurs through sudden empathic identification with some new aspect of a value conflict. The process can best be illustrated by drawing an unusually clear example from our case files. A young woman in college was the younger of two children in a business family of highly conservative outlook. She felt that her brother was very much the favorite child and that she had been treated quite unfairly at home. One summer she served as a volunteer aide in a community hospital near her home. She was astonished and outraged when she realized that patients in private rooms were given far more care and attention than the patients in the wards. Nurses sprang to answer the private-room bell calls while ward patients might be kept waiting for half an hour. She suddenly began to question an economic system which produced so much unfairness in ministering to the common needs of the sick. It was clear that this challenging of received values became possible for her because of a powerful empathic response toward the ward patients. As a victim of domestic unfairness, she burned with wrath at the plight of the less favored sick people. Empathy is often of crucial significance in breaking the hold of an unexamined value system. It enlarges one's personal outlook and makes it possible to see the conflicting human claims that offer the real challenge to any value system.

The trend toward the humanizing of values does not take account of everything that happens in the growth of value systems. It needs to be supplemented by another trend, one that has been described by Allport as moving toward a *unifying philosophy of life.* Allport comments as follows on the nature of this philosophy:

> Such a philosophy is not necessarily articulate, at least not always articulate in words. The preacher, by virtue of his training, is usually more articulate than the busy country doctor, the poet more so than the engineer, but any of these personalities, if actually mature, participates and reflects, lives and laughs, according to some embracing philosophy of life developed to his own satisfaction and representing to himself his place in the scheme of things.[21]

The trend we have been describing here does not carry any implication about a unified result. It often happens, in fact, that when a person begins to use his own experience to humanize a well-knit system of received values his philosophy for a time becomes much less unified. This was the case with our hospital aide; she violently rejected the economic philosophy of her parents when she perceived one of its

[21] G. W. Allport, 1937, Chapter 8.

unfair consequences, but the job of thinking out her own economic philosophy proved slow and disturbing, so that for a time her views were neither stable nor consistent. Allport's remarks on a unified philosophy call attention to another aspect of development, one in which the person tries to make his humanized values work together in a common cause. The three subjects in this book exhibit to a certain extent the unifying trend, but perhaps our best example is to be found in Joyce Kingsley's father, who rejected a materialistic outlook and built up for himself a religious philosophy that drew cooperation, freedom, and spiritual needs into a unified whole.

Growth Trends: 5. The Expansion of Caring

The last of the growth trends in our provisional sketch of development during young adulthood will be called here the expansion of caring. The idea is by no means new. Something of the sort was suggested in Adler's description of *social interest,* the natural tendency which he believed flowered in all of us to the extent that we outgrew egotism and the urge to be superior. Adler indicated his meaning in phrases such as "sense of human solidarity" and "fellowship in the human community."[22] Angyal offered the concept of a *trend toward homonomy.* The individual longs, he maintained, "to become an organic part of something that he conceives as greater than himself . . . to be in harmony with superindividual units, the social world, nature, God, ethical world order, or whatever the person's formulation of it may be."[23] These broad ideas imply transcendence of the egocentrism that is natural in childhood and of the heavy concern with self that is often prominent, and not entirely inappropriate, in adolescence. Somewhat similar, though by no means identical, is Allport's more precise developmental concept of *extension of the sense of self.* The sense of self becomes extended when the welfare of another person, a group enterprise, or some other valued object becomes as important as one's own welfare; "better said, the welfare of another is *identical* with one's own."

Maturity advances in proportion as lives are decentered from the clamorous immediacy of the body and of egocenteredness. Self-love

[22] A. Adler, *Understanding Human Nature* (Philadelphia: Chilton Book Company, 1927), p. 32.

[23] A. Angyal, *Foundations for a Science of Personality* (New York, The Commonwealth Fund, 1941), p. 172.

is a prominent and inescapable factor in every life, but it need not dominate. Everyone has self-love, but only self-extension is the earmark of maturity.[24]

There is a similar flavor to Erikson's description of *generativity*, which signifies that the individual takes on the welfare of certain others, particularly those who are young and in need of nurture, as part of his own sense of identity. "Generativity," he writes, "is primarily the concern in establishing and guiding the next generation. . . . Mature man needs to be needed, and maturity needs guidance as well as encouragement from what has been produced and must be taken care of."[25]

Direction of Growth   Mindful of these contributions we shall describe our fifth growth trend as moving in the direction of increased caring for the welfare of other persons and human concerns. The point will be missed if "caring" is understood in a superficial sense. Our use of it here does not imply merely that one participates actively in the affairs of family, neighborhood, or larger community. Such activity can be motivated by escape from loneliness and boredom or by sheer pleasure in company and conversation; it does not necessarily signify real affective involvement in the welfare of others. The requirements of caring are also not met by having children or by being in an occupation like teaching or nursing, where the welfare of others is the stated professional goal. Children can be produced but their interests neglected, as we saw when studying parental rejection; jobs can be taken simply because they provide security and a comfortable income. Caring is not necessarily involved when a person expresses passionate interest in bettering the condition of the disadvantaged and downtrodden. This attitude may be used only to conduct an argumentative rebellion against the near-at-hand established order, to rap the knuckles of the bourgeoisie, or to secure advancement to a position of political power; the verbal champion may have little urge to do anything real for the cause he claims to have at heart. Caring refers only to the things one really has at heart. It cannot be safely inferred from externals. The true hallmark is in the sphere of feeling: how much the person suffers when the object of his caring suffers, how much he rejoices when the object rejoices, how naturally and spontaneously he does the things that are required to promote the object's well-being.

[24] G. W. Allport, 1961, pp. 283, 285.
[25] E. H. Erikson, 1968, pp. 266–267.

The expansion of caring is a growth trend that comes into its own during young adulthood: It is foreshadowed by the empathy and sympathic behavior that appears even in nursery school children, but at that level its manifestations are not long sustained. It is foreshadowed again in the friendships of preadolescence when, according to Sullivan, the friend's welfare becomes a matter of true concern.[26] Protective care of the partner can be an element in sexual and marital relations. The most unmistakable blossoming comes in the care that loving parents bestow on their children, when the children's welfare becomes as important as the parents' own, sometimes even more important. Taking care of the young is undoubtedly the biological root and purest expression of caring, but in the wide spectrum of human culture there are many things besides children that need care. A great variety of cultural products and institutions would never flourish if a certain number of people did not have their welfare deeply at heart. In childhood and adolescence we take our privileges for granted. Our youthful cognitive maps include park, playground, swimming pool, waterworks, library, schools, and arts center in the same impersonal way as the surrounding hills and valleys. They are simply there to be used. Only gradually does it dawn upon us that such institutions did not just happen. They owe their beginnings to remarkable bursts of human initiative, and their continuing existence signifies that some group of people is devoted to their care.

Looking at our three cases, it is natural to think first of Joyce Kingsley, who gladly gave up the career she had started in social work and submitted to the irksome procedures of adoption in order to provide herself with the opportunity for maternal caring. Talking about herself in the follow-up meetings turned out to be in fairly large part talking about her children. With Hartley Hale the objects of most intense caring were bound up with his profession. The incident of the injured jeep driver, to whose recovery he devoted himself heart and soul, was only the most dramatic example of his involvement in the welfare of his patients. Hale's research, although it was a channel of his desire for professional advancement, entailed also a cherishing of the integrity of scientific knowledge; it will be recalled that he sacrificed an honors degree rather than submit uncertain findings. Joseph Kidd reminded us that concern can spread to less dramatic activities such as

[26] H. S. Sullivan, *The Interpersonal Theory of Psychiatry* (New York: W. W. Norton & Co., 1953).

caring for one's community: some things in his city, he said, "are living and breathing now because I started them."

Process of Growth What kinds of experience are critical for the expansion of caring? There is certainly a cognitive element in the process: one learns gradually to perceive the large amount of devoted caring that is necessary to maintain civilized institutions and an environment suitable for raising the next generation. Becoming a parent often produces a fairly sudden enlargement of one's cognitive map. Pediatric services, household helpers, and sitters spring into one's life as vital supports in child care. Taxes, hitherto an arbitrary imposition, may come into perspective as paying for things one wants for the children. Frustrations like the closing of a museum or the discontinuing of concerts one has enjoyed during brief respites from home cares may bring insight into the fact that cultural institutions are maintained by money and, back of that, faithful care. The expansion of caring thus depends upon the growth of cognitive maps that show what is worth caring about. In this respect it is no different from the other growth trends we have described. Indeed the five growth trends are quite similar in their cognitive aspects: in all there is movement toward a more discriminating awareness of actuality, whether it be one's own nature, other people, objects of interest, values, or the things that need care. The years of young adulthood can be a time of great progress in firsthand understanding of the nature of reality.

The essence of caring, however, is not cognitive; it is a matter of feeling. The development of feeling is less easy to trace. We are tempted to fall back, not without a certain justification, on what we take to be innate biological factors: the power of small helpless creatures to evoke maternal feelings and of beautiful young people to call out erotic ones. But if caring can apply to institutions we must not rely too heavily on biological attraction. If it is more than metaphorical to say, for instance, that a headmaster loves the school he founded and has directed for many years, we cannot derive his love from stimuli that are biologically primitive. More to the point in such a case are the actions that have been taken in behalf of the object of care. The headmaster expands his love of his school because of the succession of things he has done to enable it to grow and flourish. If he can say with Joseph Kidd that important things "are living and breathing now because I started them," he will love his school in a way that would be impossible for a man who was in it merely for the money. Similarly, a person may "love" gardens, taking delight in the color and variety of flowers; but he will have a much deeper feeling for the garden he has spaded, fertilized, planted, weeded, and tended than he would have for an identical garden cared for by someone else. Caring may start as pure feeling, but what nourishes and expands it is the production of beneficial effects upon the objects of care. There must be action and interaction if caring is to reach full development.

Critical experiences for the expansion of caring are thus those in which the needs of some suitable object evoke nurturant feelings, and in which there is opportunity for nurture to be bestowed in a manner beneficial to the object. These conditions were clearly met at the point in Joyce Kingsley's life when her young cousin Philip unexpectedly entered the family: her nurturant feelings went out to him and she took over a substantial part of his care. In the case of Kidd's devotion to city government they were more obscurely met: following the boost to self-esteem given by his election, he needed a period of time to overcome his awe of fellow council members, with some testing of his own power of initiative, before he felt moved to become the guiding hand of needed city projects. Kidd's example serves as a reminder that many kinds of feeling stand in the way of the expansion of caring. Social anxiety, desires to be cared for, preoccupation with self, envious rivalry, and wishes for personal triumph are all inimical to identifying one's welfare with the welfare of others. One more example, if it be needed, that personality is a complex organization.

The Nurturing of Individual Growth

Following a study of growth trends, nothing is more natural than to ask what are the ideal directions of growth. Can we take the end point of each trend as desirable, and the sum of them as describing the ideal person? It is difficult to think of growth without imagining some ideal goal such as perfect maturity or, to take Maslow's expression, a fully self-actualizing person. With an effort we can be dispassionate observers of human development, regarding it simply as what happens, for better or for worse; this attitude has utility in obtaining clear understanding. But superhuman detachment would be required to study the growth of personality, especially through detailed case studies, without thinking of oneself as another case and wondering how best to steer the future development of that case. So we shall close by considering the implications of what we have been studying for self-guidance.

Growth Trends and Ideals It is well to begin this topic with a clear recognition that growth trends cannot substitute either for ideals or for ethics. Nowhere is this plainer than with the trend toward increasing competence. Considering the long road a child has to travel from initial helplessness to physical, mental, and social competence, considering also that it is through competence that a person masters anxiety, gratifies needs, and attains self-esteem, it seems in order to count all movement in this direction as a good thing. But competence has no inherent moral value. It can be used as easily for antisocial purposes as for prosocial ones. Growing physical competence may prompt a boy to become a bully. Ripening social skill may tempt a girl to promote rivalry and break hearts. Emerging executive ability may lead a man into business channels where price-fixing agreements, tax frauds, and marketing of false corporate image are accepted as part of the game. The great villains of history have often been uncommonly competent. Even in terms of personal development, competence may not be an unmixed blessing. The well-muscled boy might develop better in the future if he had not done so well as a bully, the suave-tongued girl if she had not been such a successful flirt. High competence sometimes fixes a person in a sphere of early success and thus forecloses desirable long-term developments.

Similar considerations apply to the stabilizing of ego identity. Anyone who has struggled to find the makings of identity in himself and his world is likely to view stabilizing as a joyful relief. Yet there is a distinct possibility that the firming of identity during the twenties will go too far, leaving no leeway to respond to later opportunities for new experience. There are people whose ego identities have remained unstabilized, not always to their comfort, through the thirties and into the forties, after which they have belatedly found themselves and gone on to productive careers. How soon and how fully one's identity should be stabilized is a matter for careful judgment in each individual case. We cannot simply say the more the better; the end point of this trend is not an unquestioned virtue or an unchallengeable ideal.

The use of a concept like maturity, implying good advancement in all important growth trends, is most appropriate in the early part of life. It becomes increasingly inappropriate as one advances into adulthood. To be sure, we can speak of certain general qualities which we consider desirable at any age, qualities like confidence, flexibility, tolerance, judgment, warmth, and interested responsiveness. Yet even these may not be the first things we consider when we undertake to describe the course and shape of an individual life. It seems irrelevant to raise questions of flexibility about Mahatma Gandhi, whose greatness lay in being inflexible at crucial moments of history, or to accuse Eleanor Roosevelt of intolerance toward evils she tried to combat. The point is that each of us leads a particular life—particular in time, place, circumstances, and personal history—and that success in leading it depends upon a *pattern* of qualities appropriate to that life. In youth, when many paths seem possible, it may be hard to accept the idea that only a few can be followed. But no one person can lead everyman's life, and some maturities are bound to be more relevant than others.

Self-Actualization Recognizing the individuality of people's lives makes it impossible to formulate a standard description of strengths and goals. No notion of complete maturity, unless it is washed out to a few pale generalities, will be right for each individual. To perceive this limitation more sharply, while at the same time enlarging our view of possible human excellencies, let us look at Maslow's description of self-actualizing people.[27] Maslow's ideas were based on informal studies which included historical figures as well as people known to him. To be a truly self-actualizing person was, in his view, a rare achievement. Among historical figures, for instance, he rated Spinoza, Thomas Jefferson, Albert Einstein, William James, and Eleanor Roosevelt as self-actualizers, but other well-known names, such as Beethoven, Henry David Thoreau, Franklin Roosevelt, and Sigmund Freud did not qualify and were classed as only partial cases. Possibly some readers will feel that they would like to have been Beethoven or Thoreau even if it meant imperfect or one-sided development. For Maslow, self-actualization implied a well-rounded personality, all that a human being could become when conditions were favorable for the fullest possible growth. In effect he described an ideal type which few real people could closely approach, and he meant ideal in a psychological sense—the peak of psychological well-being and full-functioning.

In the cognitive sphere, self-actualization implied a perception of reality that was efficient, objective, free from distortion by desires, anxieties, and rigid habits. It also implied what Maslow called "large-

---

[27] A. H. Maslow, *Motivation and Personality*, 2d ed. (New York: Harper & Row, Publishers, 1970).

ness of outlook," which signified "living in the widest possible frame of reference" and thus easily distinguishing what was important from what was not. With respect to behavior he described a number of qualities indicative of naturalness, spontaneity, and stabilized identity: freshness of appreciation for what is new, beautiful, and interesting; openness toward one's own feelings; guidance by one's own experience and convictions in all matters of importance. In social relations, self-actualization signified what Adler meant by social interest, a high degree of empathy and sympathy for other people, indeed for all of humanity. But Maslow did not believe that superficial social contacts, however wide, contributed much to this quality. He mentioned depth of friendship as a mark of self-actualization, but preserving one's privacy was equally important, implying ability to keep out of trivial social interactions without feeling guilty about it. With respect to the surrounding culture, Maslow described a sort of philosophical detachment which was consistent with conformity in small ways but which permitted resistance to cultural expectations when it really mattered. Full self-actualization implied transcending local and national cultures to become "members at large of the human species."

Individuality of Life Patterns An ideal so broad, serene, and noble is much to be admired, but it must be used with caution in the study of individual lives. Maslow allowed that self-actualizing persons should be "strongly focused on problems outside themselves—problem-centered rather than ego-centered." To be problem-centered, however, means behaving in ways that are relevant to the problem. It implies bringing to bear not an abstract list of virtues but a pattern of qualities appropriate to the problem one is trying to solve. When the focus of concern moves from self to problems outside the self, it likewise moves, speaking strictly, from self-actualization to whatever one is trying to actualize in the world. It is doubtful that Thomas Jefferson, William James, and Eleanor Roosevelt would have judged their own lives in terms of self-actualization. They were all focused on problems outside themselves, concerned with what they could accomplish that would be of value to mankind. If we are readers of biography, we can also well doubt that these self-actualizers had the whole array of qualities given in Maslow's description. There were plenty of confusions, evasions, neurotic episodes, and vanities in the life of William James; the wonder is that he worked out a pattern of existence which made it possible, in spite of these faults, to be a great thinker and teacher.[28] One of Eleanor Roosevelt's most conspicuous traits was an iron self-discipline in scheduling her daily life, a quality which taken out of context might signify extreme rigidity, but which was directly instrumental to her having the kind of influence in the world for which she is now remembered.[29] There is doubtless an ideal way for each person to live his life; but it is his way, his own synthesis of personal qualities and life requirements, and it will not be quite like anyone else's ideal way.

There is a further difficulty in using general ideals like maturity or self-actualization when thinking about individual lives. Is it possible for all desirable qualities to coexist in a single person? Research has not reached final answers, but there is a good deal of reason for a negative reply. No doubt it would be pleasant to have the rugged fortitude, ego strength, and control that characterizes people who, like astronauts, work under great stress, and also to possess the keen imagination, sensitivity, and verbal skill that lead to honors in a liberal arts program. But the combination is certainly infrequent, and it may actually be impossible for any person to reach maximum development in both directions. Constitutional predisposition, which may have a voice in the matter, cannot be expected to favor everything. In view of this, we can be glad that no one life has to be everything. If fortunate, we can capitalize on our strengths and work out a pattern in which our weaknesses do not much matter.

Encouraging Individuality These considerations lead to the conclusion that in the guidance of growth there should be encouragement for individuality. In thinking about one's own life, in bringing up children, in counseling young people, there should be warm hospitality to individual differences. The goal of guidance is not to produce a standard article but a real individual, and this implies that the makings of individuality must be noticed, accepted, and given support. This is easier said than done. We are all fearful of deviance, forms of which can indeed spell trouble, and we are all prey to anxiety if in certain respects we lag behind other people. Both perceptiveness and confidence are required to accept those departures from average patterns out of which individuality is made. A sharp lookout should be

[28] G. W. Allen, *William James: A Biography* (New York: The Viking Press, 1967).

[29] J. P. Lash, *Eleanor: The Years Alone* (New York: W. W. Norton & Co., 1972).

kept for potential strengths and unusual gifts, for whatever seems to come most easily and naturally. Attention should be paid to areas of competence and to talents that are already showing signs of growth. Strong special interests should be valued as possible assets for the future rather than condemned as eccentricities. One's eye for assets should be at least as sharp as one's eye for liabilities.

About forty years ago psychiatry began to be popularized in publications telling people how to guide themselves and their children toward mental health. Although much of this teaching was valuable, certain aspects were distinctly frightening. Parents were given to understand that they had a tremendous influence on their children's emotional development; everything depended on the atmosphere they created in the home. It was implied that failure to provide the right atmosphere would push the child straight into neurosis or psychosis. Many parents were intimidated by these teachings. Reading about parental rejection, they came to dread showing annoyance or even feeling annoyance, believing that the child would read the signs, feel rejected, and go to emotional ruin. Learning about the relation between repression and neurosis, they concluded that all discipline and restraint were evil, and that if a child refrained from tearing the nursery to pieces it was a danger signal of disease. Discovering that schizophrenics were withdrawn and socially inept, they noted with alarm any tendency toward solitude and rushed to the rescue by pushing the child into a round of social contacts. Many parents were robbed of the courage to be themselves, to use discipline sensibly, to await social growth, and to perceive the constructive uses of solitude. So patent became this miscarriage of mental health teaching that writers on the subject changed their tone and began to provide parents with more reassuring messages. Children, it was pointed out, can be quite resourceful in resisting ruin by their parents.[30]

As a result of this change of emphasis parents became more relaxed about mental health, but the trend of economic and social conditions provided new cause for alarm. In recent years young people have often reported that their parents brought them up with comfortable permissiveness in most respects but hounded them unmercifully on two points: they must get the best marks in school, and they must

---

[30] The turnabout was exemplified in D. W. Baruch, *New Ways in Discipline* (New York: McGraw-Hill, Inc., 1949) and H. Bruch, *Don't Be Afraid of Your Child* (New York: Farrar, Straus & Giroux, Inc., 1952).

constantly mingle with other children. These pressures resulted from increasing emphasis on diplomas and degrees as credentials for desirable employment and from the growing necessity to get along well with lots of other people in large organizations. Parents feared that their children would not understand these conditions of ultimate success and would fail to build up the requisite school record and social skill. Thus even in nursery school there was distress at home if a child was reported to need help in adjusting to others instead of displaying instant social virtuosity; and if in first grade he did not bring home top marks, he might fall under pressure that would continue relentlessly throughout his whole educational career. Parental anxiety over scholarship and social participation blocks awareness of individual differences. Joseph Kidd complained that his ambitious parents did not care about what was going on inside him. What goes on inside is apt to contain the best clues to individuality.

According to the ideas developed in this book, the task of rearing and guiding children can best be represented by the metaphor of raising plants. This should be encouraging because raising plants is one of mankind's most successful activities. Perhaps the success comes from the fact that the husbandman does not try to thrust impossible patterns on his plants. He respects their peculiarities, tries to provide suitable conditions, protects them from the more serious kinds of injury—but he lets the plants do the growing. He does not poke at the seed in order to make it sprout more quickly, nor does he seize the shoot when it breaks ground and try to pull open the first leaves by hand. Neither does he trim the leaves of different kinds of plants in order to have them all look alike. The attitude of the husbandman is appropriate in dealing with children. It is the children who must do the growing, and they can do it only through the push of their own budding interests.

Parents who are not intimidated can respect unusual interests in their children. They will not be afraid of deviations from neighbor patterns, and they will therefore not crush nascent interests, like Hartley Hale's in mechanical objects and radios, which may later evolve into professional activities of the utmost value for mankind. They will also be able to await the sprouting of interests which do not come quickly to the surface, even if this means that the child drops behind other children or falls below group norms. They will wait for social interest to manifest itself, for instance, so that the seeking of social contact shall come from the child's own motives and contribute to his initiative and ego identity. It will be recalled that Hartley Hale was anything but appreciative when his mother tried to find him suitable friends. It was not that he did not want friends; he merely wanted them to be of his own choosing, the products of his own social initiative, even if it cost him effort and frustration to find them.

When considering the next steps in one's own development one should be similarly hospitable to individuality. New kinds of behavior may be desirable, but not just for the sake of conformity, marketability, or some abstract conception of maturity. As in children, the impulse toward growth must come from budding inclinations of one's own. If one wishes, for instance, to become more expressive in human relations, this should be because there are feelings one is aware of wanting to express, not because someone has said it is bad to be shy. And if one undertakes to change one's behavior in this direction, there will probably be need for the long patience of the husbandman. Social initiatives may be hard to mobilize and at first hard to do well; it may be some time before they produce the consequences one desires. But if they spring from a real internal wish, a felt necessity for one's own growth, persistence will be possible without an immediate shower of rewards. Looking for progress every day may be as discouraging as watching for daily growth in a plant, but over a span of time the growth of plants is impressive.

Until recently the scientific study of human behavior leaned toward a one-sided determinism. All three views—the social, the biological, and the developmental—represented the person as the hapless product of forces external to himself and neglected the corresponding study of the person taking action to modify these forces. We have insisted in this book that the scientific approaches were sound; they reveal much that is true, and they properly warn us not to look upon change with blind optimism and a buoyant disregard for the difficult nature of the human undertaking. But we have equally insisted that natural growth and the activity of the person be put back into the story. Lewis Mumford calls man "the unfinished animal" and says, "Unlike other organisms, the final stage of his growth is not determined by his biological past: it rests with himself and is partly determined by his own plans for the future."[31] Even though he be a nexus of biological, developmental, social, and cultural forces, a person

---

[31] L. Mumford, *The Conduct of Life* (Harcourt Brace Jovanovich, Inc., 1951), p. 36.

serves as a transforming and redistributing center, responding selectively to create a new synthesis. Under reasonably favorable circumstances personality tends to continue its growth, strengthen its individuality, and assert its power to change the surrounding world. We are capable of natural growth and action, and no facts about us are more important for our ultimate welfare.

SUGGESTIONS FOR FURTHER READING

The concept of growth trends is widely used in developmental psychology, but research interest has concentrated on the earlier and simpler manifestations of growth rather than its continuation in adult life. A conspicuous exception is Jack Block's research study, *Lives through Time* (Berkeley, Calif.: Bancroft Books, 1971), a chronological investigation that extends from childhood into the thirties. A recent textbook by Leon Rappaport, *Personality Development: The Chronology of Experience* (Glenview, Ill.: Scott, Foresman and Company, 1972), is especially strong in contrasting the outlooks of different periods of life. Leon J. Saul's *Emotional Maturity: The Development and Dynamics of Personality* (Philadelphia: J. B. Lippincott Co., 2d ed., 1962) is organized on a principle very similar to that of growth trends. Abraham Maslow's study of self-actualizing people describes qualities that could easily be cast in the same form (*Motivation and Personality*, New York: Harper & Row, Publishers, 2d ed., 1970). For a fuller study of growth trends and ideals, see the chapter on the diversity of life patterns in R. W. White, *The Enterprise of Living: Growth and Organization in Personality* (New York: Holt, Rinehart and Winston, Inc., 1972), Chapter 19.

Adler, A. *Understanding Human Nature*. Philadelphia: Chilton Book Company, 1927.

————. *Superiority and Social Interest*, ed. by H. L. Ansbacher and R. R. Ansbacher. Evanston, Ill.: Northwestern University Press, 1964.

Allen, G. W. *William James: A Biography*. New York: The Viking Press, 1967.

Allport, G. W. *Personality: A Psychological Interpretation*. New York: Holt, Rinehart and Winston, Inc., 1937.

————. *Pattern and Growth in Personality*. New York: Holt, Rinehart and Winston, Inc., 1961.

Anastasi, A. *Psychological Testing*, 3d ed. New York: The Macmillan Company, 1968.

Angyal, Andras. *Foundations for a Science of Personality*. New York: The Commonwealth Fund, 1941.

Ansbacher, H. L., and R. R. Ansbacher. *The Individual Psychology of Alfred Adler*. New York: Basic Books, Inc., 1956.

Baldwin, A. L. *Behavior and Development in Childhood*. New York: Holt, Rinehart and Winston, Inc., 1955.

Baldwin, A. L., J. Kalhorn, and F. H. Breese. "Patterns of Parent Behavior," *Psychological Monographs*, 1945, Vol. 58, No. 3.

Bandura, A., and R. H. Walters. *Adolescent Aggression*. New York: The Ronald Press Company, 1959.

————. *Social Learning and Personality Development*. New York: Holt, Rinehart and Winston, Inc., 1963.

Baruch, D. W. *New Ways in Discipline*. New York: McGraw-Hill, Inc., 1949.

Baumrind, D. M. "Child Care Practices Anteceding Three Patterns of Preschool Behavior." *Genetic Psychology Monographs*, 1967, Vol. 75, pp. 43–88.

Becker, W. C. "Consequences of Different Kinds of Parental Discipline." In M. L. Hoffman and L. W. Hoffman (eds.), *Review of Child Development Research*, Vol. 1. New York: Russell Sage Foundation, 1964.

Bennis, W. G., E. H. Schein, D. E. Berlew, and F. I. Steele (eds.). *Interpersonal Dynamics*, 3d ed. Homewood, Ill.: The Dorsey Press, 1973.

Berg, J. H. van den. *The Changing Nature of Man*. New York: Delta Books, 1964.

Block, J. *Lives through Time*. Berkeley, Calif.: Bancroft Books, 1971.

Brown, C. *Manchild in the Promised Land*. New York: The Macmillan Company, 1965.

Bruch, H. *Don't Be Afraid of Your Child*. New York: Farrar, Straus & Giroux, Inc., 1952.

Bruner, J. S. *Beyond the Information Given: Studies in the Psychology of Knowing*. New York: W. W. Norton & Co., 1972.

Carthy, J. D., and F. J. Ebling (eds.). *The Natural History of Aggression*. New York: Academic Press, Inc., 1964.

Cattell, R. B. *Personality: A Systematic Theoretical and Factual Study*. New York: McGraw-Hill, Inc., 1950.

Chess, S., A. Thomas, and H. Birch. *Your Child Is a Person*. New York: The Viking Press, 1965.

Cohen, A. K. *Delinquent Boys: The Culture of the Gang*. New York: The Free Press, Inc., 1955.

Commager, H. S. *The American Mind: An Interpretation of American Thought and Character Since the 1880's*. New Haven: Yale University Press, 1950.

Cooley, C. H. *Human Nature and the Social Order.* New York: Charles Scribner's Sons, 1902.

———. *Social Organization.* New York: Charles Scribner's Sons, 1909.

Dailey, C. A. *Assessment of Lives: Personality Evaluation in a Bureaucratic Society.* San Francisco: Jossey-Bass, Inc., 1971.

Davis, A., and J. Dollard. *Children of Bondage.* Washington, D. C.: American Council on Education, 1940.

Deutsch, H. *The Psychology of Women: A Psychoanalytic Interpretation.* Vol. I. New York: Grune & Stratton, Inc., 1944.

Dewey, J. *Interest and Effort in Education.* Boston: Houghton Mifflin Company, 1913.

Diamond, S. *Personality and Temperament.* New York: Harper & Row, Publishers, 1957.

Dill, W. R., T. L. Hilton, and W. R. Reitman. *The New Managers.* Englewood Cliffs, N. J.: Prentice-Hall, Inc, 1962.

Dollard, J., and N. E. Miller. *Personality and Psychotherapy: An Analysis in Terms of Learning, Thinking, and Culture.* New York: McGraw-Hill, Inc., 1950.

Douvan, E. "Commitment and Social Contract in Adolescence." *Psychiatry,* 1974, Vol. 37, pp. 22–36.

Ellis, H. C. *Fundamentals of Human Learning and Cognition.* Dubuque, Iowa: William C. Brown, 1972.

Erikson, E. H. *Childhood and Society,* 2d ed. New York: W. W. Norton & Co., 1963.

———. *Identity: Youth and Crisis.* New York: W. W. Norton & Co., 1968.

Escalona, S. K. *The Roots of Individuality: Normal Patterns of Development in Infancy.* Chicago: Aldine Publishing Co., 1968.

Escalona, S. K., and G. Heider. *Prediction and Outcome.* New York: Basic Books, Inc., 1959.

Eysenck, H. J. *The Structure of Human Personality,* 3d ed. London: Methuen & Co., Ltd., 1970.

Fiske, D. W. *Measuring the Concepts of Personality.* Homewood, Ill.: The Dorsey Press, 1970.

Freud, Anna. *The Ego and the Mechanisms of Defense.* London: Hogarth Press, Ltd., 1937.

Freud, S. *New Introductory Lectures on Psychoanalysis.* New York: W. W. Norton & Co., 1933.

Friedenberg, E. Z. *Coming of Age in America: Growth and Acquiescence.* New York: Random House, Inc., 1965.

Fromm, E. *Man for Himself.* New York: Holt, Rinehart and Winston, Inc., 1947.

Garfield, S. L. *Introductory Clinical Psychology.* New York: The Macmillan Company, 1957.

Garrison, K. C. *Psychology of Adolescence,* 6th ed. Englewood Cliffs, N. J.: Prentice-Hall, Inc., 1965.

Gergen, K. J. *The Concept of Self.* New York: Holt, Rinehart and Winston, Inc., 1971.

Gewirtz, J. L. (ed.). *Attachment and Dependency.* New York: V. H. Winston & Sons, 1972.

Glass, D. G. (ed.). *Biology and Behavior: Genetics.* New York: Rockefeller Univerity Press and Russell Sage Foundation, 1968.

Goethals, G. W., and D. S. Klos. *Experiencing Youth: First Person Accounts.* Boston: Little, Brown and Company, 1970.

Goodstein, L. D., and R. I. Lanyon. *Personality Assessment.* New York: John Wiley & Sons, Inc., 1971.

Grey, A. *Class and Personality in Society.* New York: Atherton Press, 1968.

Grinker, R. R., and J. P. Spiegel. *Men under Stress.* New York: McGraw-Hill, Inc., 1945.

Gross, N., W. S. Nason, and A. E. McEachern. *Explorations in Role Analysis.* New York: John Wiley & Sons, Inc., 1958.

Grossman, S. P. *Essentials of Physiological Psychology.* New York: John Wiley & Sons, Inc., 1973.

Hall, C. S., and G. Lindzey. *Theories of Personality,* 2d ed. New York: John Wiley & Sons, Inc., 1970.

Hanfmann, E., and J. Kasanin. "Conceptual Thinking in Schizophrenia," *Nervous and Mental Disease Monographs,* 1942, No. 67.

Heath, D. H. *Growing Up in College.* San Francisco: Jossey-Bass, Inc., 1968.

Hollingshead, A. B. *Elmtown's Youth: The Impact of Social Classes on Adolescents.* New York: John Wiley & Sons, Inc., 1949.

Hollingshead, A. B., and F. C. Redlich. *Social Class and Mental Illness: A Community Study.* New York: John Wiley & Sons, Inc., 1958.

Homans, G. C. *The Human Group.* New York: Harcourt Brace Jovanovich, Inc., 1950.

———. "Social Behavior as Exchange." *American Journal of Sociology,* 1958, Vol. 63, pp. 597–606.

Horney, K. *The Neurotic Personality of Our Time.* New York: W. W. Norton & Co., 1937.

Hughes, E. C. *Men and Their Work.* New York: The Free Press, Inc., 1958.

Hunt, J. McV. *Intelligence and Experience.* New York: The Ronald Press Company, 1961.

————. *The Challenge of Incompetence and Poverty.* Urbana, Ill.: University of Illinois Press, 1969.

James, W. *The Principles of Psychology.* New York: Henry Holt and Company, 1890.

Johnson, R. N. *Aggression in Man and Animals.* Philadelphia, W. B. Saunders Co., 1972.

Jones, H. E. *Development in Adolescence: Approaches to the Study of the Individual.* New York: Appleton-Century-Crofts, 1943.

Kagan, J., and H. A. Moss. *Birth to Maturity.* New York: John Wiley & Sons, Inc., 1962.

Kahl, J. A. *The American Class Structure.* New York: Holt, Rinehart and Winston, Inc., 1957.

Keen, E. *Psychology and the New Consciousness.* Belmont, Calif.: Brooks-Cole Publishers, 1972.

Kelly, E. L. *Assessment of Human Characteristics.* Belmont, Calif.: Brooks-Cole Publishers, 1967.

Kelvin, P. *The Bases of Social Behavior.* New York: Holt, Rinehart and Winston, Inc., 1971.

Keniston, K. "Youth: A 'New' Stage of Life." *The American Scholar,* 1970, Vol. 39, pp. 631–654.

Kerckhoff, A. C. *Socialization and Social Class.* Englewood Cliffs, N. J.: Prentice-Hall, Inc., 1972.

King, S. H. *Five Lives at Harvard: Personality Change during College.* Cambridge, Mass.: Harvard University Press, 1973.

Kluckhohn, C. *Mirror for Man: The Relation of Anthropology to Modern Life.* New York: McGraw-Hill, Inc., 1949.

Kluckhohn, C., and H. A. Murray (eds.). *Personality in Nature, Culture, and Society,* 2d ed. New York : Alfred A. Knopf, Inc., 1953.

Kohlberg, L. "Development of Moral Character and Moral Ideology." In M. L. Hoffman and L. W. Hoffman (eds.), *Review of Child Development Research,* Vol. I. New York: Russell Sage Foundation, 1964.

Köhler, W. *The Mentality of Apes.* New York: Harcourt Brace Jovanovich, Inc., 1927.

Kohn, M. L. "Social Class and Parent-Child Relationships: An Interpretation." *American Journal of Sociology,* 1963, Vol. 68, pp. 471–480.

Krutch, J. W. *The Twelve Seasons.* New York: William Sloane Associates, 1949.

Lash, J. P. *Eleanor: The Years Alone.* New York: W. W. Norton & Co., 1972.

Lecky, P. *Self-Consistency: A Theory of Personality.* New York: Island Press, 1945.

Leeper, R. W. "Learning and the Fields of Perception, Motivation, and Personality." In S. Koch (ed.), *Psychology: A Study of a Science.* New York: McGraw-Hill, Inc., Vol. 5, 1963, pp. 366–487.

Leeper, R. W., and P. Madison. *Toward Understanding Human Personalities.* New York: Appleton-Century-Crofts, 1959.

Levinson, D. J. "Role, Personality, and Social Structure in the Organizational Setting." *Journal of Abnormal and Social Psychology*, 1959, Vol. 58, pp. 170–180.

Levy, D. M. *Maternal Overprotection.* New York: Columbia University Press, 1943.

Lewis, O. *The Children of Sanchez: Autobiography of a Mexican Family.* New York: Random House, Inc., 1961.

Linton, Ralph. *The Cultural Background of Personality.* New York: Appleton-Century-Crofts, 1945.

Longstreth, L. E. *Psychological Development of the Child*, 2d ed. New York: The Ronald Press Company, 1974.

Lynd, R. S. *Knowledge for What? The Place of Social Science in American Culture.* Princeton, N.J.: Princeton University Press, 1939.

Madison, P. *Personality Development in College.* Reading, Mass.: Addison-Wesley Publishing Co., 1969.

Marcia, J. E. "Development and Validity of Ego Identity Status." *Journal of Personality and Social Psychology*, 1966, Vol. 3, pp. 551–559.

Maslow, A. *Motivation and Personality*, 2d ed. New York: Harper & Row, Publishers, 1970.

McArthur, C. C. "Personality Differences between Middle and Upper Classes." *Journal of Abnormal and Social Psychology*, 1955, Vol. 50, pp. 247–254.

McClelland, D. C. *Personality.* New York: Holt, Rinehart and Winston, Inc., 1951.

———. "Testing for Competence Rather than for 'Intelligence.'" *American Psychologist*, 1973, Vol. 28, pp. 1–14.

Mead, G. H. *Mind, Self, and Society.* Chicago: University of Chicago Press, 1934.

Miller, G. A., E. Galanter, and K. H. Pribram. *Plans and the Structure of Behavior.* New York: Holt, Rinehart and Winston, Inc., 1960.

Mumford, L. *The Conduct of Life.* New York: Harcourt Brace Jovanovich, Inc., 1951.

Murphy, L. B. *Social Behavior and Child Personality.* New York: Columbia University Press, 1937.

Murray, H. A. *Explorations in Personality.* New York: Oxford University Press, 1938.

Murstein, B. I. (ed.). *Theories of Attraction and Love.* New York: Springer Publishing Co., 1971.

Musgrove, F. *Youth and the Social Order*. Bloomington, Ind.: Indiana University Press, 1965.

Newcomb, T. M. *Social Psychology*. New York: Holt, Rinehart and Winston, Inc., 1950.

Newcomb, T. M., R. H. Turner, and D. E. Converse. *Social Psychology: The Study of Human Interaction*. New York: Holt, Rinehart and Winston, Inc., 1965.

O. S. S. Assessment Staff. *Assessment of Men*. New York: Holt, Rinehart and Winston, Inc., 1948.

Overstreet, H. A. *The Mature Mind*. New York: W. W. Norton & Co., 1949.

Parke, R. D. (ed.). *Recent Trends in Social Learning Theory*. New York: Academic Press, Inc., 1972.

Parsons, T. *The Social System*. New York: The Free Press, Inc., 1951.

Peterson, D. E. *The Clinical Study of Social Behavior*. New York: Appleton-Century-Crofts, 1968.

Piaget, J. *The Moral Judgment of the Child*. New York: Harcourt Brace Jovanovich, Inc., 1932.

Ralston, N. C., and G. P. Thomas. *The Adolescent: Case Studies for Analysis*. San Francisco: Chandler Publishing Co., 1974.

Rappaport, L. *Personality Development: The Chronology of Experience*. Glenview, Ill.: Scott, Foresman and Company, 1972.

Ravven, R. M. *The Phrase Association Interview*. 1951, unpublished thesis, Harvard College Library, Cambridge, Mass.

Redl, F., and D. Wineman. *Children Who Hate: The Disorganization and Breakdown of Behavior Controls*. New York: The Free Press, Inc., 1951.

Reich, C. A. *The Greening of America*. New York: Random House, Inc., 1970.

Riesman, D. *The Lonely Crowd: A Study of the Changing American Character*. New Haven: Yale University Press, 1950.

Roe, A. "Artists and Their Work." *Journal of Personality*, 1946, Vol. 15, pp. 1–40.

———. "A Psychological Study of Eminent Psychologists and Anthropologists and a Comparison with Biological and Physical Scientists." *Psychological Monographs*, 1953, Vol. 67, No. 2.

———. *The Psychology of Occupations*. New York: John Wiley & Sons, Inc., 1956.

Roe, A., and M. Siegelman. *The Origin of Interests*. Washington, D. C.: APGA Inquiry Studies, No. 1, 1964.

Rubin, Z. *Liking and Loving: An Invitation to Social Psychology*. New York: Holt, Rinehart and Winston, Inc., 1973.

Sanford, N. (ed.). "Personality Development during the College Years." *Journal of Social Issues*, 1956, Vol. 12, No. 4.

Saul, L. J. *Emotional Maturity*, 2d ed. Philadelphia: J. P. Lippincott Company, 1962.

Sheldon, W. H., S. S. Stevens, and W. B. Tucker. *The Varieties of Human Physique*, New York: Harper & Row, Publishers, 1940.

Sheldon, W. H., and S. S. Stevens. *The Varieties of Temperament*. New York: Harper & Row, Publishers, 1942.

Singer, J. L. (ed.). *The Control of Aggression and Violence*. New York: Academic Press, Inc., 1971.

Skinner, B. F. *Science and Human Behavior*. New York: The Macmillan Company, 1953.

Smith, M. B., J. S. Bruner, and R. W. White. *Opinions and Personality*. New York: John Wiley & Sons, Inc., 1956.

Spiegel, J. *Transactions: The Interplay between Individual, Family, and Society*. J. Papajohn (ed.). New York: Science House, 1971.

Sullivan, H. S. *The Interpersonal Theory of Psychiatry*. New York: W. W. Norton & Co., 1953.

Sutton-Smith, B., and B. J. Rosenberg. *The Sibling*. New York: Holt, Rinehart and Winston, Inc., 1970.

Symonds, P. M. *The Psychology of Parent-Child Relationships*. New York: Appleton-Century-Crofts, 1939.

Tolman, E. C. "Cognitive Maps in Rats and Men." *Psychological Review*, 1948, Vol. 55, pp. 189–208.

Trieschman, A. E., J. K. Whittaker, and L. K. Brendtro. *The Other 23 Hours*. Chicago: Aldine Publishing Co., 1969.

Viscott, D. S. *The Making of a Psychiatrist*. Greenwich, Conn.: Fawcett-Crest, 1972.

Warner, W. L., and associates. *Democracy in Jonesville: A Study in Quality and Inequality*. New York: Harper & Row, Publishers, 1949.

Wenar, C. *Personality Development from Infancy to Adulthood*. Boston: Houghton Mifflin Company, 1971.

White, R. W. "The Personality of Joseph Kidd." *Character & Personality*, 1943, Vol. 11, pp. 183–208, 318–360.

———. "Motivation Reconsidered: The Concept of Competence." *Psychological Review*, 1959, Vol. 66, pp. 297–333.

———. "The Dangers of Social Adjustment." *Teachers College Record*, 1961, Vol. 62, pp. 288–297.

———. *The Enterprise of Living: Growth and Organization in Personality*. New York: Holt, Rinehart and Winston, Inc., 1972.

———. "Critical Events in Life Histories." *Annals of the New York Academy of Sciences*, 1972, Vol. 193, pp. 248–252.

———. "The Concept of Healthy Personality: What Do We Really Mean?" *The Counseling Psychologist*, 1973, Vol. 4, pp. 3–12.

White, R. W., and N. F. Watt. *The Abnormal Personality*, 4th ed. New York: The Ronald Press Company, 1973.

Whyte, W. F. *Street Corner Society*. Chicago: University of Chicago Press, 1943.

Whyte, W. H., Jr. *The Organization Man*. New York: Simon & Schuster, Inc., 1956.

Woodworth, R. S. *Dynamics of Behavior*. New York: Holt, Rinehart and Winston, Inc., 1958.

Wright, D. *The Psychology of Moral Behavior*. Baltimore: Penguin Books Inc., 1971.

Yalom, I. D. *The Theory and Practice of Group Psychotherapy*. New York: Basic Books, Inc., 1970.

Zaleznik, A., and D. Moment. *The Dynamics of Interpersonal Behavior*. New York: John Wiley & Sons, Inc., 1964.

INDEX